The rise of market culture

The rise of market culture

The textile trade and French society, 1750–1900

WILLIAM M. REDDY

The right of the
University of Cambridge
to print and sell
all manner of books
was granted by
Henry VIII in 1534.
The University has printed
and published continuously
since 1584.

CAMBRIDGE UNIVERSITY PRESS

CAMBRIDGE

LONDON   NEW YORK   NEW ROCHELLE

MELBOURNE   SYDNEY

EDITIONS DE LA MAISON DES SCIENCES DE L'HOMME

PARIS

To Charles

Published by the Press Syndicate of the University of Cambridge
The Pitt Building, Trumpington Street, Cambridge CB2 1RP
32 East 57th Street, New York, NY 10022, USA
296 Beaconsfield Parade, Middle Park, Melbourne 3206, Australia

© Cambridge University Press 1984

First published 1984

Printed in the United States of America

Library of Congress Cataloging in Publication Data
Reddy, William M.
The rise of market culture.
Includes bibliographical references.
1. Textile industry – France – History. I. Title.
HD9862.5.R43   1984   381'.45677'0944   83-25232
ISBN 0 521 25653 4

Contents

Figures and maps

vi

Abbreviations

ADHR	Archives départementales du Haut-Rhin
ADM	Archives départementales de la Marne
ADN	Archives départementales du Nord
ADSM	Archives départementales de la Seine-Maritime
AMR	Archives municipales de Roubaix
AN	Archives nationales
BN	Bibliothèque nationale
BSIM	Bulletin de la Société industrielle de Mulhouse
ERDP	France, Ministère du commerce, *Enquête relative à diverses prohibitions établies sur l'entrée des produits étrangers, commencée le 8 octobre 1834 sous la présidence de M. T. Duchâtel, Ministre du commerce*, 3 vols. (Paris, 1835)
Gaz. Trib.	*Gazette des Tribunaux*

Preface

The history of the industrial revolution has been rewritten in the last twenty years. The focus has shifted away from factory workers toward artisans, and the character of the social crisis has been rethought. It was not so much a decline in the standard of living, not the drudgery of machine-tending, nor the poor housing of factory towns that afflicted society during the early phase of industrialization, but a loss of independence, the violation of old moral standards by unrestricted competition, the displacement of skilled by unskilled, the disruption of shop custom, insecurity of status. Conscious laissez-faire reform played as much a role in overturning the old order as expanding commerce; technological advance, while important, was limited in its impact. The per-capita growth rate of France was as great as that of England in the first half of the nineteenth century, and artisan experience in both countries was extremely similar.[1]

Even the new factory workers of Lancashire can no longer be seen as the faceless proletarians of legend; their grievances, on closer examination, appear to have been nearly the same as those of artisans. Machine tending in the early days was organized like artisanal labor; and the operatives struggled (in the end with moderate success) to keep it that way.[2]

This study examines the parallel experiences of French mill operatives; but it also aims, at the same time, to push the whole discussion of the nature of industrialization a step further. A detailed study of the French textile trade seems well-suited to the accomplishment of this latter aim for two reasons. First, the case-study method lends itself to the kind of methodological experimentation required by the current state of the social-historical art. A picture of the aggregate has been built up; reevaluation of the abundant sources requires that one set arbitrary limits on the scope of any single inquiry. Second, the significance of textiles within the whole process of industrial transformation cannot be emphasized enough. No trade employed more people outside of agriculture in the pre-industrial period; no trade was more profoundly reshaped than textiles by the swelling current of international commerce in the eighteenth century. This was as true of the French case as it was of the English. After 1816, French textiles experienced a rapid, if belated, industrial revolution of its own: mechanization proceeded apace, output mushroomed, prices to the consumer dropped dramatically – all the characteristics of rapid transformation were present. The French textile trade is therefore perfectly suited to an inquiry into the gamut of change that industrialization brought to European society.

A number of northern regional centers in France spearheaded the drive to mechanize in the early nineteenth century: Rouen, Reims, Lille, Roubaix, Armentières, Saint-Quentin, Mulhouse and their dependencies became the miniature Manchesters that brought France into the age of steam between 1816 and 1848. They specialized in mass-production goods of cotton, linen, and wool. The great bulk of this study is devoted to occurrences in these towns. Lyon, the center of an international luxury silk trade, had a very different historical experience; the town's silk weavers led the French working-class movement for a time. They have been the subject of numerous studies and receive only passing attention here.[3] The woolen centers of the south, expanding in the eighteenth century, stalled and stagnated in the nineteenth; Christopher H. Johnson is currently engaged in research on this area, and it too will be referred to here only as a point of comparison.[4] The transition to mechanized factory production and all its attendant cultural and social changes are the subject of this study. The northern focus was therefore a natural choice; and the unity of experience in these northern centers emerged clearly in the course of research.

None of the methodological approaches employed in this study are new in themselves. Social historians have been particularly active of late in attempting to apply the methods of cultural anthropology to their work, and it was within the now broad streams of mutual influence between anthropology and social history that the present research project was originally formulated. The idea was to collect information about the forms and occasions of social conflict in a single trade over a long period and, by careful anthropological interpretation, to trace the transition from a precapitalist to a capitalist culture. The author believed from the outset that this transition extended over a longer period and raised greater difficulties than is normally supposed. The evidence uncovered, however, suggested a startling alternative, that is, that this transition was never accomplished, at least not in the manner originally envisioned. French textile laborers failed to develop a social identity commensurate with the idea of wage labor, even by 1900.

It was at this stage that recent research in the economics of labor distribution came into play. Many economists appear now to believe that the market model – or the model of marginal productivity – has only a limited utility in explaining labor distribution in industrial society.

The theory of segmented labor markets is by now quite well established and has attracted widespread attention. This theory denies that modern industrial economies have a single market for labor. Instead, labor is seen as divided into distinct segments within which laborers have quite different expectations as to pay, working conditions, and job security. Competition between these segments is muted.[5]

Closely associated with the study of market segmentation has been the investigation of institutional employment practices and the attempts by economists to fit nonmarket models to them. Such models have been popularized most effectively by two economists, Michael Piore and Lester Thurow. The former expounded the concept of the "internal labor market" over twelve years ago; the latter, his theory of the "labor queue" in 1975.[6] In both of these theories, empirically identified hiring practices are analyzed and shown to fit only poorly the model of competitive bidding inherent in the classical notion of the market, and both Piore and Thurow propose specific alternative models of hiring and labor-use practices that seem to fit the evidence better.

Here lay a possible explanation of French textile laborers' persistent failure to develop a fully mature identity as wage earners: Their real relationship with their employers had never been a wage relationship pure and simple because the competitive exchange of labor never developed along the lines of classical economic theory. This conclusion about the economics of labor distribution, in turn, had consequences for the interpretation of culture and for understanding the structure of politics in industrial communities.

The study, therefore, is intended to make a contribution on several fronts at once. In interdisciplinary work like this there is always the danger of sounding a false note from time to time, but the potential benefits seem well worth the risk. The reader's indulgence is therefore requested in advance for the unavoidable confusions that arise, especially over terms like culture, market, labor, ritual, entrepreneur – all of which are used here in very specific ways. Every effort has been made to clarify their use in advance; occasionally a purposeful effort is being made to change or add to the usual resonances these terms have. This was an inevitable consequence of trying to break new ground.

The author has accumulated many debts since he began this project. Four institutions have contributed materially to its completion. A Duke University travel grant and two brief fellowships at the Max-Planck-Institut für Geschichte in Göttingen, West Germany, were a great help in the later stages of writing. The bulk of the research behind the study was made possible by a Fellowship for Independent Study and Research from the National Endowment for the Humanities in 1979–80. The original conception of the study stems from a year as Member of the School of Social Science at the Institute for Advanced Study, Princeton. Archivists and librarians of numerous institutions including particularly the Bibliothèque nationale, the Archives nationales, and the Archives départementales du Nord, contributed their unending and patient help.

The individuals who have helped with their ideas and reactions are too numerous to list here. Fellow participants in a seminar on cultural anthropology at the Institute for Advanced Study in 1975–6 helped in the initial formulation of method and of questions to be answered. Among them the author began to find at last an intellectual home. Conversations about the project with Michelle Perrot, Pierre Deyon, and Serge Chassagne were extremely useful at an early stage. Significant portions of the manuscript have been read by David Sabean, Hans Medick, Alf Lüdtke, Gerald Sider, Gary Kornblith, James Epstein, Sarah Maza, John Cell, Sydney Nathans, and David Brent, as well as members of the Triangle labor history seminar – all of whom gave significant ideas and criticisms, often well beyond the author's ability to respond. Several others have contributed by example and by active support in a special way, including Joan Scott, Robert Bezucha, Eva Gumprecht, Dorothy Sapp, Donna Slawson, and most particularly William Sewell, whose unstinting help and criticism over a long period provided a fixed compass point by which a young scholar navigated through uncertain seas.

Introduction

In contrast to what we normally hear, market society did not come into being in Europe in the nineteenth century. Attempts were made, yes, to create a thorough-going market economy, but they failed. These attempts are well known to historians, they constitute a principal element of the economic and political history of the period. But astonishing as it may seem, neither economic nor social historians have ever systematically considered the question of whether these attempts had the desired effect. The guiding assumption of the age of laissez-faire was that completely unregulated trade equals competitive, self-regulating markets. This assumption still has a profound hold on us today. Hence the tendency to accept as self-evident that laissez-faire reform created a market system. But nothing could be further from the truth.

Attempts to create a market society did transform Europe in the early nineteenth century, of this there can be no doubt, but the results in no way resembled the image that inspired these attempts. Rather than speak of market society for the new social order that resulted, it would perhaps be better to speak of "market culture."

The advantage of the word *culture* is that it at least raises the possibility of a disjuncture between perception and reality and forces us to interpret rather than blindly accept language used to describe or restructure social life. When a doctor administers a drug we say he is healing; when a medicine man recites his spell, we say it is his culture. Both have cultures, yes, but the doctor also has penicillin. In the nineteenth century certain medicine men saw a market society emerging and since then many have concurred. But they were deluded. Market culture, therefore, in the simplest terms, consisted of three elements: a set of (wrong) perceptions, a language through which these perceptions were formulated, expressed, and debated, and a set of (misguided) practices partially but imperfectly shaped in accord with these perceptions. Market society was a mirage. Market culture was the social order that emerged when the language of

1

this mirage insinuated its assumptions into the everyday practice of European society.

Unfortunately, historians have done much in our own century to keep the mirage before our eyes. As recently as the 1940s, the belief in market society received powerful reinforcement from two scholars who, in other respects, were as different as night and day, Karl Polanyi and T. S. Ashton. Each of these economic historians wrote synthetic works on the industrial revolution in England that remain widely read to this day.[1] Polanyi saw the period from 1760 to 1830 in England as an unexampled catastrophe in human history. Ashton saw the same period as the harbinger of unlimited human progress. Yet both agreed substantially on what had happened. Both believed that a traditional English social order had been set aside. Rapid and often painful changes were carried out that made it possible for the basic factors of production – land, labor, and capital – to be put up for sale to the highest bidder in a competitive market. The enclosure movement transformed the use of the land. The developing banking system mobilized liquid capital. And the laissez-faire reforms of Parliament shook people loose from the paternalistic shackles of the past so that they could seek out the highest bidder for their services. The benefits in terms of sustained economic growth were well worth the price of momentary upheaval and dislocation in Ashton's view. In Polanyi's view, the continuing suffering and uncertainty created by forcing nature, man, and money into the mold of freely exchangeable commodities was enough to damn the whole experiment from the beginning. The rapid shift to protective reforms after 1834, in Polanyi's view, only proved that the effects of free competition were not bearable even with the pay-off of economic growth. Whatever side historians have favored in this ongoing debate, few have questioned the basic notion that land, labor, and capital had been changed to make them into commodities sold at competitive prices in open markets. But this never really occurred.

That this same interpretation could readily be applied to Continental society was demonstrated by Eric Hobsbawm in 1962 who spoke in his *Age of Revolution* of a dual revolution that had swept over Europe between 1789 and 1848, of which England had provided the economic, and France the political component.[2] For France, Hobsbawm found a ready-made interpretation of the Revolution that perfectly suited his needs. Georges Lefebvre and Albert Soboul, the two great students of the French Revolution in this century, both spoke of 1789 as having set the stage for capitalism.[3] The Revolution had swept away the vestiges of feudalism – seigneurial dues and ecclesiastical estates in the countryside, guilds and venal office in the towns – and replaced them with perfect freedom to dispose of self and property and perfect competition in the marketplace. That no industrial revolution occurred immediately in France could be attributed to exogenous factors: the impact of war, difficulties of transport, shortages of raw material, entrepreneurial timidity. French society was nonetheless, like English, a market society by the time of Napoleon's fall and nothing that the restored monarch attempted could change this fact. In spite of all the qualifications that have since been made concerning Lefebvre's or Soboul's views of the origins of the Revolution, no one has successfully challenged their estimation of its results.[4] Yet the creation of a market system in France was never accomplished, however "free" property and labor had become.

Problems with this powerful synthesis have only emerged gradually since the 1960s. The seeds of these problems can be seen in E. P. Thompson's *The Making of the English Working Class*, which first appeared in 1963, and offered, among many other things, detailed accounts of the impact on certain artisanal trades of Parliamentary reform and Parliamentary resistance to popular lobbying.[5] The catastrophes that were befalling these trades, on close examination, resembled hardly at all what the effects of a free market ought to look like. And the demands for strong governmental control, made by artisans in the name of what Thompson called a moral economy (as opposed to the political economy of Smith and his followers), seemed strikingly practical and reasonable in view of actual economic conditions. Thompson's example inspired other studies of artisanal trades both in England and in France, and from these studies as well as other inquiries into women and the family that have since been carried out, a consistent picture emerged that is now there for anyone to see.[6] No market for labor was ever created in either of these countries. In this crucial sense the market system failed to appear.

The precise meaning of this claim will be laid out and documented in depth in this study insofar as the French textile industry is concerned. But it is important that its theoretical implications and its general applicability be understood from the outset because it is a claim not just about economic conditions in a particular time or place, but also a claim about the role that culture plays in human society as well as the role that social class and social conflict play in the formation of culture. How people came to accept that markets existed when they did not and to think of their defining social relationships exclusively in terms of commodities and exchanges when they continued to involve so much more – loyalty, deference, faith, fear, hostility – are the questions that must be answered. The implications are not just substantive, involving the way one sees this period in history, but also methodological. The simple act of reading a document needs to be completely rethought if one follows through all of the ramifications of this claim about markets.

Introduction

No market for labor was ever created. To see what this claim means, it would be well to consider for a moment the famous case of the English handloom weavers, not because it proves anything one way or another, but because, being well known and thoroughly researched, the case provides the necessary ingredients for a thought experiment about the idea of a market.

The handloom weavers have long been cited as the first great instance of mechanization forcing a whole trade community into obsolescence. The superiority of the new steam-powered loom developed in the 1780s was decisive and it drove several hundred thousand independent weavers in England into unemployment and penury between 1800 and 1840. The merit of Thompson's exploration of this case lay in his underscoring of certain neglected facets of it.[7] First of all the power loom's advantage was not so great; it could out-produce perhaps four to six handloom weavers on common grades of cotton cloth, but no more. Handloom weavers remained competitive if they accepted wage cuts of 60 to 80 percent. Countless weavers did just that, as earnings dropped from 18 to 14 to 4 shillings a week in the first decades of the nineteenth century. Secondly, a power loom was an expensive piece of equipment which, once purchased, had to be kept going constantly in order to pay for itself. Clothiers preferred, therefore, to buy only a few of them, lest they be caught out by the next slump; and they continued to turn the major portion of their raw materials over to handloom weavers in dispersed cottages. Wages became severely depressed long before the power loom had become a significant factor in production. Merely the threat of its introduction induced weavers to accept cuts. Their willingness to do so, in turn, severely limited the profitability of the power loom, thereby slowing its introduction to a snail's pace. Thirdly, the weavers turned to Parliament for minimum-wage legislation, something that Parliament had often granted in the eighteenth century but now, citing Adam Smith, refused. Had the minimum-wage been granted, the power loom would have been introduced much more rapidly because the weavers would not have been allowed to undersell the machine. Their long drawn out decline, which more than anything made them the object of public attention and official inquiry, was itself as much a result of political influence and commercial timidity as of technology.

The question that has preoccupied both contemporaries and historians, however, is why weavers in such great numbers stayed in the trade when their wages began to fall below a minimum subsistence level. Even unskilled field work could bring in 8 shillings a week, twice what weavers were earning by the 1820s. This violated expectations. Why did the weavers not seek to sell their services in other ways? A variety of explanations have been put forward over the years. Thompson cataloged them as follows: Many weavers lived in isolated villages that had only one industry. Weavers' hands were without callouses, their backs stooped; the shift to field or road work was difficult for some, impossible for others. At first they had a stiff pride in their trade and to the end they continued to value the independence of working at home on their own schedule. Other skilled trades retained their strict apprenticeship requirements longer than the weavers' trade, so that shifting to a new occupation of equal status was only rarely possible. A combination of distance, physical debility, rank consciousness, and desire for independence, in other words, locked many thousands in the trade at four shillings a week. Some of these factors came to light at the time, others have been pointed out by historians.[8]

But what these factors add up to, quite simply, is that the handloom weavers were not disposing of their labor in a market.

This is a contentious claim. But it is also a claim that pivots ultimately on the use of terms rather than on empirical evidence, because a judgment about the motives of human beings is involved and no such judgment can ever be finally settled on the basis of empirical evidence. One thing is certain: Handloom weavers did not respond to wage levels very strongly when disposing of their labor. How one interprets this fact is another matter.

In itself it is not very remarkable; economists have long held that wage level is only one of many factors determining job choice. Even classical political economists claimed only that wage levels would tend to equalize the mix of nonmonetary advantages and disadvantages of different jobs. A very unpleasant, or dangerous, or dishonorable occupation would pay relatively well; a pleasant, safe, respectable occupation, relatively poorly. The handloom weavers would therefore appear to be an extreme of the latter sort. This was precisely the conclusion of a Parliamentary investigation, later cited with approval by John Stuart Mill:

> He can play or idle as feeling or inclination lead him; rise early or late, apply himself assiduously or carelessly, as he pleases, and work up at any time, by increased exertion, hours previously sacrificed to indulgence or recreation. There is scarcely another condition of any portion of our working population thus free from external control ... The weaver will stand by his loom while it will enable him to exist, however miserably.[9]

More recently economists have added the notions of information cost and psychic costs as possible factors in such a situation.[10] The cost of gaining information about alternative employment or the psychic pain associated with leaving the loom may have been great.

There are two problems with this method of accounting for responses to wage levels, however. In the first place the idea of nonmonetary advantages and costs is, in fact, merely a metaphor, an interpretive device rather than an empirical claim.[11] There is no imaginable human decision that cannot be spoken of in terms of maximizing advantages and minimizing disadvantages. If the handloom weavers' wage had dropped to zero this would only show that the nonmonetary advantages of the occupation were infinite or that the "psychic costs" of quitting were insurmountable. To explain any conceivable behavior one can invent counterbalancing nonmonetary advantages and costs at will and attribute them to the weavers' subjective calculations. The equation will always come out right. Whether use of such an interpretive device really represents the high road to understanding human motivation is another matter. It is completely empty, provides no new information, and only paltry insights about where to search for new information. The bald implication is that every human experience – of pleasure or pain, honor or shame, moral anguish or ecstasy – can be meaningfully compared with a particular wage differential and is so compared by human actors in society. Clearly this cannot get us very far. Of course, there is no way to prove that it cannot, nor to prove that it can. Human motivation is not accessible to outside observation; claims about it can never be definitively disproved.

The second problem with this approach to accounting for wage levels is as follows: Even if one accepts that wages operate to equalize the nonmonetary advantages and costs of different jobs, it does not necessarily follow that wage levels can smoothly fulfill the function of balancing supply and demand for labor within the economy. By any account, this did not happen in the handloom weavers' case. The nonmonetary costs to the weavers of leaving their occupation were evidently high. A precipitate drop in wages failed to induce them to deploy their labor services elsewhere. Others were dissuaded from entering the trade, true. But the result was that a large labor force was only shifted out of weaving when death finally ensued.[12] In a proper market, price is supposed to ensure that demand and supply balance each other out. If it takes the loss of a generation for the price mechanism to do its work in balancing supply and demand, then one has a very inefficient labor market. So inefficient, surely, that one can deny with justice that *market* is the proper term to use for describing this form of labor distribution. In effect, even if one admits the utility of the notion that wage levels balance out nonmonetary costs and advantages, it is still necessary to recognize that the market model may apply only very poorly to the social reality of the handloom weavers' case.

Some may be inclined at this point to object that the case of the handloom weavers is an exceptional one, an extreme that hardly serves to test the existence of a labor market in England during the industrial revolution. But at the time, and down to the present day, it has overwhelmingly been treated not as an anomaly but as an exemplary instance of the functioning of the new order.[13] Unregulated competition was the engine of progress; in the case of the handloom weavers, machine was competing directly against man, and man was losing. Nothing could be more natural, or more salutary in the long run. Here again, however, a term is being used in a way that shades into metaphor. The notion of competition, like the notion of nonmonetary cost or advantage, is a loose one. In this case, handloom weavers were competing against the machine because they refused (or were unable) to deploy their labor in a competitive manner. The kind of competition that is supposed to characterize the market system did not exist here. This is why the weavers "competed" with the power loom. A competition that results from people not acting in a competitive manner cannot have the beneficial equilibrating effects within the economy that are normally claimed for it.

A market economy does not exist unless entrepreneurs are forced to buy all the factors of production in competitive markets and to sell their products in a competitive market. Not just here or there but at every stage of the production process, markets must exist in which supply and demand are balanced by free-floating prices – balanced not over decades, or generations, or centuries, but from day to day as in the highly regulated stock or commodity exchanges of our own time.[14] Here lies the problem with a whole still-potent myth about the industrial revolution. Free competition is said to have unleashed the drive for productivity, and the widespread introduction of labor-saving devices that followed brought unprecedented prosperity. Something like this did happen in some trades, notably in textiles. But it was a much less common occurrence than is normally supposed. The opposite effect was also possible, and terribly frequent. For example, if certain entrepreneurs can buy their labor over a long period at prices well below what others pay, they are at a comparative advantage that will allow them to put off introducing beneficial new production methods. Progress is delayed, not hastened; entrepreneur and consumer enjoy a false prosperity that really stems from the deprivation of those who work.

The clothiers in England who kept handloom weavers' wages at 4 shillings a week were able to avoid investing in risky new machines for decades. Progress was slowed down by this competition of man against machine because a competitive market for labor – one of the key factors of production – was not functioning.

There was nothing exceptional about the failure of wage levels to affect the handloom weavers' disposal of their labor, moreover, as studies of the last twenty years have shown. Wage levels throughout the economies of Europe in the early nineteenth century served a host of functions that impeded them from operating smoothly to balance supply and demand for labor. For one thing, wages served as powerful markers of familial status, of gender, and among adult males of social status. Since Hobsbawm's pathbreaking essay on this matter, "Custom, Wages and Workload," a great deal of detailed evidence has been gathered on the role that customary expectations associated with rank, trade, sex, and age played in determining wage levels.[15] Hobsbawm's emphasis on this role looks now, if anything, understated, for he assumed that bargaining and market forces grew in importance as the century wore on. More recent study does not bear out his idea; rather, bargaining appears to have come into play later in the century as a means of expressing and defending customary expectations or applying them to newly created job categories.[16]

What the early nineteenth century brought everywhere in Europe were legal reforms that wreaked havoc with those customary wage expectations. Everywhere in Europe laws that governed wage levels, production methods, and access to trades were summarily repealed. Women and children were quickly drawn into some of the biggest trades: the new factory industries, garment making, mining, shoemaking. They were given secondary or subdivided tasks requiring no training. Where training was required as in garment making, it was training that did not customarily confer status. (Women were expected to know how to sew a proper seam.) Wage levels for women and children in these industries remained one half or less of the rates paid to the adult males they displaced. But if they were in such demand, why did their wages not increase? True, population was growing rapidly in this period, but so was per-capita gross national product, even in France.[17] The most likely conclusion is that, here again, a competition of a dysfunctional nature was at work. Women and children did not aggressively follow up on their advantage. Neither they, nor their families, nor their employers expected them to ask whatever the market would bear. They were socialized out of such behavior or too young to know what it consisted of. Ironically, the customary low value of female and child labor only made sense in a context in which adult males were responsible for providing the bulk of the family income. In other words, adult males were in this case subsidizing the competition. The hardships experienced by thousands of displaced male tailors and shoemakers in both England and France bear witness to the real damage caused by such a free, but nonetheless nonmarket form of labor distribution.[18]

That this great influx of women and children into manufacturing resulted in higher productivity is also highly questionable. Subdivision of skilled jobs into a series of unskilled tasks did result in some increase in productivity, to be sure, but only at the expense of quality. Shoddy cut-ups (stockings), ready-made suits and shoes bore no comparison with made-to-order goods. What made these shoddy goods acceptable to the consumer and profitable to the entrepreneur were not productivity increases but the lower customary wage of women and children, which made prices even lower than shoddy methods alone ever could have.

Certain categories of adult males were played off against each other in similar fashion. In woodworking, shipbuilding, metallurgy, and construction entrepreneurs were now free to prefer unapprenticed males to apprenticed ones because they accepted lower pay.[19] But their cheapness was a matter of custom, not of the cost of acquiring a skill. Apprentices acquiring skills by every indication worked less hard and were better treated than unapprenticed child laborers.[20] The nonmonetary costs of not serving an apprenticeship should have resulted in higher pay, not lower.

Across a broad front, then, in the economies of England, France, Belgium, and to a lesser extent Germany, the stripping away of trade regulation between 1789 and 1815 created, not a competitive labor market, but a wide variety of distortions in the distribution of labor. Free trade provided ample opportunity for entrepreneurs to profit, not by increasing productivity, but by the adroit playing off of various customary categories of laborers against each other. Of course the very term, customary categories, implies an interpretation of the motives of laborers that is, like any other, open to question. But it is surely also a significant improvement on the idea, implicit in the notion of a competitive labor market, that all human beings without reference to age, sex, or life experience are avid barterers.

Contemporaries knew that these sorts of distortions in labor distribution and wage determination were occurring. But again, as in the case of the handloom weavers, there was a tendency to see these phenomena as a function of the proper operation of competition. When the great controversy over child labor arose throughout Western Europe in the 1830s and '40s, both advocates and opponents of legal restrictions on the use of children in manufacturing spoke as if the market system was functioning properly when children were drawn into industry.[21] In France, the Baron Charles Dupin, for example, an advocate of child labor legislation, believed children were paid less because they had less physical strength than adults. In his view, entrepreneurs had the evident interest of obtaining "intelligent collaborators whom youth and weakness render less expensive and more docile ... "[22] But the lesser physical strength of children did not really make them cheaper to house, clothe, and feed. Their wages were low only because they were supplemented by those of others in the household. And if their docility were an advantage, then, in a proper market, it should have earned them higher wages, not lower ones. Opponents of child-labor legislation, likewise, warned the government against interfering with the free operation of the market. "Let us not forget," said a member of the Chamber of Commerce of Rouen in 1837

> that we owe in large measure the present state of prosperity of our country to the immense progress of industry. It has already caused us problems, but we have been able to overcome them. Let us not forget, further, that this progress only dates from that recent period when tardy but salutory reason unleashed industry from that cowardly and ridiculous swaddling in which our old guild system restrained it, limiting it over the centuries to a few meagre steps forward.[23]

This statement brings us to the heart of the matter. The facile equation implicit in it, that free trade equals competitive markets equals progress, gained sway over much of the thinking of the nineteenth century, more because of its weaknesses than its strengths. These weaknesses were concentrated in two deceptively flexible ideas. First was the notion that all people sought to maximize comparative net advantage – that is, that the motive of gain was the mainspring of human behavior. But this was an interpretive strategy rather than an empirical finding, based on metaphor rather than measurement.[24] Anything which a human being might want – honor, pleasure, security, salvation – could be categorized as a gain or advantage. This in itself is quite harmless. But when the mind is brought by degrees to think of all forms of gain as having money equivalents the metaphor has become a trap. The fact that propositions about basic human motivation are impossible to disprove further clinched the trap's hold on many minds, since converts could find any amount of evidence that did not contradict (and therefore appeared to conform with) their views.

Second, the notion of competition was made to cover too broad a range of phenomena, not just those in which it ensured the rapid dissemination of new techniques or the efficient balancing of needs with resources but also those – as in the case of the handloom weavers or that of child labor – where competition resulted from the failure of balance. The sinking wage of the handloom weaver failed to redistribute his energies; the low wage of the child was dictated by expectation rather than demand. In each case competition occurred, but the wrong competitor won. Handloom weavers successfully undersold power looms, children successfully displaced adults because each was failing to calculate how to maximize his monetary income, for whatever reason. Because this could be construed as competition, however, it was taken to be a normal consequence of economic law, even by those who wished to interpose a salutary human law to protect the young.

These two ideas, that gain was the basic human motive and that unregulated competition brought maximum progress, acquired tremendous power in the nineteenth century, such power that it is justifiable to view them as fundamental elements of a new culture, market culture.

Knowledge about the why and wherefore of another's actions is never certain nor complete. At the same time, merely in order to get through life from one day to the next, it is necessary to feel relatively sure why people around us are acting as they do. The erection of great institutions such as states, churches, corporations, or political parties is a matter not just of the consolidation and centralization of power but also of the dissemination and routinization of certain schemas for talking about the nature of the cosmos, human society's relation to it, and the internal relations of human groups. These schemas simplify the problem of knowing what another person is up to. This is one reason people often remain devoted to them even when they have lost all intellectual respectability. Such schemas are seldom perfectly uniform or univocal; credos, declarations, constitutions, and sacred scriptures are always filled with potential ambiguities and contradictions. These are what give coherence to conflict, provide it with organizing principles and rallying cries.[25] (Where would the Soviet – U.S. rivalry be without the principle of private property?) Culture is as good a word as any for referring to the state of affairs that arises when certain schemas are so widely accepted that they provide a background for the coherent carrying on of human affairs, including deceit and violence, or the pursuit of power.

In Western Europe, the transition from medieval Christian to modern secular culture pivoted on a reversal in notions about human motivation. In the Christian schema, good was pitted against evil; motives were either pure or despicable. The individual was expected to struggle against forbidden desires and strive to have only approved ones. By the eighteenth century, however, a new schema had been evolved, cynical by contrast, although at base it was not cynical so much as mechanistic. Attempts to approve or control motives were abandoned. The twin impulses of a growing world commercial system and a new mechanistic cosmology offered by seventeenth-century science sparked the formulation of a new world view that promised to find internal coherence in all these phenomena, from the orbiting of the planets to the circulation of wealth. By this view humans interacted with a purely mechanical nature, and society itself was a kind of mechanism in which the centrifugal force of self-interest (or comparative net advantage) was just balanced by the gravity of competition.[26]

It is true that the upper strata of society were beginning on their own to speak of prices, interest rates, and property in new ways by the end of the seventeenth century, and nascent political economy drew on this evolving common sense to elaborate its vision. But classical political economy also systematized this new common sense and linked it to Newtonian science and moral reflection, providing the kind of breadth and coherence that is necessary for the establishment of a new world view.[27]

The basic terms of market culture constitute a set of categories. Every human activity and almost every feature of the natural world can be readily categorized according to its potential place in a market system. A particular activity may be an exchange or a production process or consumption, it may be creating supply or demand. A particular object may be a raw material or a finished product, an asset or a liability, a commodity or a piece of capital or a waste product. Unlike similar categories originating in earlier periods – noble and common, sacred and profane – the categories of market culture may all be expressed in numerical form, representing a real or potential exchange price, and, therefore, they may be added and subtracted, substituted, or canceled out. This was a considerable source of prestige in the post-Newton era.[28]

Clifford Geertz has said that culture provides both "models of" and "models for," both cognitive and prescriptive structures.[29] The prescriptions generated by market categories are mathematically precise, easy to arrive at, easy to refine. But this stunning advantage on the prescriptive side is balanced by a severe handicap on the cognitive side. Only those numerical aspects of an activity or object that might affect an exchange can be taken into account. A production process that produces 85 shirts a day must be preferred to one that produces only 65 shirts with equal input because 85 is larger than 65. It is impossible simultaneously to take into account other features of the two processes (for example, environmental damage) unless these too can be conceived of as a form of exchange. But many things simply cannot be so conceived.

This is easy to see in the case of a common household activity like cooking. If cooking is treated as a production process, then market categories generate prescriptions to maximize output and minimize input. A form of cooking will be preferred if it results in 20 biscuits per hour instead of 10. But it is possible to recognize even today that cooking may be something more than just production, it may serve other ends besides output: symbolic, emotional, or aesthetic ends that cannot be quantified. The only way to handle this within market categories is to shift cooking to the consumption column and treat it as a leisure-time activity. Then every caprice of the cook becomes the object of anxious concern on the part of suppliers of cooking utensils and groceries. All concern about efficient output is set aside. But both of these alternatives are bad; cooking

12

is, under normal circumstances, both a kind of production and a kind of consumption. It can fulfill many ends harmoniously all at once. But applying market categories makes it impossible to improve the harmony. Almost inevitably, market prescriptions disrupt it, by subordinating all other ends of an activity to the terms of a real or hypothetical exchange.

One of the most important ways in which market culture has led to destructive consequences has been its treatment of production strictly as a means to more advantageous exchange. All the anticapitalist prophets have decried this aspect of it. What has seldom been realized, however, is that because production and consumption cannot in reality be so neatly separated, it follows that production never has been successfully turned into a mere means. The prescriptions of market calculation assume it is a mere means, but they are wrong. Just as with cooking so with handloom weaving or the factory laborer's work, even in a Ford assembly plant, it has always had and will always have many other purposes and ends besides the mere assembly of Model Ts. Market calculations have been destructive because they have never taken these other purposes into account, not because they have eliminated them.[30] As long as one goes on using the terms of market culture to talk about work, one simply cannot see them. It is only possible to sense the inappropriateness of such terms for an activity like cooking because monetary exchanges do not enter into the daily domestic routine. The assignment of numerical values appears artificial and slightly odd.

In the period with which this study begins, all work within the textile trade, with minor exceptions, was carried out within households just as cooking is today. Not only men and women cottagers but even merchants would have found the terms of market culture to be odd in the extreme when applied to their lives.[31]

Researchers thoroughly wedded to market culture themselves have failed to realize that its features may at one point have seemed strange and unfathomable or that its application to social practice was ever problematical. But this was indeed the case. Even those who may differ with the analysis of labor distribution patterns presented here will be able to appreciate the unmistakable evidence of a long period of fumbling and uncertainty in the French textile industry over exactly how a capitalist production process ought to be organized. At the outset it was not certain what authority property rights ought to convey, what control over the production process ought to be exercised, or what the implications of technical change for workplace organization were. Above all, it was unclear how to treat labor as a commodity up for sale in an open market. How was this intangible commodity to be measured? At what times was it being delivered? How were its specific forms in different tasks to be compared and evaluated? What elements of the laborer's behavior were purchased? Did these elements include only a minimum compliance with the wishes of the employer or active loyalty?[32]

None of these questions were answered by deliberate consideration or conscious choice. Instead they were resolved piecemeal as developments in the industry forced them on the attention of entrepreneur and laborer. They were settled for the most part through conflict. There was no means other than open conflict for resolving uncertainties and contradictions which, for various reasons, remained invisible to one side or the other until a crisis arose. But the resolution of these difficulties was absolutely necessary so long as textile goods themselves were being disposed of in a competitive national market and so long as innovations were constantly challenging the reign of established practice. Resolving these difficulties by extending the terms of market culture, moreover, was tantamount to resolving them in favor of the entrepreneur. Fitfully, over the course of the nineteenth century, the French textile trade found ways of bringing practice ever more closely into line with the abstract notions of commodity, exchange, price, and so on, that were the basic building blocks of classical political economy. In this sense, market culture was made within and through the practice of this whole trade community.

That a similar story of gradual and fitful application of market terms could be told for other industries seems quite probable. No attempt has so far been made to see industrialization in precisely this way. Nonetheless it is evident from several recent studies that the overall evolution of workplace practice in the English textile trade, in particular, was not dissimilar.[33] Doubtless it could be interpreted along the same lines.

It is certain that conflict was an endemic feature of early nineteenth-century industrialization, and that the popularization of political economy cannot be understood except in the context of endemic conflict. Reducing the complexity of production processes to a few numbers on a page inevitably favored those who had no direct stake in them and whose only connection lay in the exchange and distribution of capital and goods. Owners of capital could afford to move to the suburbs if the smoke of their new factories became unbearable. The disastrous side effects of their market calculations fell on others. The basic terms of market culture systematically obscured these side effects from view; for this reason, these terms were taken up with alacrity.

Since Thompson's work, it has been repeatedly demonstrated that laborers resisted commercial and technical change at first in the name of an older cultural ideal, a moral economy, which was implicit in older social relations and inimical to the free reign of supply and demand. Laborers subsequently elaborated their own counter-theories. The working-class movement in England developed a notion of unequal exchange that far more satisfactorily represented the real economic conditions of artisans and outworkers than any concept of a competitive market.[34] The vast Chartist movement was intimately linked to aspirations for an entire reorientation of economic policy away from laissez-faire.[35] In France the battle cry of freedom of association, the numerous experiments in People's banks and associative production, and the struggle for a democratic and social republic in 1848–49 represented analogous attempts to remold a still living set of practical principles into a whole alternative cultural and social order.[36]

These movements have so far been seen, however, as a kind of conscious and cultural resistance against a quasi-automatic economic process or, at best, against a combination of automatic economic change and self-serving political repression. Little attempt has been made to see the whole range of political upheavals of the first half of the nineteenth century as a confrontation between two alternative cultural orders. Implicitly students of working-class resistance have too often admitted that markets were real, that industrial development was more or less irresistible, more or less beyond human control. Laborers are inadvertently cast in the romantic role of representing the human, the cultural, the fallible, the vulnerable, whereas their opponents were every bit as fallible and just as much agents of their own cultural project. The terms of market culture were not written in nature but applied piecemeal, haphazardly, unreflectively to a complex array of social practices that resisted simple categorization. Market culture was made by conscious human actors in the same sense that Thompson insisted the English working class was made. The whole history of the industrial revolution ought to be treated in the first instance as a cultural crisis that yielded cultural change.

This is not to say that material conditions played no role in the outcome of the struggle. Quite the contrary. But the aim of this study is to show that there is very little dependable knowledge of what the actual material conditions then were. Nor will such information become available until the whole accretion of pseudo-knowledge of economic conditions couched in the misused and misleading categories of market culture has been jettisoned.

LANGUAGE AND CLASS

It will not be possible to begin rebuilding knowledge of material conditions without a new way of reading documents. In France from roughly the 1780s on, the terms of market culture progressively infiltrated all the discourse that shows up in documents. It is true that the new language that gave rise to and was disseminated by the Revolution has now become the object of intensive historical investigation.[37] More than this is needed, however. The temptation remains strong, when dealing with mundane productive and commercial relations in the Revolutionary era and after, to accept the new conceptual structure that appears in the sources as a perfectly adequate window on reality. However, simply because observers began dividing up the social world before them into production and consumption, labor and leisure, costs and benefits, it does not follow that such divisions suddenly became real in some new sense. In the treatment of documents from this period, it is necessary to maintain a vigilant skepticism about the propriety and utility of the new categories of thought spreading through the literate strata that generated the bulk of surviving documents. A struggle is required at every step to get beyond the documents, to ask how the conceptual apparatus apparent in any given source actually applied to the complex social reality it pretended to report on.

No act of observation is neutral. No observer has ever recorded information merely for its own sake. Observers, in the act of observation, are engaging in social action; their desire is to change as much as to see. Their success in either endeavor is always limited. Culture is primary, therefore; no source no matter how deceptively simple may be safely used for another purpose until it has been subjected to cultural interpretation. The weaknesses of much cultural theory, which are largely responsible for its being viewed as a narrow specialty of limited interest, ought not to be confused with the power of the interpretive method, a generally applicable and indispensable tool.

The interpretive method is founded on a recognition of the uncertainty that attaches to any characterization of human intentions, and it uses awareness of that uncertainty to its advantage.[38] Such uncertainty has practical consequences, after all; history may in large measure be seen as a long, fruitless struggle to banish it once and for all from human affairs. Market culture is only the latest in a long series of failed experiments.

This study will show that in France the language of market culture was present in the documents only in isolated fragments scattered here and there before the 1780s. From 1790 on, however, a dramatic integration of its various elements took place, without at first any corresponding change in the practical details of production and exchange in the textile trade. This gulf between language and practice and its consequences will subsequently be a major theme of the inquiry.

Forewarned of the existence of this gap, it is possible to reconstruct an idea of the real nature of economic conditions within the textile industry, an idea free of the tendentious abstractions of market culture. Such reconstruction shows clearly the failure of a market system to emerge and links that failure in part to the behavior of laborers and in part to

16

the habits of owners and the policies of the state. In other words, these economic conditions cannot be understood in isolation from the cultural and political dimensions that played as lively a role in shaping them as did the wider world commercial system.

These matters will be explored, as has been noted, through examination of an unfolding sequence of conflicts, which provide the surest source of information not only about actual conditions in the trade but also about the motivational horizons of those involved in it. It is necessary, therefore, to say something about the general framework in which the problem of conflict will be approached.

It is accurate to say that this study is an examination of class conflict so long as the term *class* is not allowed to become tainted with certain implications. Too often, the word is used in a way that lets the whole of market culture in the back door after it has been shut out by the front. Classes are too often understood to have interests that motivate their actions in a way precisely analogous to the self-interest attributed to individuals by classical political economy. However, the difficulties that may be raised with respect to the individual apply with equal strength to classes, with the difference that groups of individuals present problems of even greater complexity.

Collective interests cannot even be identified without organization; likewise, once an organization exists individuals have much to gain from participating in it, even if its goals provide only a poor fit with the individual's aspirations or grievances. This is because organization takes work; communication and mutual understanding are material (as well as social) processes; conventions, rituals, and procedures on which there is wide agreement constitute a huge capital investment, so to speak. A community of laborers cannot act in concert in any way until some cultural work has been done among them. They must signal to each other, search each other out, test their mutual concerns, find an idiom in which to express them. By the time conflict breaks out, some of this preliminary work must have already been done.

The basis on which any collective unity is founded, the justifying principle, the sense of right or grievance, is a collective product. It is not entirely appropriate to judge such a product by the same criteria one uses to evaluate the theories and reasonings of individuals. The demands or strategies of a large group may appear at first glance ill-conceived or misguided. But almost always, they turn out to be rooted in the circumstances and experiences of the community; they generally prove to be a guide to its point of view on everyday practice; often they leave unmistakable traces of the work that was done to make a collective consciousness. The actions of a crowd may show that such work has been only half completed or has run up against an unexpected obstacle; ambiguity and contradiction can stymie or dissolve unity momentarily achieved. These mischances can also happen, for that matter, to a police force or a group of mill owners. For the historian who would understand all of this, facile abstractions about class are best left at the door.

French textile laborers certainly came to have, by the end of the nineteenth century, a strong consciousness of their membership in the working class. But this consciousness was as different from theoretical expectation as their own experience of work in industry was from the categories of classical political economy. The historian therefore has much to learn from attending to the development of this consciousness, to its flavor, to its strengths and to its fissures; they are instructive not merely about the laborers' experience of industry but also about certain realities of industrial society that have heretofore been poorly understood.

PART ONE

A world without entrepreneurs, 1750–1815

Money is not a mere "voucher for unspecified utilities," which could be altered at will without any fundamental effect on the character of the price system as a struggle of man against man. "Money" is, rather, primarily a weapon in this struggle and prices are expressions of the struggle; they are instruments of calculation only as estimated quantifications of relative chances in this struggle of interests.

Max Weber, *Economy and Society*, I, 108[1]

The idea of a market system implies the idea of an active entrepreneur who, besides buying all the factors of production in competitive markets, also controls their combination in such a way as to minimize costs and maximize profits. Because he must sell his products within a competitive market, in which price is set by the free play of supply and demand, the only way open to him for maximizing profits is through control of costs. This he can achieve only through tirelessly studying the production process and actively directing those changes in it that he deems necessary for reducing costs.

The idea of a market system, therefore, also implies a particular kind of relationship between the entrepreneur and the laborer he hires. Both parties must understand that he has complete control over the exact shape that labor will take within the production process. Otherwise, he will not be able to alter the process at will, which is a precondition for minimizing costs. In the end, labor must be understood as being delivered to him like a raw material, in a shapeless, unrealized form, malleable, abstract.

This notion of entrepreneurship and this notion of labor as an abstract factor of production played no role in the day-to-day practice of the French textile trade in the ancien regime. It might be possible to isolate a few exceptional enterprises in which the owner seemed to exercise control for the sake of minimizing costs. The important thing, however, is that possessors of capital within the trade felt little incentive to seek control over the production process. Likewise, there was no public recognition of the existence of entrepreneurship of this kind as a crucial social function. It is impossible to appreciate how market culture came to the French textile industry without a thorough understanding of this all-important status quo ante.

If anyone exercised entrepreneurship, it was the laborer; he was in control of production, and he bore the main financial risks associated with that control. Possessors of capital systematically sought to shift these burdens off their own shoulders and onto those of the laborer. In fact, the textile laborers of the eighteenth century, whether urban masters or rural cottagers, were active in the defense of their interests as entrepreneurs. Repeatedly they engaged in collective action over issues involving factors of production and production processes. Their consciousness of these interests was not formulated in these terms, however; neither they nor their contemporaries nor historians subsequently have ever identified their grievances or their protests as entrepreneurial in nature. In a limited sense, however, they were; and this fact underscores how great a distance, both culturally and materially, still existed between eighteenth-century textile production and industrial production as it is now organized.

Economic historians, when looking at this period, emphasize the imminence of transformation. In their eyes, the eighteenth-century economy appears poised for flight; the knitting together of international markets for finished goods and the development of regional supply bottlenecks for certain factors of production, it is known in hindsight, were destined to call the factory system into being. Outworkers in their dispersed cottages, it is said, were already reduced to what amounted to wage–labor status; the merchant manufacturers who supplied them were already thinking and acting like industrial entrepreneurs.[2] But this view of eighteenth-century industrial organization is anachronistic and misleading; it ignores certain crucial structural features and downplays a whole lost, older culture within which those features were experienced and which gave life to them.

The textile laborer was also entrepreneur in the eighteenth century because production was still lodged firmly in the household as a spacial, social, and economic unit. The capital and operating costs of production did not appear distinct, within the laborer's life, from the other needs of his household. Entrepreneurship, likewise, did not appear distinct to him from life itself. But this is tantamount to saying that entrepreneurship did not exist. When laborer and entrepreneur are one, then the decisions to act cannot be distinguished from the act. Nor can the criteria that guide these decisions be reduced to pure profit, since they arise from the whole sphere of the laborers' interest in a particular kind of life. Household expenditures to support that life cannot be distinguished from those that feed the production process. This is not an inferior form of economic organization; it is simply one in which the quantitative criterion of minimal production cost must vie with other criteria in determining what action is worth doing. Whether one should take an hour break or an hour-and-a-half break at noon will not be decided solely in terms of its effect on unit cost, as it will when the entrepreneurial role becomes a distinct facet of social organization. As laborer and consumer, the cottager has other interests that will play their role in the decision. In fact, separating out these diverse interests would have appeared to him as abstract and artificial, even dangerous.

Only the introduction of new spinning technology from England late in the eighteenth century finally challenged this age-old arrangement. And even this decisive challenge was muted and delayed in its effects by the onset of revolution and war. Down to 1815, it is hardly possible to speak of entrepreneurship – in the strict sense implied by the notion of the market system – in French textiles. However, these same years saw a revolution in thinking and in legal principle which, along with the technology, would ensure rapid change thereafter.

1 Commerce as conflict

If entrepreneurship was not a distinct activity in eighteenth-century textile production, then one cannot expect it to have left any documentary trace. And this is indeed the case for eighteenth-century France. A few merchant manufacturers, as they are called, have left some papers behind. In reality these people (misleadingly called *fabricans* in eighteenth-century records) were not manufacturers at all but merchants who contracted out for certain manufacturing processes. Their accounts were kept accordingly and do not reveal the kind of calculation one would expect an entrepreneur to depend on for decision making. Philippe Guignet, for example, has found the account books of a lace-dealing enterprise in Valenciennes for the period 1748 to 1775.[1] The Tribout family bought lace yarn, put out the yarn to individual lace makers (along with a pattern they were to follow in making the lace), and bought the finished lace back at a price negotiated on the spot on the basis of the quality and quantity of the finished product. Madame Tribout kept a single account book, entering all transactions (putting out and buying back) in chronological order. Lace makers were understood to hold their yarn on credit against return of the finished piece; the pattern too was considered to be property of the Tribouts. In theory, lace makers could sell the lace to someone else and pay off their debt; in practice the high nominal value set on yarn and pattern in Madame Tribout's books made this unprofitable. Nothing was produced or transformed on the premises. Open–market price changes for lace were immediately passed through to the lace makers. These are the books of a merchant operation not an industrial one. Nowhere can one find traces of even rudimentary entrepreneurial calculation; no breakdowns for material, labor, storage, or unit costs were made. Labor was not paid for directly; instead lace was purchased at a standard markdown from the market price, taking material costs and expected profit both into account simultaneously. (In fact part of the expected profit was expressed through the inflated material credits.) The lace makers, the real entrepreneurs, kept no accounts at all.

22

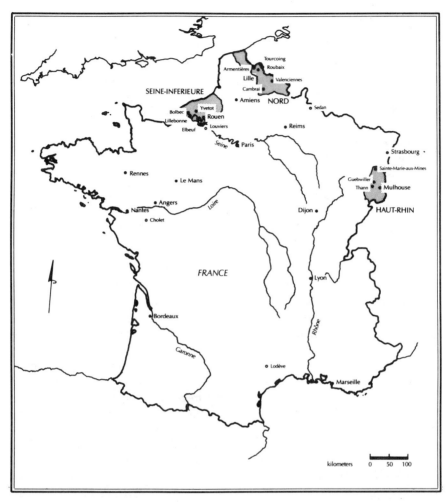

France showing principal cities and major textile centers of the late eighteenth and nineteenth centuries. Shaded areas indicate the three departments of Seine-Inférieure, Nord, and Haut-Rhin.

The same observations apply by and large to all the myriad forms of putting–out operations that grew up during the eighteenth-century textile boom. The structure of putting–out operations ranged from loose to tight, from complex to simple depending on the cost of raw material and the quality of the product desired; but in all cases the bulk of what one could call entrepreneurial decisions was left to the laborer.[2]

A world without entrepreneurs, 1750–1815

Putting-out operations were loosest in the Normandy cotton trade; there they were almost indistinguishable from open–market transactions.[3] A cheap raw material (cotton) was worked up into a low quality product (*siamoises* or *rouenneries* – that is, coarse cotton cloth, plain, striped, or plaid, sometimes with a linen warp – or plaid kerchiefs). Merchant manufacturers in Rouen, Yvetot, and elsewhere, placed raw material on credit with *courtiers*, "factors" – that is, a person with a bag or cart who carried the material out into the countryside and placed it in turn with strings of cottagers. Like a milkman the *courtier* proceeded along the rural road making his deliveries and picking up, not empty bottles, but finished goods at a previously agreed on price. These he returned once a week or once every two weeks to the merchant manufacturer. Each party, merchant and *courtier*, kept a running account of debts and credits and cleared the account when convenient. Merchant manufacturers with fixed shops rarely had any direct dealings with spinners or weavers. Some *courtiers* even placed their material through other, smaller *courtiers*, so that two or three transactions, and twenty or thirty miles' distance, might stand between warehouse and workers.[4] There were also thousands of spinners and weavers who dealt directly with local markets.[5] This entailed the loss of one day a week, more or less, depending on the distance to be traveled. (But such a loss was not necessarily unpleasant, especially in good weather.) These independents, scattered in considerable number over the whole of lower Normandy by 1760, were served by small-scale merchants who made the weekly round of local market days, converging on Rouen on Friday morning, loaded with cloth and looking for fiber to buy.[6] Their number had increased so rapidly between 1700 and 1730 that the government in 1731 had forced the Rouen guilds to set aside one day each week to allow the country dealers into the Cloth Hall, hub of the regional cotton trade.[7] This was the most progressive and most rapidly expanding sector of the whole French textile industry in the eighteenth century, having grown from nothing in 1700 to an industry providing work for perhaps three hundred thousand cottagers by 1780.

The one great danger that a rural cottager faced within the eighteenth-century putting–out system was being shut out of a local market either by distance or legal maneuver. In that case, he might be forced to get raw material from a specific *courtier*, who could then lower his offering price at will without fear of competition. A whole village might fall into dependency on such a supplier (as often occurred in the Nottinghamshire stocking trade in England by the end of the eighteenth century, where the bagman became a hated figure in popular lore).[8] Pierre Goubert has noted cases of this kind of dependency in the Beauvais region late in the

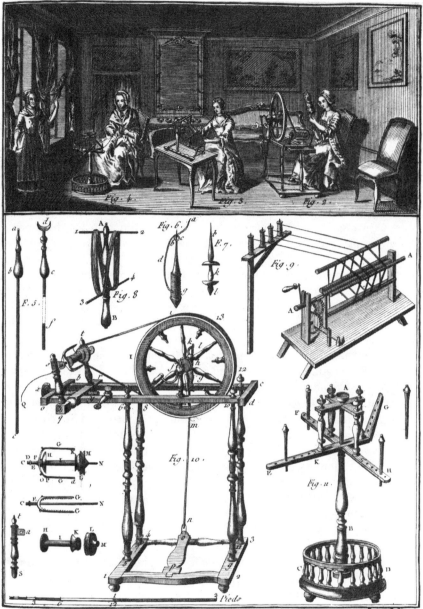

Figure 1. Spinning equipment of the eighteenth century. "Figure 10" in the plate shows a fully assembled spinning wheel. "Figure 9" shows a Manchester reel, reeling off four hanks at once (note the cog wheels set to ring a bell every 80 revolutions). From *Recueil de planches de l'encyclopédie [méthodique] par ordre de matières*. Tome sixième (Paris, 1786). These were the accompanying illustrations to Roland de la Platière's volumes.

seventeenth century (among coarse woolen producers); Serge Chassagne has signaled its existence among cotton weavers to the south around Cholet late in the eighteenth century.[9] But the Normandy trade in its heyday appears to have supported so many dealers and local markets that cottagers had little to fear from monopsony. If they did not like the terms offered by a specific *courtier*, there were others to choose from; or as a last resort, one could always choose the weekly trip to market. *Courtiers* therefore had to offer prices attractive enough to keep the weavers and spinners at home on market day. Spinners were in a particularly advantageous position since yarn was always in short supply. (It took six spinners more or less to supply each loom.) Rouen merchants routinely had to round out their yarn supply with open–market purchases of yarn imported from distant regions.[10] The simple wheel became an ubiquitous fixture of rural homes all over western France by the end of the century.

At the other extreme of organization from the Rouen cotton trade were certain town-based luxury wool and linen trades, all old and most of them stable or declining in contrast to robust cotton. These existed in Le Mans, Amiens, Lille, Valenciennes, Sedan, Cambrai, Elbeuf and numerous other provincial towns.[11] Relations between merchant and weaver were often extremely tight in these towns. The raw material was expensive, the weaving complicated and requiring considerable skill. Lille production of *camelots* (a fine, open-weave woolen cloth), for example, was organized as follows. Weavers owned only the loom frame and received from the merchant a harness made up of warp, reed, and heddles ready to be installed on the loom frame. The weaver was not trusted to wind his own warp or thread it through the heddles; this was done by specialists in the merchant's shop. Thus the merchant could control the variety and fineness of the cloth produced, even though production went on across town in the weaver's home. There was no danger that the weaver would cheat on the weight of the yarn (by adding water and then cutting off ends of yarn to sell to peddlers), because the whole warp was measured and prepared before it left the merchant's premises. From the weaver's point of view, the danger of dependency on a single supplier was counterbalanced by the strength of urban guild institutions – which set prices, limited shop size, specified production procedures to the last detail and controlled access to the trade – as well as by the scarcity of his skill.[12] Both of these bulwarks were under challenge in the eighteenth century, but not because of declining vigilance by guild authorities within the towns. Instead, merchants were increasingly finding weavers in the countryside with sufficient skill to work up luxury goods, and fashion simultaneously was slowly turning its back on the highest quality cloths.[13] Within the towns, neither merchants nor individual weavers had much in the way of entrepreneurial decisions to make; these were already made for them, in effect, and exhaustively specified by guild regulation. The merchant manufacturer's sphere of control was limited to choice of the grade and guaranteeing the quality of the product. Merchants who turned to rural weavers were not exercising entrepreneurial control either, so much as looking for better deals. In fact, the lower costs of rural weavers were offset by a considerable loss of control over production. Rural weavers could not be closely supervised, and it was too expensive to transport whole harnesses out to them; some or all of the set–up procedure had to be entrusted to them. The product was almost always of distinctly lower quality.[14] Isolation gave rural weavers ideal opportunities for pilferage, as well.[15] The weight of wool in particular could vary up to 40 percent depending on how much water vapor the fibers had absorbed.[16] Large quantities of wool could be clipped away and sold and water added without the merchant being able to tell. (Spinning offered even greater opportunity for this kind of pilferage.)

The eighteenth century saw the development of large populations of adequately skilled rural weavers producing better grades of cloth around towns like Le Mans, Valenciennes, Saint-Quentin, Sedan, Lille, or Reims. The lower price of these goods offset the loss in quality as compared to urban guild production. At the same time in the wool-producing centers a whole underground rural trade in pilfered fiber and cloth made from pilfered fiber developed with its own peddlers, merchants, warehouses, and customers.[17] As a result, rural weavers always had an obvious recourse if they did not like the prices offered by the merchants in town.

In the fine-linen producing regions, which depended on fiber from local flax crops, merchants had absolutely no control over the flow of goods, however much they struggled to exercise such control. Even where guilds strictly regulated who could deal in finished cloth and who could not, illegal dealing was rife. Outside Valenciennes, for example, country weavers bringing their fine linens to market would be accosted by *courtiers de cabaret*, unauthorized small-scale merchants, who offered to save them the rest of the trip to town with a favorable price. Valenciennes authorities were also deeply concerned about peddlers who came across from the Austrian Netherlands and bought up scarce linen yarn from rural spinners. But nothing could be done to stop such practices.[18]

The well known and oft-hailed decline of the guilds in eighteenth-century France did not, therefore, mean a concomitant rise in entrepreneurial control of merchant manufacturers over the production process. If anything, the opposite was the case. The putting–out system remained to the end of the century one in which merchant manufacturers had only limited influence over production. Structural conditions ensured, moreover, that they felt no need to seek out greater control. They were not

Figure 2. An eighteenth-century handloom. From *Recueil de planches de l'encyclopédie [méthodique] par ordre de matières*. Tome sixième (Paris, 1786).

Pl. 3.

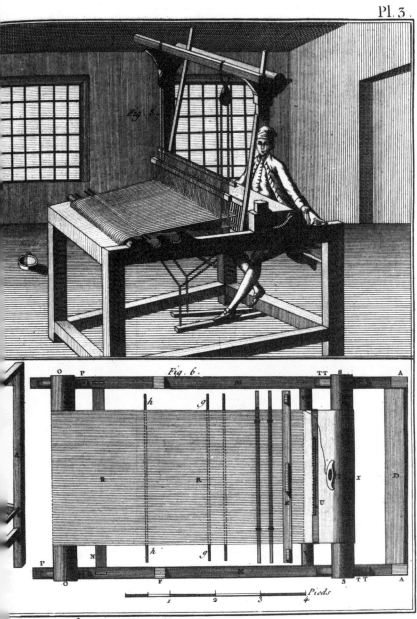

Fig. 5.

Fig. 6.

Pieds

sserand.

in a position to benefit or to suffer from a particular laborer's decisions about his own work. So long as the prices paid to the *courtier* were in line with open–market prices, it did not matter to a merchant manufacturer whether the laborers who worked up his cloth were lazy or assiduous, worked two hours a day or fourteen, worked in his garden or at his loom, worked rapidly or languidly. All this was utterly left to the cottager to decide.

Some may find these claims too extreme. Recent studies of Sedan and Lodève, for example, have shown merchant manufacturers not only breaking guild monopolies by the mid-eighteenth century but also vigorously asserting direct control over production. At Lodève the trade went through a process of reurbanization, as Christopher Johnson has put it, in which rural weavers were drawn in to work in centralized loom shops in the city "under the eye of the boss and operating on his time schedule."[19] But it is important to know exactly what motivated this centralization. Lodève merchants lived from large government contracts, producing unchanging runs of coarse woolens for military uniforms. The initial outlay of capital to operate on this scale must have been considerable; contract deadlines or the need for rapid turnover of operating capital may have been the factor that urged merchants to impose time discipline on their weavers. If so, this was an important step toward entrepreneurial control but not fully equivalent to it. Entrepreneurs seek to change the process, to advance productivity, in order to reduce factor costs; this is much more than a mere concern for turnover, which is characteristic of a merchant outlook.

At Sedan, merchant manufacturers also centralized production processes, but only finishing processes. In the production of the town's fine woolens, finishing the cloth – cropping and dyeing – cost three times as much as weaving. Centralized shops for finishing were a way for merchant manufacturers to break the control of the croppers' guild on this costly final step. Here centralization served the same limited aim for the finishing stage as rural production did for weaving. Sedan merchants were also concerned about capital turnover rates; their raw material – fine Spanish wool – was very expensive and they sought to minimize the time it sat on their weavers' looms in the country by setting strict time limits for the cloth's return.[20] One can see steps being made toward entrepreneurial control in both these towns, steps that set them apart from the general practices of the period; at the same time these were only limited steps, motivated by concerns characteristic of merchant bookkeeping.[21]

Across the whole spectrum of organizational structures that flourished in the putting–out phase of textile production, entrepreneurial control remained lodged, not with the possessors of accumulated capital, but elsewhere, either with guild institutions or with the humble cottager himself. The weaver might be thirty miles away from his urban merchant supplier, dealing through two layers of *courtiers*, or just across the street, under the watchful eye of shop clerks and guild officials. He might be working on the coarsest grade of cotton *siamoises* or on fine linen *batiste* gauze. At either extreme and at any point in between he controlled the pace, application, care, timing, and sometimes even the technique of his work.

AN ENTREPRENEURIAL RIOT

The embedding of entrepreneurial controls within the everyday life of the laborer was not without consequences for that life. Along with control come risks; the size of the market within which textile laborers operated was steadily expanding and so were the dangers associated with such operation. Many textile laborers were new to the trade, drawn away from subsistence agriculture or from other by-industries. Now, in unprecedented numbers they had become dependent on a money income from a trade that stretched across vast distances linking poor people continents away from each other into a vital interdependency. The consequences of small price variations could be unexpectedly drastic.

It is extremely difficult to say how this change was experienced by laborers; their entrepreneurial activity no more than any other feature of their lives was the object of routine written expression. Nonetheless, records of a few episodes of collective protest are highly suggestive. The 1752 disturbance at Rouen is particularly revealing and repays detailed consideration.

A piece of text, which André Rémond came across in his research on Rouen, sheds a glimmer of light into the obscurity surrounding the daily lives of Rouen cotton spinners who by the 1750s were apparently quite numerous within the town itself. The spinners were all female and all operated independently of any organized putting–out system. The text speaks directly about the typical spinner's daily entrepreneurial planning:

> If she has only enough money to pay for three pounds of raw cotton, she buys no more. She works with this small amount, and works with care. When the cotton is spun she sells it that much more advantageously as her work is perfect. From the proceeds, she subtracts enough for her subsistence, and if her small capital has now increased, she buys a larger amount of raw material.[22]

From another source one learns that small peddlers plied Rouen streets selling small amounts of raw cotton out of a bag and buying yarn.[23] John Holker, the English expert who was advising the royal government on trade policy and was stationed in Rouen at that time, spoke disparagingly of this whole system of cotton peddling. The merchants were without a uniform yarn measurement system, he said; they needed to establish a standard reel circumference and standard ratios of yarn weight to yarn length, so that yarn could be accurately graded. As it was, he complained, chaos reigns in production standards, spinners produce whatever kind of yarn they prefer, peddlers are skimming profits out of the system, and the larger merchants are never able to predict what quality or grade of yarn will be available.[24]

At the end of April 1752 a new royal ordinance was posted in Rouen requiring all trade in cotton fiber or yarn to be confined to the Cloth Hall and specifically forbidding trade with unauthorized peddlers.[25] (Whether this ordinance antedated or followed Holker's memoir is not clear.) The following day a crowd of several hundred cotton spinners, having gathered at the Cloth Hall to attempt to sell yarn, became angry and began overturning stalls and pillaging (a word used rather loosely in eighteenth-century accounts of riots) guild members' wares. Later that day, a large crowd of spinners gathered in front of the Palais de Justice, seat of the Parlement de Normandie, highest royal court in the province. They began breaking down the doors; but at the last moment the president of the Parlement, from a second-floor window, promised that the offending ordinance would be revoked.

Spinners gathered again the following morning at the intendant's office, awaiting the official word. According to one spinner who was later arrested and interrogated before the Parlement, a number of the crowd, including herself, entered the building, where nervous officials gave them money and begged them to go away. When she got back outside, she said, someone in the crowd had cried out, "It is not cotton that we want, but grain!" The spinners, joined by certain men about whose identity one can only guess, left the intendant's office and attacked a royal granary down near the river, where purchases intended to ensure the supply of Paris were stored. Another witness interrogated before the Parlement, who worked at a coal storehouse on the wharfs, denied that she had told the crowd where to find the grain but admitted, under persistent questioning, that she had in several instances told them which warehouses did not have grain – that behind one door they would find coal, behind another door wine, and so on. The official reports state that the crowd "pillaged" the grain. It is clear from the testimony of other witnesses, however, that first windows were stoned and doors broken down, and then the grain sacks were removed, torn open and their contents strewn in the streets. Several other grain storage points met with the same fate before the day was over. That afternoon a placard announcing the intendant's revocation of the ordinance was posted throughout town. But by then it was too late.

This incident has been called a food riot, categorized, that is, as one of many hundreds of episodes that made the food riot the most common form of collective protest of the eighteenth century.[26] This in itself is not objectionable. If, however, one argues about this incident, as certain historians have argued about food riots in general, that the participants were moved by "consumer" grievances, then one is making a serious error. Within the terms of market culture, it might be more appropriate to refer to this as a raw-material riot or perhaps a factor-of-production riot, and to see the spinners as being moved by entrepreneurial grievances. The vitality or morbidity of their household enterprises was determined by the price spread between raw cotton and grain on the one hand – the factors of production that kept them alive and kept them working – and cotton yarn on the other – the product that generated their earnings. The records indicate that grain prices were unusually high in Rouen that spring. The first effect of high grain prices would have been to drain the spinners' fund of working capital. The more spent on grain, the less available for raw cotton. That precarious balance, so vividly described in the quote cited earlier in this section, by which spinners sought to accumulate the stocks necessary for production, would have tipped against them. Beyond a certain point they would have been deprived of the ability to work at all for lack of money to buy fiber. In this context the royal ordinance came as an aggravating factor. Cloth Hall prices were apparently not as favorable as the peddlers'. Someone was trying to make a killing out of his guild privileges; the injustice of the maneuver was all too obvious. So the spinners sought to impose a popular justice; they demanded the reinstatement of free trade in the factors of production.

Even this corrected economic analysis of their grievance would be incomplete, however, if one failed to recognize that all these abstractions are inappropriate to a proper understanding of the spinners' motives. The spinners did not engage in distinct entrepreneurial, labor, or consumer functions. They were not trying to maximize profit as entrepreneurs or maximize purchasing power as consumers or minimize labor time as laborers. They were all of these things at once; and they necessarily reconciled conflicts in their daily lives between these diverse functions (for example, the desire for earnings versus the desire for leisure time) in terms of some higher notion of a way of life, a pattern, which they sought to achieve. One can know little about what the pattern was, but it is certain that it existed. There can be little doubt, for example, that these spinners were tied into a web of mutual social obligations, familial and otherwise, that determined their need to work in the first place and provided criteria by which to decide how much work and what kind of work they would do.[27]

Likewise they did not present their grievance in the streets by reference to a specific economic function. They did not beseige the Palais de Justice as angry entrepreneurs or angry consumers. The idiom of their protest was not economic at all; it was couched in terms of a failure of reciprocity between the king's government and his loyal subjects. Royal grain was a handy symbol of that reciprocity. The spinners could have attacked any number of grain stores; they had their ways, as the record shows, of finding out where grain was kept. They could have marched to the Grain Market a few blocks away. They could have attacked the royal wine kegs or the royal coal. But they chose the royal grain store, created by the king's servants precisely to ensure the well-being of his people in times of hardship. When questioned before the Parlement, one woman arrested for gathering up pillaged grain out of the gutters insisted that the grain was not the king's, but "God's property." Another, when asked why she had come to the intendant's office on the second morning, said "I came to sell my cotton, since I could not sell it to the peddlers."[28] Behind the obvious sarcasm and defiance of this last comment lay a deeper message: "To whom else but the king's representative should I turn when my survival was threatened?" The king's long-standing and extensive intervention in matters of production and exchange had always derived its most fundamental justification from his duty to ensure the temporal well-being of his subjects.[29] The spinners thus saw their grievance in moral, not just in economic terms; they took action to rectify an injustice done them by the king's government. They did not see their action as collective bargaining by riot, or bargaining in any form, but as the concrete rectification of a moral imbalance.[30] It is inappropriate to impose exchange interpretations of whatever kind on their actions or to try to characterize them in strictly economic terms.

THE GUILD AS ANTIENTREPRENEUR

The spinners' protest of 1752 aimed at the same thing that the whole guild system was intended to provide its members. All the previous observations about the practical realities of their working lives apply equally well to independent guild artisans. They did not make decisions about their productive labor in terms of any single criterion; their "profits," the "purchasing power" of their "wages," their enjoyment of "leisure" were all utterly indistinguishable. Within the terms of market culture, an urban weaver who spent the Monday after Easter in a bar (a habit sanctioned by long tradition), could be construed as failing to rationalize his use of time (assuming one accepted – quite irrationally – that monetary gain is the sole criterion of rational use of time). Or he could be construed as maximizing comparative advantage by forgoing money income for a more pleasant alternative. Or he could be construed as engaging in a farsighted entrepreneurial calculus: by relaxing on Monday, he knew he would be willing to work harder on Friday and Saturday. Any particular weaver was probably doing all of these things, in one sense, and yet none of them in the sense that he did not use such abstractions to think about his life.

In strictly economic terms, guild institutions could be said to have systematized these quasi-entrepreneurial, quasi-consumer decisions in such a way as to prevent petty producers from doing each other inadvertent harm. The exact mix of monetary and nonmonetary advantages that they wished to achieve had to be collectively determined, otherwise each individual was insecure. If one weaver decided to work longer than others, for example, he might place his fellows in jeopardy by underselling them or by accumulating capital to enlarge his shop and engross the market. Most guilds as noted earlier had strict limits on the number of looms allowed per shop, to prevent just such a possibility, and those limits were a subject of frequent contention among members.[31] Likewise, the large number of guild–sanctioned holidays in Catholic Europe could be seen as a kind of collectively imposed expenditure of profits. The same could be said for the guilds' elaborate rounds of banquets and rituals, or the expensive beautification of guild chapels.[32] Such activities served the twin function of draining off threatening accumulations, and imposing identical entrepreneurial decisions on all members at once. The elaborate specification of production standards, established in uneasy cooperation with the royal government, was a necessary outgrowth of the guilds' other entrepreneurial functions. Seen in this way, a guild was a fortress built to keep market forces out and to protect the entrepreneurial function from feeling their stimulus, so that this function could remain slumbering within a form of life that guild members had collectively established for themselves.

To explain guilds in this way, however correct in terms of the basic concepts of market culture, is nonetheless anachronistic. Since a guild member's every action was at once that of an entrepreneur, a laborer, and a consumer, it made no sense for him to distinguish these functions in the first place. The form of consciousness that flowered within this regulatory fortress saw work and exchange as either good or bad in a spiritual sense, and the fortress of guild controls was viewed as providing the necessary discipline to ensure that each kind of work achieved its own proper degree of perfection. The requirements that guild members celebrate the feast day of their patron saint or attend the funeral of a deceased colleague were of a piece with the detailed specification of product design and quality. All were elements of a moral correctness. No one thought of guilds as aimed at preventing the differentiation of a distinct social function (entrepreneurship); instead, they saw any deviation from guild production standards as morally suspect, as fraudulent behavior aimed at fooling the customer.[33]

Guild members stood in a publicly acknowledged relationship with both sovereign and church. They took an oath on entry as did candidates for the priesthood or the magistracy; guild statutes were sanctioned by the crown; each guild was also a religious confraternity. The Parlement of Paris argued against the dissolution of the guilds in 1776 by predicting rampant deception of the consumer and a breakdown of social deference.[34] The journeymen of Paris showed that they agreed on this last point by celebrating wildly when the edict of dissolution was forcibly registered. They knew that now police agents would no longer be able to throw them out of bars during guild-mandated work hours.[35]

Arguments similar to the Parlement's were adduced in a flood of memoirs submitted to Necker in 1779 when he proposed reforming the regulatory apparatus.[36] Regulation, said the summary report, creates commerce and can "disturb only the manufacturer of bad faith." Without regulation fraud and suspicion would dry up the flow of trade. Every form of production whether in the country or the town constituted "*corps politiques* which cannot exist without regulation because public security is at stake." Even new industries born to serve the taste of the consumer try to give their work "the proportions of a durable cloth."[37] Innovative cost cutting, which within market culture can only be seen as the essential feature of entrepreneurship, appeared to the writers of these memoirs as a kind of criminal activity, dangerous to public order and to commerce. The guilds, which appeared to so many later observers as sleepy, stagnant backwaters existing only to monopolize trade and stifle creativity, appeared to their eighteenth-century defenders as indispensable bulwarks against a threatening flood of deception and insubordination. Today we see work discipline, quality assurance, and fair dealing with the public as elements of the entrepreneurial role imposed by competition. In the eighteenth century these "entrepreneurial" functions, carried out by guilds and government in conjunction, were seen as antithetical to any form of cost-cutting innovation.

There is abundant, if patchy evidence that the humble urban weaver shared the outlook of these articulate conservatives to the last detail. In Rouen, as the flood of rural production into the Cloth Hall rose after 1730, elected guild officials sought to resist it by enforcing production standards with ruthless precision.[38] The warp yarns of every piece of rural product were counted; one yarn short of the specified number was sufficient grounds for confiscation of the cloth and a fine imposed on its owner. The quality of dye was tested with care; the length measured to the last *pouce*. Perhaps it is obvious that guild members would have tried to resist the spread of rural production; but it is not obvious that the manner they chose would involve a rigorous enforcement of quality standards. This choice reflects their immediate assumption that products from outside the guilds would necessarily be deficient in quality. It was, moreover, a completely inadequate form of resistance.

The guild members of Lille engaged in an unremitting struggle throughout the eighteenth century to protect their privileges, even after these privileges had become worthless scraps of paper.[39] They continued fighting and winning battles in court long after they had lost the war. That the humble guild weavers of the town failed either to give up the fight or to adopt new strategies is suggestive of how deeply wedded they remained to the guild outlook.

In view of these struggles, which yielded only a heavy burden of court and lawyer fees for the guild members of Lille, it is perhaps no accident that Lille popular literature in the eighteenth century is dominated by a single theme, that of ridicule for country bumpkins. The village of Turcoing, a center of illegal wool weaving, was singled out to stand for the whole surrounding Flemish plain, and hundreds of anonymous broadsheet songs were printed poking fun at its rustic inhabitants.[40] There is the story of the Turcoing lad who ate a spider in his soup, another about the Tourcennois who went to Paris to become a priest and ended up in a "convent" full of prostitutes, or one about a Tourcoing farm boy who came to Lille to pay the rent on his father's farm but got lost once inside the town gate. Every building looked so fine he thought it was a church. He wandered aimlessly until a gracious member of the lace-yarn-makers' guild (a *filtier*, as they were called) showed him the way to the landlord's house. There the boy kept slipping on the waxed floor and thought the wine he drank at dinner was a magical water.[41] This popular teasing breathes of the guild spirit. Quality, sophistication, and noblesse oblige are the characteristics which, by contrast to the rustics from *extra muros*, the humble Lillois claim for their own.

Philippe Guignet has studied the accounts of the Valenciennes linen weavers' guild and provided a detailed, quantitative picture of its decline in the eighteenth century. This guild, too, engaged in expensive lawsuits. To pay for them, while continuing to support the redecoration of its chapel and its annual procession and banquet, the members kept raising entry fees just as rural production was making membership worth ever less. To the end they believed their decline to be due to a failure of quality control. In reality, it was simply the new taste for plainer, cheaper products of the country that did them in.[42]

True to the guild outlook, urban weavers sought to control events through more vigorous enforcement and through adjusting their regulations to the harsher climate.[43] Their ultimate aim was not really any different from that of the spinners of Rouen in 1752. None of these people were attempting to defend their interests in any narrow economic sense of the word; they were seeking to gain or retain a place within the moral framework of ancien régime society, a framework that linked every subject to the king through a great hierarchy of corporate bodies. For any one of them as an individual, the maximization of gain would have urged an immediate renunciation of the guild regulations they clung to.[44]

THE POLITICS OF PROTO–INDUSTRIALIZATION

The guild system of production was destroyed by the spread of rural commerce. But it would be wrong to assert, as some have done, that its downfall was inevitable, the result of a quasi-automatic, blind process of economic growth. The guilds suffered a political as much as an economic defeat, at the hands of the people whose outlook was not very different from their own.

The importance of political influence to the spread of rural production is difficult to gauge; but the traces of it are unmistakable. In 1725 the king granted the Rouen merchant guild of *merciers–drapiers* the power to create *ouvriers* (workers), who could work "in the capacity of *maître drapiers* (master weavers)," but would be forbidden to train apprentices, band together, or elect representatives, that is, to create a guild of their own. The justification was that these weavers "whether from the town or elsewhere" did not work on their own account. Obviously some sort of putting-out operation was being legalized. In 1731, as noted in the earlier section, The Putting–Out Wilderness, the government opened the Cloth Hall to rural products, to the dismay of Rouen weavers but much to the delight of Rouen merchants. In 1749, the lace-makers' guild was given permission to deal wholesale in any kind of product. (Heretofore they had been limited to buying raw material and selling the products of their own labor.)[45] In 1752, the intendant issued the disastrous ordinance limiting cotton dealing to the Cloth Hall. These actions show that in the first half of the century different groups of Rouen merchants were able to win concessions from the royal government sanctioning their growing volume of trade with the countryside. They did not favor free trade as such but freedom for their own trade and restrictions for others. Either by means of political influence or convincing argument or both, they brought the government to see their point of view. The highest aim of royal policy in this period was maximizing national prosperity. Colbert had believed that this could only be done by careful surveillance of quality; because the guilds already carried out such surveillance they were convenient instruments of royal will.[46] But this did not mean that they were to be favored under all circumstances. Apparently in Rouen prosperity might also be increased by specific exceptions to the town guilds' monopoly of production in favor of specific merchants' guilds.

In Lille a three-sided struggle developed. Lille merchants enjoyed a legal monopoly of all trade in textile goods between the Chatelenie of Lille and the rest of France. They naturally stood to gain from any expansion of rural manufacturing. Lille guilds, however, enjoyed a monopoly of textile production within the Chatelenie (with a few exceptions). Therefore Lille merchants had to pass off all rural products as having originated in town. At the same time rural merchant manufacturers in the villages of Roubaix and Tourcoing, besides defying the Lille guilds' monopoly, chafed at having to deal exclusively through the tight-knit group of Lille wholesalers. Claim and counter-claim, suit and counter-suit dragged on before the courts from 1717 to 1776 without sign of let up.[47] The guilds retained their monopoly, but nothing was done to enforce it. The Lille merchants retained theirs as well, and it continued to have real meaning. Rural production expanded rapidly. Finally in 1776 the merchant manufacturers of Roubaix and Tourcoing were granted permission to engage in the trade that they had by now built up into a flourishing industry. They proclaimed to the world that this victory was due not to the high principle of freedom of trade but to their carefully nourished reputation for high-quality goods.[48] As late as 1789, however, they may be found petitioning the National Assembly to release them from the requirement of dealing exclusively through Lille. (Meanwhile other side battles were being waged, for example, that between lace yarn makers in Lille and Armentières.)[49]

Again one finds the strong imprint of a specific urban merchant elite on the trend of royal policy. A similar story with variations could be told for Valenciennes, Sedan, Le Mans, Saint-Quentin, and doubtless other towns as well.[50] Whether the government consciously encouraged rural production before 1760 is unclear; the import of hundreds of local decisions was nonetheless to allow it and to help certain merchants dominate it. The guilds were politically outmaneuvered; by the 1750s their monopolies on production were severely weakened or entirely gone.

In spite of government help, however, the urban merchants did not have it all their own way either. Rural production spawned rural merchants; factors, carters, storekeepers were attracted into the trade. For them it was an easy matter to skirt the legal markets, to deal in cloth that did not meet legal production specifications, to escape, in short, from the whole regulatory mechanism if they desired.[51] Increasingly town merchants realized that sustaining their own volume of trade required them to deal with these new entries. Valenciennes weavers complained of certain members of the merchants' guild who dealt openly with illegal *courtiers*.[52] In Rouen the constant escalation of sanctions against dealing outside the Cloth Hall shows how futile it was to try to stop it.[53] Urban merchants in the end undermined their own monopolies of trade by the success of their attack on guild monopolies of production. There was no way to ensure that rural production would all be funneled through town markets where royal inspection bureaus served as the linchpin of the whole regulatory mechanism.[54]

That neither merchants nor government fully understood the implications of the end of guild monopolies is strongly suggested by circumstances surrounding the 1752 riot in Rouen. The government was totally unprepared for what happened. After issuing the ordinance, the intendant had left town. On the second day of the rioting his assistant hesitated for several critical hours to repeal it without his express authorization. A perfect opportunity to appease the spinners was missed. For three days the crowds controlled the streets because the nearest royal troops took so long in arriving. Neither the intendant nor the Cloth Hall interests who urged this move on him had any idea of the impact the ordinance would have on the lives of the cotton spinners.

After 1760, however, blind and piecemeal chipping at the guild system was replaced by a concerted royal policy to promote rural production. All rural areas were freed of prohibitions on production in 1762.[55] In 1765, a strict edict came down from the Conseil d'Etat forbidding elected guild officials from interfering with rural commerce. They were not to prevent rural producers from buying raw materials in the legal markets nor fraudulently remove seals or labels from rural cloth. Under certain circumstances they were no longer allowed to participate in the inspection process.[56] Their sole remaining weapon against rural products was stripped away.

THE MYOPIA OF PHYSIOCRACY

These bold measures were taken due to the growing influence of a new school of economic thought in the capital. This school, the Physiocrats as they came to be called, advocated complete freedom of trade, but they did not do so because they had a clear idea of a market system. In view of the contemporary structure of production and exchange, it is not surprising to discover that the Physiocrats failed to develop a consistent notion of entrepreneurship.

This school's view of manufacturing was shaped by the contemporary drama of guild decline and the lessons they drew from it. Free trade should exist in manufacturing, they believed, because the consumer ought to be able to choose whatever level of quality he wished and not be forced to pay a high price for goods produced according to the strict standards of the guilds. Turgot, in his 1759 eulogy of one of the pioneers of the new economic thought, Vincent de Gournay, explained the advantage of free trade in just this way.

> M. de Gournay thought that every citizen who worked deserved the gratitude of the public ... He thought that a worker who had fashioned a piece of cloth had added something of value to the state's wealth, that if this cloth was inferior to others, it could find its way among the multitude of consumers to someone who thought this inferiority preferable to a more costly perfect. He was far from supposing that this piece of cloth, because not in conformity with certain rules, ought to be cut into fragments and the one who made it charged with a fine that could reduce a whole family to beggary.[57]

This is an argument aimed against guild regulation and the guild monopoly. The "every citizen who worked" was the rural weaver; the "others" who make superior cloth were the members of urban guilds resentful of rural production. The assumption is that price and quality are tightly linked. But this assumption leaves certain entrepreneurial activities out of account; the entrepreneur in a market system must look for ways of achieving equal quality at a lower cost. The assumption of this passage is also that individual producers deal independently with a complex commercial system through which the product must "find its way" to the consumer.

It is a statement perfectly attuned to the changing conditions of the textile trade in that period. The entrepreneurial function is not seen because it had yet to differentiate itself; free trade is advocated because everyone should be free to add "something of value to the state's wealth." The Colbertian notion that regulation of quality maximizes prosperity is the obvious target of Turgot's statement. Implicitly the accomplishments of those town-based merchants who pioneered rural production are being hailed. Nor is this surprising as de Gournay himself, Turgot tells us, rose from the ranks of the merchant class and had wide experience of commercial activity.

Quesnay, the leading thinker of the Physiocrats, was acutely aware of the importance of the entrepreneurial function of cost cutting. But he failed to see this function as the province of a distinct individual with a proprietary interest in the production process; that is, he failed to speak of the entrepreneur as such. Quesnay argued vigorously that only agriculture added value to the work put into it because of the productive power of nature that human beings merely channeled. Manufacturing was a sterile activity that resulted in no increase in value. Of those who resisted his arguments he said:

> They agree that the more one can save on costly outlays or on labor in the fabrication of artisanal products, the more profitable are such savings due to the reduction in price of these products [*plus cette épargne*

est profitable par la diminution du prix de ces ouvrages]. Nonetheless they believe that the output of wealth that results from the work of artisans consists in the increased monetary value [*valeur vénale*] of their products; these contradictory ideas exist in the same head, bouncing about continually, without any inconsistency being perceived.

For Quesnay, the former of these propositions was true; therefore the latter had to be false:

> This drinking glass costs only one pence, the raw material is worth a farthing, the work of the glassblower quadruples the value of the material. Here is [some would say] a production of wealth which has realized a triple increase. [But by this reasoning] it would be very disadvantageous if one invented a machine that made, at no cost or at very little cost, beautiful lace or excellent paintings. In fact the invention of the printing press gave rise to serious misgivings over the reduction in work for scriveners. However, after examination, it was adopted everywhere.[58]

From such arguments, Quesnay concluded:

> The monetary value of such commodities is nothing more than the value of the raw material and of the subsistence which the laborer consumes during his work; and the sale of this marketable value by the worker is nothing more than a re-sale operation. [Can one believe that] to re-sell is to produce?[59]

Quesnay fails to distinguish here between cost of production and price. In the first citation he does not say to whom cost-cutting measures are beneficial, obscuring this all-important issue behind the ambiguous phrase "the more profitable are such savings due to the reduction in price of these products." In the third citation he implies that any cost cutting that occurs in the production process is immediately reflected in the price of the final product. But the difference between the cost of producing a thing and the price that is charged for it is the life blood of the entrepreneur's existence. It is here that profit is squeezed out. It is to increase this difference even if only temporarily that entrepreneurs engage in any cost-cutting activities at all. It might be said, therefore, that Quesnay saw the importance of cost cutting in the production process, but did not see who would engage in cost cutting or why. Nor did he analyze the production process further than to distinguish labor input from raw materials; a third and crucial factor of production, the tools and techniques, that is, fixed capital, is passed over in silence. But it is principally by an investment in this factor that the industrial entrepreneur seeks to minimize the costs of the others.

The Physiocrats' emphasis on agriculture was closely linked to a failure to appreciate the full scope of the entrepreneur's role. In agriculture the land was a piece of fixed capital that the Physiocrats could not ignore;

they fully realized the importance of managing its use according to informed techniques.[60] Such management ought to be rewarded, and therefore regulation of the grain trade should be abolished. The price of grain would then rise, spurring the manager of farm land to greater efforts, creating a greater output of food for the nation's population. Paradoxically they foresaw a drop in the prices of manufactured goods if all trade were freed of restrictions. Their eyes saw no manager of production who needed to be spurred on nor any fixed capital to be managed in manufacturing. A drop in prices of manufactured goods was therefore to be welcomed, manufacturing was only a question of reselling. This was an admirable way of characterizing the activities of a merchant manufacturer, but it ignored the complex balancing act which any outworker depended on for survival.

The famous weakness of Physiocracy, its failure to see manufacturing as an independent source of value, is therefore based on a selective sensitivity to the interest and activities of possessors of capital in the contemporary French economy. Large land owners did engage in entrepreneurial activities, and the Physiocrats fully recognized the importance of these activities for the productivity of agriculture. Large merchant manufacturers did not engage in entrepreneurial activities; in manufacturing the entrepreneurial function was invisible to the Physiocrats. It got lost in the shuffle of sentences; the advantages of cost cutting were construed as proof of the essential sterility of manufacturing. The theory also had the advantage of accounting for the known effects of the elimination of trade restrictions. Unrestricted trade in grain did result in higher prices; the spread of rural manufactures beyond the reach of the guilds likewise resulted in lower prices. Both of these results were advantageous to the possessors of capital; Physiocracy made them appear to be the natural outcome of economic law, advantageous to the nation as a whole, and therefore to the crown.

THE MYSTERIES OF PRODUCTION

But it would be oversimplified to suppose that Physiocracy represented in any direct way the interests either of big landowners or of urban merchants. Landowners were notoriously noncapitalist in their outlook in this period; maximizing return was the smallest part of their concerns.[61] Likewise, French merchants were extremely conservative in their attitudes toward production methods. They adamantly refused to adopt standardized yarn rating systems, despite the fact that the technology was available and despite active government backing for the idea from the 1750s. They stuck with their old local units of measure, their uncertain reeling techniques, and trusted to inspection "by eye" – as one official disparagingly put it – to determine the proper value of a skein of yarn.[62] The Englishman Holker fought an uphill battle as a government promoter of diverse Lancashire technical methods for over thirty years before the Revolution. He had brought a whole bag of new tricks with him from England, most of which were greeted with profound circumspection.[63] Merchants feared their customers' reaction to even the slightest change in appearance or wear of their products.[64] Even when Holker's hot calender for finishing was gradually accepted, for example, merchants put out their cloth to calender operators rather than risk purchasing one of the things themselves.[65] English techniques in general were considered cheap, flashy, and deceptive.[66]

Merchants were not anxious for complete freedom of trade, either. In 1789, Albert Soboul reports, "of 943 *cahiers* [*de doléances*] drawn up by the guilds of 31 towns (185 of them representing the liberal professions, 138 representing goldsmiths and merchants, and 618 the various trade associations) only 41 advocated the suppression of the *corporations.*"[67] Under Napoleon, merchants continued petitioning the government for a revival of the old production regulations. A private bureau of inspection was tried in Valenciennes as late as 1822.[68]

There are good indications that Physiocratic influence after 1763 was not at all appreciated. Unable to carry out sweeping reforms, the Physiocratic party had to be content with piecemeal measures; as their influence waxed and waned, the future of the regulatory apparatus became progressively more uncertain, upsetting all attempts to carry out business planning in a normal way. The 1770s were particularly bad in this regard, as reformers and conservatives held power in rapid succession. The guilds were actually dissolved in 1776 only to be reinstated a few months later. By the time that Necker launched his investigation of the guilds in 1779, merchants were apparently embittered against the government. Many refused point blank to provide information on their operations to royal inspectors.[69] Nonetheless, Necker's extensive inquiry into merchant views and preferences resulted in a reform proposal that yields intriguing suggestions about thinking on production in this period.

Necker's program, to establish what he called an "intermediate system" – neither free trade nor strict regulation – would have left the government's whole regulatory apparatus intact but made it optional. All would still be required to bring their cloth to royal inspectors before selling it, but each could choose whether to submit to inspection or not. Those pieces that passed inspection would be given a lead seal with the name of the town and the year indicated as usual. Those not submitted to inspection would be marked *libre* ("free") with place and date also marked. This would remove any possibility of fraud. The consumer could immediately see what quality of cloth was before him.[70] It brings to mind the current French legal system for classifying wines. Wine is either marked *appellation controlée* (name controlled) accompanied by a place name and date of vintage, or else it is unmarked, ordinary wine of uncertain provenance.

That Necker's genius for compromise arrived at such a system for regulating cloth production in 1781, after an extensive inquiry by his staff, and that the system was put into effect without significant opposition, suggests that merchants of the time were prepared to regard cloth production much as wine production is regarded today, as something slightly mysterious, varying with geography and time, with features only cognoscente can appreciate.[71] Innumerable textile products did in fact carry place names in the eighteenth century, just as wine still does. There were *valenciennes* (lace), *rouenneries* (stripped fustian), *indiennes* (printed calico), *nankins* (fine, yellowish plain cotton), or *siamoises* (plain fustian), to name but a few salient examples. Even when place names were not used, vocabulary was linked to precise locale. Why was a plain, fine woolen cloth from Lille called a *camelot*, while the equivalent article from Le Mans was referred to as *étamine*?[72] Why were *serges* made in Lille called *saye*?[73] What was the difference between *drap de Levant* made in the Midi and *drap* made in Elbeuf or Sedan?[74] One answer obviously was that these terms all had legal definitions contained in the local production codes of each guild and town.[75] But this was obviously not the whole story. Even though the distinctions are now frequently opaque, it is probable that a knowledgeable merchant could tell at a glance whether a particular cloth revealed the idiosyncrasies of an Elbeuf weaver as opposed to his Sedan colleague. Any extensive change in production techniques, any systematic search for innovation, would have disrupted this whole accumulation of expertise. No wonder new English techniques were so consistently denounced as fraud, just as French wine producers today denounce the innovations of California.

Merchants, after all, often had so little control over the production process that it was reasonable for them to regard cloth as the outcome of a mysterious folk wisdom, as uncertain and unpredictable in its own way as the subtle marriage of vine, soil, and climate in the production of grapes. There is record of one case in which Rouen merchants, due to a regulatory change, put out the word to have their cotton kerchiefs produced in new dimensions, rectangular instead of square. Two years later they were still receiving square ones from the country.[76] Merchant manufacturers seldom knew exactly how many weavers they had working for them, much less who they were or where they lived. Their only sure form of control was inspection after the fact. If the government was willing to carry this out in the official marketplaces, it meant yet one more burden of production shifted onto someone else's back. All the better if, as Necker proposed, cloth that did not meet official standards could be freely marketed at lower prices.

The merchant outlook was therefore not entirely compatible with the programmatic approach of the Physiocrats. Merchants had already created de facto freedom of manufacturing in the countryside with the tacit support of local royal officials before the Physiocrats appeared. Complete freedom of trade as advocated by the Physiocrats could therefore offer little to merchants and only annoy those who still enjoyed advantages from their own local monopolies. Merchants, after reflection, would not have agreed that manufacturing was nothing more than re-selling, however well this term characterized their own role within manufacturing. Merchants in practice were acutely aware of the impact on value of each detail of the production process. This is why they always placed the most critical work with urban weavers who were more careful about uniformity and appearance. If quality was not for them a moral issue, it was nonetheless one in which the local character of the producer found reflection in manifold ways in the character of the cloth. This attitude was completely compatible with the silent and successful campaign to destroy guild monopolies of production that merchants waged throughout the century. The guilds declined, but neither free-trade doctrine nor the stirring of a new entrepreneurial spirit had anything to do with it.

THE MISSING INGREDIENT

The textile trade in the eighteenth century harbored great diversity of outlook and sensibility within it. Outworkers, guild members, urban merchants, Physiocratic theorists – plus a host of figures not expressly dealt with here: factors, dyers, croppers, peddlers and countless others who found their livelihood within the trade – had their own habits of mind, their own conception of the way of life textile production ought to support, their own criteria for evaluating day-to-day practice. This diversity of views gave rise to conflict and the rapid expansion of rural commerce was a barometer of merchant success: before the courts, in the corridors of the royal administration, in the markets, and on rural roads.

However diverse in their conceptions of the textile trade, merchant, guild member, and outworker had very similar views of the social order in which they sought to hold a place. (Perhaps the only difference was that merchants hoped someday to rise out of their guilds into the landed nobility.)[77] But merchant success meant that both guild members and outworkers found it increasingly difficult to maintain their place. The spread of Physiocratic influence within the government brought additional cause for grievance and conflict spilled into the streets.

Besides freeing rural manufacturing from its remaining legal bonds, a succession of Controllers General experimented with unregulated trade in grain after 1762. The complex police rules aimed at ensuring regular flows of grain to weekly markets at reasonable prices were lifted.[78] Poor harvests under such circumstances proved particularly disastrous for out-workers newly attracted into textiles in town and country and dependent for all their food on local markets. Textile regions were especially prom-inent in the great episodes of grain riots of 1768, 1771, and 1775. The orderly behavior, selective focus, and limited aims of these rioters as well as the community support they enjoyed have prompted historians to see these actions as expressions of a certain moral standard, a sense of justice about food distribution that Physiocratic policy violated.[79] To this one must add only that the sense of justice in question was the same one that inspired guild members to finance their law suits or cotton spinners to pillage the Cloth Hall in 1752. Consumer and entrepreneurial interests were not distinct in these peoples' lives; both were expressed not in economic terms but as a desire for a secure place within the framework of reciprocal moral bonds centering on the king that was French society.

However great the diversity of experiences and hopes within the trade, however consequential the outcome of conflict was for the future of the industry, all these groups were alike in not perceiving a distinct entre-preneurial role within manufacturing. This uniform failure was perfectly in accord with the state of the trade; entrepreneurship, the management of a production process for the sole purpose of creating monetary profit, did not occur. As long as growth could be contained within the limits of the current organization, there was no reason for it to occur.

2 The design of the spinning jenny

The entrepreneurial function did separate itself out and become a distinct role within society: This is a historical fact of the greatest significance. It was not just a matter of specialization, that is, of the differentiation of a task that had previously been performed by the individual producer. Separating out entrepreneurial decision making meant transforming this task and transforming the whole social organization of production along with it. The artisan made decisions about the use of resources according to a whole range of diverse criteria, none of which ever predominated over any of the others. But the entrepreneur's sole measure of success is profit and the sole threat to his existence is the failure to profit. Owning the work process without himself being engaged in it directly, an entrepreneur has an overwhelming interest in only one aspect of it, the spread between unit price and unit cost. Everything is measured in terms of its impact on this one variable. Unfortunately laborers continue to experience the multiplex reality of work directly and they try to satisfy their need for a coherent way of life by appropriately shaping the diverse features of the work experience. Here, rather than merely in the area of remuneration, is where the inevitable antagonism between capital and labor arises.

The emergence of the entrepreneurial role, in any case, involved the creation of a whole new mode of production. Once established somewhere in an economic system of the eighteenth-century type, such a mode of production proliferates by two means. Within any industry that feels its effects, competition in the sale of finished products compels others to adopt the new industrial organization or to go under – at least to the extent that price efficiently translates the advantage of the new mode of production. At the same time, there is the effect of example. Success sets others to thinking, principles are formulated, emulation and discussion spread new assumptions; language is put to new uses. In other words, it is wrong to see the impact as unidimensional. One kind of effect is felt in a very direct way through the "struggle of man against man," as Weber

48

put it, of the price mechanism. At the same time word and observation convey new possibilities in a diffuse and unpredictable way, well beyond the narrow range of direct effects. Both these forms of proliferation may be seen in the impact of the spinning jenny and associated new spinning technology in France in the last three decades of the eighteenth century. The invention of these machines in England was directly connected to the emergence of the entrepreneurial role in the cotton trade; and their proper use – assuming a competitive environment – required entrepreneurship. In fact in France the new machines were not properly put to use until after a competitive environment was created. It appears that the machines themselves, outside the society in which they originated, were not enough to lead to the grand social transformation they made possible.

ENGINEERING AS FOLKLORE

The two greatest entrepreneurs of the eighteenth-century textile trade were English artisans. Richard Arkwright was a barber; James Hargreaves was a country weaver. This fact speaks volumes about both the similarities and the differences between French and English putting–out operations by mid-century. In England just as in France, entrepreneurship was embedded within the daily round of the artisanal way of life. But in England, it successfully emerged from this chrysalis to fly free. Lancashire was a wide-open frontier by comparison with anything that existed in France; there were no guild institutions to seek control of the new cotton trade. There was no central bureaucratic state attempting to impose its policies. French overseas dependencies were dwindling to the advantage of English ports like Liverpool. Supply bottlenecks developed, of a seriousness unheard of in France. Hargreaves and thousands of other hand-loom weavers by the 1760s lived a life plagued by the search for yarn.[1] Putters–out shoved their supply problems onto their weavers (in a manner that calls to mind the inclinations of their French equivalents). Weft yarn was often left for the weaver to find on his own, however he could – by walking three miles to see a spinner he knew, by promising presents or extra pay to her, by waiting. In his idle hours, like many other Lancashire weavers, Hargreaves tinkered. He tinkered with ways of speeding up the spinning process so that his wife could produce more yarn in an equal number of hours. His crowning achievement after years of tinkering was a simple, yet revolutionary device, the spinning jenny. At first attacked by hostile spinners in Hargreaves' village, the device was quickly taken up by hundreds of unnamed imitators who made numerous improvements. (C. Aspin has shown that the initial device was very difficult to work.)[2] By 1775, seven years after Hargreaves' breakthrough, the jenny

49

Figure 3. The spinning jenny in a form current in Lancashire by 1775. Roving comes up from lower (slanted) set of spindles (E) to clamp device (set on four wooden wheels, two of which are visible on the front). Hand crank (A) turns upper spindles (L) as the clamp device is first pulled away from them and then run back toward them. From Richard Guest, *Compendious History of the Cotton Manufacture* (London, 1823).

had been enlarged, the drive reorganized, the carriage improved. The jenny developed like a folksong passing from one artist to another; authorship becomes an inappropriate concept. By 1780 there were over twenty thousand of them in existence, most being used by spinners in their own cottages. The early jenny was cheap, easily turned by hand, and quickly repaid the investment by tripling the yarn output of a spinner. Jenny-made yarn was less sturdy than handspun, but the adaptation of Arkwright's rolers to create the "mule jenny" had solved this problem by 1780. (It was another obscure cottager, Samuel Crompton, who did this.)[3] Slowly, after that date, larger shops were built that could undersell cottage-operated jennies. Steam was finally adapted to run mule jennies only after 1785. For over ten years, in other words, the principal beneficiaries of the increased productivity of the jenny were the entrepreneurs of the cottage, that is, the outworkers, not the possessors of capital. Nothing could more clearly demonstrate the real locus from which the entrepreneurial function emerged within the putting–out system.

It would be futile to try to isolate economic from cultural factors contributing to this peculiar evolution within English society, and then to weigh the separate contributions of each. It is enough to say that

The design of the spinning jenny

English society was by 1760 different from French society from top to bottom.[4] In the same years that Hargreaves was tinkering, Adam Smith was composing a masterful treatise that would place the productivity of labor (not of agriculture) in the center of all future economic thought.[5] Trade was indeed less restricted; the shortage of spinners was indeed causing hardship to cotton weavers. But such mundane facts are not enough to explain why Hargreaves thought tinkering might be of any use. Surely it is not irrelevant that he had no annual banquets or guild chapels to go to, could not, in other words, find a secure identity within society from membership in a trade community. However finely one cuts it, cultural and economic differences from the French situation cannot be separated.

A DESIGN FOR SOCIAL CHANGE

In any event, the French did not themselves share in the folkloric proclivity to tinker of Lancashire weavers and carpenters. For the moment it is necessary to take this fact as a given. The spinning jenny came to France from the outside and its revolutionary implications were not widely appreciated for a long time. Even the French experts who first witnessed its operation were a bit awed by the simplicity and power of the thing. The *encyclopédiste* and royal inspector of manufactures at Amiens, Roland de la Platière, pretended he had understood the principle of the jenny the first moment he heard of it and ordered one built without ever having seen it.[6] But Roland was an ambitious man who had a long-standing feud with the Holkers father and son, who smuggled the first jenny into France in 1773. His claim is doubtless exaggerated.[7] The royal inspector at Nîmes was more honest in expressing his astonishment. "I swear that this species of mill," he said, "is an ingenious little machine, although quite simple; and after seeing it in operation we were all astounded that we had not guessed in advance how it works."[8]

This comment is significant: The design of a machine is more than just functional, it can also carry information. The jenny carried a message to France about the nature of production for which many French were not quite prepared. The jenny simply imitated and multiplied the actions of the spinner's hand. Clamps held the roving instead of thumb and finger; for each clamp there was a spindle. (In the earliest designs there were twelve spindles; within a few years sixty was a common number.) The clamps were mounted on a piece of wood that the spinner pulled along rollers away from the spindles, just as on the wheel she had pulled on the roving itself. Nothing could have demonstrated more graphically the potential fecundity of cost cutting in production. Instead of one human hand working there were sixty wooden ones, yet the expenditure of human effort remained nearly the same. This much was easy to see by looking at it.

But it was less easy to see the potential for a revolution in the social organization of the textile trade implicit in this machine. If the device could be further improved and if many other such devices were possible for spinning and weaving processes, then the management, ownership, maintenance, and improvement of such machinery was a full-time job in itself and required access to capital, technical expertise, and ceaseless activity. The jenny and the improved successors that quickly flowed out of Lancashire called for entrepreneurial care. Their proper use soon required centralized shops and therefore the loss of entrepreneurial control by the laborer of his own labor.[9] Their labor-saving features promised sizeable profits; and the mule jenny also offered improved quality of yarn. The separation of the entrepreneurial function was implicit in the design of these machines. The design of the machine was a design for social change.

But to read the design correctly, society itself had to change. For a long time this fact seems not to have been appreciated in France. Between 1773 and 1786, 13 years in which over twenty thousand new spinning devices were put into operation in Lancashire, the number of jennies in France increased to no more than six hundred. The great majority of these were built under the auspices of the royal government and only because they brought the builder an income from royal coffers.[10]

The government had long sought improvement in industry by favoring exemplary establishments either with subsidies or tax exemptions. The most favored status was that of royal manufacture which meant tax exemptions and frequently subsidies as well. It was a system well adapted to the promotion of quality. Royal favor was a reward for unusually refined products. The "perfecting" (*perfectionnement*) of manufactures was the word ever on royal administrators' lips when speaking of their aims in favoring certain establishments.[11] The hundreds of petitions and briefs requesting such favors spoke to this idea. Techniques, processes, or devices were referred to as particularly excellent or yielding results of unusual distinction. Seldom, if ever, did the applicant provide or the government request a breakdown of the effect on factor costs of the applicant's innovation.[12] The modern researcher constantly wonders, if the device were so superior, why was there any need of government money? But perfected in eighteenth-century parlance did not mean only more profitable.

Of course when the spinning jenny arrived in France, royal officials were prepared to see that the particular form of perfection that it offered was the saving of labor, which was readily admitted to be a worthy aim. They were anxious to promote the jenny as one of a host of English technical tricks that the Holkers and others had smuggled across the Channel, most of which involved finishing techniques for woven cloth, and did not affect productivity in any appreciable way.[13] When an Arkwright carding machine for preparing cotton roving was introduced in 1779, administrators were happy to learn that it carded as much cotton as 24 people working full time. The introduction of such machinery was crucial to the domestication of a full-fledged factory system. But Rémond reports that high government officials continued to see the main advantage as the freeing of hands for employment in agriculture.[14]

Nor were officials surprised that the jenny was not quickly taken up by the trade at large. They were accustomed to seeing their new promotions received with a profound skepticism. How could one know whether something that worked in a heavily subsidized shop would be able to pay its own way on the outside? How could one be sure that customers, especially foreign customers, would accept the slightly altered nature of the product? The royal administration in its promotions and demonstrations consistently neglected the most obvious concerns of the commercial community. Under these circumstances the jenny appeared as just another of those suspect gadgets that the government was constantly trying to push on sensible businessmen. Besides, even the subsidized shops where it was put into operation had troubles with it. Jenny yarn was inappropriate for knitting frames, for use in warps, for fine grades of cloth.[15] Supplying jennies with sufficient roving of uniform twist strained existing preparation methods.[16]

The trade at large did not turn in earnest to adoption of the jenny until after May 1787 when the new commercial treaty with England went into effect. Suddenly Manchester cotton yarn – by now being produced cheaply and abundantly on water frames of the Arkwright model, on jennies, and mule jennies (both of these latter still operated by hand) – began to flood the French market, paying only a 12 percent duty. It was with a certain bitterness and in an atmosphere of crisis that the French now began turning to the jenny as the only way to save their trade. But in the two remaining years before the Revolution, the pace of adoption was only mildly increased; perhaps three hundred additional jennies were set to work.[17] England in the meantime was estimated to have well over twenty thousand jennies, nine thousand of the newer mule jennies, and two hundred mills on the Arkwright model by 1789, while France still had no mules and only eight operating water-frame mills.[18]

MACHINES AS POOR RELIEF

The impact of direct competition with England at least made the new spinning devices stand out from the other innovations the government had long been touting, thus setting minds to think along new lines. One is struck for example, by the contrast between the annual reports of the Rouen inspector of manufactures before and after the implementation of the new treaty with England. Goy de Fontenoy was acknowledged as one of the best inspectors the government had. He was one of the new breed of the 1770s who had imbibed the spirit of Enlightenment and who were enthusiasts for empirical observation. His reports are full of firsthand description; in preparing them he traveled widely through the Normandy cotton-producing region, asking questions, observing market days, and rather desperately trying to estimate quantities (of laborers, of cloth, of value), because no one knew quantities. His lengthy report of 1781 spoke not a word of the spinning jenny, although there were certainly by then over fifty in operation in and around Rouen. In 1787, however, he devoted considerable space to a discussion of the changing techniques of yarn production. He took pains to describe the most advanced enterprises. At Louviers, for example, a cotton spinning mill, the first of its kind, had been recently put into operation; 18 drum-type carding machines, machines for preparing the roving, and 36 jennies of 48 spindles each were set in motion by water power.[19] The mill employed 200, including many children. Goy was impressed by the technical complexity of the operation. It could produce yarns from No. 12 to No. 60 (by the local rating system); most output was between Nos. 20 and 26. In order to alter the output from one numbered grade to another, it was necessary "to change the cog settings of every machine." In all of Goy's previous experience it had taken merely a change in the pressure of the spinner's fingers to achieve such a result.

Goy explained that, apart from the appearance of such advanced operations here and there, the use of the jenny for cotton spinning was spreading rapidly in Normandy, with English competition as the spur:

> One must not be afraid today of occupying fewer laborers in our manufactures because we cannot for most kinds of cloth compete with England except by reducing the price of labor in order to lower that of the products. Since such things are done step-wise, the surplus laborers can be occupied effectively with other labors, with the advance of agriculture, with the clearing of land. After all, when stocking frames were introduced into France there were very strong complaints at the time, but they turned out to be baseless.[20]

This passage reflects the widespread sentiment in Normandy by 1787 that resistance was pointless, that English methods had to be adopted or the trade would go under.[21] Here surely, as well, are all the ingredients of a modern understanding of technical change. In order to remain in business, one must adopt the latest techniques; laborers that are displaced will not lack for employment in other areas of the economy. True, Goy does not argue, as had Holker in 1773, that the expansion of the textile trade itself would absorb the excess hands, a view which could arguably be said to represent a greater sophistication in thinking about such matters.[22] But Goy clearly grasps the essential significance of the new spinning techniques. Compared with his report of 1781, where production costs played virtually no role in his discussion of a fast growing industry, it is as if he has learned a whole new language. But he also spoke in a knowing tone, as if he expected the reader to have had the same thoughts already or to have heard them over lunch or in a salon last week.

Noteworthy also is the manner in which he states the aim of the new machinery: "reducing the price of labor in order to lower that of the products (*diminuant le prix de la main-d'oeuvre pour pouvoir baisser celui des marchandises*)." We think of machinery as reducing the *amount* of labor required for a specific amount of product, not as reducing the labor's *price*. But in the eighteenth century this term was exact. The immediate consequence of setting up a shop full of jennies and operating them, as the Holkers and others first did for the government in the 1770s, was that the price per pound of yarn paid to the spinners had to be reduced dramatically to reflect the increased productivity of the machines. This was the first effect of the new machinery on relations between owners of capital and laborers. The spinners had to enter centralized shops, to accept a monopsony situation in which the shop owner gave them raw material free and was the sole purchaser of the finished yarn; and the prices paid for the yarn were cut far below prices prevailing in putting–out operations. The transaction at the end of the week, in which yarn was evaluated and a price set on it, remained exactly the same in form as an open–market yarn sale.[23]

The organization of the earliest shops under royal sponsorship reveals a strong desire to stick as closely as possible with the familiar. Likewise, in spite of the dramatic change in inspector Goy's thinking, he had obviously not yet thought through all of the implications of the new machines for the social organization of production; doubtless neither had many of his contemporaries. There was a widespread tendency to continue seeing laborers as receiving prices for their goods just as in the putting–out system rather than seeing them as receiving a wage for the delivery of that abstract, formless stuff we call labor – a necessity if entrepreneurial control is to be complete.

This conclusion is borne out by evidence stemming from an ambitious program organized in Rouen to deal with the crisis caused by imported English yarn. After the commercial treaty with England went into effect, a Bureau of Encouragement was formed, a kind of committee to save the Normandy cotton trade that included merchant manufacturers, members of the Rouen Chamber of Commerce, and government officials.[24]

This committee was granted 300,000 livres from the royal treasury in the spring of 1788 to help finance the retooling of cotton spinning in the region. Plans were made to build over six hundred jennies and distribute them at less than cost. An export subsidy was to help Normandy compete in foreign markets until the jennies brought local yarn prices down to levels commensurate with those in Manchester. Displaced spinners were to be retrained to spin linen yarn, once a staple in Normandy but now almost forgotten. (No jenny had yet been developed that could work successfully with linen fiber.) Five hundred of the jennies were to be of thirty or so spindles, small enough to be distributed in the countryside. A selling price of 120 livres was set for these. Several noble landlords stepped forward and promised to buy a certain number and distribute them to tenants as a charity. Initially 25 of the jennies were to be large models intended for use in urban shops.

The program was only a limited success, however, because there were not enough buyers. The Rouen merchant manufacturers who were behind the committee's formation do not appear to have rushed to participate in its subsidized sale of fixed capital assets. But, then, this had never been the committee's intention; they had only hoped to provide interim help to the needy, to "procure for the neediest class of people the temporary means of providing for their own subsistence."[25] There are records of four or five shops in Rouen that were set up with one, three, up to five jennies in each. A few jennies were sent out into the country. Perhaps one hundred fifty new jennies in all were put into operation, far short of the committee's goal.[26] The deeper reason for the program's relative failure was that it represented an attempt to integrate the new techniques into the trade without altering its structure, that is, without altering the relationship between laborers and owners of capital, without turning the former into sellers of labor and the latter into entrepreneurs. Merchant manufacturers were, in effect, looking for someone else to adopt the new machines to whom they could continue putting out raw material as before. They saw the problem more as one of poor relief than of transformation. Rather than building factories of the new type, they applied themselves to distributing cheap jennies to others, much as one would distribute cheap grain after a harvest failure.

But then, given the existing structure of the trade, this was a reasonable attitude. Merchant manufacturers had no compelling reason to alter their own methods of business. Their survival was in no way threatened by the influx of English yarn; quite the contrary. The prices they paid for yarn were open–market prices, whether or not they put out fiber. When cheap English yarn began to depress open–market prices, merchant manufacturers in response simply adjusted downward by an equivalent amount the rates they paid for yarn returned by their factors. If the factor refused to accept the lower price, the merchant manufacturer could simply stop dealing with him and buy English yarn. Factors were forced in turn to pass the price drop through to their spinners. It was the spinners in the end, the cottage entrepreneurs, who competed with English machinery, and they alone who suffered.

One Rouen merchant reported to the Bureau of Encouragement on a test shipment of English yarn that he ordered from Manchester in the fall of 1788. Making allowance for transport, for the 12 percent import duty and for a 15 percent profit, the Manchester yarn could still be sold in Normandy at 20 to 30 percent below a price that allowed spinners using wheels to make 15 *sous* a day.[27] At most a spinner could earn 4 or 5 *sous* a day while selling her yarn at prices competitive with the imported yarn. During the long boom in the cotton trade that preceded the 1780s, spinners in Normandy had been able to make as much as 20 *sous* a day, enough to support a whole family.[28] Of course, in reality, the impact may not have been this harsh; dealers in English yarns probably took larger profits; there were still grades of yarn that the new techniques could not be applied to; and some merchants needed to order specific kinds of work from spinners who were close at hand. On the whole, earnings may only have dropped 30 to 40 percent for Normandy spinners by the summer of 1788.

In the long run of course all spinning would be brought into factories; the only question was whether all the factories would be located in Lancashire or some of them would also be in France. Had the Revolution not intervened to disrupt international trade for an extended period, doubtless Lancashire would have won out easily, judging from the inadequacy of the French response to this challenge before 1789. France faced the dilemma so familiar to underdeveloped countries of our own day; more time was needed to assimilate the lessons of the new machinery, to work out their full social implications, and to defeat if possible the formidable political resistance that was bound to arise from these implications. But direct competition did not allow time; with the treaty in place, the market for yarn became too efficient to allow for such development in France. Of course England was not a monolith in this respect; lags, disruptions, resistance occurred there in abundance as well. In France, nonetheless, the balance as of 1789 was still decisively towards these latter phenomena.

MACHINES THAT STEAL BREAD

The Revolutionary crisis of course upset all calculations; in the end it brought greater economic disaster than mere competition with Lancashire could have. But because of its outbreak, it is possible to get some evidence on a related and highly important question: How did the outworkers themselves respond to the new technology? Apparently, in the defense of their cottage enterprises they were prepared to resist the introduction of the jenny by any means. At the same time, every indication is that they were no more penetrating in understanding the jenny's real implications than their social betters.

From the point of view of outworkers in the cotton trade, the disastrous harvest of 1788 presented a familiar problem. Increased grain prices from November on created an imbalance between raw-material and food costs that was bound to deplete the small capital they needed to keep going. Only now for spinners this came at a time when yarn prices were already depressed due to the competition of the new machines.

The *cahiers de doléances* of the Rouen district, lists of grievances drawn up for the Estates General in the spring of 1789, are full of bitter denunciations of new spinning technology. The new *mecaniques à filer* (spinning machines) were singled out for denunciation in 68 out of 153 parishes, and by 17 of Rouen's 68 guilds.[29]

The most eloquent description of the spinners' plight is found in the *cahier* of the village of Perriers-sur-Andelle:

> They [the members of the Third Estate of this village] represent that the harvest was a bit mediocre this year and that there was a fifth less than the usual harvest, which has raised wheat to an excessive price ... A great number have been reduced to beggary, and what causes their misery is that most of the local taxpayers subsisted by means of cotton spinning, which today brings no profit. Trade has sagged since they have set up those machines and since foreigners have begun bringing in their finished muslins. All the work is of poor quality. [*Tous les ouvrages sont de mauvaise qualité.*] And half of this province can no longer get by, nor pay taxes as a result, until trade picks up again. There ought to be a certain balance between the price of bread and the profit to be had from the spinning of cotton. The delegates [to the Estates General] are asked to launch a vigorous plea, either to outlaw these machines or else to find work for those who cannot earn a living because of the low price of cotton yarn and the dearness of life.[30]

Most references to the jenny were at once shorter and less moderate. Article 7 of the *cahier* of Saint-Jean-sur-Cailly, for example reads: "Let us forget the very name of these spinning machines which have stolen the bread from innumerable poor citizens who have nothing but cotton spinning as their sole resource."[31]

It should be noted that the complaint was not that the machines had brought unemployment. It was that, in lowering the price of yarn on the open market, they had "stolen the bread" from those who lived by the wheel. The grievance was in effect the same as in 1752, "There ought to be a certain balance between the price of bread and the profit to be had from the spinning of cotton." The implication of the complaint from Perriers-sur-Andelle was that once the price of wheat began to spiral upward the previous fall, many spinners had given up their work as not worth the effort. Many of them must have exhausted their working capital buying grain instead of raw cotton to spin and now were, as the *cahiers* repeated constantly, "without resource," "idle hands," (*sans ouvrage*). It was not unemployment, but the "bad quality" of the "work" (*ouvrage*) that they blamed on the new machines.

It is possible to see two stages in the grain rioting that plagued the Rouen area in the spring and summer of 1789. The first lasted from March through June and represented a very practical reaction to severe shortages. When poor laborers showed up at the markets only to find grain supplies already exhausted (or even totally lacking, as happened at Darnétal, for example on 3 March), they organized themselves into groups to search for alternative sources. They scoured the surrounding farm lands, terrifying farmers by their arrival, conducting searches, buying grain at fixed prices if they found it.[32]

During July, however, a political and expressive element was added to these crowd actions, especially after Rouen organized a voluntary militia to protect grain stores. The action taken makes clear how closely outworkers associated conditions in the cotton trade with those in the grain trade.

Early on the morning of 13 July, militia members drove off a large crowd attempting to break into a storehouse in Rouen's Saint-Sever district south of the river. Some of those in the crowd broke away and proceeded to a shop not far away that belonged to the English artisan George Garnett who was making jennies and carding machines for the Bureau of Encouragement.[33] If the grain stores were out of reach, then destruction of the Englishman's machines was the next best thing. The crowd, made up predominantly of women, began throwing paving stones at the door and windows of the shop at 8:30 A.M. on Monday, 13 July, according to Garnett's own account. He armed himself and his three workmen with rifles and appeared at the door, announcing that he would shoot the first one who tried to come inside. The crowd advanced angrily; Garnett and his three assistants opened fire. One man was wounded; the crowd retreated quickly, taking the man with them. He bled to death shortly thereafter. The following morning another, much larger crowd appeared outside the shop. This time Garnett was in hiding; the shop was broken open at 10 a.m. and for three hours the crowd did what it pleased with his machinery. Later Garnett estimated the damage at 9,700 livres; five carding machines, five jennies, numerous brass wheels, metal spindles, packets of cotton yarn, and carding needles were lost or destroyed. The wooden frames of the jennies were carried to a nearby square called la Demi-Lune; the metal parts were apparently scattered through the streets (not unlike the royal grain had been in 1752). As cannon shot and rifle fire echoed through the Place de la Bastille in Paris, 150 kilometers away the crowd set fire to the pile of wooden jenny parts at the Place de la Demi-Lune and watched them burn.

During the remainder of the summer and fall, throughout the Rouen area, shops where the new jennies were in operation were frequent targets of popular anger.[34] On 20 July at least three such shops were attacked and the jennies broken; on 3 and 4 August another round of attacks spread through Darnétal and Saint-Pierre de Franqueville; this time reels and looms along with jennies and carding machines were dismantled and burned. Six shops were attacked on 17 October in the last of these incidents, following the same pattern. Jennies were dismantled, and their wooden components burned in the streets. Between 1789 and 1791 there are records of one or more similar incidents of crowds taking action against the use of jennies in Lille, Troyes, Paris, and Roanne.[35] There was, from our vantage, more agreement than disagreement between the members of the Bureau of Encouragement who hired Garnett and the crowd that burned his machines. Both were concerned solely with the effects that this machinery would have on open–market prices for cotton yarn. Neither even saw, much less took a position on, the social change that adoption of this new machinery would eventually entail. Neither yet foresaw that there would have to be a fundamental reorganization of social relations within the trade, which would mean for the spinners the yarn market would become a distant and irrelevant abstraction because they would become sellers of labor, rather than the yarn they spun. In this sense the Bureau of Encouragement, the royal government that financed its projects, and the French Luddites who dismantled and burned its jennies in the summer and fall of 1789 were all part of an age that was coming to an end. The government's policies and the crowds' resistance to them only made sense in terms of that age's assumptions; both misread with perfect unanimity and consistency the concentrated message that the jenny had brought from Lancashire.

3 New terms and old practices

The Revolution brought disaster to the French textile trade in every imaginable form: currency disorders, radical changes of fashion in clothing, loss of foreign customers, severe raw material shortages. Hundreds of thousands of cottagers were forced to abandon the trade; bankruptcy swallowed up hundreds of merchant houses.[1] In another sense, however, the Revolution brought the trade just what it needed, an extended respite from direct competition with England. The impact of the new English machinery had been painful; now it was withdrawn – but not forgotten. The new mode of production continued to make its influence felt on thinking, but not on prices. Recovery and response became possible.

The response on one plane at least was not long in coming. A direct result of the reforms of 1789 was the creation of a legal foundation for entrepreneurial control within French industry. The new law of property gave producers absolute and unlimited control over use and exchange of their stock and equipment. Clarification of this law required the National Assembly to define and regulate labor for wages as the free exchange of a commodity for a price. In law, therefore, by the end of 1791, anyone who operated a production process had the power of an entrepreneur over the process and purchased labor from competing individuals as one factor of production among others.

It is important to realize, however, that these reforms bore no simple relationship to existing economic practice; there was no industrial capitalism in embryo straining to be free, no entrepreneurial class lobbying for its interest in the Tennis Court or on the night of 4 August. Nor did these reforms call such a class or such a system of production into existence. The impact of eighteenth-century economic development made itself felt on the Revolutionary program only indirectly, through the tendentious theoretical reflection that commercial change had stimulated. The absolute right of property presented itself to the reformers of 1789 as the solution to a motley array of difficulties that the generalized crisis of the ancien regime had thrown up together. No one consciously seized on this principle as the legal cornerstone of a new form of entrepreneurial control in industry, although that is what it became. The reforms themselves helped to stimulate a great shift in the language and perceptions of the ruling elite with respect to commerce during the course of the Revolutionary decade. Real change in the practices of production was, however, much slower in coming.

ABSTRACT EQUALITY

It has been fashionable to claim that the National Assembly acted without real conviction when it abolished privilege on the night of 4 August 1789; the peasants had forced their hand by refusing to pay seigneurial dues and burning a few chateaux.[2] But this view of the matter is no more satisfactory than one that would derive the whole of the Revolution from the head of Locke or Rousseau. The Assembly did not stop with seigneurial dues but rushed onward unaccountably to end the tax exemptions of Church and nobility, venal office, hunting rights, tithes, and the special status enjoyed by provinces, towns, provincial estates, and corporations.[3] Why did they do so?

For thirty years royal ministers had been frustrated in their attempts to make reform of any kind stick. After two experiments with free trade in grain, regulation had returned after the fall of Turgot in 1776. Restrictions were loosened again in the 1780s, but Necker reinstituted strict controls in the autumn of 1788.[4] Likewise, after extensive chipping away at guild monopolies by reform bureaucrats, a large part of the structure still stood, in law at least, as the Revolution began.[5] Finally, the bankrupt government had been repeatedly stymied between 1786 and 1788 in its attempts to establish a uniform land tax that would apply to church and noble property as well as to that of commoners. The institutional experiments associated with the struggle over tax reform – Calonne's Assembly of Notables, Brienne's provincial assemblies – had brought into question the very legitimacy of the current governmental structure.[6]

The solution that the nascent National Assembly adopted to this long chain of frustrations was to institute reforms in all these areas, unconditionally, in a single stroke. All those interests that had resisted them piecemeal now suffered equally, thus no single interest could justify putting in a veto in its own case. Because the peasants were in open revolt, seigneurial dues were added to the list (to be abolished only with generous provision for compensation). But this radical strategy worked only because the Assembly succeeded in pinning the single label of *privilege* on all the diverse exemptions, controls, institutions, and monopolies that it eliminated.[7]

Appropriate enough in a sense, the label was nonetheless arbitrary to a significant degree. Tax exemptions had been attacked by the crown for centuries, as had seigneurial dues and tithes (as well as royal taxes) by the peasantry without anyone seeking to call these things by a single name. Most important in the present context, the Physiocratic doctrine of free trade had been derived from close attention to the commercial activities and needs of large landowners and, to a lesser extent, of merchant manufacturers. No attention had been given to the diverse aims of popular productive activity in town and country. Free trade represented a severe threat to the whole way of life of the popular masses in the name of an abstract, generalized large owner of capital. It was therefore anything but equal in its effects on citizens; it privileged those with large property or stocks; and it struck at those who subsisted out of their own immediate labor, and whose decisions were not uniformly motivated by a search for monetary profit. Why should this new form of privilege have been deemed to cohere with the abolition of venal offices or hunting rights?

Sans-culotte spokesmen would later learn to make much of this new form of inequity.[8] But in 1789 the delegates of the Third Estate, most property owners themselves, chosen through a two-tiered electoral process that diluted the influence of the poor, were in no position to appreciate the subtle bias of free-trade theorizing. An equal and unconditional right of property with an equal share in the burden of taxes appeared as the single coherent principle that justified the sacrifice of all special interests.

The need for coherence in its own right played a powerful role in determining the course of events in 1789, as William Sewell has rightly emphasized.[9] But equally this need did not arise in a vacuum; it came after three decades of stalemate between the interests of king and subjects on a variety of fronts. The new definition of property that emerged doubtless failed to please all merchants and landowners; many would lose privileges of their own; even those who benefited immediately must have paused before the incalculable consequences of the total abrogation of the existing system. At the same time, this new definition of property married theoretical doctrines concerning the commercial interests of merchants and landowners to the king's need for a wider tax base. This is just one of the ways in which it seemed happily to resolve the unresolvable conflicts of the past. Thus a distant but distinct ideological echo of the eighteenth-century victory of merchant over guild in the French textile trade found its way into the Declaration of Rights of Man and Citizen.

But further refinement of the new regime of property was soon necessary. After the guilds were explicitly abolished with the d'Allarde law in the spring of 1791, masters and town governments were confronted with an unexpected increase in journeyman activism.[10] Freed of guild discipline, journeymen quickly organized themselves and advanced collective grievances. But this threat of new unresolvable disputes was quickly solved by a simple extention of the property principle. Labor itself, the reformers explained, was a form of property. It thereby became the only form of property under the new regime that was not some tangible piece of nature – a strange exception. But the anomaly bothered no one in the Assembly, where labor was warmly defended as one more victim of the old privileged order. "The capacity to work," said one delegate, "is one of the primary rights of man. This right is his property, and without doubt ... it is the primary property ... the most sacred and the most inviolable."[11]

But it followed that, once sold, labor became the inviolable property of the purchaser whose money was also sacred and inviolable. Therefore laborers could not be allowed to combine or cooperate in resisting the authority of their masters. Labor like other forms of property must be freely bought and sold among individuals. The Le Chapelier law of 1791 spelled this out lest there be any doubt. Article four of the law stated that for citizens to accord at a set price, that is, a price not determined by the bargaining of an individual laborer with an individual master "the aid of their industry or of their works (*le secour de leur industrie ou de leurs travaux*)" was not only illegal but "unconstitutional, an attack on liberty, and contrary to the Declaration of Rights of Man and Citizen."

Of course this law of 1791, just like the reforms of 1789, represented an opportunistic application of principle. It would have been more consistent to insist on the right of laborers to associate and sell their property together just as merchants did in partnerships and joint ventures of all kinds. (Eventually this idea would be used to justify legalizing unions in France.) Instead the Assembly reenforced the advantage of the large owner over the small – of those who owned capital over those who owned only labor – doubtless because of an inchoate sense (arising more from sentiment than from principle) that the new regime must have some way of ensuring the subordination of the humble classes to the great. By yet one more twist, the equal right of property was made to create a disadvantage for the poor.

PRODUCTIVITY AND SOCIAL CLASS

These legal principles were admirably suited to the effective use of the new spinning technology in France. Competitive operation of this technology required entrepreneurial control of workplace and of labor; by 1791 the law had made such control into a sacred right. One may speculate whether the example of the jenny and its offspring did not play some role, however small, in the thinking of Revolutionary reformers. It is certain, in any case, that once the new laws were in existence, their framers showed a new appreciation of the importance of machinery in industry.

The jenny had attracted the attention of the reforming intellectual elite before the Revolution, this much is certain. Turgot and Malesherbes were given a demonstration of the device in the 1770s; Condorcet and the Academy of Science ruled favorably on certain improvements to it in 1785.[12] Roland de la Platière published a description of it in 1780, and featured it in his section on textiles in a successful early volume of the *Encyclopédie méthodique* published in 1785.[13] Goy de Fontenoy, as mentioned in Chapter 2, spoke familiarly of the jenny in 1787, as if it was a topic of common discussion. The scattered incidents of Luddism against jennies between 1789 and 1791 must have attracted further public attention. After 1789, successive governments consistently promoted experimentation with the new devices in and around Paris, providing, if not money, at least rent-free space in nationalized convents and monasteries.[14] Likewise in its questionnaires on industry, the government consistently asked pointed questions about improvements in machinery. "Have they [the local industries] made any progress in the art of diminishing labor by mechanical means?" asked the Committee of Public Safety in 1795.[15] Minister of the Interior Neufchâteau, in the prologue to his questionnaire of 1797 reminded his respondents that "the means which have been found to save the labor of men by supplementing it with machines or with animals" were of particular interest to the government.[16] In 1798, the abbé Grégoire, in defending the establishment of the Conservatoire des Arts et Métiers, spoke as if the significance of machinery ought to be perfectly obvious to all by now.

> Does it take a great effort of genius to see that we have more work to do than hands to do it with, that in simplifying labor one diminishes its price, that it is an infallible method to establish lucrative trade, crushing foreign industry by diminishing the competition of its products?
>
> The employment of machines ... has as its aim: (1) to obtain more work [*plus d'ouvrage*] by saving on the human strength and the number of individuals required; (2) to give the work greater perfection without requiring greater skill of the laborers.[17]

A dramatic shift in government concern with machinery coincided with the Revolutionary crisis. Increased labor productivity, heretofore considered just one of the advantages offered by technical change, was now elevated to a central position in the thought of government officials about commerce. All sign of Physiocratic prejudice against manufacture was gone.

Discovering why this happened is difficult. Any particular individual could have come to this position as easily by reading Adam Smith as by observing a jenny in action. Like as not, some individuals did both and others heard of both in conversation. Still others could have discovered the significance of labor productivity by hearing of Cort's puddling and rolling process for iron production or seeing one of the rare steam engines brought to France before the Revolution. War may have played a part in this shift in thinking as well. After 1792 the Revolutionary government had to become an entrepreneur in its own right, organizing production of arms and clothing for its multiplying forces. Conscription meanwhile caused shortages of labor that brought administrators face to face with the question of productivity much as Hargreaves had been in the 1760s.[18] It would take a separate research project to identify and evaluate all the strands that fed into the important change in government thinking about production that occurred between 1789 and 1795. In any case, the language of Revolutionary legislation on property helped push the mind in this direction; it was now perfectly natural to talk of labor, equipment, and materials as properties purchased at competitive prices and combined in the most economical way possible.

The first sustained exposition in French of the principles of political economy was written by a revolutionary politician. J.B. Say's *Traité d'économie politique*, first published in 1803, destined to become the standard reference work in French on this subject, was built upon mature reflection not only on the thought of Adam Smith but also on that of revolutionary reformers. Say's vision of a social order based on the market system borrows equally from Smith and from Sieyès.[19] Society was made up of three kinds of persons, according to Say, defined by their function vis-à-vis the creation of wealth. There was, first of all, the *savant* dedicated to the study of the law of nature. Secondly,

> Another profits from this knowledge to create useful products. This is the cultivator of the soil, the manufacturer, or the merchant, or, *to refer to them by a common term, this is the entrepreneur of industry*, he who undertakes to create on his own account, for his own profit and at his own risk, a product of whatever kind. Another, finally, works according to the directions given by the first two. This is the laborer.[20] [Emphasis added.]

The centrality of the entrepreneurial function, here enunciated by Say in an almost explicit rejection of Physiocratic shortsightedness (and in a deductive manner that Adam Smith would have eschewed), arose inevitably out of the legal principles that the Revolution had laid down. The unrestricted control over property in a social order in which property ownership was almost the only formal means of determining rank was bound to make of the entrepreneurial maximization of profit a high, even an ennobling function. This is exactly how Say saw it. His was a vision that stands in stark contrast to the old guild idea that entrepreneurship unleashed was antisocial, corrosive of good order and morality, inevitably leading to fraud, destructive of trade.

BALANCE SHEETS AND CONTRACTS

If by 1803 the entrepreneurial function had been elevated to the highest social rank in Say's mind and in the minds of his fellow *Idéologues*, elite politicians, and administrators, in the lived reality of industrial practice almost nothing had changed. When full mechanization finally came to the textile trade, something loosely resembling the vision of entrepreneur and laborer that Say elaborated would eventually, hesitantly, after considerable struggle and confusion, come into being. But in the present this transformation had not yet begun. Therefore Say's language, his basic terms – entrepreneur, laborer, savant, wage, market, and so on – only awkwardly fit social reality, and only at some expense of insight, at least insofar as the textile trade was concerned, the "leading sector" of industrial advance.

The traces of this important disjuncture between the social thinking of the elite and the practical realities of industrial production in textiles can be seen in two areas. They can be found in the confused descriptions of industry made by government officials after 1800. And they can be found in the odd melange of ingredients that went into Napoleonic labor law between 1802 and 1806, which would remain the basic law governing industrial relations for the rest of the century.

The contrast between the kinds of information on industry gathered by the French government before the Revolution and that gathered from 1795 on is unmistakable, and reveals the abstractness of the new outlook. The circumstantial, detailed, eyewitness accounts based on yearly tours that the old inspectors of manufacture made of their territories give way to administrative questionnaires.[21] The government's competence is now circumscribed; it no longer needs to regulate every technical detail or every commercial relationship; these matters now fall within the sphere of action of individual citizens. But the government does need to monitor the overall production and distribution of wealth, a vital national concern. For this purpose, however, information need only be collected about overall quantities of goods and values, their direction of flow, and the growth or decline of trade. Such information is best presented in a balance-sheet format, as if France itself were a grand enterprise requiring proper management.

The influence of these new assumptions shows up clearly in the statistical reports of Napoleon's first generation of departmental prefects, written between 1802 and 1804. The prefects were to provide general surveys of local industry, paying special attention to the progress or decline that had occurred since 1789. The following is a synopsis of the comparative table which prefect Dauchy drew up on linen production in the Aisne department:

1789	Year 9 [1801–02]
Region had 12–14,000 looms.	2–3,000 looms still weaving.
Weavers earned 20–25 sous per day; were found in both town and country.	Weavers all in country.
Spinners numbered 65–70,000, earned 10 sous a day.	Spinners far fewer, earn 3 or 4 sous per day.
Many employed in bleaching and finishing.	Bleaching and finishing abandoned, some now beg.
150–160,000 bolts per year produced, 12–15 *aunes* long.	Year 10: 30–35,000 bolts produced.
Three-fifths of total exported overseas.	Caribbean islands and South America now closed.[22]

This simple table gives a compelling picture of the extent of the disaster which the Revolution had brought to the textile industry. But this particular tabular form is something new. The number of laborers and their average daily earnings are here listed along with other quantitative information about production levels, as if one were aiming to provide a kind of regional summary of credits and debits. While ancien regime observers often reported daily average earnings of laborers who were essentially independent outworkers, they never entered them in lists of this sort along with other production items.

But in the prefects' reports, such tables became the norm. Bruslé, reporting on the Aube department, went so far as to provide in his large table on cotton output a breakdown of average unit costs of materials and labor for each variety of cloth locally produced. Of course the labor costs in his table represent rates paid to independent cottage weavers, as he himself implies, and are therefore not strictly speaking labor costs at all. (In another context he refers to them as the "profits [*bénéfices*]" of the weavers, also not strictly correct.) For both 1784 and 1802 he calculates the total value of local production, subtracts the cost of imported raw materials, and designates the resulting figure as the total "profits" generated for the region by this industry. The result, 1784: 6,016,494 francs; 1802: 2,674,010 francs.[23] Obviously the implicit aim is to provide two more items for the grand accounting of the wealth of the nation. Luçay, reporting on the Cher department, estimates "the money which [Vierzon forges] pump into the countryside in payments of wages and purchases of wood," and calculates the total payroll of a cotton printing enterprise, both as estimates of the total wealth these trades produce locally.[24] One can multiply such examples indefinitely.

The most elaborate calculations of this kind are found in prefect Dieudonné's report on the department of the Nord. For each industry of the department a detailed accounting of the various operations involved culminates in a large table that literally takes the form of an accountant's balance sheet of input and output. Dieudonné's work is studded with these tables. The compiler went to considerable effort to make all figures in them add up and cancel out, whether or not the information was of equal value.[25]

In the great majority of these prefects' reports, it is assumed that all laborers are wage laborers. The exact nature of social relations only comes up when reality seems to defy this assumption. The anomaly must be explained. Jerphanion, reporting on wool production in the Lozère department, remarks with apparent surprise: "It is nonetheless not rare to find the same individual harvesting the wool, passing it through all the preparatory processes, working it up and selling it, so that the cultivator is at the same time producer and merchant." And thus local production "is not directed by the so-called producers (*fabricans en titre*)."[26] Obviously the assumption is that the entrepreneur should be giving the orders. Likewise Bruslé feels it necessary to explain that in the Aube department "the [cotton] spinner buys each week the amount she can spin and resells it at the following market to weavers. It acquires more or less value according to the yarn's beauty." The weavers also operate independently, a fact that Bruslé finds deplorable: "The class of producers is composed entirely of workers without fortune; their position is an obstacle to the improvement of production because they cannot try the slightest experiments without ruining themselves."[27] After all, as everyone now knows, entrepreneurs are supposed to take risks.

Dieudonné, intent on providing average daily wages for every category of laborer, occasionally must calculate them himself from overall output figures, however inaccurate, because the laborers actually work as independents and therefore no one knows how much they earn. In these cases he gives details on their commercial situation, apologetically, as it were. For the Armentières region, for example, he does not even attempt an estimate. Here, he explains,

> where each producer works for his own account, the salary cannot be evaluated according to the number of days that he works but only on the basis of the price he receives for the piece of linen he has brought to market, with deductions made for the cost of the yarn and the upkeep of his tools.[28]

Yet many of the cases where Dieudonné and others confidently give average daily wage figures were in reality little different from that of Armentières weavers. The figures reported would have meant nothing to the laborers involved, whose earnings were directly linked to open–market cloth prices. The uninformed reader of these prefects' reports could easily fail to realize that virtually all French weaving and most spinning were still carried out in the home by independent or semi-independent operators. If one is informed of this in advance, however, hundreds of details passed over as unimportant or of little interest leap off the pages. The language is capitalist, the point of view is entrepreneurial, but the reality is still proto-industrial.

A similar bias undoubtedly explains the peculiar findings of two inquiries carried out on the cotton industry in 1806 and 1807.[29] The first, the so-called Champagny inquiry, found that the average number of workers per firm was 60.4; the second, a year later, revealed the same figure to be 13.3. Serge Chassagne's discussion of these two reports suggests that the discrepancy resulted from inconsistencies in the inclusion of outworkers. Some respondents included them; others did not. The original questionnaires were ambiguous; no one had recognized that there might be a problem deciding who was and who was not a wage laborer.

The true locus of entrepreneurial functions in the textile trade in 1802–04 remained largely where it had always been, serving the diverse non-monetary ends it always had. The disappearance of the guilds caused some change, but in the intervening years markets had been too uncertain for anyone to undertake really dramatic reorganizations. In the meantime the prevailing language of law, politics, and administration had undergone a revolution. Entrepreneurship was now assumed to go with ownership of capital; the aim of production was assumed to be the maximization of monetary yield. Laborers were assumed to sell their labor. Most of the time the failure of these assumptions to fit reality was not even recognized. When failure was noticed, however, it was remarked as an anomaly. Merchant manufacturers ought to "direct" their operations. Producers ought not to be without capital, since it discourages experimentation. Political economy, which set out merely to describe, was now becoming so thoroughly entrenched that it had begun to prescribe. Thanks to the Revolution, the model of had become a model for.

Merchant manufacturers, however, had by no means been so quick to adopt the new viewpoint as the Revolutionary elite. It did not fit their experience or their inclinations. They wished to stick to the known until the known became unprofitable. As late as 1792 the National Assembly was still receiving petitions from merchants asking for the reinstatement of government regulation.[30] Receipt of such requests picked up again after 1798. These petitions did not ask for a simple resurrection of the guild system. Merchant manufacturers wanted only certain facets of the old system to be revived. Like the hundred thirty *marchands et négotians* of Le Mans who applied to the ministry of the interior in 1803, they wanted to be able to form local Chambers of Commerce to serve at least consultative and informational functions.[31] Like the *fabricans d'étoffes de la commune de Reims*, who petitioned the government in October 1802, they wanted reactivation of the old product specifications and of the inspection bureaus that enforced them.[32] Their trade, the Reims merchants claimed, was threatened with destruction; the familiar anxieties of the ancien regime were rehearsed again: "the producer cheats, the consumer is fooled," they said, soon business will be at an end. Like the Rouen manufacturer who wrote in 1798, they wanted "to reestablish subordination between the worker and the head of the shop."[33] Like the Sedan wool producers who wrote in 1802, they wanted special powers to repress wool pilferage and trade in stolen wool in the countryside.[34] Merchant manufacturers did not want to give urban masters or out-workers the ability to organize; but they did want such ability for themselves, and they wanted the government to discipline labor and enforce production standards on labor. In effect, they wanted the government to continue carrying out crucial entrepreneurial functions that they remained little inclined to carry out on their own, given the continued predominance of the putting–out form of production in the trade.

To these ever more numerous requests, Napoleon's government responded. It was a time for reconciliation between old and new. The church had been induced to settle by 1802, royalists were receiving amnesty. Between 1802 and 1806 a series of laws were introduced modifying the regime of the Le Chapelier law in such a way as to give merchant manufacturers most of what they wanted without disturbing appearances. The principles of free trade and freedom of contract were reconciled with a heavy dose of de facto collective control over production that violated the spirit of these principles in a number of ways.

In 1802, the question of labor discipline was dealt with. Minister of the Interior Chaptal resurrected a law of 1781 (one of Necker's reforms), requiring the use of *livrets*, booklets that would serve as work passports for the registration of hirings, dismissals, and debts.[35] Laborers remained free to contract the best conditions they could with employers. But once hired, they could not go elsewhere until the employer returned their *livret* to them with written indications that they had fulfilled all obligations under the contract. It was understood that the obligations would usually include obeying work rules of the kind once enforced by the guilds and giving advance notice of one's intention to quit. If a laborer quit before having paid back all advances on wages made by the employer, then the debt could be registered in his *livret* and paid off by a lien of 20 percent on future earnings. Chaptal's justification for these measures: The market could not work if there were no means to ensure that engagements once undertaken would be carried out.

Collective regulation of production was provided for in a round-about way five years later with the formulation of laws to allow creation of so-called Conseils des prudhommes. These were local arbitration boards intended to rule on all disputes between workers and those who gave them work. Their jurisdiction covered product quality, wage agreements, notice periods, breach of contract, use of the *livret* and, if the worker was employed on the premises of the employer, workplace discipline and hours as well. The Prudhommes could impose fines, even short prison terms to back up their decisions. Their policies were to be based on what was considered accepted local practice. They were composed of merchant manufacturers and (to represent labor) independent artisans or shop foremen – thus preserving at least a pretense of impartiality. These councils were extremely popular in large putting–out centers; the first one was formed at Lyon in 1806; by 1813 Sedan, Saint-Quentin, Mulhouse, Carcassonne, Reims, Lodève, Lille, and Bolbec had all formed their own; others followed in time.[36] The advantage of a Conseil des prudhommes from the point of view of a merchant manufacturer was that accepted local practice could be construed to cover a wide variety of things, including specifications governing the exact form of local varieties of cloth, quality standards, fine schedules for flawed or inferior pieces, time limits for return of yarn put out, and so on. In other words the same range of entrepreneurial decisions once handled by the guilds and the government could now be enforced by the Conseil des prudhommes. Weavers who shifted suppliers frequently would now find that all imposed uniform conditions and expectations. A weaver who failed to live up to these expectations or disputed these conditions could be brought before a public body, his *livret* confiscated, a fine imposed, and his opportunities to work for anyone else closed off. In the woolen centers, the Prudhommes authorized the same kind of repressive measures against pilferage as were once handled by the guild; arbitrary house-to-house searches, seizures, fines, even prison terms were now possible again to prevent trade in stolen wool or the products made from it.[37]

All of this was reconciled with free trade on the grounds that any laborer was free to refuse these conditions; once he agreed to work, however, he was deemed to have agreed to abide by all of them even if this was not explicitly stated. All workers would soon come to know there were local regulations they must obey.

Rather than providing a government inspector to certify quality, the government made arrangements for a system of legal trade marks so that any individual merchant or producer could give to his products an exclusive proprietary label. Conditions for the formation of Chambers of Commerce were eased. Merchant and manufacturing communities could now form public bodies to gather and disseminate information, represent their interests before the government, and serve as a convenient meeting place.[38]

Almost every facet of the old system that had ever been of interest to merchant manufacturers was thus salvaged without breaking, at least on paper, with the sacred principle of private property established by the Revolution. Where the laborers were concerned, the regime of free trade was applied in its most extreme form. Even to discuss wage levels together remained formally illegal. For the owners of property, however, every possibility of softening its strictures, of facilitating collective control and consultation, of reducing competition over pay scales or over product quality was exploited under the new Napoleonic legal regime, a regime which would last out the century with only minor changes. Yet all the appearances were preserved, the new language of free contract, competition, markets, entrepreneurship, and the rest, could continue in use without fear of contradiction. The heavy hand of collective privilege was perfectly reconciled with the rule of legal equality.

The government did make one concession to labor. Mutual aid societies for the provision of disability and death benefits were legalized. The statutes of such societies were carefully limited; no discussion of religious, political, or trade matters was allowed at their meetings. Funds could be used only in cases of sickness, retirement, or death. These societies were therefore on paper no more of an impediment to free trade than were the Conseils des prudhommes or Chambers of Commerce.[39]

How this whole system worked in practice is another matter. The *livret* law was almost as easy for workers to subvert as it was for employers to abuse. *Livrets* could facilitate blacklisting and helped constrain workers to a single job, severely limiting the free movement of labor. At the same time a laborer whose *livrets* had been retained or marked with a derogatory comment by a previous employer could easily get a new clean one at the local town hall by claiming he had lost his or by using a false name. Conseils des prudhommes were extremely diverse in their behavior; some became quite active agents of local merchant and manufacturer policy, others were inactive. In some areas the whole system was simply ignored; in others it was tightly enforced.[40] The whole question is therefore both complex and important. A poorly enforced or easily abused set of laws creates a social situation very different both from that which it intends and from that which would exist without it. There is more discussion of this matter in Chapters 5 and 7. The point to be appreciated here is the vast gap that had opened up between political and administrative language on the one hand and the real spirit of labor law formulated in response to merchant manufacturers' demands on the other.

ODD ASSORTMENTS OF MACHINES

But what of the new machines? If the government could not create a capitalist industrial order from above, then surely advanced spinning technology would force one on the textile trade from below. Or at least the two working in tandem were bound to bring about dramatic change. To an extent this is correct, but real change would not begin until the 1820s. The reign of Napoleon introduced three factors that exercised a restraining influence on the transformative impact of the new technology: (1) continued protection from British competition, (2) a glittering court life that resurrected a taste for luxury and fashion after a decade of revolutionary austerity, and (3) chronic market instability.[41] In this environment, French producers were encouraged to concentrate their efforts not on the commonest, cheapest grades of cloth that made Manchester's fortune, but on those that satisfied eye, vanity, and a taste for change. This is not to say that the French public was not price conscious. There was plenty of encouragement to bring the new labor-saving devices into play. But protection, the pursuit of fashion, and market instability made it possible to do so haphazardly, without great attention to detail or the latest advances. War and political upheaval created an atmosphere of uncertainty, a speculative fever that discouraged wasting one's time on cost-conscious management. The scarcity of credit encouraged smallness. If one could just get a set of the new spinning machines into operation, one was assured a handsome profit.

Already before 18 Brumaire roughly seven to ten thousand hand-operated jennies were in use, the greater part having been built or imported since 1796; in the same period perhaps a hundred water-frame mills of the Arkwright variety were established. Throughout the troubled 1790s, raw cotton, linen, and wool had remained at roughly double their prerevolutionary price, yet, thanks to the new spinning machinery, the price of cotton yarn rose only by about 25 percent.[42] Cotton was therefore a relative bargain and the ready availability of machine-spun yarn stimulated a massive shift from wool and linen over to cotton production. Weavers had suffered terribly in the early 1790s from lack of raw materials and of demand, but now they saw new hope in the production of cotton muslins, *nankins*, velours, and calicoes.[43] The complexion of whole regions changed overnight. After 1800, cotton prints became even cheaper to produce thanks to the spreading use of chlorine bleach and roller printers.[44] The establishment of the Empire in 1804 therefore coincided with an extraordinary revival of interest in *indiennes*, the light printed cottons so fashionable during the eighteenth century, only now cheaper and more abundant. To supply this taste, the cotton spinning capacity of France grew from two or three hundred thousand mechanized spindles in 1800 to nearly a million by 1810.[45] Domestic cotton spinning by women was effectively eliminated in these same years.

Perhaps twenty thousand looms in Normandy and an equal number in the Saint-Quentin region turned to the production of calicoes, with a further twelve thousand set up in the Cholet region, thousands more around Tarare, in Lille and Roubaix, in the outskirts of Paris, and in the Vosges mountains.[46] Alsace, which had specialized in the printing of *indiennes* since the mid-eighteenth century, now found itself unable to buy enough calico inside the Empire to supply its printing operations, in spite of this expanded production. For Alsace printers, no price was too high to pay for calicoes, since it was possible for them to turn 100 percent profits on operating capital during the peak period of the Empire's cotton boom. After the 1806 prohibition on imports, smuggling of English calicoes into Alsace to pick up the slack of French production was quickly organized; but Alsace entrepreneurs began, as well, to build their own spinning mills and set up looms in their own hinterland, as quickly as their resources allowed.[47]

Another of the period's fashions, cashmere wool shawls imported from the orient, were successfully imitated by an entrepreneur at Reims named Ternaux in 1802. The following year he came out with an imitation merino wool cloth as well. Ternaux's imitations were an immediate success. Two machine builders had managed to adapt carding machines and jennies (but not mule jennies) to the production of wool yarn by this time and Ternaux had made use of the economies brought by these machines to produce an acceptable cheap facsimile of a luxury good that, like the new *indiennes*, could appeal to a larger market. Ternaux was himself, in turn, imitated; and wool thus found a modest place in the boom of 1806–1810, recovering a part of its former importance.[48]

The boom ended abruptly in 1810. Conditions worsened in 1811 when the Emperor took new steps to ensure that British ships were not allowed into Continental ports. The British retaliated with search-and-seizure tactics against neutral shipping headed for the Continent. These transport difficulties in turn forced the price of raw cotton up to quadruple its 1806 level. A bad harvest and a series of Paris bankruptcies followed, and the whole flimsy financial structure on which the boom had been based came tumbling down. Full recovery would have to await the secure installation of the Restoration regime after 1816.[49]

Strictly speaking, then, one could say that the factory system made its first appearance in the French textile industry during the period 1796–

1810 as machine processes were adopted for the spinning of cotton and wool yarn on a large scale. A closer look at these "factories," however, reveals that the structure of relationships within the trade had hardly changed at all from the earlier putting–out phase. Yes, entrepreneurs were buying machines and hiring labor to run them; this is surely industrial capitalism. But when one looks at the actual means by which this was achieved, one finds little evidence to suggest that entrepreneurs had taken control of the process of production or that any of them was systematically using such control to maximize output and minimize costs. One finds little evidence of any practices that would correspond to Say's notion of wage labor. Instead, entrepreneurs were evading control wherever possible, eschewing any appearance that their laborers were dependent on them, and making arrangements that utterly defied comprehension within the neat new categories of post-Revolutionary thought on labor and industry.

The first respect in which these "factories" of the Napoleonic era deceive expectations is in their size. According to the Champagny inquiry into the cotton trade of 1806, there were 1,037 establishments operating mule jennies and water frames in France (excluding conquered territories). Five hundred twenty-five of these shops were located in the Seine-Inférieure department, which included Rouen and most of its dependent cotton-producing region. For this department there is slightly more information than for the rest of France; these 525 shops operated a total of 297,900 spindles, 87,940 on water frames and 209,960 on mule jennies. The average number of spindles per shop was therefore 567. Only 21 of the shops had over one thousand spindles; altogether these larger shops accounted for 79,040 spindles (average per shop: 3,763). The remaining 504 shops with less than one thousand spindles averaged 434 spindles per shop, and these smaller establishments accounted for 73.4 percent of the region's capacity.[50]

Four hundred thirty-four spindles represents an extremely modest array of equipment. A document of 1814 from Rouen shows that over 80 percent of mule jennies in the town at that time had between 90 and 132 spindles.[51] Therefore the average shop in 1806 was equipped with no more than four mules. These machines and their ancillary equipment could have fit into a small barn.

Even more revealing about the state of the trade at this time are the technical implications of such small size. Mule jennies required carefully prepared roving to operate properly.[52] They could not be operated in cottages, like the earliest jennies often were. The only way to prepare roving was to have a carding machine and a slubbing billy (*métier en gros*), or even better two carding machines, a coarse and a fine carder. Carding machines had large heavy tumblers on which steel needles were mounted; they were impossible to turn by hand. In order to operate four mule jennies successfully, it was mandatory to have the cards, the slubbing billy, and a power source for the cards: a water wheel or horse treadmill. Altogether these were more expensive than the mules themselves by far. What is odd about the number of four mules per shop is that technical manuals advise one to expect a carding machine to supply enough roving for ten to twelve mule jennies. In other words, the average shop in 1806 did not have an optimum assortment of machines, in the language of the trade.[53] Their roving preparation capacity was far greater than their spinning capacity, or else their preparation equipment was being operated at very low efficiency or with very poor results. Both were probably the case. The early carding equipment was very sensitive, easily damaged, and difficult to gear properly for those without great experience, as most of these new French shop operators must have been.[54] But this means that 80 percent of the spinning capacity in the largest yarn-producing center in 1806 was in the hands of very small operators, whose equipment was far from technically optimal. Most of the cotton was being imported from the Caribbean or the Near East, sources whose cotton was known for poor quality, dirtiness, and shortness of fiber.[55] There were improvements in equipment being made at this time; another document shows that Rouen area shops had raised their average capacity up to about seven hundred spindles by 1815.[56] But this was still far below the number corresponding to a minimum assortment. From other sources there is evidence that Lille and Roubaix shops were much the same size, and that only in Alsace were proper assortments put into operation from the very beginning.[57] These observations all point to a single conclusion: Prices for cotton yarn were so high during the boom years 1806–1810 that no one concerned themselves in the least with production costs. Even with a poorly arranged and extremely small array of equipment profits were high and, over the years, most profits were taken immediately out of circulation. (Otherwise, shop size would have grown much more rapidly.) Likewise, the slumps of 1811–12 and 1814–16 did not stimulate a search for efficiency; they merely discouraged further investment of any kind.

If such tiny shops were, as it appears, economically viable in the boom years, then one may imagine that the few properly equipped mills were extremely profitable, which may explain why, alongside these thousands of small entrepreneurs, the Empire period gave rise to a few huge and hugely successful firms like Tiberghien et Bardel, operator of a Saint-Denis mill with 26,260 spindles in 1806 or Richard-Lenoir et Dufresne which controlled over a hundred thousand spindles in five mills by 1812 and in addition marketed its own line of spinning equipment.[58] Yet the reversal of 1811–12 was so severe that many of even these big operators were forced into liquidation within a few months. The market in this

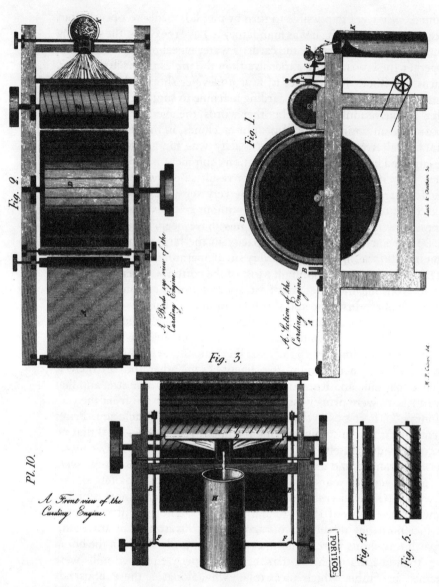

Figure 4. An early carding machine. The steel teeth mounted on the rollers gradually brush the fibers straight to form a roving ready to be spun. From Richard Guest, *Compendious History of the Cotton Manufacture* (London, 1823).

period, in other words, was not well organized enough to provide that stable competitive pressure that one usually supposes to be the chief virtue of the market system; and as a result the processes of production could be operated in a most negligent fashion, without attention to any of those elements of discipline and order so intrinsic to what industrialism is supposed to be. Machinery investments – like government contracts, smuggling operations, or currency manipulations – were simply another one of those sources of windfall, another one of those risky gambles that characterized commercial life under Napoleon.[59]

The human hand that operated the machinery was even less important. About work relations in these shops, two things need to be noted: (1) the modest technical requirements of mule–jenny operation at that time required no time discipline or supervision from the shop owners and offered the widest scope to independent initiative on the part of each mule spinner; and (2) the method of payment for yarn remained exactly the same as in the open markets and putting–out networks of the eighteenth century, providing the shop owner almost the same protection from the bad work habits and inefficiency of the laborer as merchant manufacturers had always enjoyed.

Mule jennies of up to one hundred spindles were operated by hand by a single individual (in practice always male) without any outside power source.[60] On the advanced designs of the late eighteenth century the crank was carefully placed in such a way that the spinner could comfortably turn it while guiding the movement of the carriage with the weight of his body. For mules with well over one hundred spindles it was possible to do without artificial power simply by having a separate (male) laborer to turn the crank under the command of the (male) spinner. Virtually all mule jennies in France before 1820 were operated in this way.[61] During the 1790s Manchester machine builders perfected the necessary gearing to provide mule jennies with power assists so that artificial power could be used to turn them. On these improved machines, as the spinner tugged on the carriage that pulled the spindles away from the rollers (to a distance of 5 to 10 feet), he would get help from a slipping belt drive attached to a distant treadmill, water wheel, or steam engine. These power assists were of no help, however, during the "winding on," the second phase when twisted, stretched yarn was now wound on the spindles to form a neat, tight "cop." This step was as important as the first. Even a slight let up in tension (if the carriage moved back too fast, for example) could ruin the yarn, allowing it to knot up (as when the tension goes out of a yo-yo string). Gearing that was sophisticated enough to drive a mule jenny through both these steps without constant assistance was only first developed by Roberts and Sharp of Manchester in 1830 (this was the "self-acting mule") and for many decades afterward even this advance

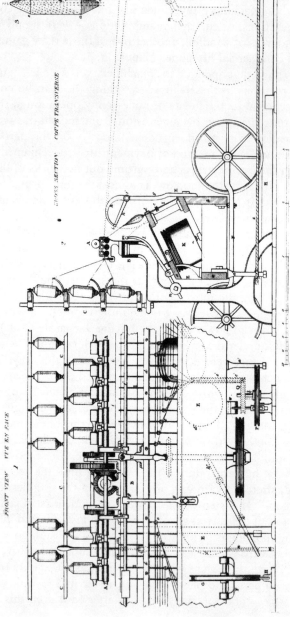

Fine Spinning Mule. ENG.   Métier à Mull-Jenny ou fin FR.

FRONT VIEW   VUE EN FACE

CROSS SECTION   COUPE TRANSVERSE

Figure 5. An advanced, power-assisted mule jenny. Carriage is shown at the beginning of the stretch. Dotted lines show its position at the end of the stretch and beginning of the winding-on. Roving passes between the rollers at A (upper left in the cross-section drawing), which squeeze and pull it, locking fibers together. It is then stretched and twisted as the spindle turns and the carriage rolls away from the rollers. During winding-on it is finally wound into a cop on the spindle as the carriage returns to original position. Shape of cop is shown in insert at upper right. From Andrew Ure, *The Cotton*

left much to be desired.[62] Mule spinners were highly skilled laborers both in France and in England through most of the nineteenth century. But particularly in the Napoleonic era in France, before power assists were in use and hand cranking remained general, the mule spinner's work had a markedly artisanal character. When he entered the shop to run one of its handful of machines, there was no steam engine or water wheel to set the pace, and no whistle to blow. There was roving ready for spinning that was probably of highly uneven quality, made of the world's worst grades of cotton smuggled past English ships from no one knew where. There were, as well, assistants dependent on him for their livelihood – one or two piecers (usually children of either sex who replaced bobbins and repaired broken yarns) and perhaps a crank operator. They had to be paid out of his own receipts at the end of the week. In the winter the mule spinner had to have a lantern and oil to light his workplace morning and evening and often had to pay a fee for heat as well. These all represented fixed costs that had to be met before he earned anything. He therefore had his own reasons for getting down to work with dispatch.[63]

On pay day he would find that all his cops of yarn produced during the week would have been rated and weighed in the same manner that stallkeepers in old marketplaces and factors in the countryside had rated and weighed yarn in previous centuries. He then received a certain price per pound of yarn. Here is the only place in the pay procedure that differed in any way from the cottage phase of yarn production: The price he was paid was much lower, reflecting the roughly twenty-fold increase in productivity that the hand-cranked mule brought vis-à-vis the spinning wheel.[64]

Yarn rating systems had been improving slowly since about 1750 and this is perhaps worth mentioning, since it was one way, albeit a highly indirect way, in which the shop owner was able to increase his control over the production process. Yarn was rated according to its coarseness or fineness, finer yarn being more difficult and time-consuming to produce and therefore necessarily more expensive. There were a bewildering variety of methods for rating yarn in eighteenth-century France, all based on a weight–length ratio. (A pound of fine yarn is obviously much longer than a pound of coarse yarn.) Equal lengths of yarn were wound onto a reel and then weighed. By the Manchester rating system slowly introduced into France after 1750, each grade of cotton yarn was assigned a number according to the number of hanks of that yarn which it took to add up to a pound (each hank being 840 yards long). If two hanks of a yarn weighed a pound, it was a No. 2 yarn. If it took thirty hanks of a yarn to weigh a pound, it was a No. 30 yarn. And so on. (See Fig. 1 for a drawing of a Manchester reel.) The advantage of the Manchester system arose from its simplicity and uniformity and from the fact that it was used with a reel geared to ring a reminder bell when the hank was wound off. Mental counting of the turns became unnecessary.[65] Using such reels shop owners were in a position to specify with precision exactly what grade of yarn their mule spinners were to produce and to check with equal precision whether they had managed to do so. A loose hand on the crank or a negligent pushing of the carriage would show up in uneven or improperly coarse ratings later on. The price for the yarn could then be adjusted downward accordingly. Mule spinners had to anticipate the discerning tests of the reeling and weighing-up time as they worked. In this indirect way their work was closely controlled. Of course, there were ways of fooling the reel and cheating the scale that any good spinner knew about.[66] It is particularly significant to notice in the present context that such a method of rating and paying for yarn involved the commodity of labor only indirectly. Labor was only measured and paid for through its outcome. Laborers, as in the rural cottages of the ancien regime, were left very much to their own devices as to how their labor was to be transformed into a tangible product, and how they were to divide up the proceeds among themselves and their assistants, while still covering their heat and lighting costs.

These "factories," it seems, were organized in almost every respect possible like putting–out systems. But for the fact that the mule spinner had to come to the shop, and that the price per pound he received was only a small fraction of those once paid to female hand spinners, the organization remained the same. For that matter it would have been perfectly possible to install one of these mules in the spinner's own home and provide him with roving from the cards every day, so long as the distance from the shop was not too great. One can speculate whether the tiny average shop size might not have resulted in part from such arrangements. One thing is certain, and that is that these peculiarities were never reported to the government and will never show up in their files; common sense now dictated that labor was a commodity that employers purchased and that industry was made up of entrepreneurs and laborers. Nothing further needed to be known in this area.[67]

AMBITIOUS WEAVERS

The steep economic peaks and valleys of the twenty-five-year period from 1789 to 1814 remind one how fragile a human institution any large-scale distribution system is. Whether it will operate to disseminate useful competitive pressures or not is anything but clear. At least for part of this period, from 1796 to 1811, the distribution of textile goods on the Continent created sufficient pressure to ensure that the mule jenny was able once and for all to displace the hand wheel. But then it does not take great market efficiency for prices to reflect a twenty-fold advantage in productivity.[68] That mule jennies were profitably operated throughout this period with complete negligence toward the simplest technical requisites of efficiency shows that even at its best the system did not distribute competitive pressures very effectively. Its highs were too high and its lows were too low.

Nonetheless the guilds were gone and their absence made a real difference, especially for weavers. Suddenly they had to make calculations and decisions that the guilds and the slower pace of change had made for them before. Even if the new Conseils des prudhommes dictated exactly how a piece must be produced, no one could any longer say what a weaver must produce. The massive shift to cotton therefore came in the form of thousands of individual business decisions prompted by lucrative suppliers' offers. Fashion-conscious merchant houses were attracted to Saint-Quentin-area weavers, for example, because of their former reputation for producing fine quality linens. Oberkampf began buying calicoes there in 1796; Richard-Lenoir et Dufresne entered the region three years later and managed to convince four thousand area weavers to turn to calico production for its factors in the next few years.[69] Meanwhile other local merchant manufacturers had imitated these trend setters, lest they steal all their weavers away.

In Normandy for a short while it was possible to earn up to 35 francs a week in calico weaving; weavers saved, bought small plots of land; some tried their hand at becoming suppliers themselves. Artisans and apprentices from other trades bought looms and set themselves up as calico weavers. Hundreds of small merchant manufacturers were successful for short periods, but were wiped out by sudden price fluctuations in raw cotton. In this situation of flux, with its extraordinary opportunities and dangers, the usual social cleavages were blurred. If anything, as a local merchant said looking back on the period later, the weavers who saved their earnings and bought land were the winners, not the merchant manufacturers who were struck down in great numbers in 1811–1812.[70]

There are scattered indications that the fly shuttle came into general use in the period after 1796 as well. This device, known in France since 1760, was easily added to existing hand looms and could provide an increase in the speed of shuttle strokes up to 50 percent. But it had been strangely neglected. If the evidence of its spread after the Revolution is correct, it was certainly the result of weavers making individual decisions to use it. There are no records of merchant manufacturers or factors promoting it. The very scarcity of records on this issue is an indication that it was left up to individual weavers to use it or not.[71]

In the weaving branch, therefore, although its organization remained unaltered, Revolutionary reforms had by 1800 brought a new, quicker pace of change. Aggressive merchants and shifts of fashion were not unknown before the Revolution, but at least then there had been the guild institutions whose officials and lawyers slowed the whole process of change down, softening its impact. Now calico weavers all over France would suffer physically from the consequences of their own personal business decisions when the crisis came. In the new order this was no longer a scandal, this was freedom.

THE NEW STATUS QUO

Up until 1815, nothing had occurred to bring about a fundamental change in social relations in the French textile trade. Despite the revolution in elite outlook, in the 1790s the entrepreneurial role remained undifferentiated within a trade still based exclusively on putting–out. The Empire boom gave the French textile industry its first real taste of unrestricted trade; but, because entrepreneurship remained an undifferentiated function within the trade, everyone felt the prick of competitive opportunity equally, bankers, merchants, shop operators, mule spinners, and cottagers alike. Even while the new spinning technology was integrated on a considerable scale, each individual remained responsible for the advantageous management of his own sphere of activity. Now at last the spirit of Lancashire found some echo in the hearts of French cottagers. Following fashion became a necessity; Kay's fly–shuttle was finally taken up with alacrity.

Under the Restoration, when the bottom dropped out of Normandy calico prices, those who could jumped into the production of the new *rouenneries* with pink stripes that began selling so well. No one blamed the merchant manufacturers for lowering their rates on calico to starvation levels. They were merely passing through the market's commands. The thousands of weavers who by now knew only calico weaving or were too tired or too old to change made no protest against their fate. In law they may have been required to carry the *livrets* of wage laborers; in their own minds they were independents who had gambled and lost.[72]

Doubtless this fact would have astonished the prefect Dieudonné, the economist J.B. Say, or Chaptal, architect of the *livret* law. Little people were not supposed to be entrepreneurs. Numerous considerations had led the elite to embrace an abstract market language that fit only poorly with existing social reality. First of all, absolute property had been the simplest consistent principle available for reconciling the diverse pressures brought to bear on the National Assembly in 1789. Such sweeping change as the Assembly enacted had to be justified by clear and consistent principle. The new notion of property used to justify the National Assembly's diverse reforms entailed a thoroughgoing laissez-faire economic policy of the kind long advocated by the Physiocrats. But such a policy, as discussed in Chapter 1, indirectly advantaged a group in society that had previously been advantaged directly by privilege and exemption, that is, the large owners of capital, landed or mobile. Privilege took on a new form; it hid behind a mask of equality but it did not disappear entirely. The known social world was not totally overturned; there continued to be great people and humble people. Authority and deference continued to have a familiar shape. The revolutionaries systematically favored this outcome, not so much because of the influence of some mighty material interest, surely, as simply because their minds recoiled before the unknown. How could a society exist without hierarchy and strong differentials in access to resources?

Secondly, the Revolution took place at just the time when the writings of Adam Smith and the new technology of spinning were arriving on French shores. Both gave a strong impetus to the recognition of labor productivity as a crucial factor in production; and the latter evidently required entrepreneurial control to realize the potential advances in productivity that it promised. At the same time the new property law, especially after the passage of the Le Chapelier law, provided a strong basis for the assertion of entrepreneurial control. These diverse trends in elite thought during the Revolutionary years, which it has only been possible to sketch in briefly here, culminated in the tripartite social vision of J.B. Say, in every sense a worthy successor to the medieval orders. The *laboratores, oratores,* and *bellatores* of the ancien regime were relayed by laborers, savants, and entrepreneurs. This was an elegant but also an inapt vision. Even if the Revolutionary crisis had not ensued, there can be little doubt that such a vision would have remained distant from practical conditions in textiles. The elements for establishing a factory system may have existed for cotton spinning, but cottage weaving was destined to remain the norm for another half century and in either branch real entrepreneurial control of production would take decades to work out.

Under these circumstances, the direction taken by Napoleon's revision of labor law is not surprising. Since most property owners in textiles were still merchants and merchant manufacturers, not entrepreneurs, they continued to desire from the government a legal apparatus like the old one perfected by Necker, which ensured collective and public fulfillment of certain entrepreneurial functions without giving cottagers any say in the decision making. Napoleonic law answered perfectly to their needs while ostensibly limiting itself to the regulation of free contracts between equals. At the same time, it was flexible, it was there to be used if a local merchant community chose to use it, or to be ignored if they did not.

And it could provide powerful public pressure to prevent laborers from freely disposing of their services if that was what owners of capital wished.

The stage was now set for the enactment of that peculiar travesty of a market system that the French textile industry was to become in the nineteenth century. Only one thing was needed before the curtain could rise, the return of reasonably stable markets for textile goods, which came soon after the final fall of Napoleon and the return of peace.

PART TWO

Uses of the market idea, 1816–1851

> Our relations with them [our employers] are a sort of market which is imposed on us by force, by violence, because we are compelled to work; this market enriches those who do nothing and allows those who work to want for everything. Were it voluntarily contracted by us, if there were any mutual obligation involved, it is we who would be the object [of enrichment] on the part of the idle.
>
> Charles Noiret, *Aux travailleurs* (1840)

By comparison with the ups and downs of commerce under the Empire, the business cycle during the Restoration and July Monarchy was orderly. The lows were not necessarily more shallow nor the highs less steep (although often they were), but the causes of these alterations were identifiable and, to a certain extent, systematic. War was replaced by poor harvests and bank failures as the triggers of periodic slumps. Price formation was erratic and unpredictable, but it did occur. Producers could use price information as a guide to planning over longer terms and thus could find profit in exploiting smaller price differentials. Speculation plagued the international supply lines for raw cotton and wool, occasionally creating purely artificial scarcities that defied all planning efforts, but in the intervals, supply was very steady and abundant, better than it had ever been in the eighteenth century, in fact. Yarn markets were more regular still. Trade in finished cloth became highly organized although prices remained erratic due to a new factor promoted by the merchants themselves: the increased pace of change in fashion. The greatest problem of all, however, was the occasional prolonged slump in aggregate demand that, by a chain reaction, disrupted the normal flow of commerce and investment. The brilliant Simonde de Sismondi as early as 1819 attempted to explain this recurrent phenomenon as a necessary result of what would now be called market inefficiencies in the distribution of manufactured goods.[1] Producers constantly seeking to maximize output, he explained, were bound to outstrip consumer desire for their goods, even at lower prices; when the threshold was reached the message would not get back to the producers until it was too late and vast resources had been committed to the production of goods no one wanted. His conclusions were hotly disputed, but the notion of crises of overproduction was soon in the air, and French textile manufacturers were soon habitually discussing the danger of the *trop plein* – the "too full" market that led to ruinous losses.[2] It is clear, in sum, that markets for textile goods in the 1820s and '30s were organized and operating, that prices could be easily discovered and used as planning devices – within a strictly limited scope and at considerable risk. The limited orderliness of these markets was nonetheless sufficient to cause a remarkable transformation in the scale and methods of textile production between 1815 and 1834. Indicative of this transformation were two changes: At the consumption end, fashion took on an entirely new significance; at the production end, labor conflict made its first appearance. Linking these two developments was the emergent range of activities that in the twentieth century is called "management" and is characteristic of the task of the entrepreneur. Something like a market society was coming into being. But this emergent social order was fundamentally different from the one which was envisioned by the prophets of market culture, if for no other reason than because nothing faintly resembling a labor market made its appearance. Even the boom-and-bust markets for manufactured goods of these pioneer days were efficient by comparison with what happened to labor. People, the most important resource of all, were not distributed in this society as in a market. The maximization of profit, therefore, proceeded along very different lines from those of theory; and the structure of society changed in ways quite different from what is normally supposed. In the meantime the useful but deceptive language of the market system made great progress.

4 The first crisis of management

By 1820 it was not necessary to read J.B. Say to understand what the new structure of life was supposed to be. It was only necessary to perceive how odd the Bourbon court looked grafted back onto *la Grande Nation*. Those ex-Revolutionaries and ex-Napoleonic officials who, now out of jobs, began to form themselves into a party and to call themselves liberals were anxious to interpret their accomplishments to a wide audience. The reforms of 1789, which the restored monarch made no attempt to undo, had won out, they said. Privilege was at an end. Liberty, according to the liberals, was the liberty to excel. Napoleon himself was made into the prime example. A rosy legend soon surrounded his memory, according to which he had risen from obscurity by his own talent and exertion to rule Europe and to protect the Revolution from its enemies. The message was spread not only through learned treatises and newspaper articles but also through popular fiction, the reminiscences of army veterans, vivid printed portraits and battle scenes.[1] Stendhal's Julien Sorel was not the only young man who devoured avidly the stories of Napoleon's exploits.

It is true that Stendhal in *The Red and the Black* pilloried Restoration society for its clericalism and its conservatism. The only avenue open to success under the restored Bourbons, he implied, was within the hypocritical and obscurantist Catholic hierarchy, and even here arbitrary obstacles of birth and wealth blocked the ambitions of the self-made. But Stendhal's spleen is a less dependable guide to the feeling of life in post-Napoleonic France than Balzac's frenzy for success, a trait he shared with all his young heroes. The example of Napoleon and of the hundreds who had risen with him could not be erased. Rank no longer need be inherited; there were other, quicker avenues. The Bourbons ruled at sufferance; when Charles X finally tried in 1830 to break decisively with the legacy of the Revolution, he was overthrown within hours. Louis Philippe from the throne he had won in the streets touted to the world, as Napoleon had done, his approval of an open society in which wealth wedded merit.

89

Uses of the market idea, 1816–1851

CAREERS OPEN TO TALENT

The mordant desire for upward mobility affected both entrepreneurs in the textile trade and consumers of its products. Producers of the Napoleonic period had already succeeded at amassing fortunes by appealing to a taste for imitation luxury among the not-so-rich. Under the Restoration, this trend continued and widened until it transformed the social meaning of clothing entirely.

Government policy toward the textile trade could not have been more favorable to the business of making more and cheaper luxuries available to all. After a brief flirtation with an open import policy, by February of 1816 the government had resurrected Napoleon's absolute prohibition of yarn and cloth imports. But Louis XVIII, unlike Napoleon, imposed no significant barrier to the entry of raw fiber. For the first time in history, textile producers had not only freedom from internal constraints and protection from foreign competition, but stable access to the best foreign sources of raw cotton and wool. In 1834 before a government board of inquiry, mill owners and merchants from all over France were unanimous in their praise of Restoration trade policy. As the Alsatian mill owner Roman testified,

> One of the needs we feel most strongly in France, and one of the causes that has contributed most to our state of malaise, is the difficulty of finding social positions.

But thanks to Restoration trade policies,

> Our cotton industry, and industry in general, has offered immense resources in this respect in the last twenty-five years. How many individuals of every class, above the working class, have found in industry the means to an honorable existence for themselves and their families!

Or, as a Rouen merchant manufacturer put it, the 1816 import prohibition "is our industrial Charter" (referring to the Charter of Liberties granted by Louis XVIII on his return to France in 1814).[2]

Under the cover of yarn and cloth import prohibitions, textile producers continued to make their fortunes by catering to ambition. The only difference from Napoleon's era was that the times required a new tone in fashion. Men on the way up in the 1820s had to wear more subdued colors, more conservative cuts, and avoid cotton in favor of the traditional fibers, especially wool. With the old hereditary nobility installed at court, it was impossible to announce one's warm aspirations with bright calico prints, lustrous satins or cotton velours.[3] It was the ruin of Amiens, in fact, that cotton velours were rejected in favor of traditional, dark woolens for men's pants.[4] But the same change brought the languishing trades of Sedan and Elbeuf back to life.[5] Imitation cash-

90

meres and merinos for women survived the initial transition to conservatism, much to the relief of Reims, as did the fine white cotton muslins of Saint-Quentin. But calico prints did not. At first they were rejected outright. Then, gradually they came back into use among a lower class of clientele, those who did not mind imitating the faded glory of the past (or could not afford to do otherwise).[6] This shift represented a significant challenge to the cotton industry; cost-cutting became crucial to survival. Paris spinning shops, the most advanced of the Empire period, were forced into liquidation because labor costs were too high there. The other two important centers of calico production, Rouen and Mulhouse, managed to adapt, each in its own way, to the new conditions. In doing so they created a new vocation for the cotton industry – supplying peasants and artisans with bright, pretty, abundant cloth whose price moved steadily downward. Like Manchester manufacturers a generation earlier, they discovered that demand was very elastic among the poor. Slight decreases in price brought large increases in consumption.

Gathering statistics had by this time become a field unto itself avidly pursued not only by government officials but by doctors, lawyers, and amateur savants. Entrepreneurs willingly volunteered general statistical information about their town or region or sometimes even about their own operations. Hence it is possible to trace the breathtaking growth of the cotton industry under the Restoration by citing figures that are doubtless accurate enough for present purposes. Tables 1 and 2 show that in the 10 short years between 1816 and 1826, cotton consumption increased by 170 percent, yarn prices for the common grades dropped 30 percent, and spinning capacity increased by 140 percent. Most of the new capacity was concentrated in northern provincial towns and their near suburbs, where the average capacity per firm rose to at least three thousand spindles and in some towns to as high as eight thousand spindles.

Shops of this size consisted of twenty to sixty mule jennies where typical shops of the Empire had only had five or six. (One wants at last to begin using the term mill or factory to speak of them.) On average, output per spindle was up, by some 30 to 40 percent. The larger shops were able to prepare the fiber better, for one thing. For another, the best American grades of cotton from Georgia and Louisiana were again available, at lower prices than ever before. Carding these grades was easier; a single pair of cards could supply more mules. Such advances in output coupled with the lower raw material costs made it possible to offer constantly lower prices on finished yarn. Much of the initial growth in firm capacity, up until about 1820, was made possible by the sale of used equipment from Parisian and Belgian firms in liquidation.[7] But by the mid-1820s, there were numerous French concerns building machinery for the industry that was considered almost as good as British.[8]

91

Table 1. *Imports and prices in the French cotton industry, 1816–1826*

| Year | Cotton imports[a] (000s of kg) | Raw cotton prices[b] | | Yarn prices[b] (No. 30 warp, francs per kg) |
| | | Lowest | Highest | |
		(francs per kg)		
1816	12,115			12.50[c]
1817	13,370			
1818	17,034			
1819	17,010	3.00	3.40	9.30
1820	20,003	3.00	3.40	8.90
1821	22,587	3.00	3.05	8.20
1822	21,572	2.20	2.90	7.75
1823	20,384	2.55	2.90	6.90
1824	28,630	2.50	2.85	6.70
1825	24,667	2.30	4.00	7.30
1826	31,914	1.75	2.40	6.40

[a] Maurice Bloch, *Statistique de la France*, 2 vols. (Paris, 1860), I, 133–4.
[b] ERDP, III, 488.
[c] Ibid., p. 354.

The most dramatic development of all, as the figures show, was in Alsace. In Mulhouse and its surrounding villages, well financed cloth printing firms reacted to the need for lower prices on calico prints by setting out to achieve self-sufficiency in cloth production. They built their own spinning mills and established their own networks of weavers all with an eye to gaining technical parity with Great Britain. Half a million spindles were set in operation in the region between 1815 and 1825; the number of looms engaged in cotton weaving (calicoes, percales, muslins of all grades) rose from ten to about fifty thousand.[9] Growth in Normandy was less dramatic but vigorous, nonetheless. In both areas, the inflated prices paid to weavers for producing calicoes under the Empire were cut drastically in 1818 and further cuts followed. Such cuts, along with continued mechanization in spinning, were an essential feature of the overall strategy of achieving rapid growth by taking advantage of elastic demand. Rouen producers switched to coarser grades of yarn as another means of keeping costs down. Where Normandy calico weavers had earned as much as 100 francs per piece (for about twenty days' work, that is) in 1816, they were fortunate to be making 30 francs by 1822. Those who knew how went back to weaving traditional *rouenneries*. In the same period the price per meter of printed calicoes dropped from over 2.50 francs to less than 1.65. Similar cuts in rates paid to weavers

Table 2. *Capacity of various centers of cotton spinning in France in 1810 and 1826*

Center	Spindles in 1810[a]	Spindles in 1826	Average spindles per firm, 1826
Lille–Roubaix	200,000	500,000[b]	3,300[b]
Normandy	350,000[c]	800,000[d]	3,500[d]
Amiens	75,000	68,000[e]	2,200[e]
Paris	250,000	—	—
Saint-Quentin	60,000	275,000[f]	8,000[f]
Alsace	45,000	570,000[g]	8,800[g]

[a] Maurice Lévy-Leboyer, *Les banques européennes et l'industrialisation internationale* (Paris, 1964), p. 59.

[b] ERDP, III, 184–90.

[c] Average 700 spindles per firm in 1815 (AN, F[12]1585).

[d] ERDP, III, 269–70.

[e] Ibid., p. 415.

[f] Ibid., pp. 517, 520; Charles Picard, *Résumé d'une étude sur la ville de Saint-Quentin* (Saint-Quentin, 1880), p. 111.

[g] Achille Penot, *Statistique générale du département du Haut-Rhin* (Mulhouse, 1831), p. 372.

occurred in Saint-Quentin and Tarare (where the finest grades of calicoes and white muslins continued to be produced) and Alsace (where immigrant Swiss weavers, ruined by the 1816 import prohibition, provided a ready pool of laborers for the new vertically integrated firms).[10] Thus growth was maintained despite the fall from fashion; by the mid-1820s yesterday's finery had come within the reach of peasants and artisans. At import levels reported for the year of 1826, the industry was producing over five meters of cotton cloth for every man, woman, and child in the country each year.

In the midst of this heady prosperity, the cotton industry experienced in 1825 a foretaste of crises to come. Speculative buying forced up the price of raw cotton to its highest levels in a decade. Speculators knew the mill owners had to buy some cotton to keep their machines going. But consumer resistance kept the costs from being passed through; orders for raw cotton dropped off, and the speculators had to take heavy losses in the end. (See Table 1.) The whole episode was over in a few months. But certain structural peculiarities of mechanized production were made painfully apparent. Mill owners were compelled to buy some cotton; they could not refuse simply because they had to keep their expensive machinery going. This novel vulnerability now began to tempt speculators.

This time the stockpilers lost out; those who bought as little as possible were rewarded with lower prices. But what would be the correct strategy the next time? [11]

There was nothing in the other sectors of the textile trade to equal the explosive growth of cotton production. Wool producers were barred from taking advantage of elastic demand to the same degree as cotton producers by the high cost of raw wool. Wool that sold for 10 francs per kilogram when clean and ready for spinning yielded woolen cloth that sold for about 13.40. The same amount of raw cotton would have cost 2.50 francs and sold for 8.00.[12] The process of production only added about one third to the selling price of the wool, where it trebled that of cotton. Cost-cutting measures in production therefore had only a minor impact on the final price of woolen cloth, which remained well above the price charged for an equivalent grade of cotton cloth. Wool had come back into fashion with the Restoration, but only for a clientele that could afford to pay extra. Elbeuf woolens for men's pants were 25 francs per meter in 1822 (equal to at least two weeks' pay for a mule spinner, and this without taking into account the cost of garment making).[13] As a result, by comparison with cotton, pressure to improve production procedures was not very strongly felt. Nonetheless, there were enough savings available through mechanical spinning (especially in the production of lower-cost flannels) to attract investors into this area. Typically, wool spinning mill operators owned only their machinery, however; they processed wool belonging to merchant manufacturers for a flat rate per kilogram, arrangements not unlike those that continued to prevail among female hand spinners.[14] Until 1825, only carded wool was machine spun; longer, more expensive combed wools (called worsteds in English) still employed a great army of women spinning in their cottages. Because Reims producers specialized in flannels and imitation cashmeres that used carded wool, Reims had led the way in mechanical spinning since the early years of the Empire. By 1820, there were already 40 small mills in the town; by 1827 there were 200,000 spindles for wool in the Reims area, more than all the other northern centers – Elbeuf, Louviers, and Sedan – combined.[15]

SELLING UPWARD MOBILITY

Beginning in 1824, Reims merchant manufacturers pioneered a marketing revolution of extraordinary importance for the future of the textile trade in France. Seeking to take advantage at once of wool's favor with fashion and of the growth potential cotton producers had discovered in lower prices, Reims producers launched a new cloth, called *circassiennes*.[16] The warp yarns were cotton, the weft wool; once fulled (an expensive process of teasing and trimming the wool fibers), the wool nap tended to cover up the cheap cotton warp yarns, so that the cloth had the appearance of an all wool article. But it could be sold profitably for much less. *Circassiennes* were an immediate success in Paris. Other Reims merchants quickly followed the lead, introducing a carded-wool cloth called *napolitaines* that could be made entirely of machine-spun yarn.[17] Because this cloth was simply not fulled, it had some of the look of the more expensive merinos (worsted cloth made of merino wool). The public greeted this new article, too, with enthusiasm. *Circassiennes* were overproduced during their second season; merchants were forced to let them go at 20 to 30 percent discounts; and in subsequent years their reputation never quite recovered from the blow. No one wanted to pay full prices for something that had been sold off at discounts the year before; besides, the depth of the discounts had revealed just how inexpensive *circassiennes* were to make. *Napolitaines*, however, once their novelty wore off, won the loyalty of a wide public. They became, as one merchant put it, "the merino of the middle classes"; by 1834 they were the single largest selling article produced in the Reims area, retailing for under 4 francs per meter (where merinos often cost over 10, down from a high of 30 francs per meter under the Empire).[18]

The following year, 1826, cotton struck back, entering once again into the lists of fashion with an article created in an Alsatian town, Sainte-Marie-aux-Mines. The new article, called *guinghams*, had a less expensive but dependable No. 40 warp and fine weft yarns of No. 100 to 120. The yarns were dyed in advance, so that *guinghams* came in a wide variety of solids, stripes, and plaids, the fine weft yarns giving them the look of expensive muslins and percales. Again the pattern was repeated: *Guingham* was at first a dizzying success for its originators; merchants of the German-speaking Alsatian town learned French and began opening bureaus in Paris to take orders and better anticipate changes in taste. But they and their imitators also overproduced in the second season, a situation likely to win the contempt of consumers. In this case, however, *guingham* was able to continue finding appreciative buyers, at lower but still profitable prices, for years to come.[19]

With hindsight, it is easy to see that these new varieties were all repeating the pattern set originally by printed calicoes, beginning as fashionable successes, ending by finding buyers of slimmer means who were content to follow, rather than to make, fashion. With their initial success behind them, each was able to provide profits at prices lower than those of the articles whose look they imitated. But this hindsight must not obscure the impact of the initial discovery in the mid-twenties. Merchants realized that what had happened to *indiennes* could be repeated on other, ever new varieties of cloth.

In the same years a whole new field of possibilities for new articles was just opening up, since machinery capable of spinning combed wool became available after 1825. A rush began to establish new mills and reconvert old ones for this purpose. In the vanguard were Amiens with 75,000 spindles, Reims with 55,000, and Roubaix with 17,000 by 1833, virtually all set up since 1827.[20] Thanks to these mills the elegant look of combed wool was available in abundance at prices 10 to 20 percent lower than previously. The town of Roubaix proved most versatile in putting the new yarns to use in cheap combinations. Between 1827 and 1830 Roubaix launched two new articles that proved of durable appeal: *lastings*, an all-wool cloth in stripes and solids for men's coats and pants, and *stoffs* (cotton warp, combed-wool weft) which challenged the reign of *napolitaines*, selling for as low as 2 francs per meter, and therefore accessible to a wider public. In addition, Roubaix began experimenting with silk yarn and jacquard looms for producing silk-and-cotton brocades for men's vests. (Six hundred jacquards were in operation by 1833, 2,500 by 1835.) Roubaix's new course was set; the town became the capital of popularly priced imitations, especially in woolens. Cotton yarn and calico production in Roubaix languished.[21] Saint-Quentin was not far behind in coming out with new varieties – half-wool or all-wool muslins suitable for printing to replace their fine cottons. From 1828 on, fashionable worsteds were offered in new combinations every season to ever lower strata of buyers.[22]

The success of all these mixed-fiber and imitation articles depended on the activities of a new kind of retailer, the *marchand de nouveautés*. By making high-volume purchases, by advertising fixed prices in newspapers, by using special sales to increase stock-turnover rates on slow-moving items, these precursors of the department store stimulated a taste for fashion among customers who heretofore could not have aspired to it. These retailers pioneered as well the ready-to-wear garment industry in the late 1820s. At first confined to work clothes, the new technique of sewing clothes with standardized patterns soon expanded to include suits and dresses in imitation of the current fashionable cut. The new cheap cloths were an obvious choice for these garments. Ready-to-wear drew the poor away from their traditional supplier, the *fripier*, or used-clothing dealer, and appealed to those of straitened means who aspired to something better: clerks, shopkeepers, declining *rentiers*, impoverished law students. All of these novel retailing techniques would have been against the law under the old guild system; now there was nothing to stop them.[23]

By 1830, the merchandise available from most *marchands de nouveautés* must have fairly shouted the assumptions of the age at any customer who examined them. By that date, the products of the textile trade had themselves accomplished the transition to market culture. They appealed to the consumer's vanity, to his hopes for the future, to his admiration for wealth and success. Many in the end must have come to believe that it was perfectly natural to have such feelings, that it was inherent in the human condition. Calicoes in the meantime had come within the range of the working-class purse. Laborers of the burgeoning textile towns by the 1830s, at least judging from a few indications, preferred to have bright calico shirts or dresses, even if it strained their budgets, in order to distinguish themselves from the peasants and country weavers who were their parents.[24]

Clothing is such an intimate feature of personal identity, it would be impossible for a social revolution to occur without transforming collective attitudes toward it. Already in the eighteenth century, it is possible to identify an increased pace of change in fashion. The old sumptuary laws fell into neglect; artisans were occasionally seen aping aristocrats in culottes and silk stockings.[25] The Revolution put its stamp of approval on this trend, abolishing all sumptuary regulation as another attack on individual liberty. The 1790s saw a riot of color spread over Paris.[26] But the Restoration brought a more subtle, more profound embedding of the new order's assumptions in the prevailing habits of dress. Conservative tastes now prevailed; but any citizen could choose to wear conservative finery. The ambitious advertised their ambition and the parvenues their success by wearing only the latest fashions. Those of lesser talents or means were offered imitations, clever new innovations, the democratizing fruits of economic progress available in a dazzling array of prices and styles.

AN INCREMENT OF CONTROL

The successful pursuit of fashion required of merchant manufacturers not only creative marketing or the ability to drive a hard bargain with both weavers and wholesalers; it also required greater control over production itself.[27] The merchant of Sainte-Marie-aux-Mines, worried over the success of his latest *guingham* pattern, had to assure himself that his weavers knew in which order to weave the stripes. His Roubaix colleague who had set out to produce a line of pinstripe *lastings* faced the same problem. There were at least four different kinds of solutions to this problem, none of them new, that were applied in differing degrees from region to region. The result was a greater level of control than had ever been exercised over weavers in the past, but one which still fell short of strictly defined entrepreneurial control.

Normandy merchant manufacturers continued to suit the article to the skills of the locale. More difficult articles were kept in Rouen, simple

97

stripes and plaids went to the Pays de Caux, plain-weave calicoes, easiest of all, to Picardy and beyond.[28] Alsace saw the proliferation of small workshops of ten or so looms, beginning by about 1826, run under the direction of a "foreman" (*contre-maître*), actually a subcontractor who took in work on commission from the large houses in Mulhouse, Sainte-Marie, or elsewhere. The success of *guinghams* was a particularly strong spur to this trend, for a whole community of weavers had to be trained to weave them. A few of the larger firms in Mulhouse tried uniting large numbers of hand looms under one roof in order to maximize supervision; but the number of such large shops remained very small. In fact, a large majority of the region's 50,000 looms in 1830 remained in the cottages of individual weavers. But obviously the more difficult, more fashionable articles were assigned by preference to the shops.[29] Similar loom shops proliferated in luxury woolen production, as well, in the early decades of the century, to the point where they predominated in the production of *nouveautés* in Elbeuf.[30]

At Roubaix, two different methods were used. Numerous merchant manufacturers built their own housing tracts clustered around their warehouses and warping and dye shops. Rent was deducted from pay, and the threat of eviction added to the arsenal of control. Detailed supervision was easy: In the mid-1820s the Roubaix Conseil des prudhommes drew up the most elaborate code of its kind for regulating relations between merchants and their outworkers. Every change of address or change of supplier and every arrival or departure of a weaver at Roubaix was to be registered in books held at the town hall as well as in the weaver's *livret*. Conditions of notice and of pay, grievance procedures, and the rights of all parties were elaborately specified. In theory, nothing was to escape the notice and control of the Prudhommes; in practice the compliance rate was about 60 percent, perhaps the highest of any textile town in the country.[31] These various strategies – increased control by Prudhommes, the use of housing tracts or workshops, and the suiting of articles to the skills of the weavers – were used to one extent or another in almost every center.

But these techniques fell short of full entrepreneurial control for several reasons. First of all merchant manufacturers still had much to gain from leaving a heavy burden of responsibility with the weaver. Most weavers continued to own their looms (or in shops, to rent them) and to supply light, heat, shuttles, sizing, and bobbin winding out of their own pockets. Most continued to have the final say over what they would produce. It was as necessary for them to second-guess fashion as it was for the merchants; a price change on an article in Paris could result in rate cuts in Champagne or the Vosges within days.[32]

Secondly, this new measure of control was not aimed at increasing productivity so much as at ensuring quality and uniformity of an article whose success depended heavily on appearance. The stakes were high; the woolen centers of the south, for example, gradually lost out in the struggle to attract the discerning buyer. By 1834, their trade with the eastern Mediterranean was being taken over by English competitors; within France northern competitors gradually forced them to turn to heavy, common articles without much future. The result was a steady decline. The reasons for this are not entirely clear; but it is certain that the northern woolen centers did not win out due to an advantage in labor productivity.[33] There are no traces of merchant manufacturers anywhere in France seeking for that special control over labor that allows for experimentation and technical advance. Power looms had, of course, appeared by 1820, but they were suited for production of only the plainest middle grades of cotton cloth and therefore were not very attractive within the special market conditions of France. They spread more slowly even than in England.[34]

Weavers did feel the change in status. Their suppliers were driving harder bargains than ever before. In the new game of fashion, the merchant had the upper hand. He offered enticing rates on new articles, attracting large numbers of weavers to them; then, when the market was saturated, he slashed his offering rates. Many weavers, having just learned how to produce the new cloth, were reluctant to leave it – that is, until the next craze came along. The slump of 1827–32 interrupted this rhythm somewhat; merchant manufacturers did not hesitate to allow their weavers to feel the full brunt of the market. The rate for weaving calicoes in Rouen dropped in 1831 to 8 francs for a warp of 130 meters, less than 2 sous a meter. At that price, said one merchant, "they preferred to beg."[35]

Roubaix merchant manufacturers' reaction to the slump stands out as a significant exception to this general pattern. In 1827, under the auspices of the Prudhommes, over one hundred twenty firms in the area signed a contract that bound them to pay their weavers according to agreed rates for the duration of the crisis; and the Prudhommes continued to set official price lists for the town through 1831.[36] The fear was that their community of weavers would be destroyed and dispersed, leaving them with no labor force at the end of the crisis. In taking such action, Roubaix merchant manufacturers revived an old guild practice in a time of stress; at the same time, however, they moved a step closer to treating their weavers as sellers of a commodity, labor, which had its own price and its own costs of production independent of the value of the product. Elsewhere, throughout this period, weavers continued to be treated as independent operators just insofar as doing so justified lower rates and frequent changes in article, and were also subjected to tighter controls just insofar as fashion demanded.

THE ANATOMY OF A SLUMP

In the cotton-spinning sector a much more significant change occurred. By 1827 the opportunity for entrepreneurial control had been put into the mill owner's hands by mechanization and centralization of production. But after 1827, finally, competition forced him to assert it. And the response of his laborers was to resist.

Now at last, one may say that the market system was functioning as theory predicted, forcing the reorganization of production and the recasting of social identities in the workplace. But to understand the change that occurred in cotton spinning after 1827, it is necessary to appreciate, on the contrary, just how weak the force of competition was and how much real diversity the price-clearing mechanism of the yarn markets tolerated throughout this crisis.

As noted above, average output per spindle increased in the cotton spinning industry between 1816 and 1826 by 30 percent. But this average increase in output concealed a marked diversity: Some mills had not shown much improvement at all, while others had made rapid strides achieving advances in output well beyond the average. Achille Penot, a Mulhouse savant and social reformer, in his 1831 statistical study of the Alsace region provided a detailed discussion of advances in spinning technology since the Empire. "The cards and the mule jennies built now," he said, "are hardly different from the ones built in 1806." But significant advances had occurred in the intermediate processes carried out on the carded fiber before it went to the mule; the newer machines were vast improvements over the old. In addition artificial power sources had been applied to the mule jenny. "At first slubbing billies [*métiers en gros*] and mule jennies were cranked by the spinners. A water course or horse or ox tread mill turned the carding equipment." But by 1827 virtually all mule jennies in Alsace's mills were equipped with power assists and moved by water or steam instead of by hand. When the power assists were first introduced, the old mules of 120 spindles had been linked together in series, since the limitation of hand power no longer applied, making a mule of 240 spindles that could be operated by a single spinner. Artificial power for the mules and improved rovings had greatly enhanced the output potential. "On a mule of 240 spindles in 1816 and 1817, it was difficult to produce more than 3 kilograms per day of No. 32 yarn; whereas now it is possible to obtain 8 or 9 kilograms, that is, almost triple, and of better quality."[37]

Penot's estimate of triple the output seems a bit excessive, but his figures are not greatly different from ones found in other sources that suggest that 3.5 kilograms per day from 240 spindles under the Empire was not uncommon and that 6 to 7 kilograms on power-assisted mules in 1830 was frequently achieved.[38] Hence, in Alsace output was generally increased between 1816 and 1826 by 100 percent or more, thanks to the introduction of new preparation equipment and of power assists for the mules. Output per spinner, since each spinner tended double or even quadruple the number of spindles tended under the Empire, must have increased much more, bringing unit labor costs down dramatically. Alsace was favored not only with large, well-financed firms, but with an abundance of swiftly running streams in the Vosges mountains, ideally suited for providing cheap power. By 1826, with the exception of a handful of mills, none of the other regions had either of these technical advances – improved preparation machines or power assists for mules. Few of the rivers in Normandy, and none of those in the Lille–Roubaix area provided enough power to make possible the shift to power-assisted mules. The steam engine was almost nonexistent in these centers before 1825. Roubaix did not have water to fill the boilers; of 200 mills in Normandy, no more than ten were equipped with steam power by this date.[39] Yet mills in both of these areas were making adequate profits in 1826 which, by all accounts, was a boom year for the cotton trade.[40] Alsatian mills, producing at double the output per spindle and perhaps triple the output per spinner of other regions, must have been yielding extraordinary returns on investment.

Under the circumstances, new cotton mills must have seemed like a sure investment, although in view of what followed this was far from being the case. In fact, from the vantage of 1834, mill owners lamented the "fever of production" that had "won over every head" by 1825, leading to the establishment of numerous new mills.[41] It was during this rapid expansion that a mediocre harvest in 1827 touched off an overall sag in demand for manufactured goods. Table 3 shows what happened in cotton spinning over the next seven years. Overall consumption did not drop more than about 14 percent in the worst year of the slump, 1828, by comparison with 1826. But in order to find buyers for all this cotton, mill owners had to cut prices back from 6.40 francs per kilogram of No. 30 warp in 1826 to 4.40 francs in 1828, to 3.80 francs in 1832, the first year in which consumption passed the 1826 mark. This represented a sustained reduction in prices of 30 to 40 percent. After this ordeal, the high prices and record output of 1833 and 1834 must have seemed like the return to a forgotten paradise.

To appreciate the impact of the slump on the way mills were operated, one must put oneself in the position of a mill owner in 1827. When

Table 3. *Imports and prices of cotton in France during the crisis of 1827–32*

| Year | Cotton imports[a] (000s of kg) | Raw cotton prices[b] | | Yarn prices[b] (No. 30 warp, francs per kg) |
| | | Lowest | Highest | |
		(francs per kg)		
1826	31,914	1.75	2.40	6.40
1827	26,694	1.80	2.00	5.30
1828	27,375	1.80	2.00	4.40
1829	31,889	1.75	1.90	4.00
1830	29,260	1.70	1.95	4.00
1831	28,229	1.70	1.80	4.10
1832	33,636	1.70	1.90	3.80
1833	35,610	1.80	3.10	4.75
1834	36,035	2.20	2.80	5.15

[a] Bloch, *Statistique*, I, 133–4.
[b] ERDP, III, 488.

demand began to sag, the pressure was felt first of all on liquidity. As yarn sales fell off, firms at first faced rising inventories and shortages of cash to pay off their own creditors. Because credit was extremely limited, firms often had only one means of generating cash, moving inventories of yarn at cut-rate prices, even selling at a loss, in order to continue operating. In other words, the permanent credit famine meant that price was very sensitive to shifts in demand. If enough troubled firms took the course of cutting prices, the result was a rapid, downward price spiral. All crises generated by sagging demand in the first half of the century took this form at the beginning.[42] In 1827, the better equipped Alsatian firms were able to continue profitable operation, even at the lower price levels. But many of the others were forced to take serious losses. The least competitive mills began at once to be squeezed out; 80,000 spindles were idled at Saint-Quentin, 100,000 in the Lille-Roubaix area, and an equal number in Normandy.[43]

Those mills without competitive equipment but which were well financed enough to survive the initial shock were faced with a dire necessity. For the time being they had to cut costs wherever possible. As the months dragged into years with no improvement in yarn prices, mill owners realized that only improvements in their plant would enable them to ensure profitable operation, and hence survival.[44]

At the heart of both these policies, cost cutting and utilizing improved equipment, lay the labor process itself. Hitherto neglected and poorly understood by the mill owners (who as a body had only a meager technical education), the mule spinner's job and how he carried it out suddenly became the key to survival in an altered economic climate.

Mill owners in Roubaix began drawing up formal work rules for the first time at the onset of the crisis. The local Conseil des prudhommes insisted on having copies of all such rules in its files, since they fell within the Prudhommes' jurisdiction over work contracts; some of these files have survived.[45] The earliest set of rules in the files dates from August 1826, and it served as a model which most other owners copied, perhaps on the Prudhommes' recommendation. The average Roubaix mill at this time had about four thousand spindles, roughly thirty mule jennies; the largest mill in the town had about thirteen thousand (about one hundred machines). Only two or three of the town's forty mills had steam power.[46]

The earliest set of rules, from the Delerue firm, was clearly intended for an operation without steam power. The rules reflect only a casual interest in punctual arrival at work; the hours of operation are not even listed. Three rules out of sixteen deal with lateness or early departure from the mill. Only three deal with comportment inside the shop; two deal with the notice period for quitting (one of these clearly violates existing statutes). The remaining eight concern technical aspects of machine operation, tool breakage, use of lamps, and handling of raw cotton. Four rules bear directly on the operation of mule jennies. Spinners were not in any way to adjust the gears or cords of their mules without authorization. Technical manuals of the period list a number of ways in which a mule spinner could enhance his pay by tampering with the machine. One of the most common was to place a piece of leather around one of the drive wheels – making the spindles spin faster – just as one was spinning the last few hundred yards of the cops. When sample hanks for measurement were later wound onto the reel, the yarn would measure several grades finer than the bulk of the yarn in the cop. The spinner would then be paid as if he had achieved a finer number of yarn, that is, his rate of pay per kilogram would be higher by 5 to 10 centimes. A later set of work rules from Roubaix, modeled on Delerue's, specifies that "Any spinner who adds a pinion or uses other means to spin finer yarn at the end of a *levée* will forfeit his pay on the whole *levée*."[47] (*Levée* was the term for the removal and testing of finished cops.) Spinners were also subject to fines for worn bobbins (resulting from failure to oil contact points on the spindle) and for loose, dirty, or poorly wound cops (resulting from negligent bumping of the carriage back into place during winding-on, a procedure that could reduce breakage but resulted in weak yarn). Spinners were also forbidden to put out their own lamps, probably because they paid for the oil themselves and therefore tended to extinguish them even when doing so led to inferior work.

The highest penalty, a 4 franc fine and immediate dismissal, was reserved for those who pilfered raw cotton and took it home. The second highest, a 3 franc fine, was for smoking. (Cotton dust and floating tufts of cotton created a serious fire hazard in the mills.) The third highest penalty, a 1 franc fine, was inflicted for writing or drawing on the walls, adjusting one's machine without permission, or missing a day of work. One of the lowest fines of all, 20 centimes, was the penalty for leaving work early.

Subsequent rules in the Roubaix Prudhommes' files vary from the original usually in the extent to which they specify procedures for handling machinery and fines for mishandling it. Not until 1836 is any penalty specified for leaving one's machine or talking to other laborers; not until 1839 is there any explicit reference to a bell for signaling the beginning and end of the work day, not until 1847 is there a rule against laborers spelling each other on the mules.[48]

At Roubaix, formal work discipline was a product of the crisis of 1827 – or so this material would suggest. Owners trying to tighten up their operation turned to writing codes of rules where before they had depended on personal authority and surveillance. In the early years, they concentrated on measures affecting the quality of work carried out on the machines; and only gradually and reluctantly did they later extend their control – beyond obvious rules against fist fights and graffiti – to the personal conduct of their laborers with the aim of increasing their application to work (that is, increasing the intensity of work). It is important to remember, as well, that posting a set of work rules was by no means the same thing as enforcing these rules. In almost all of the rules from Roubaix owners made reference to "my foreman," in the singular, with the implication that there was only one foreman in the shop. From other evidence of the 1830s, it appears that laborers at Roubaix and elsewhere, even in the strictly run mills of Alsace, honored "good Monday" by leaving work at noon on the first day of the week, or not showing up at all, that spinners often left their piecers to tend the mules in order to take unofficial breaks, that talking, singing, and laughing above the noise of the machinery were common. One indication worth citing at length is the following passage from a technical manual published in 1839 by a retired Alsatian mill director named Oger and found in the section entitled "On the duties of directors and foremen":

> When the director has developed a style of command that is brief and to the point, and engages in no idle conversation, the rest of the employees are compelled to do likewise and order reigns in the shop. How many directors have noticed that, when they engage in a conversation that is a bit long with one of their foremen, the workers take advantage of the occasion, neglect their work, and start chatting with one another in a manner which becomes at times so noisy that it is necessary to

104

punish them in order to arrest a disorder of which the director himself was the origin.

Complete silence must reign in the shop; the worker who is less distracted accomplishes his work with more care and attention . . .

In certain industries where noise causes no trouble, singing is tolerated because it makes tiresome work easier to put up with. But in spinning mills singing's role ought to be filled by the regular pace of the machines and the rhythmic return of the same sounds. I have often been convinced [sic] that this beating of the measure, as it were, relieves the worker and sustains him in his work.[49]

It is allowable to doubt whether the ideal here described was ever achieved even by Oger himself.

Besides attempting to reduce unit costs through tightened discipline, mill owners responded to the crisis by trying to catch up with Alsace, purchasing and installing improved models of preparation equipment and sources of artificial power strong enough to replace crank operators on the mule jennies. A large Paris machine manufacturer that specialized in the new models of preparation machines reported the value of its deliveries of new textile machinery between 1821 and 1833 as follows:

1822	39,816.08 francs	1828	623,067.54
1823	68,900.28	1829	716,099.88
1824	100,383.30	1830	898,483.56
1825	319,234.62	1831	1,389,933.57
1826	559,715.70	1832	2,340,208.02
1827	447,812.28	1833	2,526,665.88[50]

There was indeed a spurt of spending before the crisis in 1825 and 1826, the result of that "fever of production" sparked by the high potential profits of newly equipped mills. After the onset of the crisis, machine deliveries dipped, firmed, then resumed rapid growth. Most of this new buying was, as the firm's owner pointed out, for "additions, changes, eliminations of old equipment" at existing mills.

It is difficult to get direct evidence on the installation of power assists for mule jennies, but an indirect trace of the rapid shift to this new method of moving the jennies after 1827 shows up in the steady elimination of treadmills in favor of water wheels or steam engines. At Saint-Quentin in 1825, 14 of the 29 mills in the town itself still operated with treadmills; by 1834 the proportion of treadmills in the area's mills had been reduced to under 10 percent. In the Lille-Roubaix area, the number of mills equipped with steam engines leaped from under 15 to over 82 of the area's 150 mills between 1827 and 1834; at the later date 17 more were in the process of being installed. In Normandy, some 10 water wheels and 25 steam engines were installed in the same years so that by 1834, perhaps 50 percent of the area's 240 mills had artificial power sufficient to turn their mules.[51] Although this proportion is comparable to that of the Lille-Roubaix area, Normandy's rate of conversion to artificial power was the lowest of all the major cotton-spinning regions. As late as 1847, a significant proportion of Normandy mills (83 out of 293 mills) were still operating with treadmills and hand-operated mules.[52] Even in 1834, all of these areas were still behind Alsace. There were some compensating factors. Both Lille and Saint-Quentin specialized in the finer yarns; mules built for such purposes had much smaller power requirements than those used to spin common numbers. Mill operators in these two towns might have legitimately feared to disrupt their delicately balanced production systems by converting to artificial power when crank operators could turn up to two hundred spindles on fine-yarn mules.[53] Normandy supplied a market that was not very demanding – southern peasants (and after 1830 Algeria); operators here may have hoped to cut costs by less capital intensive means that resulted in a lower quality of yarn.[54]

THEORY AND PRACTICE AT THE MULE

However great these regional differences, the shift to power-assisted mule jennies was still undoubtedly the most common successful response to the prolonged slump. But this was a technical innovation of a particular kind, much like that of providing sewing machines to seamstresses or jackhammers to road crews or computerized switchboards to telephone operators: The device made it possible for laborers to work more intensively and thus to produce more in an equal time (as well as providing some increase in output for equal effort). But to make the conversion profitable, it was necessary to ensure that the laborer take advantage of this possibility. This was the most difficult challenge facing mill owners in France between 1827 and 1834. For the first time, they would have to manage labor, to alter its forms, to control and reshape it in order to ensure a profit. This kind of control would take more than simply issuing work rules or intensifying surveillance; it would take active intervention in the mule spinner's relationship to his machine.

The responses of mill owners to this challenge varied as greatly from region to region as did their willingness to adopt the new equipment in the first place. Overall it is possible to conclude that they were not very successful at reshaping spinners' behavior. But it is also necessary to be aware of the regional variations in strategy if one is to account for the exact geographic and temporal distribution of the outbreak of collective resistance.

Just how undermanaged mule spinners were in these mills even after the general adoption of power assists is clear from scrutiny of evidence on output. The most detailed evidence of this kind comes from the 1834 government inquiry into industry, which also provides a vivid picture of regional variations in entrepreneurial style. Mill owners turned over great masses of evidence to a government commission of inquiry in that year in an attempt to convince the new government that the old prohibition on imports of English goods dating from 1816 remained absolutely necessary to the industry's survival.

Output reports from specific mills found in this document and a few other sources can therefore be compared with ideal output levels provided in technical manuals of the same period, yielding a rough idea of labor intensity in the mills. Oger gives recommended machine speeds and expected rates of output for spinning No. 30 warp and No. 100 warp cotton yarns. (These numbers were based on the now standard French metric rating system. Five hundred grams of a metric No. 30 yarn is thirty thousand meters long. This was a common calico grade; a square meter of the resulting cloth would weigh about one hundred fifty grams.) Oger recommends an optimum velocity for the final set of rollers on the mule of 4.033 meters per minute. This was not a maximum; Oger counsels against running either faster or slower, slower because output drops, faster because increased breakage will result causing an equal drop in output. Allowing for one seventh of total spinning time for winding on, he calculates that a single spindle in a year with 300 work days (six days a week with allowance for holidays) would produce 16.586 kilograms of No. 30 yarn. Of course, no spinner could actually achieve such a level of output since it would require the mule to be running nonstop, 13 hours a day, six days a week, all year.[55]

In another technical manual published in 1843, one finds calculations of output based on what one could actually expect a mule spinner to achieve, taking into account actual experience in operating mills. The authors of this manual find that a No. 30 yarn can be spun at a rate of about 7.1 kilograms per spindle per year (using the same conventional 300-day year), and recommend that this rate be used for the setting of pay scales. This is less than half of the theoretical ideal calculated by Oger.[56] (Both of these manuals assume that the mules have power assists.)

Actual reports from mill owners about their output achievements varied over a great range, a fact which is at first bewildering. Some of these reports are displayed in Table 4, along with the figures from the two manuals. (All have been converted to the form of kilograms per spindle per year assuming a year of 300 work days; Achille Penot's estimates, quoted in the preceding section of this chapter, are repeated at the bottom in this standard form for ease of comparison.) None of the estimates in

Table 4. *Output reports from various sources for mule-spun No. 30 cotton yarn*

Source	Kg per spindle per year
Oger's ideal estimate, based on optimum roller speed and allowance of one seventh of time for winding on; technical manual of 1839.[a]	16.6
Jullien and Lorentz's estimate of practically achievable output, technical manual of 1843.[b]	7.1
Reports from 1834 ministerial inquiry:[c]	
Nicholas Koechlin's (Mulhouse) estimate of own best output.	12.5
Koechlin's estimate of Rouen-area standard.	7.5
Roman's (Mulhouse) counter-estimate of Mulhouse standard.	10.0
Fouquet-Lemaître et Crepel's (Rouen) estimate of own output.	13.9
Sanson-Daviller (Gisors) estimated output of a "good" spinner.	9.0
Sanson-Daviller's estimated output of an average spinner.	6.0
Reports from earlier sources:	
Achille Penot's estimate of Empire-period average.	3.8
Achille Penot's estimate of 1827 average.	11.3
Méquillet-Noblot's (Héricourt) initial maximum on newly bought used equipment with inexperienced spinners, 1819–20.[d]	5.3
Horrockser, Miller & Co. (Lancashire), pay book record of 7 April 1819.[e]	7.7
(Hand wheel, eighteenth century.[f]	30.0)

[a] Oger, *Traité élémentaire de la filature du coton* (Mulhouse, 1839), p. 272.
[b] C. E. Jullien and E. Lorentz, *Nouveau manuel complet du filature* (Paris, 1843), 108.
[c] ERDP, III, in order of appearance in table, from pp. 630–1, 613, 270, 484.
[d] Claude Fohlen, *Une affaire de famille au XIXᵉ siècle: Méquillet-Noblot* (Paris, 1955), 30.
[e] Each spinner operating two mules of 352 spindles, according to report of A. Andelle to the Ministry of the Interior, AN, F[12]2295.
[f] Based on memoir of Holker *fils* of 1773 in AN, F[12]2295, assuming spinner earned 10 sous per day.

fact exceed Oger's ideal, but a number of them come disturbingly close to it. Of the six reports taken from the 1834 ministerial inquiry into the textile trade, two come so close to it that they are difficult to accept.

Evidence from the 1834 inquiry is particularly revealing because the political aims of the mill owners reporting on their own operations are quite evident. The new minister of commerce, T. Duchâtel, a doctrinaire advocate of political economy, wished to revamp foreign trade policy and to replace the absolute prohibition on imports of British goods with an import duty. The vast majority of spinning mill owners argued forcefully against such a step. Before Duchâtel's board of inquiry in 1834, they tried to demonstrate on the one hand that the French textile industry had benefited greatly from the prohibition, which had made possible constantly lower prices on an expanding volume of goods, but that on the other hand the British were still too far ahead for the French industry to stand up against direct competition. Duchâtel personally cross-examined many of the mill owners who testified, providing invaluable evidence on how they thought about their operations, what accounting methods they used, and what kind of control they exercised over their laborers.

Fouquet-Lemaître et Crepel of Rouen, for example, spewed forth figures on Normandy and on their own operations before the board of inquiry in an utterly nonchalant manner.[57] Their clear rhetorical aim was to impress the board with the immense value of the interests committed to the spinning industry, the great progress they were making, and the large capital improvements that were under way. When, therefore, they remarked in passing that their 45,000 spindles (in four different mills) produced 12,500 kilograms a week, all of it of common grades around No. 30, it was difficult to say whether this was a calculation of capacity or a report of actual production figures. But this level of production works out to almost 14 kilograms per spindle per year, nearly twice what one manual considered practical for No. 30. One suspects therefore that this is a report of a theoretical capacity, not of actual output achieved at the firm's mills.

Nicolas Koechlin, of Mulhouse, one of the rare supporters of a prohibition repeal, tried to prove to the board of inquiry that Alsace mills were competitive with the British; their higher fuel and transport costs were compensated, he said, by cheaper labor, while technically their mills were on a par.[58] He reported that at his own mill he had preparations equipment so well run, and mule spinners so deft, that he achieved rates of one kilogram of yarn per day for every 24 spindles (equal to 12.5 kilograms per spindle per year); he chided the inefficient mill owners of the Rouen area, who only produced a kilogram for every 40 spindles (equal to 7.5 kilograms per spindle per year). Was it his fault, he asked, that others did not replace their old equipment? Besides, the present prohibition on imports encouraged wild speculation on raw material within France that made it impossible to sell at competitive prices abroad. Koechlin wanted into the world market, where he believed his own firm would thrive. Other Alsatian mill owners were not so optimistic. The Mulhouse Chamber of Commerce in 1833 had voted to support Koechlin, but then had backed out, reversed their position, and in 1834 went so far as to report figures from Koechlin's own mill that belied his claims. Roman, the Chamber's spokesman, estimated that Alsace mills averaged only 10 kilograms per spindle per year.[59]

The Paris firm of Sanson-Daviller, with a large mill at Gisors, provided evidence on their experience that contradicted both Koechlin and Fouquet-Lemaître et Crepel.[60] Sanson-Daviller claimed that their best spinners working mules with 400 spindles produced eleven to twelve kilograms of No. 30–33 yarn per day (9 kilograms per spindle per year). But the rest, "despite all our efforts, our supervision, suggestions, bonuses or other stimuli," produced from one third to one half less. Sanson-Daviller demonstrated that they had very close ties with Lancashire firms, had taken pains to equip themselves with identical machinery, and were very concerned about the output rates achieved by their mule spinners. They lamented their own inability to produce roving as good as that of certain British firms – even with the same equipment and better grades of fiber. They did not yet know how to fine-tune the interdependent processes of fiber preparation; they needed more experience. Sanson-Daviller did not oppose lifting of the import prohibition if it were done under certain conditions.

The Sanson-Daviller testimony provided the most detailed, most careful discussion of mule spinning in the whole inquiry; it yields results that correspond to information provided by technical manuals, as does, by the way, evidence from a Lancashire mill in 1819 which, one can assume, was equipped comparably to French mills in 1834 (see Table 4). Every report of higher outputs on closer inspection raises serious questions about its dependability, often on internal grounds alone. Fouquet-Lemaître et Crepel, for example, reported that their mule spinners made an average of 3 francs per day. But they also reported that their *prix de façon* for No. 30 yarn was 35 centimes per kilogram. But, at 35 centimes, their own output figures would have yielded average pay of 3.89 francs for spinners working on mules of 240 spindles (a size which Fouquet-Lemaître et Crepel reported that they used). The figures they provided to the board simply do not agree with one another, unless one assumes that this firm had very small mules for the time, of about 160 spindles, which they operated at breakneck speeds producing a very inferior yarn. But even under these conditions, their report of output is hard to believe, since Oger asserted that at such speeds breakage of roving would in the end result in a drop in output. One must suppose that this firm simply did not keep very close track of its own arithmetic and did not expect anyone else to.

The best evidence leads to the conclusion that mills of the period with power assists for their mules experienced output levels of about 6 to 9 kilograms per spindle per year, on average. If the mules were set to operate at speeds anywhere near the recommended optimum of Oger, that is, around 4 meters per second for the final roller pair, it follows that these mules were running from 36 to 54 percent of the total time that the mills were open. A combination of the following factors must have forced output levels down below one half of Oger's ideal: (1) Mule spinners took more than one seventh the draw time to accomplish the winding on, slowing down to piece, to form good tight cops on the spindles, or for a variety of other reasons. (2) Down time for replacing bobbins, cleaning, lubrication, piecing, repairs, and other ancillary tasks added up to a considerable portion of work time, perhaps as much as 25 percent. (3) Unofficial resting, whether in the form of a slow pace of work, unnecessary lengthening of down time, or outright absence from the machine must have been common.

The evidence of extensive down time is all the more remarkable when it is recalled that mule jennies were operated by teams made up of spinners, piecers, bobbin boys, and often crank operators. All knew at least the rudiments of the others' tasks so that team members could and did spell each other when the mule was running smoothly.[61] If the mules operated only 60 percent of the total time at work, then the mule spinners and their teams may individually have been running their machines for less than 50 percent of the average work day.

It seems likely that direct supervision was loose or nonexistent in most of these mills, that mill owners continued, as under the Empire, to depend on payment by the kilogram to ensure that spinners worked, instead of taking on the burden of some kind of direct control over the work process. This makes it possible to imagine how human beings survived the grueling work schedules of that period with their 13 hour days, six days a week. The fact is that they did not work all this time. The fact is that their work was not yet managed in any real sense of the term, and that their relations with mill owners continued to be modeled on that of outworker and supplier.

At the same time, the crisis of 1827–1832 must have sensitized mill owners, as they had never been before, to the problem of managing labor. The records of the 1834 inquiry are filled with complaints about the slowness and ineptitude of the French laborer. His inferiority to the English was, in the owners' eyes, self-evident and incurable. His one saving grace: he cost less. The English laborer, according to Roman, was a kind of cross between the French and the German, a mix of Norman and Saxon, which gave him at once "vivacity and attentiveness."[62] Sanson-Daviller saw English superiority as a result of growing up in the mills and working all one's life on a single grade of yarn.[63] These complaints were in some cases intended as only one more good argument for maintaining the prohibition against British imports. But they doubtless as often reflected a new awareness of the whole area of work, its performance, its intensity, as a factor that heavily influenced profitability during the crisis. And it also seems likely that in this area most owners still felt a real sense of impotence.

The problem of the capitalist control of labor had finally come to the fore. How French mill owners sought to resolve this problem is a question that cannot be answered directly, however. Penetrating the factory is a notoriously difficult thing for the historian to do. But in this case, indirect clues exist in abundance. Some mill owners' efforts at reform sparked bitter resistance from mule spinners, attracting public notice and government intervention. Labor management and labor conflict in the French textile mill were, so to speak, born together, a fact that deserves careful consideration in its own right.

5 Spinners on guard

The most serious episode of collective protest among textile laborers in the first months of the July Monarchy occurred among cotton spinners in the Rouen area.[1] The evidence shows that Rouen was likely to have had the greatest difficulty in adapting itself to the new conditions of the slump after 1827. The style of Rouen mill operators was at the opposite extreme from that of the Alsatians, who viewed their firms as patrimonial possessions and spared no expense in keeping equipment and methods up to date. Charles Noiret, a literate and outspoken handloom weaver of Rouen, gave in 1836 a stinging description of the quite different outlook that prevailed in the town. In the early years of the Restoration, he said: "The profits of the producers were such that they did not bother to count them: they bought, they produced, and sold according to habit and their capital quintupled in a single year ... They got rich without knowing why."

As for their treatment of labor, judging from Noiret's comments, it resembled what one today associates with secondhand car dealers rather than with managers. They bought cheap cotton, he said, mixed in waste fibers, set their machines to spin No. 30 but told the spinner it was No. 26 (justifying a lower rate of pay per kilogram), and sold the yarn to their customers as No. 34 (arithmetic reminiscent of the report of Fouquet-Lemaître et Crepel in 1834). Once their fortunes were made (and the industry ruined), said Noiret, they bought land and retired.[2]

Obviously the impact of the 1827 slump was particularly upsetting to the calculations of such owners, and adaptation was for them most difficult, because it required first of all a sizeable input of capital in the midst of a crisis, when even in the best of times they were more interested in taking it out. It also required an attempt to control laborers whom they were used to bargaining with or simply duping. Their attitude therefore changed most abruptly, and their laborers must have felt the change with particular acuteness. In the days following the July Revolution of 1830, Rouen-area laborers took to the streets in protest.

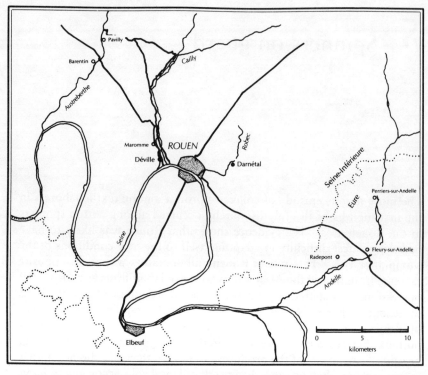

The Rouen area, showing nearby mill towns. Agglomerations and principal connecting roads drawn to approximate mid-nineteenth century conditions.

THE PREFECTS' COALITION

The revolution of July 1830 that produced the July Monarchy had come and gone so quickly that many provincial towns did not even hear of it until it was over. Three days of street fighting in Paris were sufficient to send the restored Bourbons packing; liberty had been the battle cry and the tricolor flag the banner of the victorious crowds. But the winners of this revolution were overwhelmingly the old Napoleonic elite, the liberal party, who filled the ministerial offices and the benches of the Parliament with the new king's blessing.[3]

Parisian artisans, therefore, should not have been surprised when, in the days following the fighting, their demands were rebuffed by the new government. As loyal veterans of the street fighting, printers asked that steam-powered presses be outlawed; masons asked that hours be limited and that day wages replace piece rates in their trade. Locksmiths and plasterers asked for similar changes. To these and other requests the response of astonished officials was a categorical refusal. The laborers,

114

according to the new prefect of the Seine department, "had forgotten for a moment all the principles for which they had fought and which several of them had sealed with their blood ... They had lost sight of the fact that the liberty of labor is no less sacred than all our other liberties."[4]

This was the first French insurrection in which the labor question provided the central motive of the popular masses who made it. Had the liberals properly understood this in advance, they might have hesitated to boost themselves into power on such backs. Had the Parisian artisans understood what the liberals meant by liberty they might not have fought for them with such alacrity. But this happy misunderstanding was only discovered afterward. It arose out of very recent developments, out of the same economic changes that had overtaken the textile trade in the previous fifteen years. Masons, tailors, printers, shoemakers, carriage-makers had all seen their trades transformed by competition under the impact of the boom of the early 1820s and the succeeding slump. The consequences were quite diverse from trade to trade, but also quite deeply and universally felt.

Rouen was the scene of very similar misapprehensions between laborers and elite; events unfolded in a way that strongly suggests an absence of models, a searching for appropriate organizational forms among laborers and authorities alike. The nature of the laborers' grievance was something entirely new, which neither they nor their social betters knew at first how to handle.

Parisian crowds had helped Louis Philippe and his party into office; therefore crowds everywhere, for a time at least, were to be treated with circumspection. The word came from Paris: above all, avoid bloodshed.[5] Popular sovereignty was for a time to receive at least nominal respect. The laborers must have sensed this, or else must have been genuinely moved by word of the fighting in Paris because they adopted its ritual forms to organize their own actions. Just like the Paris revolutionaries, and just like the contingent of guard who marched through Rouen to announce the fall of Charles X, the laborers formed into columns with drum and tricolor flag in the lead and marched to the town hall.

According to a letter of the prefect to the minister of the interior dated 28 August,

> A crowd of workers formed yesterday in Saint-Sever about six o'clock. *In the Saint-Sever neighborhood are situated most of the mills existing in the town of Rouen that are equipped with steam power.* The crowd marched up to several of these establishments to attract their fellows out to join them, which they did in most cases. A crowd of about eight thousand was formed in this way and filed down most of the streets of the neighborhood and some streets in Rouen proper demanding the abolition of work rules.

115

> At one point a Rouen police agent stood up alone before this crowd
> and ordered them to return to work; but they replied that they had
> grievances against their masters and wanted the government to set things
> right. He proposed that they choose a delegation to follow him to the
> town hall ... [Emphasis added.][6]

The agent promised that these delegates would be allowed to see the
mayor and that no arrests would be made. Six delegates went with him,
talked with the mayor who pledged to investigate their grievances, and
heard the prefect himself urge them to return to work. There was no
more trouble that day. In the evening the prefect issued a proclamation
forbidding assemblies in the streets.

The following day, most spinners did return to work, but about three
hundred did not. Forming a column, they marched on the town hall
carrying a tricolor flag. Six of these spinners were also admitted to see
the mayor.

On the same day, 28 August, there were two further developments.
The prefect met in his offices with a large number of Rouen mill owners
to inquire about the spinners' demands. The owners responded with
attempts to explain and defend what they were doing inside their mills;
at any rate, some of them did for they later sent supporting documents
that still can be found among the prefect's papers.[7] In the end, a committee
of owners was formed to make proposals and report back to the prefect
within a week. Meanwhile the six spinner delegates who had been chosen
to speak with the mayor the day before seem to have set themselves up
as a committee as well. That morning they came to the offices of the
major local newspaper, the *Journal de Rouen*, to ask the editor to publish
an accurate account of their demands. His earlier report on the spinners
had angered them. He had said that they wanted shorter hours, higher
pay, and the discharge of all workers who did not live inside city limits.
He had claimed that the mills were in bad financial condition and were
only operating because the owners did not want to see the laborers starve.
Both of these statements were sheer fabrication. The crisis was by this
time three years old and had entered a second stage in which survivors
were revamping their equipment in order to maintain profitability. Other
evidence makes clear that, at least in Normandy, the revolution of July
1830 was over so quickly that business had not had time to turn down.
(It was not until November and the trial of the legitimist ministers that
confidence was shaken and commerce slowed to a crawl for several
months.)[8]

As for the spinners' demands, the editor agreed to publish them, although he hesitated at first for fear of appearing partial. His paraphrase
of what they wanted appeared in the next day's edition (but even here
he failed to understand exactly what was at issue):

116

Without going into the details, we will say that they want a reduction in hours and modifications of the work rules of certain mills. According to the petitioners there are mills where the day is sixteen-and-a-half or even seventeen hours long, with one-and-a-half hours of rest time only, where fines are incurred for the slightest infraction, where an absence, whatever the cause, is punished by withholding double the amount of salary the worker would have received in that time; that in some mills a task is imposed on the workers who must complete it or be fined without regard for their particular abilities, etc.[9]

This somewhat garbled account of the spinners' grievances at least got the general nature of the problem correct. Owners were experimenting with work rules to improve their laborers' attention to work and they were lengthening hours because they had realized that doing so was an easy way to increase the rate of return on fixed capital. As the prefect notes, the trouble began in the neighborhood where steam-powered mills were concentrated. Many of these mills were burdening their accounts with large capital outlays for steam engines and new preparations equipment.

As for the report of seventeen-hour days, which is hardly credible in the form it is given, evidence from a government inquiry of 1837 given by a Rouen-area mill owner may offer an explanation. It was common practice in the area, according to his testimony, for mills with unfilled order backlogs to run until midnight or beyond on Friday nights.[10] The practice was accepted by the laborers because they had their eyes on Saturday afternoon when the week's yarn – already weighed up and tagged – was finally paid for. Monday absenteeism soared afterward because, with extra pay in their pockets and still fatigued from the end-of-the-week push, laborers stayed away from work even more frequently than usual on that day. Such a schedule from the mill owners' point of view was a partial solution to the laborers' general poor performance and high absenteeism on Mondays under the best of conditions. Rather than try to reform this ingrained weekly work rhythm, the owners took advantage of it, using the laborers' end-of-the-week anxiety about pay to induce them to work extra hours. Hence the demand was for an end to once-a-week days of seventeen hours.

According to what the prefect heard, the spinners wanted hours reduced across the board to twelve per day with no exceptions. In his report to the minister of the interior of 29 August, he offered the following commentary on their grievances: "On the first point their complaints are not groundless. They are subjected to thirteen hours of work per day . . . They incur a fatigue from this that sleep cannot repair, their health declines early in life, and their vigor is exhausted before its time." The prefect was here committing a common error by assuming that thirteen hours of boring machine-tending must drain human beings of their spirit and health. But of course, there was time for rest aplenty in those thirteen hours, given the way the mills were managed. The laborers were in fact responding to efforts to suppress this time and to push them toward the position that the prefect already imagined them to be in. He continued: "The work rules they wish to see revised are not all stamped with a spirit of exact justice; and one must concede that, applied with rigor, they would be insupportable. These rules ... establish a fine system that is easily abused." In a section of his draft report that was crossed out of the final version, the prefect continued this sentence as follows: "and a piece-rate scale [*échelle dans les prix de main-d'oeuvre*] according to which vigorous laborers who provide a large quantity of product at the end of the day are paid a higher price for each piece of work than that paid to the weaker laborer who despite all his efforts cannot manage to produce as much."[11] This crossed-out passage along with the reference in the newspaper to fines imposed for not producing certain set tasks, is explained by other papers in the prefect's files apparently provided him by mill owners. One is a piece-rate schedule from an unnamed mill with the date that it went into effect noted: 17 May 1829.[12] This schedule lists four prices per kilogram for each number of cotton yarn from No. 18 up to No. 42; each of the four prices is associated with a certain limit of kilograms that one must produce to get that price. For No. 30 yarn, the prices are as follows:

Kg	Centimes per kg
50	25
60	26
70	29
80	31
105	33

Hence, if one produced only 50 kilograms in two weeks, one would receive only 25 centimes per kilogram, or 12.50 francs; if one produced 80 kilograms in two weeks, one would receive 31 centimes per kilogram, or 24.80 francs. A 60 percent increase in output was rewarded by a 100 percent increase in pay. Another sheet of paper in the prefect's file is clearly a part of a pay book that was torn out to show him how a similar system worked in practice. This system was a simpler two-step scale; eighteen spinners working on No. 30 weft yarn were paid either 30 or 32 centimes per kilogram. An indication of the range of actual outputs can be gleaned from this pay sheet: seven spinners made less than 70

118

kilograms of No. 30 yarn in the two-week period from 13 to 27 February 1830; one made over ninety kilograms, the other eleven made between seventy and ninety kilograms. An output of 80 kilograms on 220 spindles in two weeks is equivalent to 9.1 kilograms per spindle per year, about what Sanson-Daviller considered to be good work. Just as Sanson-Daviller testified in 1834, there were a number of spinners who produced only one half as much. The four-step pay scale in the prefect's files, in fact, picks out the revelant range of outputs if spinners produced on average from 6 to 9 kilograms per spindle per year on mules of 220 spindles.

What appears to have happened is that mills adding water or steam power for their mules were seeking ways of making the spinners work with more attentiveness. They tried to elaborate new pay scales that reflected their own added capital costs in cases in which they supplied power thirteen hours a day to a machine that only operated six or seven hours in reality. They tried to raise or introduce fines for absence that would protect them from the added costs of having an increasingly expensive plant operated only intermittently. And they ran their mills more hours per week; in this way, even if output per hour did not increase, total output would, reducing certain unit costs. The spinners were opposed to all these innovations.

The prefect apparently understood something of what was going on in the mills. The fact that he crossed out his condemnation of the special pay scales from his final draft of the 29 August report to Paris suggests he had second thoughts about them and found them on balance to be not so unjust as had first appeared. The following day, he invited owners of mills in the Déville and Darnétal valleys to meet with him, that is, those whose mills operated with water power from the Cailly and Robec rivers. These were, he said, likely to be affected by the same troubles since they had similar fine systems. These mill owners, too, formed a committee to look into the spinners' grievances after meeting with the prefect on 30 August.

The spinners in the meantime were not idle. Police reported that Rouen streets were full of restless bands in the evenings during the final days of August. During these same days, the six delegates to the original meeting with the mayor took steps to put themselves in regular contact with spinners in every mill.[13] They constituted what they called a central administration and summoned senior spinners in every mill to meet with them and consider alternatives. One of the letters they sent out was intercepted and found its way to the prefect's desk; it calls on the *curés* to prepare for a meeting. (The two most senior spinners in each shop were called the *curé* and the *vicaire*.) The letter reads, with many grammar and spelling errors, as follows:

Administration of spinning mill workers.

We invite the *curé* of the mill to please appear Sunday at 7.A.M. at the Grenouille cafe; bring a petition on stamped paper [that is, prepared to be mailed] which mentions not working more than twelve hours, no more work rules, no fines, no task, etc. If there is no *curé*, then the first worker to have come and be sure to make a collection from the workers to pay the costs. You are expected Sunday without fault; without fault make sure your petition is well done. I salute you. R.[14]

Here in the spinners' own voice, the innovations are lumped together: the longer hours, work rules, fines for unexcused absence, and *la tâche*, the task system that rewarded higher output with higher prices – all are listed as if they went naturally together in a way any spinner would understand – were part and parcel of a single grievance.

This letter was intercepted on 3 September; by that time spinners' delegates had already had at least one meeting in which they designated representatives to maintain contact with the various suburbs where mills were located. Those who agreed to serve in this capacity were told that this organizing effort was occurring regularly, that is, legally, and with the approbation of the authorities.[15] The intercepted letter implies a similar presumption. It was obviously the spinners' intention to send petitions from each mill to the authorities.

It is therefore not surprising that one of the representatives, a spinner named Drely working in Barentin north of Rouen, who was asked to represent Barentin and Pavilly, felt he could assume a certain authority over the spinners in his area. The fact that he did so – and quite innocently – came out at his trial. None of the mills in Pavilly or Barentin nor anywhere else in the area had been shut down following the spinners' initiative of 27 August. But many spinners were trying to limit work to twelve hours a day. At one mill Drely intervened; the mill's water wheel had recently been stopped for repairs, idling the whole mill. Now that it was back in operation, Drely allowed the mill to work evenings to help make up for some of the lost time and lost earnings, threatening anyone who interfered with a blow from his baton. Drely assiduously organized the *curés* of his area for the meeting announced on 3 September, finding help to copy the letter summoning them, and personally reminded each *curé* to collect 10 centimes from every worker. At one mill he was reported to have asked how things were going, to have been told that everything was fine, and to have said, "Alright, relax, boys; we're going to take care of your problems back in Rouen." He was arrested on 4 September with a number of the letters in his possession and charged with coalition.[16]

In arresting Drely and a number of other spinners for coalition in the first days of September the government revealed its own confusion about the situation. The new prefect's political future at this moment depended on his ability to restore order without bloodshed. Order, he had decided early on, consisted in this case of the mill owners making some concessions to the spinners' grievances and the spinners staying off the streets and in the mills. To achieve this end, both he and his lieutenants unhesitatingly treated owners and spinners as two organized bodies – not as two groups of independent and equal players in a market. They were, moreover, organized bodies with a proper relation that was now disturbed, that is, one of authority and obedience, control and service, rank and deference.

The police agents, the mayor, and the prefect unhesitatingly summoned members of both groups to name delegates, form committees, deliberate, and communicate with each other. They did this apparently without the slightest consciousness that each such action was a breach of the Penal Code's anticoalition articles. Citizens from a single trade were not allowed to deliberate or communicate about trade matters; and those who instigated such actions were liable to two-year terms of imprisonment. Both the owners and the spinners, also without hesitation, responded to these summonses. No one reminded the prefect that he was instigating a coalition; no one objected to having a committee of owners make policy for the whole group. Among the spinners, the rudiments of an organization already existed in the recognized authority of senior spinners in each shop. No one in this situation thought for a moment of allowing the market to resolve their difficulties. There was not even an attempt to organize a bargaining session between the parties. Once the prefect got word of a formal organization being created among the spinners, however, he quickly ordered arrests to be made. Suddenly they were guilty of coalition; apparently no connection was drawn between the naming of delegates to meet with the mayor on two occasions and the creation of a chain of communication and command, which to the spinners had seemed perfectly self-evident.

On 2 September Pavilly, Maromme, and Déville erupted in their turn, just as the prefect had feared. A huge crowd surrounded the Déville town hall; a number of copies of work rules from several mills were ceremoniously torn up. When one of the spinners was arrested, the crowd angrily forced the Déville mayor to release him. Again, delegates were chosen to consult with the mayor and the crowd dispersed. There is a letter in the prefect's file of 5 September addressed to these four delegates. He mentions their grievances against those work rules that instituted a task system like that in Rouen. He speaks of the mill owners' willingness to make concessions as far as the present state of the industry allowed and expresses his hope that they would accept these limited concessions in the proper spirit.

As the crisis dragged into a second week, and the day scheduled for the owners' official response drew near, the local National Guard was growing tired and nervous. They had been on extra duty day after day under orders not to provoke the restless crowds that filled the evening streets. Determined to act with restraint, the prefect nonetheless decided that no further patience was to be shown to the spinners once the owners had announced the concessions they were willing to make.

The announcement came on the morning of 6 September. The owners ceded little ground. Fines were reduced in size; promises were made to keep hours down to thirteen wherever possible; the task system was not renounced. No one went to work that day. It is not clear whether the spinners had made plans as to what their reaction should be, but several officials were under the impression that Rouen spinners had decided to stay at home (probably because the Rouen streets were so well guarded) until reinforcements marched in from the suburbs.[17] To the northwest of town, in Déville, Maromme, and Pavilly, the crowds were large and angry, but peaceful. They did not march on Rouen. At Darnétal to the east, however, 900 mill operatives gathered in front of the town hall armed with sticks and batons. They pelted the handful of National Guard at the entrance with paving stones; guards seized two out of the crowd and dragged them inside. The spinners then broke into the town hall's courtyard and began breaking down the door. Once inside, they confronted the mayor and demanded release of the two who had been arrested. They were released. Still smarting from the indignity, the laborers asked him to turn over a member of the National Guard who had reputedly wanted to fire on the crowd. The mayor flatly refused. They demanded the Guard's drum. The mayor agreed to give it to them if they promised to march only as far as the nearby Place Longpaon and then disperse. This condition was accepted, although it seems clear that at least some of the spinners planned to continue on to Rouen and there to precipitate a decisive confrontation.

Outside, drum in the lead, the crowd formed into a column and marched to Place Longpaon. Once there, some tried to organize a further march on Rouen by finding the *curés* of various Darnétal mills, and encouraging them to bring their men up and continue the march.[18] But the group that left the square on the road to Rouen, drum still leading the way, was much smaller than the original column, for fewer than a hundred joined in.

The prefect, having heard that the town hall in Darnétal had been overrun, immediately ordered National Guard and regular troops to march there from Rouen. Fearful of the Guard's mood, he lost valuable time, however, exchanging notes with the barracks in which he requested that a regular army officer be given command of this force. The joint contingent of troops met the spinners' column on a bridge just outside of Darnétal. The laborers scattered before them, and the troops gave chase, pursuing them back to the Place Longpaon where they cleared the square of its remaining people. In a narrow side street, a knot of guards were showered with projectiles from the windows. They broke into a cafe from which a chamber pot had come flying, gaining entry just in time to see a group of laborers rushing into a back alley. Farther on they cornered the escaping laborers in a dark room off the alley. Things began hurtling at them out of the darkness. An officer fired his pistol once, and the laborers surrendered to arrest. Elsewhere, a Guard member was attacked by a spinner with a knife tied on the end of a baton; he wounded the spinner with his sword, and arrested him.[19] The laborers were routed, but there were no deaths and only minor injuries. Forty-five were arrested in all at Darnétal, 20 more in other suburbs or in Rouen itself by the end of the day. The spirit of the spinners seemed to be broken, and the prefect was highly pleased.

At his trial on 11 September, Drely misunderstood the nature of the charges being made against him. When he heard a mill owner testifying that Drely had been named to him as the "leader of the crowds," he interrupted. "But, your honor," he said, "I carefully convoked only the *curés* and the *vicaires* because I wanted to avoid crowds." Obviously he was thinking of the prefect's ordinance of 27 August forbidding assemblies of more than twenty persons in the street. But he was charged with coalition, with being an "instigator or leader" of a coalition, a crime imposing up to two years in prison. He shows no sign of having understood this during his trial. He had no counsel. His statements amounted, in fact, to an admission of guilt. Allowed to plead his own defense after all testimony had been heard, Drely said that

> He had been brought by workers to a meeting in Sotteville [near Saint-Sever] that he had there been given letters whose contents he did not understand, that he had, in fact, maintained order in Barentin and Pavilly, that it was he who had favored night work at the Lalisel mill, and that, finally, he had never brought more than two workers per mill together, not wishing to interrupt work.

This statement, again, amounted to an admission of guilt, although Drely obviously did not realize it. When he was given the maximum penalty allowable under the law, "he broke down in tears."[20]

The sixty who were arrested during the day of 6 September were kept in jail cells awaiting their trials for up to five months. The prosecutor's office explained that extensive testimony had to be sought from all the soldiers and Guard members involved in the arrests (although surely this was because their memories of the exact infractions committed by each individual prisoner were faulty). Several were in the end charged with assaulting officers of the government, an offense which carried a heavy penalty.[21]

This Rouen-area dispute was triggered by fundamental changes in the way mill owners thought about their businesses. For the first time since the industry began, they had become dissatisfied with paying for yarn at a flat rate per kilogram. In the past, this expedient alone had always been deemed sufficient – from the days of the putting–out system on – to provide an incentive for the spinner. But under the conditions created by the crisis of the late 1820s, this simple method no longer seemed enough.

Installing power assists for their mules was expensive. It doubled or tripled the power requirements of the operation as a whole, which meant new water or steam equipment had to be purchased. At the same time the mule department had to be provided with a network of drive shafts, belt drives, and pulleys, and each mule had to be altered to accept artificial power. In order for the added investment to pay for itself, it had to result in increased output per spindle. In other words, if the spinner did not achieve higher output on his mule thanks to the new power assists, then the capital investment they represented was wasted.

Mill owners, therefore, looked for a way to pay their spinners for attentiveness, instead of for yarn. Here finally a step was made toward paying for labor, rather than for its outcome. Spinners who produced beyond certain kilogram limits were paid more per kilogram. The attentiveness required to surpass these limits earned pay over and above that earned by the simple production of the yarn. The yarn was no longer a commodity because it was no longer paid for at a fixed price. Simultaneously, to encourage more spinners to attend to their work, fines for absence were increased (and enforcement probably strengthened). To reduce capital costs even when spinners showed only slight increases in attentiveness, hours of operation were extended, especially at the end of the week.

The spinners' hostility to these changes is understandable. The fines and longer hours were intrinsically unpleasant. But worst of all the task system was an attack on their independence. Spinners wished its abolition because they preferred to avoid having their attitude to work manipulated by means of variable pay rates. They resisted the combination of intimacy and callousness implicit in this new, subtle influence exercised over their motives. They mistrusted the owners and preferred dealing with them through the concrete medium of the yarn, its fineness and its weight, with no other intervening variables. Like eighteenth-century urban weavers, they did not want to be forced to calculate. When concessions were made in the other areas by the mill owners but the task system upheld on 6 September, the more determined among the spinners tried to carry out a full-scale insurrection, just like the one at Paris six weeks before.

The column of spinners marching into Rouen was to serve as a call to arms raising up the people against an unjust coalition of government and capitalists. But the effort was an abysmal failure.

Throughout this episode neither the laborers' behavior nor the treatment they received was informed by the notion of free competition. The mill owners were making a step toward a greater control of their laborers' behavior, but this step was not accompanied by any progress toward treating labor as something freely distributed within a market. The laborers did not attempt to withhold their labor service, which they were legally free to do if they gave proper notice. The government actively encouraged collective settlement of the dispute, without bargaining, by means of token concessions granted from on high by a committee of owners. Collective organization on the laborers' part was encouraged to facilitate communication with the government. But the moment it began to appear as something ongoing and independent, it was actively repressed. At this stage the anticoalition articles of the Penal Code, formally intended to enforce free individual bargaining on all parties, were applied without apparent awareness of the inconsistency involved. No *curés* or *vicaires* were prosecuted by the government. Their role in the illegal "administration" set up by the spinners came out clearly at Drely's trial. Several of them testified during the trial. But the government informally recognized the special authority of senior spinners; this was not viewed as threatening, quite the contrary. Order required that the spinners' community have some organization, so long as it did not spread beyond individual mills or arrogate special authority to itself. Senior spinners went untouched. But drawing such a fine line was bound to cause confusion and anger among the spinners. From their point of view, the government was provokingly inconsistent; it addressed them as a group but repressed all their attempts to organize as a group. Their demonstrations were illegal, they were told; but then delegates of the illegal crowd were ushered into the mayor's office. In any case had not the revolution in Paris weeks before been illegal in the same way? The mayor promised to report back to the delegates, but then the prefect arrested them for coalition. From 6 September on, protest was repressed with extremely harsh prison sentences. The new government's liberal principles were applied in such a peculiar and selective way that they maximized the laborers' sense of frustration.

PAYING FOR STEAM

There were disturbances in other cotton-spinning centers in the fall of 1830, but on a much smaller scale. In Roubaix on 10 August children and adolescents (most of them probably piecers) came out of the mills and organized a grand march through town. They stopped at the mayor's house to demand that he fly a tricolor flag over his door. At mill owners' houses (usually in these days attached to the mills), they pounded on the doors, crying for the owners to sign papers promising increases in pay. A number of owners apparently complied. (Later the *procureur* assured them that all such agreements were null.) Crowds celebrated in the streets late into the night on that one ironic day; but afterward all went back to work. It had been more like a festival than a protest.[22]

In Alsace there was trouble in the Mulhouse suburb of Dornach in November. Calico printers and spinners at several of the larger firms including Dolfuss-Meig and Schlumberger planned an action whose aim is not certain since it was deflected by the quick reaction of the authorities. Following the announcement of pay reductions in connection with a slowdown in business, laborers at the two large firms agreed to meet at a prearranged spot. Once together, they proceeded to march from mill to mill, much as had the Rouen spinners on the first day of troubles there, trying to stop work and to bring the laborers out to join them. They succeeded at one mill but ran up against resistance at a mill reputed to be staffed mostly by aliens. (Resident aliens could be summarily expelled from the country on the word of the mayor.) A contingent of National Guard arrived very quickly, chased the laborers back into their own neighborhoods and there arrested nine so-called leaders. It seems likely that the laborers wanted to march on the town hall, as a few calico printers had done at Dornach the day before. But there was no sequel.[23]

Why did nothing comparable to the Rouen incident occur in these other centers? Alsatian mills, it appears, were not engaged in extensive retooling at this time. They had started out the slump with competitive equipment; they were setting prices rather than suffering from them. Many of these mills had been originally set up with power-assisted mules. Evidence is scanty, but what there is suggests that graduated piece rate systems had also been introduced earlier. During the boom years up to 1826, it would have been easy to introduce such systems in the form of premiums paid over and above the regular rate to spinners who produced above a certain minimum. In Alsace the higher rates were called premiums, in fact. Spinner resistance to them, if it existed, has left no trace in departmental archives.[24]

The mills of the Lille-Roubaix area, however, were in the same predicament as those of Rouen. They, too, had to retool in the midst of the slump, increasing their capitalization at a time of serious uncertainty and constant liquidity difficulties. But mill owners of this region came up with an ingenious solution to the problem of motivating their mule spinners. They made no changes in pay procedures. The very same price lists for the different grades of yarn continued in effect, with a unique price per kilogram for each grade. One simple change was made; the owners introduced a charge for steam power that they levied on the pay given out to spinners. This charge was fixed at roughly the same amount as spinners had formerly paid to their crank operators, about 9 francs a week. It can be seen that this ingenious gambit combines the appearance of continued independence for the spinners with an effect on their actual earning level very much the same as the task system at Rouen. The steam charge took the form of a fixed cost that changed the spinner's actual pay per kilogram of yarn in direct proportion to the amount he produced. If he produced 40 kilograms a week and received 50 centimes per kilogram less 9 francs for steam, his actual earnings were 11 francs for the week or 28 centimes per kilogram. If he produced only 35 kilograms, however, he earned only 8.50 francs for the week, or 24 centimes per kilogram. Yet the spinners could accept the idea of paying for steam power as a logical extension of their having paid their own crank operators (although the latter would have received a variable amount proportional to the spinners' earnings). Likewise instead of introducing stiff absence fines, the Lille–Roubaix area owners simply added clauses to their work rules specifying that spinners were always liable for the full steam charge whether or not they were present for work, and in addition to any other fines for absence that they paid. The work rules preserved in the Roubaix Conseil des prudhommes files include five examples of this kind of arrangement from the 1830s, and a number of other sources speak of it as the general practice of the region.[25] As the spinners gained experience at handling their power assists, their output levels climbed and owners generally increased the steam charge. By the 1840s, 14 francs per week was a common rate. At this point the fixed fee for steam ate up over half of a spinner's usual gross earnings. No word of protest was raised against the steam charge by spinners before 1848.

Certainly there was widespread unhappiness among spinners in the summer and fall of 1830 due to the rate reductions that mill owners had been making regularly since the slump began. But only in Rouen, where much more than mere rate reductions was at issue, did cotton spinners stage a sustained, large-scale movement of protest.

DISORDERLY WEAVERS

Weavers were also suffering under the continuous rain of rate reductions in the early years of the July Monarchy. Weavers by this time were finding it less easy to change suppliers than they had under the ancien regime or the Empire. *Livrets*, Conseils des prudhommes, notice requirements were spreading. Changing suppliers had by no means ceased and remained in normal times the recourse of the dissatisfied.[26] But during a slump like that of 1827–1832, when all suppliers were reducing their rates, some weavers began turning to collective action.

At Armentières in August 1830, several hundred calico weavers from the area beseiged the town hall (in the by now familiar manner) to ask for a postponement of reductions that had been announced by their merchant manufacturer. The mayor interceded for them and secured a promise that rates would be maintained at current levels for the near future.[27] At Bar-le-Duc in December 1831, cotton weavers marched to the prefecture asking that all the merchant manufacturers of the town agree to a standard rate schedule. The prefect met with a number of delegates and explained to them that "he deeply wished to see them working in perfect harmony with their merchant manufacturers, but that the relations which they have with each other are purely a private concern." Nonetheless as a private person, the prefect said, he was willing to listen to their grievances and conciliate the dispute if possible. His decision was to send to Rouen to discover what rates prevailed there for weaving similar articles. These, he said, ought to be a fair standard for Bar-le-Duc.[28]

In Sainte-Marie-aux-Mines, the original center of *guingham* production, weavers walked out of a loom shop in July 1833 when it was announced they would have to pay 20 centimes a day for the winding of bobbins to feed their shuttles. They marched to other loom shops in the town but found no weavers willing to join them. Apparently similar changes were expected elsewhere but had not yet been announced. Finally in the neighboring village of Echery they were joined by a large number of weavers and about four hundred marched back to Sainte-Marie singing "La Parisienne" (a song that celebrated the events of 1830), and waving a black flag before them crying "*Vive le drapeau noir!*" and "*Vive la misère!*" Back in town they broke loom-shop windows, beseiged a manufacturer's house, and were dispersed by a contingent of gendarmes and National Guard.[29]

The selective application of anticoalition statutes is as evident in these weaver incidents as in those involving spinners in 1830. Government remained concerned, above all, to preserve order and was guided by a vision of order in which the idea of a market played only the most limited role. In Bar-le-Duc the prefect privately and unconsciously instigated a coalition to set prices. His aim was to reestablish subordination, work and harmony, respect for one's betters. In Sainte-Marie the weavers were in fact judged by the local Prudhommes to have been justified in leaving the shop because the owner had not given them proper notice of the new charge. Five were prosecuted for coalition, however, in connection with their subsequent actions, that is, seeking for others to join them. The weavers may have acted legally in walking out of the shop, but they felt they had rebelled against constituted authority (witness the black flag, the rock throwing, the stand off with gendarmes). The authorities were in perfect accord with this perception and quickly found the right legal technicality on which to base their repression.

EXPERIMENTS WITH REFUSING WORK

None of the incidents discussed so far, among either spinners or weavers, involved concerted work stoppages. Laborers did not leave work in order to put a stop to work; they left the shop in order to do something, to communicate with their fellows, to march in the streets, to display themselves in a body before public officials as a loyal gauge of their concern and of their desire for action, or to demonstrate their anger with official measures taken in the matter.

In none of the records concerning these incidents does any word meaning strike appear. The word in French that would later come to mean strike, *grève*, was still a piece of Parisian journeyman slang in the early 1830s; *faire la grève* was to go to the Place de Grève outside the town hall, the square where most hiring in the building trades took place. The phrase therefore meant looking for work, or being unemployed. By extension *la grève* could mean a hiring hall, unemployment, or a concerted work stoppage of a group of journeymen. The word did not come into general use outside Paris until after 1845; its modern meaning was not settled until about 1860.[30]

The idea of a concerted work stoppage in support of workplace demands was an old one in Paris and among journeymen of certain trades. Up until 1830, however, action imitated the form of a guild disciplinary measure rather than that of a market maneuver. Journeymen would pronounce an "interdict" or "condemnation" on a master, on a group of masters, or even a whole town and then they would look for work elsewhere, that is *faire la grève*. The master was punished; he was not offered negotiations.[31] How this kind of work stoppage was gradually transformed among skilled journeymen into a strike, in the sense of a bargaining tool – a refusal of a price for a commodity – cannot be traced here.[32] However, it is possible to document at least partially the development of the idea of a strike among textile laborers. By 1834, concerted work stoppages had gained limited acceptance among mill operatives in at least some provincial centers in the north.

The Paris environment could make a great difference, as the record of an 1833 incident among cotton spinners of the Saint Marceau quarter shows. During September, as a wave of large-scale actions spread across Paris, spinners at six small mills doing fine numbers in that neighborhood demanded a 5 centime pay increase (probably 5 centimes per kilogram of yarn). They made their demand known before leaving the mills, not to public officials, but directly to the owners. The six mill owners lodged complaints that their laborers were engaged in an illegal coalition. By the time of the trial, however, some sort of agreement had been reached. The owners changed their testimony, denying that anything serious had occurred. One spinner when questioned responded as follows, according to the *Gazette des Tribunaux*:

> I had a glass of wine that was going to my head. I went very politely into the widow Mignot's shop, and I saw her machinist. "Hey!" I said, "How goes it, pal? How's work?" "So-so," he answered. "Anyway, even when it's going bad, it keeps on going." Now if that's what you call a conspiracy, my goodness, I don't know what to think.[33]

The charges were dropped. Here is evidence of conscious maneuvering to obtain a higher price and of concerted, well-informed evasion of the law – to all appearances an outlook quite alien to the spinners of Rouen in 1830.

Subsequent incidents outside Paris during 1833 and 1834, with one exception, follow the Rouen pattern more closely than the Paris one, although the work-stoppage idea was gaining recognition. Excellent documentation of a conflict in Reims wool spinning mills in the spring and summer of 1834 allows one to see just how far laborers were willing to go, at this stage, to attempt such a strategy.

Rumors of a rate reduction had begun to circulate in Reims in early May. The local subprefect reported that the mills were operating at a loss given the current price levels for raw wool, and owners were looking for any means possible of relieving their situation.[34] As for the wool spinners, however, he said that "events which have recently occurred in the various big cities, and which the spinners have interpreted according to their lights, have given them courage, boldness, and a certain adroitness." They were determined, he reported, to resist any rate reductions.

But it was not at all clear to the spinners what action to take. The subprefect reported on 29 May that a meeting of one hundred fifty spinners had taken place the day before, at which it was proposed to attack a "*filature mecanique* (mechanical spinning mill)" in the suburb of Pont-Girard in order to head off a proposed rate reduction there. On 31 May a lieutenant of the gendarmerie reported that the spinners had formed a large menacing crowd the day before that threatened to break machines in "the mechanical spinning mills" of the town.[35] Again this odd term. Fourteen arrests were made that day. The reports imply that no one worked on Saturday 1 June; but on Monday the mills reopened. The subprefect reported that he feared the mill owners had given in to the spinners' demands.

One wonders why both these officials used a term that was on the face of it redundant, mechanical spinning mills, unless it had some significance in the specific context. The most likely explanation is that certain mills were introducing power assists for their mules, or that certain of the mills that had power assists were attempting to reduce rates. The fact that mules in these establishments were mechanically powered may have been the sense of the term mechanical. This hypothesis is strengthened by later references to spinner hostility towards new large mules in the mills, probably mules that had been combined when hooked up to an artificial power source. The spread of artificial power had been rapid in wool spinning as in cotton during the slump of 1827–1832. By the end of 1834, only three or four of Reims' 45 mills were still operating with hand cranks and treadmills; 30 had steam engines, 10 water wheels. Now, it appears, a surge in raw wool prices had brought pressure to make that changeover pay off more effectively, by forcing more attentiveness out of the spinners, and in some cases by doubling up the mules in series so that spinners tended twice as many spindles as before.[36]

Up to the time the conflict was temporarily resolved in early June, there had been no work stoppages other than those necessary to allow concerted action or meetings. Refusing to go to the mills on Saturday 1 June, if that is in fact what the spinners did, cannot be interpreted as a withholding of labor: Saturday was pay day, hence what the spinners were refusing to do was accept reduced prices for their yarn.

Conflict began again in late August when the mill owners announced their intention to go back on the June agreement and reduce rates after all. Several hundred spinners gathered on the morning of 24 August in a woods outside of town to decide what to do. Some wanted to break the large mules, according to the subprefect's report, but "the band's orator, a certain Gerard Silles, said that this idea must not be carried out, because the workers occupied on these machines would be thrown out of work ...

"August 25," the subprefect went on, "is the feast day of the patron saint of spinners, but it has not been celebrated since 1830. [The spinners from] one mill, Mont-Dieu, wanted to have a mass said tomorrow ... to bring their saint['s statue] out of the church [as if for the customary procession] and smash it on the steps. But this idea was not accepted."[37] The gesture of smashing the statue was apparently intended to be a threat: This is what, the spinners wished to say, we will do to your machinery if you maintain the reductions. For the spinners there was a clear connection between the rate reductions and some new technical arrangements in the mills, whether it was the power assists themselves or some new doubling of the mules. They were willing to accept the new technical arrangement, but only if customary prices continued to be paid for their

131

yarn. The spinners decided in the end to go back to work the following day, a Monday, and meet again in the afternoon (which they usually took off anyway) to decide upon some plan of action.

On Monday afternoon the spinners marched in a column into the woods to hold their consultation, chanting as they went, "Rather death than a rate reduction!" At the meeting, "Some wanted everyone to stop work and proposed that a collection then be made to help those who would be most in need. The majority were against this, however, seeing no chance that such a collection would produce a sufficient sum to support the group for very long." One group wanted to break the machinery at the Bertrand mill and to attack Bertrand's foreman, considering him to be one of the instigators of the proposed reductions. This idea, too, was rejected. Others had heard that the owners wanted to reduce hours at work starting on 1 September, whether in order to save money or to retaliate against them, no one knew. Again, the meeting broke up without any agreement as to what action to take.

Later that day a smaller group met in the woods and decided to refuse to work and to do all in their power to keep others from working. The next morning they stationed themselves near mill entrances and, apparently without violence, informed their fellows of their decision. The mills were idle that day; and they remained idle for seven more days. On the first day, senior spinners (called "*chefs*" at Reims) brought petitions from some mills to the subprefect; he urged them to exert all their influence to maintain calm and encourage a return to work. Tumultuous demonstrations in the street that day led to several arrests. The spinners had written a song to the tune of "la Parisienne" castigating the "vile" owners who had gone back on their earlier pledges: "Tremble you timorous owners / The worker demands his rights . . . Fear lest equality / Return to reign on earth. / Oh, spinners, on guard!"[38]

On each of the following three days, at meetings in the woods, the spinners decided to continue their refusal to work. The subprefect was inclined to let them exhaust their resources and return to work on their own accord; but on 31 August the prefect at Chalons ordered him to put a stop to the daily meetings. About this time the subprefect heard that certain metal workers were thinking of joining in on the work stoppage. "Those fellows are organized on military lines," he said, "with captains and lieutenants; I think they are dangerous because some come from Paris, others from Lyon, and they appear to be well practiced in the art of popular riots and capable of directing them."[39] Perhaps it was the metal workers who advised the spinners of a new way to make collections of money from property owners in town. The key was to appear at doors with a register in which one carefully marked down the names of all those who gave. Such collections were made in Reims on 31 August and 2 September. Someone apparently advised the spinners with handwritten postings, as well, to try taking up collections amongst the other laborers of the town, which they had not thought to do.[40] Some part of the money that was collected went astray. The subprefect refers in his reports to "disputes among the mutinous" over the disappearance of funds. (Labor conflicts through the 1850s were often called mutinies by government officials.)[41]

By 3 September, the spinners had lost their sense of direction since the Guard had begun breaking up their meetings, some owners had in fact offered concessions, and a general movement back to the mills began. By the fifth, all were back at work.

In contrast to the work stoppage at Paris, the one carried out by spinners at Reims in 1834 came in response to a complex grievance involving technical changes linked to pay reductions. The nature of the grievance itself seems to have played a role in the spinners' prolonged indecision about how to proceed. The idea of breaking the offending machinery was repeatedly raised. In May, spinners appear to have refused to present themselves at the mills on pay day, as a gesture of rejection for the new prices being set for their yarn. Such gestures do not reflect some kind of naiveté or failure of organization among the spinners: Through them the spinners hoped to express a proprietary interest in their machinery (by destroying it rather than letting it be rearranged) or in their yarn (by refusing to "sell" it to the mill owners on pay day). The spinners were casting about for a tactic appropriate to independent operators. Their grievance was the same as that of the Rouen cotton spinners in 1830. They were protesting the imposition of some sort of crude labor–management policy. But they found that all the property they wished to withhold from sale or break was in the shops owned by the mill owners; and they were clearly dissatisfied with merely marching through town chanting and singing. The idiom of 1830 had begun to lose some of its potency, both for them and for the authorities. The subprefect showed every readiness to allow them to engage in this sort of activity as long as they wished. But what could they do that would have a decisive impact on the mill owners?

The decision to quit work was taken as the best of a number of bad alternatives, and the advice of skilled journeymen in the town may have played a role in the decision, as well as in the strategies followed once the work stoppage began. The spinners were not ready to regard the work stoppage as their most potent weapon, as a strategy peculiarly appropriate to their position. Yet some sort of step in this direction was taken, just as the Reims mill owners were making a preliminary step toward trying to manage labor.

THE LARGER CONTEXT

The years from 1830 to 1834 were a period of intense labor protest in France, protest of a kind never seen before in French history; journeymen and laborers organized and coordinated their activities on an unprecedented scale. Stiff repression brought a temporary lull after 1834, but collective action picked up again in 1839–40 and again in 1846–8 culminating in the momentous overthrow of the Monarchy by Parisian artisans in February 1848. These developments of the July Monarchy have long been considered as the beginning of the modern labor movement.[42] At first there was concern among historians that the leading role in these protests was played by laborers whose condition least resembled that of modern industrial workers; it was not factory operatives in the new mechanized trades that stood at the forefront of the movement, but the virtually independent silk weavers of Lyon or the highly skilled carpenters of Paris with their old secret *compagnonnage* organizations dating from the time of Louis XIV.

Closer study showed that diverse forms of competitive reorganization began affecting the old artisanal trades in the 1820s; the search for profits amid the whiplash of boom-and-bust markets made no distinction between modern and traditional sectors.[43] The beginning of the labor movement therefore came to be explained as resulting from the decline of the artisan instead of the rise of the factory system.

Lyon silk weavers, for example, who pioneered the associationist ideology that was taken up by the whole French movement and who rose in insurrection twice between 1831 and 1834, were experiencing all the changes that had already transformed the rest of the weaving trade since 1700, but compressed into a single moment. Despite the disappearance of the guild, the coming of the jacquard loom after 1800 had given the urban master weaver a new lease on life. The jacquard required high skill in set–up and handling and produced brocades and pattern weaves with great rapidity. The growing emphasis of retailers on cheaper plain weaves from 1820 on, however, stimulated rural production. For these articles, rural weavers were good enough. Simultaneously, shrinking markets for fancy work induced merchant manufacturers to drive hard bargains with the remaining urban masters. These peculiar conditions prolonged the drama that had ended in the eighteenth century in most other weaving centers, the struggle of town against country. Revival of guild controls and fixed rate schedules was a living issue to Lyon masters. By 1831, they had realized, however, that such aims under the new regime of property were necessarily revolutionary in nature. So they fashioned an ideology to match. "Association" to them meant, above all, breaking the power of the merchant manufacturer.[44]

Construction workers, equally in the forefront of working-class action, were also experiencing rapid change. Subcontracting came into use increasingly after 1815. Subcontracting was, it is true, a means for a construction firm to avoid managerial cares. But the subcontractors, in order to finish work on time and under budget, had to seek new control over work. They introduced piece wages for the first time in this trade, setting them at levels carefully calculated to increase the pace of work. The need for surveillance forced them to stop working on the building themselves; as a result they emerged as a conspicuous (and often hated) new stratum in the trade. Each of these changes violated long-standing notions of honor among construction workers, as well as increasing their insecurity and intensifying their labor.[45] Here, too, skilled craftsmen were suffering a decline.

But now the thesis of the decline of the artisan has come under attack in its turn. Jacques Rancière has rightly pointed out that the most articulate and activist artisans – tailors, printers, shoemakers – came from trades that did not have very far to decline. Skill requirements and working conditions had already been minimal in these trades in the eighteenth century.[46] Christopher Johnson's work on Lodève likewise reveals how unique conditions can conspire to create a highly self-conscious group of laborers in a trade not apparently afflicted by rapidly changing management or technology. In France as a whole weavers, whether in cottages or centralized shops, did not play a significant role in the events of the 1830s. But in Lodève, woolen weavers staged protests that reveal a high level of organization and carefully contrived strategy. Weavers at one shop in January 1834, for example, demanded a rate increase, left the shop when it was refused, and set out for Bédarieux to find other work, accompanied by an escort of five hundred of their fellows.[47] Johnson reports that this was an attempt at selective pressure: One shop had been singled out for attack and the weavers there received some form of monetary support. At the same time, the departure to find other work was classic *compagnonnage* strategy, the typical follow-up to an interdiction in a provincial town. Lodève producers all worked for one customer, supplying military cloth to the government, with strict contractual time limits; they were therefore highly vulnerable to this kind of pressure, as the weavers had learned by the 1820s. Lodève weaving was on a technical and managerial plateau in the 1830s as well; its markets were insured against cyclical slumps and outside competitors. There was little pressure for bold innovation. Weavers were not experiencing any change in status. Yet they targeted a vulnerable shop and carried out their action against it with perfect coordination. Further actions in subsequent years reveal consistent unity of purpose and clarity of execution that are a far cry from what one observes in northern centers in the same period.[48] The apparently precocious laborers were therefore located in the technically stable and ultimately moribund center. Johnson suspects Lodève's later decline was directly related to a labor militancy that discouraged investment.

It may therefore be inappropriate to speak of the decline of the artisan as the key factor behind labor militancy in this period. But what does seem to constitute a common denominator in all these trade disputes, no matter what the skill level involved, is the threat to the multiplicity of purposes that work fulfilled. Even if, as with tailors, the skill requirement was already nil, the trade overcrowded, the work tedious, nonetheless it was possible still to desire continued control over one's own pace, over one's breaks, comings and goings, and methods of work. One did not have to take an artisanal pride in one's work to dislike the prick of incentive pay schemes. Tailors and silk weavers were losing control in the very raw sense that rates offered for their work were becoming ruinously low. Long hours and a desperate pace of work were required to earn a living wage. Lodève weavers were succeeding where these other laborers were not; they kept piece rates high and therefore reduced outside pressure on their behavior at work.

Mule spinners in northern centers were being subjected to closer surveillance and more finely tuned piece-rate schedules after 1827 very much as Parisian construction workers were. The attempt in Rouen to introduce multiple-tiered piece rates, probably more sophisticated and more controlling in its effects than anything attempted in other trades during this period, prompted a correspondingly vociferous response. But Lille area mill owners proved themselves to be the most sophisticated managers of all. They made their increase of control invisible by hiding it within a measure whose form respected the spinner's sense of independence, the steam-power fee. There, in the crucial years of 1830–4, the calm was almost unbroken. The spinner there remained in control of his own fate, for he saw the fees and costs of his work as elements of that fate instead of as attempts to manipulate his behavior.

It is important to recognize that under a regime of piece rates the level of earnings and the organization of work are inextricably interrelated. Establishing a particular rate of pay is usually tantamount to imposing a particular method of work. An employer can gain little from an increase in the productivity or intensity of labor if he is forced to pay the same piece rate as before. His unit labor costs remain precisely the same. By the same token a drop in piece rates can often compel the laborer to do things differently, while an increase can give the laborer at once more money, more leisure, and more control over work. The contrast between Rouen and Lille suggests that, to French laborers in the 1830s, the latter two were at least equally as important as the former. French laborers continued, like the weavers of eighteenth-century guilds, to desire freedom from the need to finely calculate the value in monetary terms of every move of the finger, every break for a little drink and talk, every decision to take an extra moment fixing up a piece of work to look the way it ought to. One did not have to be dedicated to a trade and full of its esprit de corps to want such things. One only had to be alive and to be working. There was no management scheme in existence that had so imposed itself as to prevent laborers from identifying with their work and seeking to integrate their work and their complex social identities into a single coherent way of life. Nor has one yet been invented, for that matter.

6 Visions of subsistence

By 1834, the fledgling French textile industry had made only a few fumbling steps toward treating labor consistently as a commodity independent of its products. With rare exceptions the control strategies prevalent in the industry maintained a partial independence for laborers, both in the spinning mills and in the putting–out networks of the countryside – a partial independence to which the laborers demonstrated a tenacious commitment. At the same time, any attempt to voice demands or grievances was considered by owners and government alike to be flagrant insubordination. Actual bargaining, whether collective or individual, was virtually unknown. Nonetheless in the years following the revolution of 1831, the textile laborer was suddenly made to stand before the rest of French society as the essential proletarian. In a flood of newspaper stories, speeches, government inquiries, and private investigative reports, he was portrayed, odd as it may seem, as the being who more than any other exemplified the fate of the wage laborer in a competitive market economy. Down to the present day the textile laborer of the early industrial revolution has continued to play this role on the stage of history, and any fact that might have gainsaid this view of him has been systematically ignored.

A BASE LINE OF COMPARISON

By 1830, there was a need for some group in society to play the role. In the new social order the possibility of advancement was balanced by insecurity. If rank was based solely on merit, it was as easy to move down as to move up. One's position in society was determined solely by the function one fulfilled. After the Revolution it was no longer possible to hold a position independent of one's economic function, like the impoverished nobles of Brittany who in 1789 had come to town in peasant dress to cast their vote with the Second Estate. By 1820 every citizen, artisan or landowner, noble or otherwise, was to manage his property

138

competitively; if he failed and lost his property he fell *ipso facto* to a lower status. No one could any longer be what he was merely by virtue of an oath taken or a patent from the king.

But this new idea of how society worked was bound to foster anxiety and disappointment. Whether or not there was more social mobility in the nineteenth century than there had been in the eighteenth, it is certain that more people thought about it, that it inspired a pervasive malaise. Martin Nadaud, a Paris mason, was astonished at the profits he made on subcontracting deals early in the July Monarchy and equally astonished at the dishonesty and trickery that prevailed among the rapacious contractors he had to work with.[1] In fear and disgust, he went back to working for wages. According to evidence that Jacques Rancière has recently brought forward, tailors and printers were gripped by a deep longing to get out of the trade, to find something better; artisan followers of the Saint-Simonians begged their middle-class leaders for jobs as secretaries or porters.[2] Flaubert brought together the illusions and anxieties of this period in the figure of Emma Bovary. Unable to rest satisfied with her rank as wife of an obscure provincial health officer, she sought escape in frenetic purchases of fashionable clothing and furniture (from a scheming local *marchand de nouveautés*), in a futile love affair, in advancing her husband's scientific renown, and finally in self-destruction.

Under the sway of such anxieties people needed a baseline of comparison against which to measure their own advances and retreats, an image of the lowest level beyond which one could not fall. By universal accord this lowest level was equated with the position of the unskilled manual laborer, especially the textile laborer. To be a manual laborer was to be at the bottom, to be socially nondescript. As Balzac said, writing in the fashion magazine *La Mode* in 1830: "By working with his hands, a man becomes a means ... The man-instrument is a sort of social zero, of which the greatest number never adds up to anything, even when preceded by some figures."[3] At the end of *Madame Bovary*, after Emma and Charles have both died, casualties of Emma's burning aspirations, their only child Berthe ends up in the custody of an aunt who, being poor, "has put [Berthe] to work in a cotton mill to earn her living." She was, that is, consigned to oblivion.

Dissemination of the doctrines of Malthus and Ricardo in France in the 1820s and the appearance of hundreds of steam-powered spinning mills on the horizons of northern towns after 1827 combined to make the textile laborer a particularly appropriate image of a social nullity. Whatever their differences over details both Malthus and Ricardo agreed that the equilibrium price for labor in a free market was a subsistence wage, that is, just enough income to keep alive, no more, no less. Charity only worsened the poor's condition, keeping more of them alive to compete for jobs. Ricardo further taught that accumulation of fixed capital was bound to result in greater productivity and lower prices for manufactured goods.[4] In the northern textile centers, by 1830, the visible evidence of capital accumulation, lower prices for manufactured goods, and poverty among laborers had become overwhelming. The new factories came to be viewed as monuments to the correctness of political economy, and simultaneously the popularized doctrines of political economy became accepted as guides to understanding the new factories.[5] An exquisitely balanced deprivation was in store for anyone who, like little Berthe, fell to the bottom of the social ladder; and the textile laborer became a convenient image of life in that state.

Until recently historians have accepted the contemporary judgment as a settled fact and mined the documents that set forth this judgment as if they were stock piles of dependable information.[6] In the last few years, however, this attitude has begun to change. The great mass of eyewitness accounts, of tables and graphs, of first-hand testimony on factory towns has begun to be subject to critical scrutiny. Observation of social conditions is no longer deemed to be a simple, unstructured matter. The construction of categories, the discrimination of relevant perceptions, and the use of appropriate terms are now seen as highly powerful acts that every human engages in whenever he turns his attention to a particular subject or opens his mouth to speak.[7] Even so there is an understandable reluctance to jettison all the accumulated evidence as untrustworthy. Especially with reference to the early investigations of working-class conditions, there is currently a need for in-depth reevaluation. And any reinterpretation of the experience of nineteenth-century textile laborers cannot get around this need. What, if anything, can be learned from the old investigative literature? By what methods is the wheat to be separated from the chaff? Closely linked to these questions is the equally important problem of understanding how far market culture distorted contemporary perceptions of social reality. As must necessarily be the case for any cultural construct that rests on blanket claims about the structure of human motives, the answer is, very far indeed.

FUNCTION VERSUS MORAL EXISTENCE

What ultimately prompted extensive investigation into textile laborers' wages and living conditions was not merely the fact that they had come to represent the state of labor in a competitive market. The spur to investigation arose out of profound moral difficulties raised by political economy itself in its early nineteenth-century form, difficulties which any theory that justified a totally functional social order were bound to run up against. These difficulties can be seen in nascent form in works of the mid-1820s by two champions of liberalism who exemplified and proselytized the kind of thinking that later made textile laborers into a potent symbol of the new age, Charles Dupin and Charles Dunoyer.[8]

Charles Dupin, in a work published in 1827, proposed a common unit of measure for gauging and comparing diverse social roles. The title of Dupin's book, *The Productive and Commercial Forces of France*, names what was for him the common element required by all functional activity of whatever kind, "force."[9] He distinguished inanimate and animate forces, the latter provided by both humans and animals; and he divided human force into physical and intellectual varieties. His unit for measuring force was the "adult-male equivalent." In the first part of his work, he tried to compare, point for point, the commercial and productive forces available to France in terms of adult-male equivalents with those available to Great Britain. He assumed that every child 12 to 17 years old and every man 54 to 60 years old provided France with one half of an average adult man's force. Every woman, as well, provided one half. Therefore, out of France's total population of 31,600,000, there were forces available equivalent to those provided by 17,609,057 adult males. He estimated that two-thirds of these forces were deployed in agriculture, along with horses, oxen and donkeys. To each of these latter he attributed an adult-male equivalent of force as well (1 horse = 7 men, 1 ox = 4 men, 1 ass = 1 man). He therefore discovered that French agriculture had a total of 37,278,537 adult-male equivalents available to it. The remaining one-third of human forces were deployed in industry, along with 2,100,000 adult-male equivalents in the form of horses, yielding 6,303,019 adult-male equivalents of what he called animate forces available to industry. Water power, wind power, and steam power were also each assigned an adult-male equivalent number, yielding a total of 6,233,333 in inanimate forces (ships' sails figured for three million of this total). Hence France had a total of 11,536,352 adult-male equivalents of all forms of force available to industry. Here is where the contrast with Great Britain was most dramatic in Dupin's eyes: Dupin found that British industry disposed of 19,840,000 adult-male equivalents in inanimate forces, and therefore a total of 28,228,264 adult-male equivalents of all forms. The inanimate forces were decisive to Britain's edge, he remarked.

Part Two of Dupin's essay, on the ways of ameliorating France's forces, covers two kinds of forces, "physical forces" and "intellectual forces." He discusses the improvement and multiplication of animals, the improvement of human health and stature, instruction in the countryside, the forces and position of the "feminine sex," and the application of forces in the workshop (this latter discussion consists of a call for education for the worker in mechanical and economic subjects).

In Dupin's 1827 work, society appears as an organism in vital inter-action with its environment; and he uses his notion of force to propose a kind of bioenergetics for measuring and comparing the contribution of various functional elements of this organism. The relative importance of various social groupings (women, agricultural laborers, industrial laborers and so on) could thus be compared not only among themselves, but even with the nonhuman elements of the total organism. Nonhuman force was to be improved by becoming more abundant while human force was to be improved by advances in its health and its intellectual component. This latter task was the function Dupin assigned to himself within the great organism, as shown by his teaching at the Conservatoire des Arts et Métiers and his numerous lectures and pamphlets on popular education in the 1820s.

It would have seemed odd in the eighteenth century, and it seems odd today, to reduce all the activities of men, women, children, horses, oxen, steam, wind, and water to a single unit of measure so that they could be compared and added up. But in the 1820s, this was just the sort of analysis that the mind was pushed to by the prospect of the first great advances in labor productivity. Could one not observe just at this period steam engines literally replacing both men and horses in giving movement to certain wheels in spinning mills and elsewhere? The structure of post-Revolutionary social thinking conspired with the prospect of such sub-stitutions in Dupin's mind to create an image of a vast natural and social functioning whole. The idea that an individual could change one function (read: social class) for another according to his merits, just as machines could take over certain human functions brought Dupin to search for a common underlying element to purposive action, just as it brought others to develop a taste for advancement and for the trappings of advancement. Hence the same social thinking that transformed fashion in clothing in the 1820s lay behind Dupin's attempt to identify and measure totalities of adult-male equivalents of functional capacity.

But inherent in Dupin's notion of force was an unnerving problem: Might not the deployment of humans along with machines and horses in the physical and intellectual manipulation of nature entail some danger not only to their physical but also to their moral existence? If the term "moral" is taken to refer to that which distinguishes humans from horses and steam engines (more so even than human intellectual capacity since the intellect like the horse is used primarily as a means, that is, it functions to achieve set ends), then did not Dupin's sort of thinking raise in an utterly new way questions about the moral existence of the vast majority of human beings constrained to spend their lives doing no more than carrying out certain social functions? Dupin himself eventually came to see things in much these terms. After the 1830 revolution, elevated to the Chamber of Peers in the new government, the Baron Dupin became one of the leaders in the movement to establish legal limits on the use of children in industry and legal requirements that they receive a minimum of moral and intellectual instruction.[10]

There was no hint in Dupin's work of 1827 of these later concerns. But as early as 1825, other social thinkers were giving voice to ideas that raised such moral issues in a disturbing new way. The writings of Malthus and Ricardo showed the way, by lifting to stark prominence the implications of free competition among the working classes for a limited number of jobs. Charles Dunoyer, in an 1825 piece called *Industry and Morality Considered in Their Relation to Liberty*, was one of the first to expound before the French audience the dire consequences that these English thinkers saw as resulting from such competition.[11]

Dunoyer's principal concern, as an opponent of the Restoration regime, was to argue against certain legitimist apologists and defenders of the old aristocracy, in support of the idea that industrial society was the one kind of society in which the individual was both most moral and most free. "Industrial society" was defined as that in which there was no class that was not "industrious," that is, did not live either by its labor or its property. This was tantamount to saying that industrial society was a society run according to the new functional logic. In other societies (especially monarchical ones with a titled nobility) the dominating classes lived by taking rather than by producing. This illegitimate appropriation deprived others of their liberty and enshrined immorality at the highest level of society. Only industrial society left to each the complete liberty to advance his own well being so long as it did not infringe upon the liberty of others. Only industrial society closed off all access to careers of nonproductive political intrigue.

After having explained this view at length, Dunoyer went on to regret that, although in industrial society humanity had the most liberty and was capable of the greatest morality, it was nonetheless the case that even in industrial society, there was very little liberty, and that this liberty was unequally distributed. One's liberty increases with the development of one's faculties, which is always easier if one has wealth. In the best of cases, natural inequalities will lead some to lose this necessary wealth, and to be forced to "rent their services" in order to live.

> The causes which have given birth to this class of laborers will naturally tend to enlarge it; the workers, by multiplying, necessarily force down the price of labor [*prix de la main-d'oeuvre*]. In spite of the fact that their resources diminish, they continue to breed, for one of the evils inseparable from their condition would be to lack the discipline and the virtue needed to control their tendency to multiply, to stop dumping

too many workers on the market [*jeter trop d'ouvriers sur la place*] ...
In the happiest of worlds, this would inevitably occur.[12]

Charity cannot help since it can only result in a further drop in wages.
Nor could resources ever multiply faster than population. Only absti-
nence offered any hope of improvement in the state of this laboring class.
Yet "knowledge, ability, and virtue"[13] will tend to be the preserve of
those with wealth. An initial inequality in natural capacities, therefore,
tends to magnify and reinforce itself. It is not impossible to pull oneself
up out of the poorer classes; it is difficult but in fact there is constant
movement up and down. The justice inherent in industrial society is not
that all are free, or equally free, but that those who are most active,
honest, and prudent are also most rich, happy, and free.[14] Finally, Dunoyer reviews the functional requirements that make stark social strat-
ification inevitable, here following the views of J.B. Say discussed in
Chapter 3. Industrial society naturally requires three sorts of people:
those who study nature, those who plan actions upon nature, and those
who carry these actions out. Hence any industrial society would be made
up of at least three functionally defined classes: savants, industrialists,
and laborers. Individuals must compete for positions in these three groups;
and those who fall into the third group will be forced into a downward
spiraling vortex of poverty and vice.

Dunoyer's 1825 piece brought the dismal message from England that
in the best of all possible worlds life would be very grim indeed for the
majority of humankind, integrating this message with the functional social calculus of class that he championed against the claims to inherent
superiority of the Restoration's ultra-Royalist aristocrats.

These two works were part of a larger current of theoretical discussion.
Authors like Parent-Duchâtelet and Duchâtel joined Dunoyer in describing the plight of the poor in industrial society, remarking the ravages of
wage competition, and preaching the futility of charity.[15] Even the revolutionary voices of the period spoke the language of economic function.
Sismondi's critique of political economy was carried out entirely in the
theory's own terms. Saint-Simon, like Dunoyer, distinguished sharply
between the idle and the productive classes and praised the creativity of
the entrepreneur. Comte's notion of social roles was much more supple
than Dunoyer's or Say's functional categories, but bore the marks of the
age's new habits of mind.[16]

This is not to say that a precise or thorough knowledge of political
economy had by this time become part of the common baggage of every
educated French mind, nor that there was perfect agreement about the
significance and application of the new ideas. But insofar as social issues
were discussed and, as William Coleman has recently shown, insofar as
society became the object of explicit empirical inquiry after 1820, views

like those laid out by Dupin and Dunoyer commanded uncritical acceptance and determined what issues deserved investigation.[17] These issues were overwhelmingly moral in nature. If human beings represented merely one more physical resource among others for achieving society's aims, did this not constitute a threat to their requirements as moral beings? If most human beings were doomed to live out their lives at a subsistence level, were they unable to afford a morally acceptable minimum of material goods? These were the questions that preoccupied investigators when they first turned their attention to the working class of textile mill towns in the late 1820s.

It is particularly important to recognize that investigators did not set out to prove the existence of markets or to demonstrate the functional relations that determined society's structure. They took these things as given and inquired rather to find out if a society so constituted could be a just one, if it needed reform, and if so what kind of reform.

The impact of such a starting point on the sort of evidence deemed relevant in these inquiries is plainly visible in one of the earliest examples, a report delivered to the Industrial Society of Mulhouse in 1827 by Achille Penot. Penot's *Discourse on Some Research in Comparative Statistics on the Town of Mulhouse* assumes that certain relations exist between the price of labor, the growth of Mulhouse's population, and morality.[18] As a result, he simply searches to establish indirect statistical patterns causally linked to this central set of assumptions that go untested, unexamined. He makes no attempt to study wages, cost of living, or the movement of laborers in a market. Instead he proceeds as follows: (1) He establishes that the poor of Mulhouse buy national lottery tickets one-quarter more often than the French average. (2) He shows that illegitimate births for which no father acknowledges parenthood are one-quarter more frequent in Mulhouse than in France as a whole. (3) He shows that the number of children in school is a smaller proportion of the total population in Mulhouse than in France as a whole by a factor of one quarter. (4) He remarks that inhabitants of Mulhouse consume 108 liters of wine and 131 liters of *eau-de-vie* per capita per year, without being able to produce any figures for France as a whole. However, Penot notes, most of it is consumed by adult males and most of that on Sundays. (5) He finds that one half of all children in Mulhouse die before reaching the age of 10, while for France as a whole the equivalent age is 20. Finally, he remarks the extraordinary correlation between these diverse variables, and points out that they have varied together in a worsening direction over the last 10 years as Mulhouse's population has gone from 10,000 to 18,000.

What Penot felt no need to do, because it seemed painfully obvious to him and to his audience, was to explain that behind these statistical measures lay a nexus of cause and effect of just the kind that Dunoyer had posited. The growth of the laboring population was outstripping the growth of available jobs; competition amongst laborers for work was keeping pay at a bare minimum; long work hours, lack of means, and poor nutrition were bringing neglect and ill-health for the children so that those who survived childhood became uneducated and dissolute adults. Men drank heavily to forget the helplessness of their situation, and the drain on the family budget that resulted only made more certain their imprisonment in a life of deprivation. In short, the market mechanism of supply and demand for the commodity called labor was setting up a self-reinforcing, self-perpetuating misery that grew along with the town's very prosperity. These connections were so clear to Penot that his whole exercise could concern itself merely with indirect correlations and yet he considered the demonstration complete.

It might be objected here that Penot's and Dunoyer's assumptions remain quite compelling today, and that nothing that was presented in Chapter 5 about modes of payment prevented the level of payment from dropping to that of bare subsistence as a result of competition for jobs. That is, even though the form of labor control in the mills of Mulhouse may not in 1827 have reflected a fully worked-out conception of labor as a commodity, the level of payment may well have reflected the pressures of unregulated competition among laborers. Hence Penot may have been correct in his assumptions. However, this possibility deserves to be investigated in a way that Penot himself failed to do; his indirect method and his secondary evidence in no way allow one to conclude that he was either correct or incorrect.

That Penot satisfied the members of the Industrial Society of Mulhouse is not surprising. Founded less than a year earlier the Society was made up of mill owners, doctors, lawyers, and local savants. Its chief purpose was the exchange of scientific and technical knowledge. But the Society also had wider aims in mind; in its first year of existence, one of its committees recommended that the Society inquire into the form of political regime most suited to industry.[19] Citing Dunoyer as its authority, the committee proclaimed this approach to politics to be the only worthwhile one, since it was free of that ambition for power that produces nothing.

From the very beginning, French mill owners promoted social investigators' activities in their own towns, but none more actively than those of Mulhouse. The prosperous twenties had transformed the mill-owning class from the obscure shop operators and speculators of the First Empire into substantial and highly conspicuous members of the provincial notability. The slump of 1827–32, the revolution of 1830, the cholera epidemic that swept through poor neighborhoods of every French town in 1832, and the transition to steam power with its soot and its noise all threatened to turn their conspicuousness into a severe political liability. Public responsibility was literally thrust on them. The Protestant families of Mulhouse were doubtless particularly sensitive to this sort of attention. From the outset their Society aimed at counteracting bad publicity by vigorously promoting public inquiry and moderate reform. Groups of mill owners in other towns were not far behind. They welcomed social investigators, gave them tours of the working-class neighborhoods, provided them with statistics and opinions.

Thinkers like Dunoyer obviously offered at least some Mulhouse owners an attractive apology for their own role in society as well as for the impoverished condition of their employees. The harsh realism of political economy assuaged their troubled consciences. Its doctrines were as firm and simple as the figures on their annual balance sheets. (For they had all by now been forced to adopt some form of capital accounting.) Political economy as they learned it told them that their own motives and those of their employees were identical, the pursuit of gain; and, as Dunoyer and others expounded it, it told them that such motives were politically innocent and publicly beneficial. It is not possible to explore this matter fully here, but the contrast between their views and the outlook of merchant manufacturers as recently as 1814 could not have been greater. The latter clung to the old ways of making money; they founded the Conseils des prudhommes and Chambers of Commerce and used them to retain all the vestiges of collective industrial control that they could.[20] But the large mill owners by 1830 had no need of collective control. What they needed were organs of public action like the Industrial Society of Mulhouse. Chambers of Commerce were soon turned to these new ends, as were local learned and technical societies; intercity liaisons were established. By the 1840s national lobbying efforts could be mobilized at a moment's notice.[21] Eventually every northern center was provided with its own industrial society in emulation of Mulhouse.[22]

The investigative literature is therefore as much a product of their activities as it is of the investigators' efforts. To say that this literature is riddled with errors is to say that mill owners had erroneous ideas about their own shops and employees. But this presents no problems if one remembers that claims about motives lay at the heart of all these errors. No amount of firsthand evidence can disprove a claim about motives.

IMAGINARY BUDGETS

Two of the earliest investigators to take part in this debate condemned industrial society outright as conservative defenders of the old legitimist regime and the old Catholic social order. Baron Pierre-Marie-Sebastien

Bigot de Morogues, who published in 1832 a work entitled *On the Misery of Workers and the Means by Which It May Be Alleviated*, was the first French investigator, so far as this researcher knows, to publish an eyewitness report of a visit to a factory with the sole aim of investigating the effects of free competition on laborers.[23] He was the first as well to gather empirical evidence on wages and living costs with the aim of demonstrating what a subsistence–level wage was in practice. Morogues' proposals for reform amounted to a kind of reworked Physiocracy. Open competition in industry, particularly open competition with superior foreign enterprises, spelled doom for the laborer. His wages could be forced below the starvation level and still his products would be undersold. Cries would then be raised that grain prices were too high, that tariffs protecting agriculture should be lifted (as was being argued in England) so that industrial laborers' living costs would be lower. But this would ruin the small farmer, larger farms would produce at lower cost but also at lower yields per acre, meaning less food to go around. For Morogues, the small farm was the key to national well-being. Small farmers worked their land more intensively, the farms employed more laborers, ensuring sufficient employment levels to maintain wages. The small farm, not the big factory, ought to be the object of political concern. Vigorous government intervention in the marketplace to protect the small farmer was necessary. Morogues turned the tables on Dunoyer, using Dunoyer's own view of the situation of laborers to argue against his kind of social order. Small farmers (and, implicitly, their aristocratic guardians) were the proper bulwarks of a healthy society.

Morogues used evidence on the ill-health and deprivation of laborers to underscore his argument. He presented, without discussing his sources, average wage figures from various French towns.[24] The daily wage (*prix de la journée*) in Paris, he found, was 2.50 francs to 3.00 francs; in Orléans, 1.50 francs; in the Hérault, 1.30 francs. In 1832 it had sunk as low as .75 francs in Metz and Nancy; the Vosges, Rouen, or Lyon were no better, he said, without specifying further. After a long excursus on grain prices, Morogues concluded that a bare minimum annual subsistence budget for a family of three was 860 francs, or, in extraordinary circumstances, it could be cut to 760 francs. Taking 1.50 francs as the average daily wage of adult males and appropriate values for the wages of women and children, he concluded that the same family, if all went well, could earn barely 760 francs per year in industry.[25] To Morogues this evidence seemed devastating; and he embellished his case with statistics on high crime rates in cities during economic downturns and with evidence on the poor health and weak stature of army conscripts in industrial areas. Morogues praised luxury because of the kind of trade it stimulated and predicted that the very poverty of the laborers would

148

in times of crisis bring the downfall of the mass-production industrial concerns that employed them. Morogues saw industrial society as the source of an insidious decline into poverty and degeneracy for the great majority of its members.

Morogues' wage and budget figures were extensively reviewed in a book that appeared two years later, *Christian Political Economy*, by Jean-Paul-Alban de Villeneuve-Bargemont, prefect of the Nord under Charles X and now an impassioned critic, like Morogues, of all that the new regime stood for.[26] Villeneuve-Bargemont went further than Morogues in the sharpness of his critique of the emergent liberal orthodoxy. Not only did he see the growth of Britain's cotton industry as directly responsible for the expansion in the number of poor there, but he attributed this industry's existence to the promotion of "English theories" about trade.[27] That is, Villeneuve-Bargemont blamed political economic theory itself for the appearance of a social order that mirrored its structure in England; and he decried the spreading menace of this system within France.

The menace could be demonstrated, he believed, merely by bringing together figures on the growth of the cotton trade in the department he formerly governed, the Nord, with figures that purported to show an increase in the number of *misérables* there. But, unlike Penot, Villeneuve-Bargemont was prepared to go beyond such indirect correlations and provide direct evidence on the plight of the industrial laborer. After reviewing with approval Morogues' wage and budget figures, Villeneuve-Bargemont offered findings of his own on the town of Lille, where his prefecture had been located:

> We found, for example, that to support a family of workers in the town of Lille, it was necessary to have an annual total of salaries earned by the family of at least 1,051 francs, and this supposing that the worker had no aging or infirm parent to maintain. We made no allowance for the instruction of his young children, set nothing aside for savings or for unforeseen emergencies.
>
> Yet the simple manufacturing worker of the town of Lille hardly earns in good times more than 1.75 francs per day, his wife .60 francs, his children able to work about .53 francs; total, 2.88 francs per day. Counting three hundred days of work, which is all that one could hope for, one achieves an income of only 1,051 francs per year, that is, just enough to allow the family to subsist.[28]

Here, for Villeneuve-Bargemont, was a decisive demonstration of the injustice of competitive pressure on wages, one which served as the cornerstone of his discussion. Here was direct proof from one of the centers of the new cotton industry of the precarious existence, devoid of instruction, entertainment, or security for the aged, that unregulated, competitive industry inevitably forced on those who served it.

The problem with both Morogues' and Villeneuve-Bargemont's findings on laborers' wages is that they are quite vague; and there is internal evidence that they were tendentiously arranged. Morogues' wage figures could be used to prove that all laborers in Nancy and Metz had far less than what was necessary for survival in 1832 as easily as they could be used to prove that laborers in Orléans or other "average" French towns had only just enough to survive. But since the laborers of Nancy and Metz did not all die in 1832, such a use of the evidence would have suffered from being implausible; whereas the idea that competition kept wages at subsistence levels made plausible the arrangement of wage levels and bare survival costs in such a way as to equal each other exactly. In Villeneuve-Bargemont's case, the traces of such conscious rearranging of the evidence are painfully clear because they led him into arithmetical errors; three hundred times 2.88 francs is 864 francs, not 1,051 francs. This latter figure turns out to be 2.88 times 365. Villeneuve-Bargemont forgot to leave out Sundays and holidays when he originally calculated what wage levels he needed to match with living costs. Later he changed the number of workdays in the text of his report to a more realistic 300, but forgot to redo all his other figures.

In subsequent studies of this kind, evidence on wages and living costs became much more specific, definite, and abundant.[29] But just insofar as it did so, it becomes possible to show from internal indications that the case for an open labor market as the determining factor in wage levels was never adequately established. This did not bother those who gathered such evidence, because they were not aiming to establish such a case; they fully believed it already and continued seeing the ravages of competition as the hidden determinant behind the most diverse data.

By far the largest and most thorough study of the condition of textile laborers published in this period was compiled by Louis Villermé between 1835 and 1840. While carrying out his research, he enjoyed the active support and cooperation of hundreds of local mill owners, doctors, and experts. In Alsace, he presented a list of 42 questions to the Industrial Society of Mulhouse, which were duly answered in the Society's name by Achille Penot. (The questions and answers were later published as a separate pamphlet.)[30] At Lille, Villermé was escorted through town by the mill owner and Chamber of Commerce spokesman, Theodore Barrois, posing questions for him and for a number of other mill owners, doctors, and public officials.[31] At Rouen, he gathered evidence on the earnings of country weavers directly from a merchant manufacturer and received long tables of wage figures from the Conseil des prudhommes.[32] As a member of the Institut de France, he was everywhere cordially received and warmly assisted. In his introduction he boasts that he even talked openly with laborers, sitting at their tables and speaking as equals, man-to-man.

Since the time of its publication, Villermé's study has commanded wide respect; although historians may have disagreed with his views, they have in every generation cited as authoritative his accounts of personal observations and drawn for their own purposes on his wealth of evidentiary detail. In doing so, however, they have often allowed themselves unwittingly to accept as true a larger framework of assumptions that shaped both Villermé's views and his selection and arrangement of material.[33] This is one way in which that framework, part of the foundation of market culture, has been passed down over the years and kept alive. The fact is that these two elements of Villermé's work are not so easily separable; not only did he arrange his evidence to help advance his own views; but, beyond this, the forms of evidence that he sought out and used were determined by the terms of the debate in which he engaged.

Villermé wished to walk a tightrope between two alternatives that he refused to accept. He wanted, on the one hand, to document the harsh living conditions that he believed laborers were compelled to accept in a competitive industrial order. At the same time, he wished to deny to opponents of this order such as Morogues or Villeneuve-Bargemont any moral grounds for condemning it, since he, like Dunoyer, believed it was the best that could be hoped for and that liberty (that is, the liberty to dispose of oneself and one's property in the marketplace) was worth certain sacrifices.

This was doubtless Villermé's aim from the outset, for there are indications that he construed his evidence in such a way as to make that position plausible. One of the clearest cases of this kind of construction of evidence, and one in which the inadequacies of Villermé's approach are quite apparent, is his discussion of wages and living costs in the Lille–Roubaix area.

For the whole Lille area, Villermé reports the following salary levels in spinning mills:[34]

Cotton (francs per day)		Wool (francs per day)	
Men	2.50–3.00	Men	2.50–3.50
Women (first class)	1.00–1.75	Piecers (paid by	
Women (second class)	.75–1.25	their spinners)	1.10–1.30
Children	.50– .60	Combers	1.50–2.50
		Children of both sexes	
		in mechanical	
		combing	.50–1.50

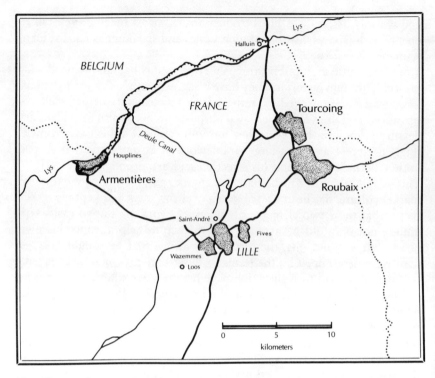

The Lille area, showing suburban and regional textile towns. Agglomerations and principal connecting roads drawn to approximate mid nineteenth-century conditions.

Calico weavers, he says, earn 1.50 francs per day and the women who help them, .40 to .60 francs per day.[35] For the individual towns, he provides more specific information as he discusses each in turn. In Lille, in 1835, men (in the textile trade) earned from 25 to 35 or 40 sous, on average about 30 sous. The strongest men could earn from 35 to 50 sous, most about 40 to 45; the most intelligent or skilled men could earn about 45 sous to 6 francs, but most earned about 3 francs.[36] Good assiduous women could earn 20 to 40 sous a day, others only 12 to 20; adolescents earned 12 to 25 sous. (One sou equals 5 centimes.)

Thus in Lille a three-member household with all members working, he concludes, could earn about 915 francs per year – assuming a year of 300 work days, with the head of the household earning 1.50 francs per day, his wife earning 1 franc per day, and a child earning .55 francs per day. But food and rent alone would cost this family 798 francs.[37] Villermé goes on to discuss how he arrived at this latter figure for basic living costs, and having done so his demonstration is complete. He is not quite as simplistic as Villeneuve-Bargemont (whose data, by the way, Villermé does not cite because of what he calls the typographical errors in it); Villermé realizes that the mere proximity of the figure 798 francs with the figure 915 francs is dramatic enough to make his case; only 117 francs – less than 35 centimes a day – are left over for clothes, medical expenses, drink, and entertainment, not to mention savings. Thus when Villermé says three pages later that "The workers of Lille are quite often deprived of a bare minimum," the reader is fully prepared to accept this statement as self-evident.

But already the reader has been taken on a dizzying dance through a maze of figures switching back and forth unpredictably from francs and centimes to sous out of which a conclusion has appeared that does not follow at all from the evidence presented. Who, after all, is Villermé talking about in Lille if not laborers in cotton spinning mills, of which there were over fifty by 1835? Yet according to his own figures on such mills in the area, the very minimum that a man, woman and child working in such a mill could have earned was, respectively, 2.50 francs per day, .75 francs per day, and .50 francs per day – in other words, 1,125 francs per year.[38] This minimum possible yearly income is 327 francs above what food and rent would have cost them, according to Villermé. Figures from the middle of the ranges he reports yield an income of 1,380 francs per year; the top income of the three people would have been 1,605 francs per year. Villermé assumed for calculating the family budget that the average man in the Lille textile trade earned only 1.50 francs per day. But who was this man, if not a mule spinner? Does he mean to imply that mule spinners in Lille earned less than the minimum he reported for the Lille area as a whole? But there were so many cotton mills in the town itself, surely they would have dragged the reported range down to their level. Does he mean to imply that the vast majority of Lille textile laborers were domestic weavers? But domestic weaving had been reduced to a very small number of looms in Lille by this time. Villermé reports that the *filtiers* of Lille, makers of sewing thread, earned only 1.50 francs per day; and it is true that since the eighteenth century the trade of *filtier* had fallen on bad times.[39] But there were simply not enough of them to establish a Lille-wide average; there were not more than six hundred of them in the town while the total number of mule spinners was definitely in excess of fifteen hundred.

When Villermé turns to Roubaix, strangely, he regales it with the opposite treatment; instead of straining to produce a low average wage, he pretends to find much higher average incomes there. In Roubaix, reports Villermé, a man whose work requires force earns 2 to 3 francs a day, a day laborer earns 30 to 35 sous (again the unit shifting), a weaver earns 30 sous. A three-member family in Roubaix needs 828 francs for food and rent, slightly higher than in Lille. But, if one assumes that all three work, the man earning 2.25 francs per day, the woman .90 francs

153

and the child .30 francs, then annual income for this average household is 1,035 francs, providing a surplus of 207 francs over bare sufficiency. And, indeed, Villermé remarks, there is a certain ease apparent in the town, by comparison with Lille.[40]

Again, similar internal problems arise. It is true that most of the region's wool spinning mills were being built in Roubaix during the 1830s; hence, mule spinners in Roubaix, if one follows the overall figures for the region provided by Villermé, would have earned on average more than in Lille. But in Roubaix mule spinners were in the minority, not the majority as in Lille. By far the great bulk of textile laborers in Roubaix and its dependent villages were the twenty thousand weavers (and their families) who worked for the accounts of Roubaix merchant manufacturers, weaving *stoffs*, *lastings*, some calicoes, cotton-silk blends, jacquard-brocades and other specialty items. Villermé put their average daily earnings at 30 sous, 1.50 francs, not 2.25 francs. What group was large enough for their earnings to have raised the Roubaix average up to 2.25 francs? The answer is that there was none. Here, again, Villermé makes no attempt to explain the relative sizes of the various groups he is reporting on, forcing us to take his word about the average he picks to work with when discussing living costs, yet rudimentary knowledge that is readily available from other sources on the sizes of these groups shows that Villermé is being far from rigorous.

Why did Villermé choose to proceed in this manner? Lille was still at this time a walled town; perhaps half the town's mills were located inside the walls, the remainder spilling out to the southeast and southwest into Wazemmes and Fives-Lille. It had always been crowded inside the walls, at least since the time the town had fallen definitively into French hands in 1667; and there had always been two or three poor neighborhoods in which drainage was bad, population dense, buildings narrow and damp.[41] Now, since 1828 or so, these areas were daily being covered over with a thin layer of soot from the nearby mill stacks. Villermé was given a tour through the narrowest alleys of one of these neighborhoods, the parish of Saint-Sauveur, and he was shown the rue des Etaques, so called because of the high numbers of poor who had died there of the plague in earlier centuries. (*Etaque* means "stake" in the local dialect; stakes were placed in front of all households stricken by the plague to warn visitors away.)[42] Roubaix, on the other hand, a mere village in 1750, now a jumbled collection of brick houses and mills that faded imperceptibly into its surrounding bourgs, farms, and hamlets, did not look nearly so bad to the casual eye. It appears from Villermé's descriptions that he was struck by the contrast, that these variations in appearance alone inspired his peculiar handling of wage evidence. If Roubaix looked better, it was because wages were a bit higher.

154

These same variations in appearance, in fact, guided him in the application of his carefully nuanced moral thesis to the laborers of the Lille-Roubaix area. Villermé's judgments about the moral condition of the laborers were designed to support two conclusions: (1) that sufficient income was a factor in, but far from being the sole determinant of, an upright existence, and (2) that vice and degradation spread by a kind of contagion of example wherever laborers were crowded together, whether in their living quarters or their workplace. Hence Villermé observes the following about Lille laborers.

> But if one sees in Lille a very considerable number of laborers like those who live in the rue des Etaques and nearby courtyards, a much larger number is far from presenting the [same] spectacle of misery and profound degradation ... even though they hardly earn better salaries. Clean, parsimonious, above all sober, they know how to find housing, clothing, better food, in a word, how better to provide for their needs with the same remuneration for a day's work ... Many choose their places of residence with a view to staying close to other laborers of good conduct, and so live in the Saint-André neighborhood [north, outside the walls] just as the *misérables* live in the Saint-Sauveur neighborhood and that of the rue des Etaques.[43]

These comments are in no way supported by what can be gleaned from contemporary police reports on the textile laborers of Lille. Lille mill hands both inside and outside the walls drank together, planned together, took action together, frequenting bars and living in tenements both in town and suburbs indifferently. To their eyes the color of the beer was the same on both sides of the wall.[44] But Villermé needed to make such a distinction in as plausible a way as possible, for it was the central aim of his study to show that existing wage levels were not so much a condemnation to a subhuman existence as a severe moral test, which those of strong character could survive. The greater space and cleanliness of the suburbs were just the sort of visual evidence that a casual observer might accept as proof of a distinct moral differentiation between two kinds of workers. Villermé could not resist turning this difference in appearance into evidence for a sweeping moral generalization that fit his own preconceptions perfectly.

Likewise at Roubaix where such differences in appearance were not in evidence, Villermé misconstrued the wage data to produce a higher average income that would account for the contrast with Lille's crowded slums. Not that Roubaix was entirely free from vice, in Villermé's view. The infectious influence of large workshops, he notes, had struck there in recent years as wool combers had been drawn into centralized establishments. Their conduct had deteriorated markedly since the days when they had all worked in their own homes. But of course nothing in Roubaix could compare with the vice, drunkenness, and promiscuity one saw inside Lille. In short, the moral test in Roubaix was less severe because wages were slightly higher, but the contagion of crowding there was nonetheless having a limited effect.

But these statements about Roubaix do not stand up either. Wool-combing machine operators were entirely different sorts of workers – often female – from hand combers (still numerous at this time); there would have been no continuity of personnel with centralization. There is evidence that middle-class newcomers to Roubaix had a habit of seeing vice where none existed. Two years after Villermé's book was published Roubaix was shaken by a series of riots when a new police commissioner tried to arrest as prostitutes two young girls on their way home from work. One of the girls was sick and died in a town jail cell two days later. The new commissioner, a protégé of the prefect, had to be withdrawn to save the town and the mills from destruction by an enraged laboring community. One imagines the reaction if Villermé had read his book before a group of local wool combers.[45]

Thousands over the years have been fooled by the abundant detail marshaled by Villermé, fooled into supposing that he was providing measured factual information about early industrial laborers. In the end, however, his evidence is no better (only more voluminous) than that of Morogues or Villeneuve-Bargemont or Penot. For Villermé, as for the others, it was enough to have been shown an impoverished neighborhood and some cotton mills within the same town. At once he perceived the dire, morally challenging impact of economic law. As for wage and living-cost figures, one could prove anything with them, provided one collected plenty of them, left out the necessary ingredients for the reader to figure the averages himself, and avoided "typographical errors." At bottom it remained, as in Penot's early study, a grandiose collection of indirect – and weak – correlations that demonstrated nothing.

One can hunt through all the studies of the period without finding an inquirer who claimed that mule spinners earned less than 2 francs per day. At the same time, there were very few who ever set up a family budget to prove that laborers' families were living at a subsistence level without placing the adult male's earnings at a level below 2 francs a day.[46] But if it was not the mule spinners working in these frightening and wondrous new enterprises who were being forced to live at what the theory dictated was a subsistence level, then whom indeed was all the concern about? It was here and only here that the fierce, technically advanced international competition was supposed to be concentrating its pressure.

Villermé in his general conclusion resisted the idea that perfect equilibrium was ever achieved in the labor market. Instead he saw a kind of two-stage oscillation in effect, although the outcome was nearly the same. In normal times, manufactures attracted workers and the presence of workers in turn stimulated more manufactures. Within the mass of proletarians thus formed a moral corruption developed. And in times of crisis "these proletarians, short of work, are prey to privations and sufferings all the greater in that, being numerous, they compete against each other [for jobs]."[47] Likewise he resisted the idea that such competition brought laborers to the bitter extreme. "Even if we admit," he said, "as some people affirm, that ... by the competition among workers their work is brought to the highest limits of human capacity and their salary reduced to the lowest possible level," even then, he insisted, direct legal intervention would do no good.[48] In reality, Villermé contended, things had not gone this far; there was still room for individual moral effort to have a real effect on individual well being. Further, there were a few small steps the government ought to take to improve matters. This was the reassuring message that Villermé's highly misleading budgets and descriptions were intended to convey. Empirical inquiry brought the reassuring message that neither side of the controversy was quite correct.

WAGES AND FAMILIES

But even this carefully nuanced view of the operation of the labor market fell wide of the mark. The gravest problem that any idea of a labor market confronts in the case of early textile laborers is that of price formation. For a market to operate there must be prices and they must be capable of being compared one with another. Published reports on laborers' wages always took the form of the average daily wage. But most of these figures show signs of haphazard formulation, for the simple reason that they had little relation to the real conditions of work. Here, for example, is a list of figures for the average daily wage of Mulhouse mule spinners from various sources of the 1830s and 40s.[49]

	Francs per day
Roman, 1834	2.00–3.00
Koechlin, 1834	2.38
Société industrielle de Mulhouse, 1835	2.00–3.00
Villermé, 1840	2.00–3.00
Penot, 1843	2.00–3.75
Dolfuss-Meig, 1848	2.65

Two of these figures stand out because they are not ranges and because they are not reported in round figures; they are in each case reports on an individual mill and thus appear to be averages worked out by means of some real clerical work on the pay books. The rest appear to be rough estimates. This is the best evidence and the only kind of evidence that survives on the mule spinners' wages in Mulhouse for this period, and similar series could be presented for town after town. Nor was it the case that individual mill owners' reports often showed signs of having been drawn from real calculations with the pay book. Quite the opposite is the case. Fouquet-Lemaître et Crepel reported that their spinners earned 3.00 francs per day when their own output reports suggested an average of 3.89 francs. Often one has the impression that the pay ranges provided are based on figures used to calculate ideal piece rates rather than on a calculation of actual earnings.[50] With the help of such figures, historians have argued with equal forcefulness that manufacturing wages went up in the course of the July Monarchy, and also that they went down.[51]

But even if accurate averages were available in abundance, there would remain the basic stumbling block that it is impossible to grasp the laborer's position by using the notion of an average daily wage. Many secondary wage earners were paid on a day basis in these early textile mills, and for them the notion has some meaning. But piecers' earnings were linked to the spinners' output, and many of the preparation workers continued to be paid by the piece, not the day, until well into the Third Republic period.[52] For the majority of laborers in textile mills, as for all domestic weavers and their assistants, pay was firmly linked to output. Spinners were not even compensated for time lost when their machines broke down. Hence earnings varied over a wide range, not only from week to week but from one laborer to the next. Villermé was aware of this problem, and made gestures in the direction of taking it into account with his talk of "strong" or "weak" laborers, but the gestures were purely rhetorical in the end, for he plowed on with his averages nonetheless.

A rough sketch of the mule spinner's actual earnings situation will suffice to show how distant was the notion of an average wage from shop-floor realities. In one mill in Rouen from which actual pay records have been preserved from a two-week pay period in early 1830, 23 spinners earned an average of 2.02 francs per day, a figure within the range of averages widely reported elsewhere in this period.[53] This figure, was, however, probably high for Rouen in early 1830, judging from other evidence available. The Rouen Conseil des prudhommes in 1835, for example, provided Villermé with a table to show the drop in average daily wages paid to mule spinners during the slump of 1827–32; as is so common elsewhere, the figures represent ranges only.[54]

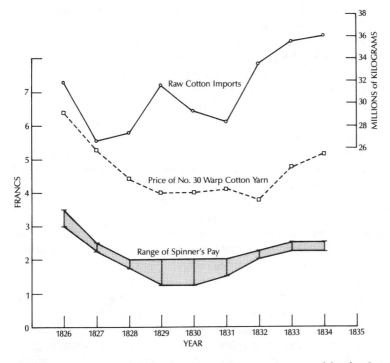

Figure 6. Comparison of spinners' average daily wage as reported by the Conseil des prudhommes of Rouen during the crisis of 1827–32 with raw cotton imports and prices of No. 30 warp cotton yarn.

1826	3.00–3.50 francs	1830	1.25–2.00
1827	2.25–2.50	1831	1.50–2.00
1828	1.75–2.00	1832	2.00–2.25
1829	1.25–2.00	1833	2.25–2.50
		1834	2.25–2.50

If these figures are even roughly accurate, it appears that mill owners in Rouen during the slump simply passed through drops in yarn prices on the open market, adjusting their piece rates in proportion. Figure 6 shows a very tight fit between trends in yarn prices and average wages in Rouen. Only the lower end of the mule spinners' pay ranges do not match the movement of prices; the upper ends fit quite well, the lower ends drop more than they should. But the Conseil des prudhommes explained that these lower ends in 1828–30 were set to reflect the fact that many mills did not work full weeks all year long. (Therefore they would not reflect changes in rates paid per kilogram.) This series of rough approximations, rare in that it purports to trace changes over a period of years, suggests that mill owners set the rate that they paid for yarn in their mills at some fixed percentage of the rates they received for their yarn in the open market. Hence, no spinner could count on earning any particular average daily wage over a year period. He had to hope that prices held in the marketplace and accept cuts in rates if they did not.

The instability and uncertainty of such cyclical market trends were overshadowed by vast variations in earnings from week to week, from one mule jenny to the next, and from one spinner to the next. The pay records of the Rouen mill from early 1830 show that mule spinners earned over a two-week period from a low of 5.50 francs to a high of 33.05 francs. In terms of daily averages, this was from a low of .46 francs per day to a high of 2.75 francs per day; that is, only half of the spinners earned amounts in the near neighborhood of the overall average of 2.02 francs per day. Some of the causes of these variations may be guessed at. A "Dutuit senior," who earned only 12.05 francs during the two weeks in question, may have been getting on in years. (His son, listed as working on another machine, earned 24.50 francs.) Another spinner was granted a supplement of 2 centimes per kilogram because of problems with his rollers. (That this supplement actually made up the difference between his actual earnings and his usual earnings on a machine in good order is doubtful; even with the supplement his average for the two weeks was only 1.75 francs per day.) Problems with machinery or with raw materials could, from week to week, seriously lower one's earnings and one's expectation of output changed with age. Arthritis in arms or fingers, for example, would have had serious, immediate effects on one's level of output.

Finally, the specific kind of yarn one was assigned to spin could be more or less lucrative. Rates for yarn in this as in other Rouen establishments in 1830 changed in simple numerical series with the number of yarn in question (with a 2 centime allowance added for those who passed their "task" limit), as follows:

No. 14 yarn	14–16 centimes per kg
No. 18 yarn	19
No. 26 yarn	26
No. 28 yarn	28–30
No. 30 yarn	30–32

Prices set this way paid, in effect, about one centime for every two thousand meters of yarn no matter what grade, since one kilogram of

No. 14 yarn was 28,000 meters long, of No. 18 yarn, 36,000 meters long, and so on. Hence equal success in keeping the jenny running in theory resulted in equal pay – except that in practice a No. 30 yarn had the strongest rovings and machines producing the coarsest grades were usually set at slightly faster speeds.[55] Even with such an apparently fair rate structure, there was always a grade that was actually the most lucrative to work on that varied from shop to shop. On fine yarns of No. 40 and above, things were even more complex because it was necessary to give added twist – more twist the finer the yarn. Hence *tarifs* in centers of fine-yarn production did not follow simple numerical progressions, as in the following example from Tourcoing in 1833:[56]

No. 40 yarn	48 centimes per kg
No. 45 yarn	55
No. 50 yarn	63
No. 55 yarn	71
No. 60 yarn	80
No. 65 yarn	91
No. 70 yarn	1.02 francs

The rate went up more rapidly than the number to compensate for the extra twist time. But again extra twist time was often at the discretion of the spinner; those who knew how to put out good yarn with less twist time were in a position to profit from spinning higher numbers.[57]

In sum, for any individual, a host of factors determined his pay level in any given two-week period, all were variable, only some were partially under his control: (1) his own age and experience, (2) the grade of yarn he was assigned to produce, (3) the state of his machinery and raw material, (4) the mill owner's readiness to pass through fluctuations in open–market yarn prices by altering his own rates, and therefore, as well, (5) the state of the cotton trade in general. It would be possible to go on listing other such variables; water-powered mills, for example, in many regions were forced to work only part time during one season of the year because there was not enough water pressure to run all the machines.[58] Part-time work was also a common recourse of mill owners when yarn prices took sudden, short-term dips, or when their own order backlogs fell to low levels: This was another aspect of the habit of immediately passing through to mule spinners even the slightest fluctuations in market conditions, a habit that reinforced the spinners' impression that they were in some sense independent operators, not wage laborers.[59] The average daily wage of a spinner in normal conditions would have been for any individual spinner an abstraction so distant from, and so irrelevant to, his own day-to-day experience as to invite ridicule.

Depending on the particular, volatile combination of circumstances he faced, the spinner could expect to earn anywhere from .65 francs to 3.50 francs per day (equivalent to from 195 to 1,050 francs per year); this was a range so wide as to have only the vaguest of relations to his subsistence needs. And on this score alone, it amounted to quite a serious distortion to apply to the real situation of the mule spinner the simplistic concepts of a labor market and of the subsistence-level wage as the natural equilibrium price for labor. The mule spinner's own subsistence needs, in fact, were equally likely to vary over a wide range during his life time, depending in large measure on his family situation.[60] Even if all mule spinners had earned on average enough income to support whole families, the variability alone of their real earnings from week to week would have required that other members of the family work to provide some insurance against a bad week. Even though in many years and in many towns, according to Villermé's own evidence, mule spinners did earn enough for a family of four to get by on (for example, in Rouen in 1826, according to the Conseil des prudhommes' figures), nonetheless available evidence indicates a general expectation among them that other family members should contribute whenever possible. Mule spinners' backgrounds, those that can be traced, were usually in domestic textiles, where the production process had always involved family collaboration.[61]

Cultural presuppositions inherited from the eighteenth century about the value of labor – what Hobsbawm has called "custom" in wage determination – had a powerful influence on the use of labor in the textile industry.[62] In textile towns, demand for women and children was always high; Tilly and Scott have shown this to be a common feature of mill towns in both France and England in the nineteenth century.[63] But women's wages never rose above a level roughly 50 percent that of adult males in the same industry, and children earned somewhat less. The fact is that demand was high for these categories of laborers precisely because price was unresponsive to demand pressures. The cultural presupposition that women and children's labor was far less valuable than an adult male's put an artificial ceiling on their wages. Demand had little effect on price, a fact which in turn stimulated demand. Women and children were valuable because they did not value themselves. Mill owners, as a result, could never hire enough of them. This is one reason mule spinners were required to find and pay their own piecers, relieving the owner of the always difficult task of finding children.[64] Diverse wage expectations, insofar as any labor market can be said to have existed, would have fractured it into separate spheres in which the different levels of pay for different categories of labor – male, female, child – had no mutual impact on each other.

Because the undervaluation of women and children made them so valuable, and because the lack of relation between mule spinners' variable earnings and their subsistence needs (also variable) forced them to depend on supplementary earnings of other family members, mill owners tended to hire by family, that is, to offer jobs to several family members at a time. For the mule spinner himself, the choice of piecer where possible would be aimed, as well, at keeping the piecer's income in the family (as well as at training one of his own children to the trade). In two instances where lists of employees are available, one from 1830, one from 1853, from 40 to 60 percent of spinning-mill laborers were related to at least one other laborer at the same mill.[65]

The same cultural presupposition that froze women's and children's earnings at one half or less those of adult males dictated that there be a strict division of labor by sex and age in the mills. This division of labor was maintained in spite of the fact that only one or two tasks in the mill required any physical strength. One of these was *battage*, beating or opening of the raw cotton; it was usually assigned to vigorous young males. Cleaning, carding, and stretching were all carried out by women and girls with male foremen and mechanics (one per department at most) at watch.[66] Carpentry, machine maintenance, and steam-engine operation were, as tasks requiring special training, exclusive preserves of males. Stock movement was consigned to low-paid *hommes de peine*. Mule spinners were all adult males, the youngest being from 16 to 18, while piecers and bobbin fetchers might be boys, girls, or if a spinner could find no child or adolescent to his liking among kin or friends, even adult women.

This established proportions of roughly one third each of men, women, and children. Said one mill owner in 1834, "It's about one third of each kind – in the same proportion as nature makes them."[67] Two hundred ten cotton spinning mills in the department of the Seine-Inférieure in 1847 were reported to provide work for 6,224 men, 6,628 women, and 5,596 children under 16.[68] A breakdown of laborers in three large Rouen-area mills in 1850 according to age, sex, and marital status is available, and is shown in Table 5.[69]

Despite marked variation from one mill to the next, certain overall features stand out: (1) the relatively small number of married women, doubtless due to a preference to care for the home once there was another old enough to work;[70] (2) the greater number of unmarried women than unmarried men, perhaps reflecting an influx into the mills of young women who wanted savings for a small dowry;[71] (3) the scarcity of children under 12; (4) the presence, apart from these exceptions, of laborers of all ages and marital statuses in proportions not very far from those one would expect in the population of a community. Only the extremes, the very old and the very young, are missing.

163

Table 5. *Age, sex, and marital status of workers in three Rouen-area mills.*

| | Married | | Unmarried | | Widowed | | Under twelve | | Total |
	Men	Women	Men	Women	Men	Women	Boys	Girls	
Rouen mill	131	71	71	165	4	16	16	8	482
Déville mill	128	34	115	32	9	2	33	44	397
Bondeville mill	130	139	79	149	15	20	60	20	612
Total	389	244	265	346	28	38	109	72	1,491

These extremes, however, may have been there and not been counted. Two reports, one from Lille in 1837 and one from Mulhouse in 1835, speak of women bringing new-born infants to the mills with them, clubbing together, and hiring nurses to watch the infants in a corner of the shop.[72] A list of laborers at a Tourcoing mill in 1853 includes a *surveillant*, age 58, living alone, who was a disabled veteran, and who apparently watched infants, not laborers, since he was only paid .60 francs per day. The same mill employed a "*commissionnaire*," aged 77, who earned .75 centimes a day; perhaps he fetched food and drink for laborers.[73]

In short, a whole human community had moved into these mills, lock, stock and barrel, distributed tasks as best as possible according to its customary notions of what was male, what female work (including the novel category of housework, now that production of commodities was moved out of the household), and accepted pay at customary levels and in customary forms (that is, in the form of prices for goods produced). With the possible exception of young single women without other options for accumulating savings, it is not likely that members of families whose principal means of support lay outside the textile trade sought work regularly within spinning mills. Mill hands, even among laborers as a whole, were set apart to a certain extent, lived a life among themselves, followed their own routines, and had their own standards. Although they were not paid as much as skilled artisans in the traditional crafts, mule spinners practiced an art that took very special skills and long experience; nor was theirs the only task of this kind in the mills. The description Oger provides in his technical manual of 1839 for the task of feeding opened fiber into beating machines (universally a female assignment), shows that it took great care and application to get the fiber laid out evenly and thickly across the conveyor belt.[74] Long practice and aptitude at concentrating through steady periods of time so as never to let the conveyor belt go empty were necessary. One could not casually enter or casually leave such professions. Thus, even though the rate of relatedness in individual mills was only 40 to 60 percent, if all the mills of a particular town could have been measured – and over time so as to take into account the family life cycle – this percentage would doubtless have been much higher, how much is impossible to say.[75]

This engulfing of a whole community by the mills is perhaps one reason that early work rules speak with greater firmness of (and impose higher fines for), talking, fighting, or tarrying at others' workplaces than they do of arriving late to work or leaving early. The difficulty was not getting this community to come to work, but limiting the time devoted to community life once all were at work. Norbert Truquin in his autobiography talks of working in an Amiens spinning mill in this period as a not altogether unpleasant experience. The most difficult part for him was getting out of bed and to the mill on time in the morning. Once inside, however,

> the worker found himself in good company. The foremen in those days were less concerned about quantity than quality. Earnings were ten francs a week, sometimes twenty. The agreed-on prices [for yarn] were paid without comment. When the foreman was not around, we told stories, talked about plays; some fellows set up a pulpit and pretended to preach; the time passed agreeably.[76]

Truquin provides an idea of what laborers did for the 40 percent of time at work that they were not operating their machines, and of how laborers tolerated 13-hour days during those precious boom periods when the mills sold all the yarn they could make. Life went on in the mills, real recognizable human social life.[77]

Of course Truquin's mill was a new one, well ventilated and well heated. One ought not to suppose that all establishments were so well set up. Heat, dampness, dust, and stench, as many witnesses testify, were often overpowering to the uninitiated and dangerous to the health of long-term employees. The point is not that the mills were physically pleasant but that, as human institutions, they were shaped more by the standards of the laboring community than by the discipline of the owners. The division of labor, the levels of pay, and the pace of work were all attuned to centuries-old popular custom and current collective needs.

The industry, with its violent growing pains, was even not yet able entirely to liberate its workforce from that "economy of makeshift," as Olwen Hufton has called it, that the laboring poor had always known before.[78] Mills went on short time, closed, or went bankrupt so frequently that it was always necessary to be prepared to find temporary work outside the trade.[79] (Here is another reason why it is impossible to analyze mill pay rates in terms of subsistence needs.) The industry's crisis years between 1820 and 1850 were almost as numerous as its boom years; for 13 out of these 30 years (1827–32, 1837, 1839–41, 1846–50), with a precarious or disastrous yarn market facing mill operators, there was no way for any mill hand to plan on an average daily income, since no one knew what would happen from week to week, and every fluctuation in demand had a direct and immediate impact on the laborers' earnings.[80] With their needs varying widely according to their ages and the makeup of their households, and their individual earnings varying widely according to the caprice of the machine, the skill and luck of the laborer, and the state of the industry as a whole, it is difficult to imagine how laborers managed to piece together a formula for survival in these decades. Doubtless, their lives went from comfort to penury and back with relative frequency, just as their workdays went from slow, short-time languor to frenzied boom-time activity according to the flow of orders and according to whether it was Monday or Friday. It is impossible to know what strategies they used to cope with such experiences because the surviving documents are impregnated with abstractions – with averages and yearly budgets that add up and cancel each other out to the last centime.

There was certainly a kind of competition over pay levels. During the ministerial inquiry into the textile industry in 1834, mill owners and merchant manufacturers from different centers reported average daily wage levels, and there was much discussion of their variations from center to center and of the quality of local spinners and weavers. It was widely believed that the West was worse off than the East, that Normandy got less work out of its spinners and weavers than the Nord or the Marne or the Aisne departments, that Alsatian laborers were the cheapest and best of all. A merchant manufacturer from Tarare complained that local weavers were all switching to silk since fine cottons no longer paid well enough.[81] A Lille mill owner complained that new spinning capacity was going to Alsace because of the better labor available there.[82] The extent to which any of these impressions were true is extremely difficult to judge. Sanson-Daviller tried to import spinners from Alsace to see if they were better, but they refused to come. Some German workers the firm recruited, it was found, in their restless and uprooted state performed very poorly.[83] The test was inconclusive. The fact that the test was carried out at all shows how little owners understood that their laborers were not atomized individual sellers of labor but members of communities. Evidence already cited here, in any case, suggests that mule spinners in Alsace were paid more, not less, than their Norman colleagues. All the evidence currently available on the origins of recruits to spinning mills shows, in addition, that northern centers drew almost exclusively on their own hinterlands.[84] Long-distance migration was rare. Even the Flemish-speaking immigrants to Lille and Roubaix came from the linen-producing region in the immediate vicinity.[85]

There was, nonetheless, pressure on the owners to equalize pay levels throughout the industry; if wages in their own center were known to be high, new investment would be attracted elsewhere. In this limited sense there was some wage competition on the national level and a kind of competitive pressure to even wage levels out across the whole country. The one single development that had surely resulted from regional pay differentials was the flight of cotton spinning mills from the Paris area in the early 1820s; Paris pay levels had been double those of other towns, and the steadily dropping yarn prices of the Restoration soon induced Paris operators to liquidate or transfer.[86] It seems likely that more than a 50 percent difference was enough to scare away new investors, more than a 100 percent difference enough to induce operators to relocate. This is a very far cry from the kind of competition that observers assumed to exist, however.

There were other phenomena one could point to that were demonstrably the result of competition as well. Defective machinery or raw material, difficult foremen, or steep fines could lead to the departure of laborers. Laborers often quit when piece rates were lowered; in boom periods they could be attracted away by higher rates in neighboring mills.[87] Monetary and nonmonetary factors thus observably affected some laborer decisions aimed at improving their lot. It was easy to assume that gain was the underlying motive of their behavior and that they were now free to pursue gain by any and all means. Mill owners and social investigators could thus talk as if the existence of a labor market were a self-evident fact. If average-daily-wage figures were only approximations of the calculations that laborers carried out in their own heads, nonetheless some such calculation was going on and approximations were good enough for general purposes.

But it was not so easy for laborers nor for any human beings to reduce all the elements of life to a single quantitative dimension. This feat was all the more difficult when the one quantity that was sure and fixed in value, money, came in such fitful spurts and starts, and in amounts varying arbitrarily according to age, sex, and family status. The solidarity of family units was a fundamental necessity under the circumstances and the larger kin and friendship networks that grew up in mill, bar, and neighborhood streets were extremely valuable both to material survival and to a secure sense of identity. Mobility was highly restricted by these things; mill owners thereby gained a certain power over those whose community and social identity were linked together through work as their employees. Human beings have other things to do besides earn; making collective identity is work in its own right, living without one is impossible. This issue will be taken up further in Chapter 9. It is enough to say here that there was no clear price for labor; that there was no developed way of measuring it; that family units were the units of subsistence not individual earners, so there was no simple way of comparing earnings to needs; that valuable human relationships were cultivated and worked out inside and outside of mills damping price sensitivity even further; that carefully nurtured skills and habits were the key to survival in the mills and could not be jettisoned lightly once formed; that long-distance migration could be extremely painful and disorienting. In short, there was no market for labor, no way for price to balance supply against demand. (Of course it is impossible to prove this – or to disprove it.)

Visions of subsistence

These things speak clearly of the immaturity of industrial capitalism in this period. The inability to formulate what exactly labor was or how to control it except through maintaining the old habits of independence, the family-based division of labor, the ferocious inefficiencies of the yarn and cloth markets, the credit-starved operating strategies of mill owners – all of these factors may be attributed to the immaturity of a system of thinking about production that was riddled with unseen contradictions that only generations of experience have managed somewhat to even out. But the investigators unhesitatingly construed all of these features of immaturity (insofar as they noticed them) as evils inherent in the proper operation of the laws of supply and demand, or even more wrongly as inherent in the extreme and unrestricted operation of these laws.

Along with the somber budgets and average daily wage information, two facets of mill operation – the long hours of "normal" times, and the employment of women and children – attracted the most attention among investigators. Both were deemed to be the result of the ruthless encroachment of the labor market upon two basic moral prerequisites of truly human life – a minimum of time for leisure, learning, and reflection on the one hand and the proper relation of parent and child on the other. Investigators saw unrestricted trade in labor as being responsible for the destruction of human community among the laborers, believing that work in the mills was as they had witnessed it on their inspection tours, constant, unremitting tedium at the machines. In fact, lack of control over labor and the absence of a functioning labor market had led to the incorporation of community into the mills, not its destruction.

In the 1830s, a growing number of mill owners, doctors, investigators, and legislators began calling for some legal limits to be placed on the exchange of labor. Only in this way could a moral minimum of human social life be ensured for the laborers. Many mill owners pleaded their own inability to accept self-imposed limits, due to the danger of competition. As early as 1827, during the first year of existence of the Industrial Society of Mulhouse, one of its members, a mill owner from Guebwiller named J.-J. Bourcart, called on the Society to support legal limits on the hours that children under 16 could work each day. He argued that laborers in the mills produced more in 12 hours than in 15, that the second generation of mill hands might turn out to be both feeble and depraved if action were not taken. He sounded the note of self-interest loudly. If the working-class youth were protected, then "the master would have a wide selection of robust workers, workers more intelligent and easier to guide. France would have if necessary *real men* to defend the homeland [emphasis in original]."[88]

A committee was formed to study his proposal. Judging from its later action, this committee was split on the issue; they reported back to the Society that they were strongly in favor of some amelioration of the conditions of laboring children, but felt themselves incompetent to judge whether the law could rightly interfere with paternal authority or the right of contract. M. Dunoyer was called in for advice, and saw no difficulty in the issue of limiting a child's labor since there were already numerous laws that limited and defined paternal authority. Bourcart therefore put the question to the Society in December 1828, and Zickel brought it up again in January 1829. Two sessions of heated discussion resulted. At one, a mill owner named Reber delivered a strong address, claiming that the poor state of the laborers was due to conditions un-related to work, that is, to food, habitation, and "the debauchery of the young." Another owner named Kestner-Rigau countered heatedly that work, cotton dust, the "emanations" of other bodies, and the mixture of both sexes together in the workrooms could not fail to have ill effects on the health and morality of children. But the motion to petition the Chamber of Deputies for a law limiting the employment of children in industry was defeated by a narrow margin.[89]

The issue did not come up again before the Society until 1833, a more prosperous year for the industry, and this time the Society came out squarely in favor of a law limiting the labor of children.[90] From this point on, the movement for a child-labor law slowly gathered momentum. Villermé, during his first tour of research in 1835, was won over to the idea. It fit perfectly with his own approach to the problem of the condition of laborers in the textile industry: A moderate reform that would limit the most damaging features of competition among laborers was just the sort of recommendation that he might propose as a result of his extensive investigation. Before the Academy of Moral and Political Sciences of the Institut in 1837, he delivered a strong speech in favor of such a law.[91] The same year a bill was introduced into the Chamber of Deputies, and a large inquiry was launched by the Bureau of Manufactures into the state of children in industry. It consisted, needless to say, of a question-naire sent out to Chambers of Commerce, Conseils des prudhommes, and other interested bodies. The issue was heatedly discussed in news-papers and the Chamber and within administrative bodies, but the bill did not win enough support to pass. In 1840, another effort was launched and this time it was successful, resulting in the passage in March 1841 of a law limiting hours of work for children under 16 working in shops with over 20 employees (that is, a slim minority of all working children) and requiring them to receive some rudimentary instruction in reading, arithmetic, and religion. Voluntary local councils were to oversee its enforcement.[92]

Although this law was never effectively enforced, its passage was a signal event. For the first time since the abolition of guilds a half-century before in 1791, the government had taken it upon itself to outlaw trade in certain kinds of labor. The dramatic difference between this new kind of regulation and the old underscores how profoundly French culture had changed in the intervening years. Before, markets had been controlled in order that they serve as the foundation for orderly trade communities who produced in their own lives and in their wares that quality that was appropriate to them. Now, trade in the labor of children was being limited for fear of its effects on the moral and physical state of laborers. The reason that children were singled out in this way may be read in the pages of Dunoyer or of any writer who reviewed the ideas of Malthus and Ricardo for the French in these years. It was among the children that the self-reinforcing cycle of impoverishment first took hold, in Dunoyer's view. Because their parents could afford no instruction, the children's virtues, and hence their liberty (as if such things were a function of formal instruction) were never developed; hence they were doomed to fall into the same marasma of poverty as their parents had. The supporters of the law wished to intervene in this cycle to give the children at least a chance of escape, so that their status, like that of all the superior classes in "industrial society," could be viewed as the outcome of a fair competitive test showing who was most appropriate to fill each social function. Competition was to be adjusted in order to make it spur on, not dampen, ambition and advancement.

The law passed within months of the appearance of Villermé's masterpiece, the *Description of the Physical and Moral Condition of Workers in the Cotton, Wool, and Silk Industries* in two volumes in 1840. In its final form, the work benefited richly from the wide-ranging discussions and investigations set under way by the 10-year-long debate that preceded the law's adoption. One of the most important aspects of this work, and of the long debate that preceded it – apart from the gathering of a wealth of misconstrued statistical evidence on hours and wages – is that it gave concrete literary form to a vision of the working class, backed by the authority of eyewitness accounts, that fit perfectly with the presuppositions about unregulated trade in labor that had been widely disseminated since the 1820s. This concrete literary form depended on two main devices: First, the use of moral indignation as a means of avoiding comparison of contradictory evidence, and second, the use of what one might call breakthrough passages of rhapsodic moral and physical disgust at some witnessed condition or event. Both devices had already been used so often by 1840 that they were in danger of becoming tiresome clichés, had Villermé not had sufficient literary skill to reinvigorate them. Because he did, however, his work gave them, in a sense, a definitive form to which all future practitioners of the art were required to turn.

The first device is easier to explain and easier to see through. Here are three examples from Villermé's work: (1) In different parts of the work, Villermé deplores the following facets of work in the mills without ever bringing them together to look at them in a single context: He deplores the fact that laborers work 13.5-hour days with only an hour and a half for breaks. He deplores the fact that laborers do not come to work on Monday, or else take themselves off to bars to drink and talk together for the afternoon. He deplores the fact that laborers must often work less than 13.5 hours due to slumps in the industry.[93] Here is one set of facts that ought to have been brought together for comparison at some point. (2) Villermé deplores the fact that laborers spend so much time in bars they have little or none left for family life. He deplores the fact that some of their family life is carried on in bars, for even the women come and daughters' marriages may even be arranged there.[94] These facts Villermé does present together, but his own attitude toward working-class bars does not allow him to see the obvious. For Villermé, family life carried on in bars was not family life. (3) Villermé imports a failure of comparison into his work when he repeats verbatim the Bureau of Manufactures' conclusion of 1837 that from one-tenth to one-half of all children in the mills work with their own parents but, usually, about a third do.[95] Following the Bureau, he points out that sometimes, out of a spirit of calculation, parents place their children in other mills so that the whole family cannot be laid off at once if the mill closes, but that in general children are better off when they work with their own parents. In making these statements, the Bureau of Manufactures and Villermé were insisting on seeing coherence in evidence that had no coherence. In response to the Bureau's questionnaire on the use of children in industry, bodies in the northern textile centers had provided a chorus of contradictory opinions, all clearly based on rough impressions. On the question how often children worked with their own parents as piecers or bobbin-fetchers, the Lille Conseil des prudhommes, for example, had insisted that parents prefer to place them with others because "when [the children] behave poorly and disobey, they fear they might give vent to their anger and be carried away, which they would not do with the children of others." The Lille Chamber of Commerce was at the same moment remarking that parents bring their children with them into the mills almost from the time they are old enough to walk; and the Roubaix Consultative Chamber was observing that children ordinarily worked under their parents' eyes, except where circumstances forced the parents to place them in a different mill. The Industrial Society of Mulhouse insisted that manufacturers did not want to use the children, but the laborers insisted on bringing them along and had large families solely out of a spirit of "deplorable speculation" on their children's earning power. The General Council of the Seine-Inférieure department said that in those places where the number of mills created sufficient competition for children to allow parents to decide where to place them, they preferred to keep them at their sides. In the same department, the Société libre of Rouen claimed that in only one in eight cases in Rouen (where there were over fifty mills) did parent and child work together, while the Consultative Chamber of Bolbec (where only one or two mills existed) insisted that all children in the mills worked with their parents. The Consultative Chamber of Elbeuf had claimed that at most one-fourth of the children worked with their own parents, because in general parents wisely sought to place them in other mills, lest everyone in the family lose his job at the same time.[96]

One could go on for pages citing this kind of evidence from the Bureau's files; every possible combination of judgment is amply represented: (1) Parents do employ their own children out of a spirit of calculation; (2) They place them in other mills out of a spirit of calculation; (3) They keep them at their sides out of concern for their well-being; (4) They place them elsewhere out of a concern for their well-being. Parents are alternatively depicted as constrained by economic necessity and as basely participating in the exploitation of children. Strangest of all, these manifold contradictory opinions, many from bodies in the same towns, gave rise to not the slightest controversy and were never remarked upon as such by the Bureau of Manufactures which, on this and many other points, concocted at its caprice a general statement made up of bits and pieces of all these discordant voices. Villermé had toured these towns and posed the same questions to the same officials; he was given full access to the Bureau's files; but in his overall statement he chose to echo word for word the utterly gratuitous conclusions of the Bureau.[97] In this way, he was able to deplore the fact that for the majority of children in the mills, who – he had decided – did not work for their own parents, conditions were not as good as they might be. This was the sort of moderate dissatisfaction that Villermé preferred to arrive at on all such questions.

As for the reality that all these contradictory statements purported to be about, there is unfortunately no better source extant for this period than these statements. The one or two cases where lists of employees have been preserved do not include most of the children, since they were considered to be directly employed by the spinners themselves. The reader is as well equipped as this researcher to attempt to make some sense out of all that was said on this issue. On a range of other issues about conditions in the mills, perplexity would be as great if there were space here to review all the things that were said. In the great rush to deplore the state of the laborers no one much cared how this state was actually described so long as, in each person's opinion, something deplorable was pointed out. This is why all these diverse generalizations, whether on the issue of bars, or hours of work, or of child labor, were never brought together and compared by Villermé or his contemporaries. All equally well served the purpose; all provided something to which one could attach one's disapproval. Whether laborers were seen as conniving in their own degradation or as victims of circumstance, all agreed that open competition for jobs had created a situation that was to one degree or another deplorable.

Villermé's other principal rhetorical strategy, the use of what could be called breakthrough passages, was also widely employed by other observers of the period, but few used them as skillfully as he. Here is a notable example. While in Lille, Villermé was given a tour of the Saint-Sauver district, which was, as mentioned in the section entitled Imaginary Budgets, the town's poorest neighborhood. He was shown the interior of one or two cellar dwellings there along the rue des Etaques, which he later described:

> Day arrives for them an hour later than for the others, and night an hour earlier.
>
> Their ordinary furnishings consist of, along with the tools of their trade, a sort of cupboard or plank of wood for storing food, a pot, a small terracotta cooker, a few dishes, small table, two or three bad chairs, and a dirty pallet made up entirely of some straw and a covering in tatters. I would prefer to add nothing to this list of hideous things which reveals at first glance the profound misery of the unfortunate inhabitants, but I must say that, in many of the beds I was just speaking of, I saw lying together individuals of both sexes and of very different ages, most without shirts and repulsively dirty. Father, mother, the aged, children, adults press upon each other there, pile up there. I stop ... The reader will complete the picture himself. But I warn him that if he wishes to keep it faithful, his imagination must not recoil before any of the disgusting mysteries that are accomplished on these impure beds in the bosom of obscurity and drunkenness.[98]

This passage is one of the most striking single examples of what had already by 1840 become a kind of literary commonplace. It should be evident by now why the term breakthrough passages is appropriate. The dry drone of statistics and of evidentiary discourse that makes up the bulk of Villermé's prose suddenly is set aside and replaced by an entirely different tone, self-consciously descriptive, rich in metaphor, poetic.

Similar shifts in tone have been noted by at least two other researchers on this period in literature from both England and France, and each of these researchers, in the service of quite different hypotheses, has claimed that the shift in tone is evidence that the observers in question had experienced a shock, had witnessed something that was difficult to master, which they expressed, in a sense, in spite of themselves in their writing. Both Steven Marcus and Louis Chevalier have argued that indeed something shocking, new, and frightening was happening in Europe's cities and boom towns in this period, and that observers were being forcibly seized by it and moved to record the change.[99]

There are at least two problems with this view. The first is that neither poverty nor slum neighborhoods were new, only larger. Nor was it new that they be observed and described, only the number of observers was greater; and the ends their descriptions were intended to serve were different. The rue des Etaques' very name revealed the agelessness of the misery it harbored; its presence within the walls of Lille in a state not very different from what it had been in Louis XIV's time was only distantly connected at best with the appearance of mechanized spinning mills there. The second objection, however, is even more telling; it is that such breakthrough passages had rapidly become stylized, even trite, as if investigators came to understand that they were expected. These passages often have little concrete detail to anchor them to a particular time or place. They float free, in the end, like pieces of standardized poetic ornamentation.

The vision of incest is one of the most frequently encountered of these literary commonplaces. Its origins go back at least to the mid-eighteenth century. In the late seventeenth century, according to Jean-Louis Flandrin, members of noble families were beginning for the first time to have separate apartments and to sleep each in his own bed, rather than all together in a single large bed in a central room with servants ranged around the wall. It was at this time, as well, according to Natalie Davis, that the literate classes were beginning to look upon the poor with new eyes, seeing them as creatures with alien thought processes and primitive social ties.[100] By the eighteenth century, then, it was possible for wealthy observers of the poor to be shocked at peasants' sleeping together, whole families to a single bed. Olwen Hufton has uncovered a number of instances in which concern over the danger of incest led observers to denounce the practice in the late eighteenth century.[101] But in the eye of early nineteenth-century observers, the one-room single-bed dwelling took on a new meaning; now it seemed to reveal the moral decay brought on by that insufficiency that competition imposed on the laborer. The image of the too-tight dwelling was enlisted (along with many others) to fill out a concrete vision of what it meant to live on a subsistence wage.

The Bureau of Manufactures' 1837 questionnaire gathered quite a number of these images of incest, none of which equalled Villermé's unique combination of vividness and discretion. There is this, for example, from the General Council of the Seine-Inférieure department: "It is principally in the towns that the laborer's family lives *pêle-mêle* in a single room in a miserable tenement [*masure*], humid, obscure, and unhealthy. Corruption passes like a contagion from parent to child in this habitual contact."

According to the Chamber of Commerce of Lille, the narrowness of their dwellings was the principal cause of the degeneracy of the laborers because it "often obliges the members of a single family to sleep *pêle-mêle* in a single room. The same lack of space causes the grave problem of encouraging women to leave their homes on days off and follow their men to the bars."

The Chamber of Commerce of Reims was in perfect accord on this point, seeing as one of the roots of working-class vice their "dwellings so often unhealthy and unclean in which they sleep *pêle-mêle* and in a single room, sometimes even with individuals from outside of the family, fathers, mothers, and children of both sexes."[102] This last instance is particularly noteworthy because it uses the same climactic word order as Villermé, piling up the kin terms together at the end. In all three of these 1837 passages, one notices the code word *pêle-mêle* that helped convey a sense of the personal disarray of the laborers. It had been much overused by 1840 and so was wisely avoided by Villermé.

The Lille mill owner T. Barrois, in his report to the Chamber of Commerce of Lille in 1837, surpassed all other authors of such passages in the directness of his language. To him, the greatest source of immorality for laborers living inside the city walls were "the dwellings so tight that the laborer often has only one room for himself and his family, where young children are witnesses of things that they ought not to know. This has grave consequences for the morality of young laborers. So much so that it is not rare that girls are deflowered by their brothers." In the margin of this report, a secretary at the Bureau of Manufactures remarked "If we publish this, we will have to delete this passage."[103] Barrois was certainly one of those mill owners who had entertained Villermé on his visit to Lille two years earlier; and his views may have induced Villermé to emphasize the danger of incest in his description of a Saint-Sauveur cellar rather than in descriptions of dwellings in other mill towns.

Not only the allusion to incest, but almost every detail of Villermé's inventory of the cellar had clear literary precedents. By 1840, there were a number of things one was expected to notice and to mention. Lack of light, inadequate beds, and the absence of cupboards had become favorite themes. This development is not difficult to trace. In 1834, two provincial doctors, Ange Guepin and E. Bonamy, published a statistical and moral description of Nantes in which the following description of working-class dwellings appeared:

> On either side of the alleyway, which slopes and is therefore beneath street level, there is a large, somber, icey room whose walls sweat with dirty condensation, which gets air from a semi-circular kind of window, two feet high at the top. Enter, if the fetid odor does not repulse you. But take care, for the uneven floor is neither paved nor tiled, or else the tiles are covered by such a thickness of filth that they cannot be seen. Here are two or three beds, worm-eaten and shaky and held together by pieces of string; a straw mattress, with its covering in tatters, seldom washed because it is the only one; sometimes there are sheets, sometimes a pillow – that is what is on the bed. As for cupboards, there is no need of them in such houses.[104]

The following description of a Mulhouse working-class dwelling, penned a year later by Achille Penot, is much shorter but reveals a definite affiliation:

> One pitiful straw mattress for the whole family, a tiny stove which serves all cooking needs, a box masquerading as a cupboard, a table and a few chairs.[105]

And Villermé himself echoed this description of the Mulhouse dwelling in 1840 as follows:

> A single, bad straw mattress for the whole family, a small stove which serves for cooking and for heating, a crate or large box masquerading as a cupboard, a table, two or three chairs, a bench, some dishes – these make up the normal furnishings of the rooms of the workers ...[106]

The similarities in the description of furnishings in these three passages are great enough to raise suspicion that the second two borrowed from the first. Doubtless to both Penot and Villermé, the evocation of the absent cupboard was an irresistible device for arousing pity in the reader. It is worth noting that Villermé could have written his passage on Mulhouse without ever having set foot in the town. Villermé's description of the Lille cellar followed a similar protocol, including the allusion to "a sort of cupboard or plank of wood for setting food on." These descriptions all worked by negation; the hidden reference was always to a middle-class home, with waxed floors and a bedroom for each individual, abundant linen, and a groaning pantry. No one describes how the inhabitants of these dwellings made do with what they had or what emotional significance they attached to their own belongings.

Villermé's description of the cellar in Lille was thoroughly synthetic. Every element, every detail, mirrored and improved on innumerable other similar passages. This was far from being a spontaneous, genuine response to an actual shock, far from being something that had, in an uncontrolled way, forced Villermé to break with his usual measured prose and burst out the awful witnessed facts. On the contrary, it had everything to do with the self-conscious manipulation of detail, the confection of appropriate metaphor, the balanced allusion to things that could not be printed, in this eve of Victorian convention. The break with expository discourse, having been practiced so often before, was itself here used as a conscious device for persuading the reader of the immediacy and empirical respectability of these ornate descriptions by negation. They served to give vividness and reality to the otherwise quite abstract notion of bare subsistence.

Descriptions of furnishings and visions of incest were not the only kinds of breakthrough passages. Sometimes specialized varieties developed for use with specific towns or specific contexts. In 1827, for example, in the report of the Industrial Society of Mulhouse's first committee on child labor, a seed was planted that was to grow into one of the most heart-rending passages in Villermé's whole study. The committee claimed to have found that:

> Many spinning mill workers live at a distance of one or two *lieues* [four to eight kilometers] and have as a result one or two *lieues* to walk in every season through all kinds of weather to get to their shop as well as to get home. Therefore, without speaking of the less than substantial nourishment which they procure for themselves, nor of the bad state of their footwear and of their clothing, we are faced with workers of every age, children in fact, who are forced to leave the paternal shelter at three or four in the morning every working day, in order to get to the shop by five, and who do not return home until nine, ten or eleven in the evening, being unable to devote more than four or five hours to rest and sleep.[107]

Villermé must have noticed this passage early on in his investigation, for in his list of 42 questions for the Industrial Society of Mulhouse submitted in 1835, he included the following as No. 22: "What precautions do they [the laborers] take against humidity, rain, cold, coming and going [to work]?" And the Society answered: "None despite special need."[108]

In 1837, Achille Penot, in a review of the situation of child labor and of the Society's efforts to support legislation on the issue, repeated the original passage almost verbatim:

> At Mulhouse, many laborers in the spinning mills, to save money and as a result of the insufficiency of housing, live at a distance of a whole *lieue* from their shops and must as a result cover this distance morning and evening, in every season and through every sort of weather, when they go to work and when they return. Thus, without speaking of the hardly substantial nourishment that their parents can give to them or

the bad state of their footwear and of their clothing, there are children who, every day of the week, are forced to leave the paternal shelter about four in the morning to get to their shops, from which they do not return until nine or ten or perhaps even eleven at night. And then, worn out with fatigue, after having quickly consumed a meager meal they cannot devote more than five or six hours to that sleep so absolutely necessary to their health and to the development of childhood.[109]

Apart from certain unimportant rephrasing, Penot has merely reduced the distance involved from one or two *lieues* down to one *lieue* only and has added to the vividness of the description by including a reference to their "meager dinner hastily consumed" while they are "worn out with fatigue." The reduction in the distance figure was perhaps related to the fact that the Society itself in 1835 had reported to Villermé that children from the farm families of outlying villages only occasionally worked in the mills during the busiest seasons.[110] Those who worked through both busy and slow seasons, the report implied, lived much closer in.

But such a report was not enough to deter the tireless Doctor Villermé once he had sensed the dramatic possibilities of the idea. Villermé does mention in his book that these outlying villages only supplied workers to the mills in the most prosperous periods.[111] But then he rushes to give us his own eyewitness account of the daily voyagers, an account rich with new, vivid details:

One must see them arriving each morning in town and leaving each night. There is among them a multitude of pale, thin women walking barefoot through the mud who, without umbrellas, pull their work smocks or their outer skirts up over their heads when it rains, to cover face and neck. And an even greater number of children no less dirty, no less pale, covered with rags soaked in the grease of the machinery that drips on them while they work. These latter, better protected from the rain by their waterproofed clothes, do not even have, like the women we have just spoken of, a basket of provisions for the day. Instead they carry in their hands or under their shirts, however they can, the crust of bread that is to nourish them until their return home.

Thus to the fatigue of an immeasurably long day, since it is at least fifteen hours, is added these comings and goings so frequent and so difficult for such unfortunates. The result is that at night they arrive home tortured by the need to sleep and the next day they leave before they are completely rested in order to get back to the shop by starting time.[112]

Once again, Villermé proved himself a master of the breakthrough genre. This is one of those passages that even today sticks in the minds of the reader, reproaching him for his bodily comforts and possessions. But in fact, there is little information in it. Villermé perhaps saw some laborers going to and from work on a rainy day and combined his memories of the scene with Zickel's and Penot's reports of children having too little time to sleep because they walk in from outlying villages. He carefully plays down the fact that this was at most a seasonal phenomenon. Even the vivid description he provides is all based on suggestions from others; Villermé saw nothing he did not know in advance he was supposed to see: Zickel's and Penot's passing references to inadequate food and clothing are transformed into rain-soaked work smocks, grease-stained tatters, and crumbs of bread. From being fatigued at day's end, the children become "tortured" by the need for sleep.

It is unfortunately quite difficult to get through to the reality behind all of these reports. Some observers made little of it, others like Villermé made as much as they could of it. Achille Penot, by 1843, had made a complete about-face on the issue; he accused Villermé of exaggerating and insisted that, in any case, by the time Villermé's book had come out, the housing situation had greatly improved and no one ever walked in from outside town any more. Clothing, he added, was also now cheaper and more abundant and no inhabitant of Mulhouse was inadequately dressed. He pooh-poohed the whole fashion of painting dark pictures of industrial towns.[113] The fact is that after the 1841 law had been passed and failed to have any measurable effect on the situation, industrialists in Mulhouse and elsewhere had lost interest in reform. Penot was doubtless reacting to this more general shift.[114] The fact that all the evidence from this period is distorted by the veering course of political fashion makes it difficult to say what is true, what untrue. But even if there were women and children who suffered in something like the way Villermé supposed, it is still necessary to ask whether the cause was, as Villermé unquestioningly believed, the self-regulating play of market forces or whether it lay elsewhere – whether, that is, it was the very unquestioning belief in the existence and power of market forces that brought down upon the laborers suffering of a kind that had nothing to do with an abstraction called the subsistence wage.

FROM RHETORIC TO LEGEND

Villermé's work stands as a kind of clearing house for all the new images and opinions of the 1820s and 1830s on the textile laborers of France. From its pages they move directly into literature, into political speeches, and eventually into the rhetorical repertoire of the socialists, all of whom, from Louis Blanc to Jaurès, drew heavily on the investigative tradition. These images became a part of the culture, of the faith in numbers and in prices that still rules over our civilization.[115] He had many imitators; some, like Le Play, refined the intruments of budgetary analysis. Others, like his colleague at the Institut de France, Adolphe Blanqui, took up the device of the breakthrough passage and carried it to evermore baroque extremes. Blanqui's 1848 study of the state of the working classes was in every respect a work of homage to Villermé. Everywhere he found what Villermé had found, except that his improvements on the master strained the limits of credibility. Take, for example, the following passages on the inhabitants of the rue des Etaques:

> This population of pariahs is not found in any other city of France, and seems condemned to miseries unknown even in the savage state ... [They are] human shadows whose heads hardly reach the level of our feet [in their cellars] where the half-flight that reaches them barely allows them to be perceived from the street ...

> If one penetrates the interior of a *courette*, a strange population of children, emaciated, stunted, crooked, with a pale and terrifying appearance, surrounds one demanding money. Most of these unfortunates are practically naked and the best dressed are covered with rags. But they at least breathe free air. Only in the depths of the cellars can one appreciate what suffering is inflicted on those who are prevented from going out by age or by the rigors of the weather. Most often, they sleep on bare earth, on rotten straw, or on dried potato greens, or sand ... The holes where they vegetate are entirely devoid of furnishing; and only the most fortunate are graced with a small stove, a wooden chair, and a few utensils.[116]

When preparing to intimate that incest is committed in the garrets of Rouen, Blanqui warns the reader elaborately in advance that his sensibilities may be offended. Before one is done with this study, the cliché-ridden artificiality of the whole procedure oppresses one far more than any of the images he so lovingly draws out.

In the same category as Adolphe Blanqui must be placed Victor Hugo who, at Blanqui's invitation, toured the Saint-Sauveur district of Lille in 1851. Hugo was a member of the National Assembly at that time, and early in 1851 he received a letter from Blanqui asking him to bring a delegation to Lille to see what poverty existed there. "I know the terrain by heart," Blanqui wrote, "and you will learn more in one day than you could in ten years."[117] Hugo came; and the great romantic dynamo saw the same things as the others had:

> mattresses whose covering, never washed finished by taking on the color of the earth.
> No sheets, no blankets.
> I approached one of these beds, and I made out a living being. It was a small girl of six years who lay there, sick with measles, trembling with fever, almost naked, hardly covered by an old wool rag.[118]

Later Hugo would write of Lille again in his endless poem from exile, "Les Châtiments," where not incest but prostitution caused by hunger caps the sufferings of the cellar dwellers of Saint-Sauveur. By this time Lille's cellars were notorious and had become the center of a strange sort of pilgrimage traffic carried on by right-thinking bourgeois reformers seeking to witness in all their vividness the ravages of the labor market's downward pressure on wages.

FOURIER ON GUARD

The image of working-class conditions constructed by Villermé and others in the 1830s is inseparable from an implicit interpretation of working-class motives. The laborers came to the manufacturing towns in search of work. Inevitably, it was supposed, they competed against each other for the available jobs, driving down wages. Moral corruption spread among them by bad example like a contagion. Low wages brought extreme deprivation, which spawned a search for illusory escape through drink, incest, and debauchery. They exploited their own children either because they had no choice or because they had no scruples. Of course, if physical deprivation was easily observable in the manufacturing towns, if alcohol consumption was high, and if there was an efficient labor market in operation, then it followed almost certainly that this interpretation was the correct one. Or, put another way, if the motive of gain was the fundamental human motive, then it followed that laborers would compete with each other for jobs in the manufacturing centers; that the resultant low wage would be profoundly, unbearably frustrating; that parents would exploit their own children for gain (whether they were compelled to by necessity would be irrelevant, and therefore not worth arguing over); that all relations of solidarity, familial or otherwise, would be at an end. In a very real sense, Penot's or Barrois' or Villermé's view of working-class life is nothing more than a projection onto their own society of the idea that the motive of gain is universal and fundamental. Their vision had nothing to do with the working class at all, except in the larger sense that it represented a prevalent way of thinking. Policy was dictated by this way of thinking, public debate informed by it; it created a barrier to any deeper understanding of working-class problems. Any notion of society built on a single formulaic idea of human motives, however seductively scientific it may be made to sound, is bound to create barriers to deeper understanding and therefore to productive change of any kind.

The aim here is not to deny that suffering or deprivation occurred, it is to point out that there are other ways of looking at deprivation. Olwen Hufton quotes the following report of an eighteenth-century priest on the needy of his parish:

> Old Pradeilhes of Lozerette, quite poor, has his father too old to work

and completely nude: the younger Pradeilhes is quite miserable, with an invalid wife abed now for over a year. They particularly need a blanket and couple of sheets ...

Old Pierre Coudère needs something to wear. Charles Coudère, a common pauper, needs a sheet for his bed.

Old Anne Delon needs food to eat. Old Baptiste Albanie, quite impoverished, needs especially things for his bed which is nothing but a bit of straw.

Old Courtez, quite impoverished, wife without clothing. Old François Chardonnet, poor, needs a shirt. Antoine Dumas of Crouzet, common pauper with several children. The old mother-in-law is neglected by her son, something ought to go to her first of all.[119]

This action-oriented list of personal needs may be contrasted with a characteristic expression of Villermé's on the bars of the rue des Etaques. Having gone out into the streets one night while visiting there, he tells us, he saw numerous bars full of people.

I would have liked to go into one of these places, where I saw through the doors and the windows, beyond a cloud of tobacco smoke, the ants' nests of the inhabitants of this hideous neighborhood; but it was obvious that in spite of the care I had taken to dress in a manner that would appear less suspect to them, my appearance in their midst would have excited surprise, mistrust. A great number were standing for lack of a seat; and one could see many women among them. All were drinking that detestable gin or else beer ... I resigned myself therefore to following people in the streets where many were stopping at corner grocers' to have a drink of gin before going to the bar, and where I heard even children using the most obscene language.[120]

Villermé was unable to see any needs here; he was unable to see in the very activities he observed a search for moral and human wholeness. Yet this most certainly was happening in the bars and streets of Lille. But then, can any group of people who are both impoverished and motivated purely by gain be anything but despicable? (This issue is taken up again in Chapter 9.)

One of the utopian socialists of the period, Fourier, understood the problem of motives with particular acuity. His imaginary phalansteries would make allowance for the complexity of human desire. In what was almost a caricature of the market idea, he posited the existence of other irreducible motives besides gain. There were in particular the three "distributive passions": The butterfly urge, or the desire to change activities roughly every two hours; the composite passion, that is, the desire to have both sense and spirit pleased in the same moment; the cabalist passion, the desire of people of different ranks to plot together to achieve some desired end. Instead of suppressing these impulses, Fourier's utopia would allow for them, exploit them, ensuring that giving them full sway would also result in the production of more good for the community. The phalanstery would beat laissez-faire at its own game.[121]

In this respect Fourier, more than Villermé or even Engels, came closest to giving theoretical expression to the grievance of Rouen spinners in 1830, when they demanded the end of the *tâche* system. No more than he, they could not rest satisfied with an institutional structure built on such an impoverished conception of the human spirit. The idea of the market gained its strength from the same source as its fatal weakness. Universally applicable, incontrovertible, easy to understand, it was also vacuous, insipid, and ultimately demeaning.

7 A search for identity

Two German historians, Martin Henkel and Rolf Taubert, recently issued a stinging critique of what they consider to be a teleological bias that plagues historical research on conflict in industrial society.[1] Unions, strikes, and collective bargaining are implicitly taken as the proper forms of working-class action; all other forms are viewed as either backward looking or forward looking depending on the extent to which they resemble the twentieth-century end point. Henkel and Taubert are particularly good at tracking down the subtle wordings, the condescending tones, and tendentious metaphors by which such judgments are often expressed. But the justice of their critique is already widely acknowledged. It is widely admitted that, in early forms of protest like food riots or machine breaking, the people involved moved in a social context entirely different from that of twentieth-century wage laborers.[2] Most now agree that protest from before about 1830 in Europe is not to be measured by twentieth-century norms.[3]

Avoiding the teleological bias becomes a problem of an entirely different order, however, when one comes to examine the period after 1830, full of incidents of protest that bear a close resemblance to modern-day strikes and of organizations that look very much like unions. There is a strong temptation to fall back on the idea that these incidents and organizations represent early, failed efforts by people who did not yet quite understand what they ought to do. After all unions, strikes, and collective bargaining did eventually become dominant. It is reasonable to assume, therefore, that at some point they became appropriate and that people then had to fumble around until they discovered the proper response. The common assumption has been, indeed, that they were appropriate by 1830. Incidents from this date on are commonly referred to as strikes and organizations as unions, however odd they appear when viewed as such.[4]

Insofar as such an assumption resembles the one that served as the starting point for social investigators of the July Monarchy, however, it must be religiously avoided. These investigators assumed that a labor market existed and they found it easy to interpret a vast amount of evidence as indicative of its workings. No evidence was found that shook their assumption because it is impossible to find empirical evidence that disproves an assumption about basic human motives. Even suicide may be seen as an attempt to maximize gain. The assumption that unions, strikes, and collective bargaining are proper forms of working-class action is perfectly analogous. It rests on the assumed existence of labor markets. As purveyors of a labor service in an open market, laborers must be prepared to refuse to sell below a certain price. To make such a refusal meaningful, they must organize selling units that have as much market power as the individual buyers they are dealing with. To get the highest possible price these selling units must bargain with the buyers, making good-faith offers, withholding the commodity from sale until the best possible price is obtained. Any other form of behavior is irrational. Strikes not preceded by negotiations are wasteful. Rioting in the streets only brings public hostility and official repression. Discipline, unity, and subordination are necessary if the laborer is to maximize his individual gain.

Few students of industrial conflict have had as rigid a notion of unions and strikes as this, but equally few have ever freed themselves from the pervasive influence of such assumptions.[5] If labor markets do not exist in the classical form, however, or even if one wishes to test whether they ever existed, then it is absolutely necessary to jettison all assumptions about the proper form of working-class action as well. Once this is done, it becomes possible to view the forms of conflict engaged in by French textile laborers down through 1851 in an entirely new light. As soon as human motives, instead of being assumed to have a standard form, are seen as problematical, one discovers abundant evidence that groups of textile laborers were themselves in fact wrestling with the problematical nature of motives. Their motives were not as clear to each other as they were to Villermé; they did not have the benefit of access to the current literature on economics. Their uncertainty about how to proceed was not contaminated by the tendentious lucidity of the market idea. The weaver Charles Noiret, who was literate enough to have glimpsed how the market was supposed to work, spoke of it publicly to his fellow workers in 1840 as something "imposed by force," rather than being the result of a natural freedom.[6] The comment recalls Villeneuve-Bargemont's confused view that it was the new theories that were responsible for the new society. But a market had not been imposed on textile laborers, something else had been which the literate classes were now referring to as free contracts. This something else was a form of relationship to their employers that was much more complicated than a mere exchange of a commodity for a price. But one of the complicating factors was that it was defined in law and spoken of in books as being just such an exchange between free equals.

Complicating matters even further was the fact that mechanized factory production had recruited a new body of laborers to serve it. Mule spinning and machine tending were unprecedented professions. Most mill operatives were of local origin and able to understand each others' dialects without difficulty, but there were nonetheless few conventions available to guide them in giving shape to their collective existence. These remained to be worked out.

Of course this approach to the understanding of human behavior is open to the same attack as the one being rejected. Because it is impossible to disprove an assumption about basic human motives, it is easy to find evidence for any claim – including the one made here, that the difficulty of interpreting human motives was a central determinant of certain behavior in the past. This claim has no advantage over the one that sees gain as fundamental – except the crucial advantage that it takes the existence of the problem of interpretation into account.

OIL LAMPS AND HIDDEN SCALES

Those cases of conflict for which the documents are most informative from the July Monarchy are also the ones that most clearly reveal uncertainty and ambiguity. The more detailed are the records available, the more obvious the confusion. The incidents at Rouen in 1830 and Reims in 1834, previously discussed, fit this pattern perfectly. Mill owners were uncertain about how to increase their control over the pace of work. (As it happened, those of Lille–Roubaix hit on a successful formula, one which eschewed any appearance of enhanced control.) Laborers were uncertain how to express their dissatisfaction and at first turned eagerly to models provided by the Revolution of 1830 – the marching of the sovereign people through the streets with drum and tricolor flag. (By 1834, however, in Reims this strategy had begun to wear thin.) Officials were uncertain how to handle the laborers' strongly felt grievances and oscillated between consulting them collectively as an organized body and repressing fiercely all traces of organization among them. In none of these cases were laborers' wages or working conditions being determined by market forces, except in the most indirect sense: Average wages of over 4 francs a day would probably have resulted in a very gradual shrinking away of a local industry, due to their indirect effect on yarn prices (assuming stable conditions in the yarn market). But for individual decision making, averages were all but irrelevant. Markets were unstable, rates were unstable, output was unstable, needs were unstable. The most powerful direct influence on the laborers' material survival was the structure of his family and his community at any particular moment. These shaped access to jobs and were in turn influenced by political relations between that community, its employers, the state, and the rest of society. It was no easy matter for individual laborers to know what their fellows felt about these diverse issues or what they wanted to do about them.

When one looks for well documented conflicts from the remaining years of the July Monarchy, two incidents dating from the crisis of 1839 stand out. It is possible to sense new ideas at work in these incidents, but the level of uncertainty remained very high; and the uncertainty itself can be shown to be a perfectly reasonable response to concrete features of industrial practice at that time.

The 1839 crisis was milder and briefer than that of 1827–32. After three boom years, speculators had driven up the cost of raw materials in the summer of 1836 and been forced to take losses the following spring. In late 1838, the cycle of speculation had started up again. Mill owners spoke angrily of being held to ransom by raw-material dealers who were keeping large stocks off the market in hope of higher prices. But demand fell off in 1839, particularly for cotton goods, and hundreds of mills began experiencing difficulties between July and August.[7]

On 28 August in the village of Radepont southeast of Rouen a mill owner named Lachêvre announced to his 27 mule spinners that beginning immediately they would be working into the evening and that they would be expected to pay for the oil used to light their lamps.[8] The oil would be charged at the rate of 2 francs per two-week pay period, the charge to be discounted from their pay. The evening hours were to begin that very night. Lachêvre made this announcement by calling the most senior spinner into his office. The spinners responded by delegating three other spinners to inform Lachêvre that they would prefer not to work the evening hours at all if it meant paying a charge for oil. Lachêvre retorted that they must either accept these terms or give notice. If they did not wish to do it, there were others who would. Later in the day, one spinner did give notice, and was informed that his *livret* would be available for him to pick up the following pay day. The other spinners worked the evening hours that night and every night until Saturday 7 September when they received their pay. Each spinner was docked 1.65 francs for oil, having worked a week and four days since Lachêvre's announcement; none protested. "It was therefore reasonable to assume," commented the *procureur* of nearby Les Andelys (Eure), "that all the spinners agreed to the oil charge and that the winter would pass without any of them quitting on that account."

The following Monday, however, after working all day, the spinners marched out of the mill in a group at the moment when they should have lit up their lamps for the evening hours. Lachêvre caught up with them at the gates of the mill; they told him they refused to work the evening hours because they did not wish to pay for the oil. The following morning when the starting bell rang (5:30 A.M.), the spinners appeared at the gates prepared to work in the usual manner, along with 78 other employees of the mill, piecers and preparations workers, mostly women and children. The spinners told Lachêvre that they would work again until sundown but no longer, unless he dropped the oil charge. Lachêvre was incensed. He told them that they had already agreed to the oil charge, having worked for 10 days under the new terms without protest, that his regulations required 14 hours of work from them which meant they had to work beyond the fall of night, and finally that if they did not work they would deprive the preparations workers of their livelihood. But the spinners marched away, and the others trailed after them. The mill, deserted by its workers, was closed up. The following morning (Wednesday), according to the *procureur*, "all the workers arrived again at work, the spinners made the same claim, the same response was made to them, and they all marched off." Each day thereafter until 5 October, that is, for almost four weeks, the scene was repeated. Lachêvre rang the starting bell, the spinners appeared, the spinners refused to work evenings, Lachêvre refused to renounce the oil charge, and the spinners retired.

Judicial proceedings were instituted against the spinners on 18 September. On 5 October they were brought to trial and 24 of the 27 spinners were sentenced to four days in jail. Apparently they went back to work on Lachêvre's terms following their jail sentences (although this is not made explicit in the *procureur*'s reports).

Until the very end the spinners firmly believed they were in the right, since it was they, not Lachêvre, who brought the dispute to the attention of the authorities. On Wednesday 11 September, two days after the work stoppage began, the *procureur* reported, "I happened to be in the Fleury area" (Fleury is an adjacent commune); "eight of the spinners sought me out and announced to me that they would not work, because this oil charge was being forced on them." The *procureur* went to the mill, questioned Lachêvre and decided that "the fault was undeniably the spinners' own. And I told them so. I made all the representations to them that seemed required by the circumstances and made them promise to return to work the following morning." Five days later, however, Lachêvre came to the *procureur*'s office in les Andelys and told him that on each subsequent day he had rung the starting bell as usual and the spinners had on each occasion raised the same claims as before and refused to work. It was at this point that the *procureur* order the local *juge d'instruction* to open an investigation. The spinners brought the government down on their own heads, because they had been so sure of the rightness of their cause.

Even after the investigation began, they remained adamantly attached to their position. On Wednesday 18 September the *juge d'instruction*, after his initial interrogation, brought the spinners all into his chambers to preach to them about their error. "He made them feel all the seriousness of their misdeed," said the *procureur*. "He reminded them that they were all married men with wives and children who depended on the fruits of their labor for survival and engaged them as forcefully as he could to return to their work the next day, Thursday. They seemed to appreciate the justice of the observations of this magistrate." But Thursday the same ritual was repeated at the mill's gate, much to the *juge d'instruction*'s surprise. On Saturday, 28 September, they went so far as to demand that Lachêvre pay them for a whole two weeks' work even though they had been out since the first day of that pay period. Lachêvre angrily offered to pay them the usual rate of 28 centimes the kilogram for the yarn they had spun that first Monday before walking out. But this offer was refused.

This is an incident that could plausibly be called a strike. The spinners held out for a month, refusing to work despite the stern warnings and paternal scoldings of employer and government officials. Only a jail sentence forced them to give up the effort. But there are certain peculiar features of the episode that are much better explained if they are taken as signs of a search for an appropriate mode of behavior. The dispute began, after all, as a disagreement over the proper manner in which to register a grievance. The mule spinners left work without warning at the old quitting time after working under the new conditions for 10 days. They were not withholding their labor, they were simply unilaterally satisfying their own unexpressed demand. Lachêvre insisted they were required to give notice; they ignored him. The next day they came to work and he shut them out because they remained unwilling to pay an oil charge. They were perfectly willing to work until nightfall, or beyond if he paid for the oil. They were ready to work, they wanted to work; 28 centimes per kilogram of yarn was acceptable to them. This was not a strike so much as a state of refusal to pay for oil that resulted each morning in a new closing of the mill.

Strictly speaking, of course, Lachêvre had acted illegally in the first place. He was required to give two weeks' notice of any change in work conditions; such notice had to be given on a pay day. He broke both of these provisions of the law. Perhaps he did not know the law very well, or felt that the oil charge was not a significant change. Perhaps the spinners knew less than he. It is possible they thought they were required to work under the new conditions until the next pay day after which they would be free to refuse, not realizing that giving notice meant to refuse now to work as of two weeks hence. They must have thought they were acting legally; why else would they have so confidently approached the *procureur* for help?

Coming to the mill each morning ready to work doubtless also helped the spinners find out what they wanted to do. Without meetings or committees, without formal grievances or declarations, they could meet in the morning outside the gate, quickly gain a sense of whether their collective agreement continued to exist, and confront Lachêvre at starting time with a semblance of unity. Doubtless there was a moment each morning when any one of them could have broken away from the group and walked into the building behind Lachêvre.

It was certainly difficult for them to know what the real provisions of the law were. Their only sources of information were Lachêvre, the *procureur*, and the *juge d'instruction*, all of whom spoke to them in condescending tones without distinguishing clearly between what they ought to do and what they were legally required to do. ("If you do not work your children will starve." "If you do not work the other employees will be deprived of a livelihood.") The authorities were also confused about how they ought to act; for three weeks they sermonized the spinners but did nothing. Each time they were astonished that the sermon did not have the expected effect. Laborers so obstinate in the end had to be punished. Neither in their sermons nor in their judicial procedure did the officials concern themselves much about the niceties of anticoalition law. It was not the market they were maintaining, but proper subordination and respect among the lower orders.

None of the parties to this episode shows any sign of having known what a strike is. The grievance did not concern the price of labor but the conditions of a subcontracting agreement; the action involved no concerted withholding of labor; no one engaged in bargaining in any direct or explicit sense. True, the spinners made an offer every morning that was rejected. But part of the problem was that Lachêvre refused to recognize their offer as having been made in a proper form; and the laborers had no idea whether to believe him or not on this point.

A conflict that unfolded in Lille spinning mills in the same weeks as the Radepont episode provides another, irresistible illustration of the reigning uncertainty over the proper form of collective action. The events at Lille eventually gained widespread attention when crowds of several thousand people beseiged the town hall for two days in a row in September, stoning the National Guard whose restraint was all that prevented serious violence. Reporting on these events, however, the *Echo du Nord*, Lille's principal newspaper, admitted that "If one asks what are the causes of this disruptive movement, we would be at a loss to say."[9] Uncertainty about the nature of the movement played a central role in determining its course. There is particularly good evidence that government officials disagreed all along about what the cotton spinners of the town were doing, that these officials unwittingly gave conflicting signals to the laborers, only realizing they had done so during the trials of arrested "leaders" that followed the crowd incidents in September. At that time, the officials involved failed to come forward, allowing perfectly innocent persons to be convicted.

At the focal point of the conflicting views of the spinners' intentions lay two meetings of 18 and 19 August in which the cotton spinners of the town decided to form an organization. The decision was almost an afterthought; it remains unclear even now what exact aims, structure, and power this organization was intended to have. There are three reports on these two meetings, and at their trials various participants testified about their actions and intentions. No simple conclusion is possible on the basis of this evidence.

Three mills in the suburb of Fives–Lille had announced without notice on Saturday 17 August that their spinners would receive rate reductions that week of 25 centimes per pound of yarn (about 30 percent). Most of the 42 cotton mills of the town were operating on reduced hours and lowered rates due to the crisis; their store rooms were full of unsold yarn; no end to the slump was in sight. A spinner named Théry later testified that he received a letter from the spinners at the Desmons mill in Fives–Lille, complaining that they had not "made up their weeks" (i.e., made a reasonable amount that week).[10] Théry admitted that he was the "dean of deans" in Lille (*doyen des doyens*) – dean being the term used in Lille to refer to the senior spinner in each shop. The letter asked him to make a collection among all the spinners of the town in order to "complete the weeks" of those spinners in Fives who had been struck by rate reductions. The following day, Sunday, a meeting was held at the cafe of M. Parsy in Lille to gather the money collected in the various mills. To Théry's surprise a great deal of money had been collected and over four hundred persons were present at the cafe. Here is where the various accounts diverge. According to a report from the *procureur* in Douai the collection gathered at Parsy's was to support the Fives–Lille spinners in a refusal to work at the new rates.[11] (We would call this a strike fund.) Two other reports from Lille police agents state that the sole aim was to make up the difference between the old and new rate.[12] Both police agents agree that at the meeting a wage-insurance scheme was hatched – "a kind of mutual aid society," said one agent – to guarantee to all spinners of the town that they would continue to be paid at current rates. Each spinner would be assessed weekly dues of 25 centimes in order to receive the insurance. In one of these reports, the agent claimed that the idea for such a scheme came up only because there was a good deal of money left over after the spinners of Fives had been provided for. Initially, the spinners wanted to turn the money over to the mayor of Lille to keep it for them in the *caisse d'épargne* and hand it out to victims of further rate or hours reductions. If this was not possible, the deans would have to return it. The deans of the 42 area mills decided to investigate and meet again Monday afternoon. "Finally," reports one police agent, "it was decided that if all the mill owners tried to lower rates," which of course would ruin the insurance scheme, "all work would cease forthwith, without noise, without scandal, until the former conditions were reestablished." Only one agent reported this detail; nowhere else in the records is there any trace of such a plan.

According to the other police agent, a charter was written up for the insurance scheme at the first meeting. Later testimony corroborates this report, and a copy of the charter may still be found in the prefect's files.[13] It provides for weekly payments and for compensation to spinners whose rates are reduced or who are unemployed for valid reasons. There is no word of concerted work stoppages. Of course, one could read between the lines and find any sort of masked intention in the charter one pleases. The prefect, when he saw the charter, was outraged; it was to him flagrant evidence of a coalition.[14]

The prefect received a copy of the charter from the mayor of Lille who had, on 19 August, received a copy from a group of deans. The spinners had decided to submit it to the municipal government for approval. They had had help in writing the charter from a man named Codron (sometimes written Caudron), who happened to be at Parsy's cafe that Sunday. Codron was variously described as a former court bailiff (*ex-huissier*), as applicant for a police agent's job, and as businessman (*agent d'affaires*). His lawyer described him as "an honest man belonging to that intermediary class who knows all too well the needs felt by workers."[15] Théry, dean of deans, said that at the meeting Codron described himself as "father of the workers who are unhappy and without work." "They said he was a lawyer," Théry added. Codron offered to help write the charter. He told them they needed a proper charter if they were to avoid trouble with the police for making collections of money and passing them out to other spinners. In his own defense Codron said: "I was father of the workers, that is possible. But instigator of coalitions, no, I was never that. In drawing up their charter I told them 'As long as you put any unsuitable provisions in your charter, you will gain nothing by it.' "[16]

There is thus good evidence that the spinners were searching for a legal way to insure their current piece rates by means of a collective fund. The mayor of Lille certainly believed this was so. Codron and some of the deans submitted the charter to him Monday and he approved it.[17] This official approbation did not come out at the trial and was not referred to by defense lawyers. But the mayor admitted to having approved the charter in a letter to the prefect dated 24 September, and he begged the prefect not to use the charter as the basis of a prosecution.[18] The request was ignored, however. As far as the prefect was concerned the mayor had been duped. The mayor silently acquiesced.

On Monday, 19 August, while the mayor was giving his approval to the charter, spinners at one of the mills in Fives had refused to go back to work at the reduced rate; and on the following day, according to the mill owner M. Desmons, "a crowd appeared in front of my mill and broke 100 francs worth of window panes. In order to help reestablish order, I took my laborers back at the old rate." Had this resistance been instigated or supported by the deans' insurance scheme? "I think that the dean of my mill was involved in the association," said Desmons.[19]

It seems quite possible that some of the spinners thought the insurance scheme was simply mutual aid while others saw it as a safety net that made resistance less risky. In other words, the same disagreement may have existed among the spinners about the purpose of this organization as existed between the mayor and the prefect. In subsequent weeks, some spinners certainly appear to have been more confident in their acts of resistance against the mill owners. Besides the incident at Desmons' mill, trouble broke out at the Toussaint mill on 19 September. The price of bread, already high inside the city, had just gone up to 55 centimes the kilogram, so that the spinners' depressed wages could buy at most two or three kilograms a day. A delegation of six spinners at Toussaint asked that he raise their piece rate in proportion, linking yarn prices in the mill to bread prices in the shops. Toussaint refused, and his 80 spinners walked out.[20]

Was this an isolated incident? Part of a larger plan? Had there been any coordination? Police agents who were keeping close watch on the spinners reported nothing of the kind. They did, however, get warrants and arrest the six spinners who had served as delegates at Toussaint. The police came to their doors at 4:00 A.M. the following morning and marched them off to the central headquarters at town hall. This is the act that precipitated a mobilization of all the spinners in the area.

The rest of the Toussaint spinners gathered at the mill entrance at 5:00 that morning. Clearly, like the spinners at Radepont, they had as yet formulated no definite plan of action for the day. A return to work was possible; it was time to consult about strategy and demands before the 5:30 starting bell. But their delegates of the previous day did not arrive. Soon someone brought word of the arrests. Disturbed and angry, the spinners retired from the entrance; there was no longer any question of returning to work. They had only one aim in mind now: to get their friends out of jail.

At such a moment a twentieth-century union, in France or anywhere else in the industrialized world, would have a single unquestioning response – a general strike. The notion of a refusal to work has taken such profound hold of the minds of laborers and their leaders as the tactic par excellence of workers – just as their status as purveyors of work is taken unquestioningly as the defining feature of their social existence – that no other response would be likely to receive even cursory consideration. But this was not the response of the Lille spinners, even if the idea of a general walkout had been broached at a recent meeting. Instead, for the spinners, the only plausible response was to go in force to the town hall, where their friends had been taken, and get them out.

The Toussaint spinners' first impulse was to get help. To achieve this they stationed themselves outside the Mille spinning mill in the northern end of town at the end of the lunch hour and intercepted their colleagues as they returned to work. Thus reinforced they began marching southward, stopping at each mill that they came to, chanting and singing, pelting the windows with paving stones to get their fellows out with them. By 3:00 P.M., now several hundred strong, they had reached the Saint-Sauveur district in the southern end of town where numerous mills were located. At 4:30 the mayor called out the National Guard and a battalion of regular troops were rushed from the citadel to the town hall. The mayor had already realized (or heard) what the spinners' ultimate goal was; and he sent a hasty note to the prefect urging him to keep the troops stationed at the town hall through the night since he foresaw serious trouble after the mills closed for the evening. At 5:00 P.M., the spinners reached the Desmons mill outside the Porte de Paris. By 7:00 (closing time) there were over fifteen hundred (one report says "several thousand") massed outside the town hall. (There were no more than eighteen hundred spinners in the whole Lille area.) Troops and National Guard confronted the angry crowd's insults and taunts for two hours as dark descended. Finally at nine, a proclamation by the mayor forbidding all assemblies in the public square was read out by the light of a torch. The three legal calls to disperse were made, and then the square was cleared. To the immense relief of the mayor and his subordinates, the dispersal was accomplished without bloodshed.[21]

The streets were heavily patrolled that night. At 4:30 A.M. contingents of National Guard took up positions at all mill entrances and most spinners returned to work that morning without incident. The presence of the Guard had deprived the spinners of their normal meeting place. However, by 9:00 A.M. there were crowds again in the streets of the

Saint-Sauveur district engaging in rock-throwing skirmishes with patrols and in attempts to besiege mill entrances. They made some progress, but there were also numerous arrests; and most mills continued to operate even with reduced personnel. At 3:00 P.M. 24 prisoners (including the original six Toussaint delegates) were moved from the town hall to the citadel, which was considered immune from any threat of crowd violence. When word of the transfer got out, efforts to gather another crowd died down.

The following day, Sunday, according to one police informant, meetings were held at various points in town to organize a gathering for Monday, at a prearranged time and place so that the Guard would be unable to thwart the spinners' efforts to muster support.[22] But nothing ever came of these plans. Sunday was calm. On Monday, 23 September, work resumed in all mills as usual. That morning Codron and several others who participated in the August meetings were arrested and charged with coalition. After such disorders, both the prefect and the *procureur* believed that the leaders of the spinners' association must be subjected to exemplary punishment.

But apparently due to personal communication with the mayor of Lille, both the *procureur* and the prefect modified their view of the whole conflict on that same Monday. Reports from each of them dated 23 September speak for the first time of spinners' grievances that were not unjustified and that had induced the mayor at first to look with favor upon the spinners' association. Up until this point, not a word had been spoken in government documents about this issue, but now suddenly the conflict is completely reinterpreted by the government. The *procureur* did not understand precisely what the mayor was talking about. He misspelled the word for bobbin, for example, in this comment: "A grievance which the workers put forward and which the municipal authority believes to be well-founded is that the weighing of their bobbins – the product of their labor – is done in a hidden place and in such a manner that in certain mills they do not receive the whole salary that is due them."[23]

In a much more lengthy discussion of the same matter the prefect explained that a number of mill owners had taken to carrying out the verification of the number of the yarn (on which the pay rate was based) in a back room out of sight of the spinners, and that there was good reason to suppose that the procedure was not entirely honest. Pay reductions could be justified in this way by claiming that the spinners' yarn had been coarser than he was supposed to make, and therefore 5 or 10 centimes were cut from the price per kilogram. It was this in particular, according to the mayor, that had spurred formation of the mutual wage-insurance scheme in August.[24]

The significance of this grievance for any interpretation of the spinners' consciousness depends on understanding exactly how the spinners were paid. Lille cotton spinners still regularly paid a fixed weekly fee for steam power, and sometimes fees for light and heat. These fees were deducted from the pay they received based on the verification and weighing up of their yarn at the end of the week. One must suppose that when mills went on short hours, they reduced the size of the steam power fee proportionately. But whenever a piece rate reduction occurred, as was happening in a number of mills in August, the fixed fees loomed larger, took up a greater proportion of the week to work off, and thus magnified the impact of the cut. If under these circumstances the mill owners added to their devices for reducing pay the removal of reel and scale to a back room where trickery could go unchecked, one can sense the anxiety that resulted. Where would it stop? What gambit would they come up with next week? One can also see why a mayor, one of whose duties was the repression of consumer fraud – false measures or watered beer or milk – might lend a sympathetic ear to the spinners' complaints.

It is revealing, however, that the spinners responded almost as one would expect a group of independent operators to respond – that is, they tried to assure for themselves by creation of a common fund a certain minimum rate per kilogram for their yarn. This was an act of people who saw themselves as petty commodity producers, not as wage laborers. At the same time, it was possible, once the association was formed, to contemplate collective resistance to the mill owners with greater equanimity. Was this an unintended side effect or a central aim of the association? Different spinners might have made opposite answers to this question, just as the prefect and the mayor disagreed. It is important not to treat this whole episode merely as some kind of proto-union's bungled efforts to organize a strike. The income insurance scheme was just that and nothing else, and it was precisely attuned to the concrete circumstances of the laborer's working lives. Its real purpose was unclear just to the extent that these concrete circumstances were ambiguous, informed as they were with heterogeneous principles; and just to this extent the laborers remained uncertain about their own identity.

When those arrested came up for trial in October, the movement had entirely died away. This, and the mayor's behind-the-scenes efforts, ensured lenient sentences. The very fact that some of those sentenced were deans was itself an extraordinary sign of official displeasure. Normally deans (or *curés*, as they were called in Rouen) were not made targets of repression at all. Their positions were recognized by the mill owners, who treated with the workers through them by choice; they were almost semiofficial representatives of the working community. Of course, strictly speaking, this amounted to sanctioning coalition. But no one engaged in such close reasoning about the matter. Unreflectively, people recognized that the laborers were, had to be, held together by bonds of community merely by virtue of the fact that they were laborers who lived and worked together. Coalition to the ruling class meant not organization as such but autonomous and independent organization. That all the deans of Lille were directly involved in the formation of the association in August demonstrates that this association itself was viewed as something to which one belonged by virtue of one's identity as spinner not by individual preference. Agulhon has characterized this kind of belonging, which he found to have played a central role in the Var uprising of 1851, as "archaic" or "folkloric" community.[25] But this is misleading, since at base all human beings in all times and places have felt strong ascriptive (as opposed to voluntary) membership in some reference group. What has characterized the modern nation-state has been an attempt to eliminate the influence of such belonging from both the economic and the domestic political spheres, to limit nonvoluntary belonging on the one hand to the nation as a whole and on the other to a private, personal, familial realm – an impossible task. Atomized individuals committed to personal gain have yet to emerge. No one can really act that way.

The trial of Codron and certain deans on charges of coalition in October can be seen, then, as one small episode in this impossible struggle, made all the more futile in that the persons on trial had acted more or less with the sanction of those social betters who were now condemning them. The result of such action could not be the advance of liberal forms of social organization (as opposed to "folkloric" ones); it could only grind deeper into the hearts of laborers that sense of injustice that always arises among people who feel damned if you do, damned if you don't. The double bind faced by laborers under the July Monarchy was that their social betters wished them to remain folkloric as long as folkloric meant humble (and therefore cheap) but denied them such a sense of membership with all the force of law whenever it gave rise to autonomous expressions. At certain moments (for example, when pay cuts were announced), they were supposed magically to become atomized, individualistic economic actors. All the rest of the time they were to remain simple, humble folk thankful for the organic tie of dependence that held them to the proprietors. Any hint that this caused them to feel a sense of betrayal (inevitable under the circumstances) attracted immediate official repression.

Of the 20 who were convicted for coalition on 12 October, two got three-day sentences, seven got eight days, 10 got 10 days. Codron was singled out, receiving a 20-day sentence.

By such means, the July Monarchy in effect created the opposition that later destroyed it. The Republican Union of Spinners of Lille formed in the days after the February Revolution nine years later wrote a charter that was almost precisely the same as that written in August 1839. As for Codron, he is quite possibly the same person as the "Caudron, shoemaker's tool merchant" who surfaced in Rouen in the early 1840s and quickly became Cabet's leading correspondent in that town, later helping to manage the Icarian Communist newspaper *Le Populaire*. Unknown, in a new town, and as champion of a new and optimistic doctrine, he again became a "father" to a group of cotton spinners. Perhaps he was one of the 19 Rouen petitioners who praised Cabet's emphasis on the dignity of all human beings in 1846, lamenting that "All our relations, whether with our masters or with public functionaries, are acts of authority that wound our dignity."[26]

THE COMING OF A NEW WORD

Numerous incidents of protest by textile laborers from the 1830s and 40s have left documentation that is not as full as for these episodes in Radepont and Lille. In some cases, the reports are so scanty, and the range of plausible interpretations so great, that they cannot be used to adjudicate between different general views of this period. This is not always the case, however; details have often survived that are at least suggestive.

Of six conflicts associated with the crisis of 1837, for example, five occurred before raw cotton prices began their decisive plunge downward in the spring.[27] All five of these conflicts involved piece-rate reductions. But frequent piece-rate reductions after the price break seem to have been accepted without opposition by textile laborers. The timing of these conflicts therefore suggests that cuts that occurred while prices were still high (but demand on the wane) were perceived as unjust, whereas those which merely reflected price changes in the open market encountered no resistance.

Among these six incidents one finds several cases of laborers marching on prefectures or town halls, three obvious cases of notice violations on the part of employers abetted by local officials, but no clear instances of work stoppages as such.[28] The one incident involving weavers (calico weavers in Armentières) revealed that they, in contrast to mule spinners, were extremely well-informed about labor contract law and were able to maneuver the local Conseil des prudhommes into ruling in their favor – an extremely rare occurrence in these years. Doubtless weavers had more occasion to learn the provisions of the law because it continued to serve as the principal labor control technique of merchant manufacturers.

In Rouen in the spring of 1839 laborers at one mill rebelled against the reimposition of the *tâche* system; there were two marches on the *palais de justice* followed by a return to work.[29] A month later in Darnétal and Rouen laborers quit work at four mills to protest rate reductions. The local *procureur* remarked in his report on this incident that the laborers stayed at home; "there has been no sign of trouble; everything is perfectly calm." He indicates that they had left work three days before, on Monday, "and have not returned either yesterday or today." Is there a note of astonishment in this phrase? The word *grève* does not appear in the report. Fourteen arrests were made. The outcome is unknown.[30]

The group with the greatest grievances in the 1840s were handloom weavers; to their growing frustration, merchant suppliers in 1840–2 did not willingly allow piece rates to rebound at the same pace as prices did. Lacking confidence themselves, the merchants were anxious to build their own cash reserves; and handloom weavers responded with repeated protests. In production of certain grades of calicoes, steam-power looms also began to provide real competition, ensuring that rates would move steadily downward.[31] Hence weaver actions were numerous in these years. Just as spinners protested rate cuts that preceded the 1837 open-market price break, so weavers in the early forties insisted on a proportionate share in open-market price recoveries. Just as Lille spinners in 1839 had opposed the concealment of reels and scales for weighing their yarn, so weavers denounced suppliers who fraudulently lengthened their warps without increasing the rate of pay. Weavers besieged municipal authorities, as in Cholet (Maine-et-Loire) in 1840 and 1841, Roubaix in 1843, or Roanne (Loire) in 1847, or paraded unfinished warps through the streets (Armentières, 1837; Elbeuf, 1846; Roanne, 1847), or besieged suppliers' warehouses (almost all cases). Actions seldom extended beyond one or two days.

October was the most common time for weaver protest because in October prices were set on winter season items.

At Cholet (just south of Angers) in October 1840 calico weavers, angered that suppliers were offering the same low rates as the previous year, marched on the town hall and won major concessions through the intercession of the mayor; a *tarif* was drawn up for the whole town specifying significantly higher rates.[32]

The following October, Cholet weavers again resisted rates offered to them for the winter season. As one local paper put it, the weavers were insisting on weaving only "the articles which pay the best and thereby are forcing their will on the suppliers."[33] A small group of weavers appeared at the town hall on 5 October and demanded a general adjustment upward. "Everyone agrees," said the *procureur* on the scene, that this has been a prosperous year and that "the worker must feel, thanks to this state of prosperity, that his salary on certain articles should have been increased."[34] Merchant suppliers had blundered, he said, in not passing through higher prices earlier. The mayor told the weavers to return to work at once, however, if they wished him to intervene; he would then be happy to hold talks at the town hall on the issue. The weavers left, but instead of returning to work they went to a number of suppliers and told them to come to the town hall. Talks held that afternoon got nowhere. In the meantime, the square outside had filled up. A rain that began to fall about 6:00 P.M. sent everybody home. But the following day there were marches through the streets. An unfinished warp, paraded through the streets on a stick, was set afire in the main square. Weavers were reported to have uttered dire threats: arson against the suppliers, an attack on the town hall. They were cleared from the square by gendarmes at nightfall.

The following two days were calm. But weavers' delegates told authorities that if they had not received increases by 12 October, "we will see what we must do." At one meeting weavers told the local *procureur* that "they will cease their work" on the twelfth. He warned them that doing so would certainly lead to "disorderly lives ... and a collision between themselves and the authorities ... which would cause great suffering and would be a terrible blow to the industry and commerce of Cholet." They countered that they were determined and that their action would be entirely "inoffensive." But on the twelfth nothing happened. Some suppliers had by then given in to the weavers' demands, but not all.[35]

Local newspapers claimed that the whole affair had been masterminded by certain instigators who forced other weavers to leave their cellars and go bargain at their suppliers' warehouses.[36] The government heard reports of a vast underground weaver organization. However, all that an investigation turned up was "certain societies of leisure ... which encourage coalitions of workers by providing them with a chance to talk over their interests and agree on common strategy. The members assemble on Sundays to play and drink together; some are held in the neighborhood of the presbytery and almost under the presidency of the *curé*."[37] There were, that is, what Provençals called *chambrées* in the area, groups of friends who met regularly to drink and play cards or *boules*.[38] Since no republicans could be blamed for influencing them, it must be the *curés* who were doing it. So went official reasoning.

As in Lille in 1839, here at Cholet certain weavers were thinking of a general concerted work stoppage, even trying to plan one, but it did not happen. Was it the idea of only a minority? Or had they won the substance of their demands by the twelfth? There is no way to know.

Records of incidents involving weavers at Roanne (1842 and 1847), Roubaix (1843 and 1846), Bitschwiller (1845), and Cholet again (1846) give no indication that weavers attempted to express their grievances by means of work stoppages.[39] In other instances the scanty records are ambiguous. At Romarantin in 1840, weavers left their shops (they did not work at home) for three days in a dispute over piece rates. At Lillebonne in 1847, weavers quit for only part of a day, but local officials reported that a collection was made to support their effort.[40]

Among spinners certain incidents in the last years of the regime took a form that in every way satisfies the modern notion of a strike. Perhaps the earliest of these were in Reims where wool spinners had already experimented in this direction in 1834. In August 1840, Reims spinners in several mills tried to organize a work stoppage against rate cuts that had been announced. Several meetings were held, but in the end only one mill was affected for one day. But the following February, in two mills simultaneously, spinners refused to work for five days in support of a demand for a rate increase.[41] The fact that they initiated the demand and then backed it up with a refusal to work (rather than responding to a mill owner's announcement of a cut) makes this incident the first of its kind in the records on textile laborers of the northern centers. It shows that an altogether new view of their situation was moving Reims spinners. But the surviving records do not indicate how they came to agree on such a view or why.

Finally, and quite without warning, the French word that now means strike suddenly began appearing in provincial records of incidents involving textile laborers in 1846. At Saint-Quentin in September of 1846, as the price of bread was beginning to inch upward, 200 cotton spinners marched out of the largest mill in the town and stayed out for two weeks demanding a return to 1841 yarn rates that had since been gradually rolled back. An official in the *procureur*'s office said of the spinners' action that they "*se sont mis en grève*" (went out on strike); and on their return that "*la grève peut être considérée comme terminée*" (the strike may be considered to be over). They won no increase.[42] Johnson indicates that disciples of Cabet in Reims and Saint-Quentin were in contact with each other, but it is impossible to say how the word or the idea of such an action arrived in Saint-Quentin.[43] The *procureur* denied that "those who practice radicalism" in the town had any part in the affair.

Weavers of *nouveautés* (fine, high fashion woolens) in Elbeuf also mounted two "strikes" in October 1846, that is, protests referred to by the word *grève* and which seem to have fit the pattern now associated with that word. These were highly skilled, well paid weavers who came from all over France to work in Elbeuf loom shops. (Some may have known of the bitter months-long weavers' work stoppage in Lodève in the south in 1845.) Prices were set at the start of each season, after a "trial piece" of the article in question had been woven. Negotiations over the price for that season were often heated, the shop owner critically evaluating quality and finish, the weaver complaining of the time and effort expended. A bad harvest and high food prices had made the weavers particularly demanding in negotiations for the winter season at the beginning of October. On 15 October, weavers in three shops met to plan joint action to win a supplement to rates they had settled for a week before. One shop owner met their demands at once, but the other two did not, and these weavers went "on strike" for three days. They returned to work on the nineteenth, it is not known on what terms.

On 27 October, a "strike" began at another Elbeuf *nouveauté* shop when weavers there demanded that the bonus they were usually awarded for a good piece be made part of their regular pay (also, in view of the high food prices). These weavers were only idle for one day, since the police decided to act against them, arresting six of them in their homes at midnight.[44]

These incidents of the late 1840s at Reims, Saint-Quentin, and Elbeuf – the latter cases involving use of the word *grève* – suggest that some sort of change was setting in as the revolutionary crisis of 1848 approached. The change remained circumscribed; in other northern centers neither the new word nor the form of protest associated with it made any appearance before the 1848 Revolution. Both Elbeuf and Reims were towns where specific lines of communication existed with the larger world of self-conscious artisans and political proselytizers. But it is difficult to say what role, if any, these contacts played in the experimentation with new forms. Nor does the documentation on these incidents allow one to get any sense of how laborers arrived at their decisions. It is difficult, therefore, to know to what extent ambiguities were being eliminated and new conventions of protest established. All of these incidents were related to the special circumstances of high food prices following a harvest failure. The initiation of demands for higher rates may have been seen as an extreme emergency measure, the refusal to work as a last resort.

Whatever the case, the overwhelming distress of the summer of 1847 led in many regions to scenes that defy any attempt to find a neat progression in popular consciousness: Food rioting became widespread. In the Lille–Roubaix area in July, large bands of spinners and weavers were seen on the roads looking for farmers who had grain stores left to sell. The National Guard was called out to protect the wheat fields from pillage as the harvest approached.[45] In Mulhouse, spinners left work on 26 June to complain at the town hall about the high price that had been set on bread by the municipality. (This price was already being subsidized.) The mayor promised to talk if the laborers named delegates and dispersed. They did so, but then turned toward other mills to bring their fellows out to join them. By noon the town hall square was full again and the impatient crowd began sacking bakeries. They moved almost in unison, "as if by signal," according to Kahan-Rabecq.[46] The National Guard by and large refused to act against them. Every bakery in town and suburbs was raided. Troops were pelted with stones; fires were set in a number of the bakery shops. There were four dead and 66 under arrest by the end of the day. These occurrences, reflecting extreme distress, were nonetheless as appropriate to the real social conditions of the time as were the strikes occurring elsewhere. They protested the breakdown of that most fundamental kind of solidarity – the fair sharing of food in time of scarcity. It was a kind of solidarity that the notables of the time explicitly espoused and took measures to enact, following policies that differed little from those of their remote forebears of the sixteenth or seventeenth century – that is, the control of prices, and the gathering and controlled sale of public stores. All were perfectly aware that the price mechanism could not be trusted to ensure the well-being of society in these circumstances; liberal notions were not even an issue (except for, perhaps, the sanctity of property, the point on which Mulhouse laborers vociferously disagreed). Hence there was nothing "backward" about food riots in 1847, unless one agrees to apply the same term to the whole of French society – in which case the characterization itself becomes suspect.

By the fall of 1847, this phase of the crisis was over. The harvest that was brought in was much better than the previous year's; food did not again become an overriding issue. Instead the February revolution brought a rapid and dramatic change of the whole social context in which the textile industry was carried on.

A REVOLUTION IN PAY PROCEDURES

Within days of the successful insurrection in Paris of 23–24 February 1848, Ledru-Rollin, minister of the interior in the provisional government of the new republic, sent what he called "commissioners" out to the provinces to replace the prefects of the previous regime in every department. Those commissioners who took power in the northern industrial centers were quick to establish ties with local laborers, allowing them a free hand to organize themselves as they wished and to formulate grievances.

The new commissioners believed it was their duty to bring about reforms in industry. But, as it turned out, they had only a short period in which to act. The power of Ledru-Rollin and his team was brought to an end soon after the victory of the nascent party of order in the April twenty-third elections. From this point on government administrators became progressively more hostile toward laborers' organizations and laborers' wishes, attempting to dismantle piecemeal their new freedoms and to beat down their new self-confidence. This was a long, drawn-out process that was nonetheless accomplished in the northern textile centers well before Louis Napoleon's coup d'état of December 1851 – hence the lack of resistance to the fall of the Republic in these centers.[47]

Even in the short period of their ascendency, it is possible to glimpse marked diversity in what the revolutionaries hoped to accomplish. Louis Blanc, apostle of the "organization of work" had been included in the provisional government from the first day. What he meant by this famous phrase was that, under free-trade conditions, work was carried out in an anarchic manner. "Organization" was the opposite of anarchy. This much was widely understood. As to what constituted organization, those who consciously pondered the matter had the greatest diversity of opinions. Textile laborers came forward with concrete proposals, embedded in their own day-to-day work experiences, while their new-found leaders persisted with quite different ideas and even misinterpreted the laborers' demands in such a way as to fit them into their own frame of reference.[48] At the heart of these misperceptions lay the simple fact that the revolutionaries often looked at the laborers through the eyes of Villermé, while the laborers aspired to the full status of independent operators that they still partially enjoyed. Had the new regime lasted long enough, had there been no common enemy, the gravest difficulty in realizing a consistent program of industrial reform would sooner or later have surfaced. As it was, 1848 amounted to an initial encounter, an interlude of hesitant discovery in which literate reformers who believed that the inexorable laws of supply and demand were responsible for the laborers' plight confronted laborers whose grievances were quite differently conceived.

Ledru-Rollin's choice for commissioner of the Seine-Inférieure department that contained Rouen and its surrounding mill towns was Frédéric Deschamps. A prominent Rouen attorney, a republican who believed that democracy would create the conditions for true fraternity between classes, he had supported Ledru-Rollin since the latter's first appearance on the political scene. In 1846, he had been connected with a project to establish a newspaper called the *Travailleur Normand*, which was to have actual laborers on its managing board. (The project never reached the publication stage.)[49] His first act as commissioner of the provisional government was to urge calm on the laborers of the Rouen area so that no one could ever accuse them of having "stained such a beautiful revolution with fire and pillage."[50] (There had been attacks on the railroad by boat operators and dockworkers.) The government, he promised, would look out for their interests; and he called on them to send petitions listing their grievances, instead of taking to the streets. In the initial weeks of his administration, he sponsored accords in a number of industries including in each case provisions for shorter hours and for minimum wages. For dyers, hours were set at 11 per day, and the daily wage at 2.25 francs. For dockworkers on the river front, Deschamps authorized a shorter work day of 11 hours and established rules that required employers to pay for a minimum of half a day of work no matter how short the time they actually used dockers.[51] In each of these cases, Deschamps responded to what he and a great number of others believed to be the principal grievance of the working class, that is, the long hours and low wages created by unregulated competition. Deschamps doubtless believed he was mitigating the effects of unregulated competition in the textile industry also when on 10 March he sanctioned a single piece-rate scale for all the cotton mills of the department (limiting their hours at the same time to 11 per day). But in fact the demand for such a scale had, in the laborers' eyes, an entirely different meaning, and its establishment had effects which entirely escaped Deschamps' awareness.

Rouen's textile laborers had played no part in the violent demonstrations of 24–25 February, but on Monday, 28 February, they broke their silence. Huge crowds of spinning mill workers organized themselves in the suburb of Maromme, to the west of town, and fanned out to surrounding mill villages.[52] A report from the mill of Renard et F. Masson fils in the village of Villers-Ecalles, seven miles northwest of Rouen, tells of several crowds in succession arriving to besiege the mill entrance that day from the direction of Pavilly.[53] At the first word of trouble, the director had shut the mill down. Later one of the crowds forced him to sign an agreement making "absurd" concessions, on pain of seeing his mill burned to the ground. There were, he lamented, no forces of order whatsoever to turn to out in the countryside. The following day the director of the mill sent an assistant to Rouen to search for news. (His laborers had not come to work.) The assistant brought word of a settlement made in Rouen that satisfied the director, who put the mill back in operation on Wednesday, planning to follow the terms of the Rouen settlement. On Saturday, pay day, the laborers at Renard et F. Masson fils, realizing on what terms they were being paid, began making difficulties. They feared a trick, the director reported, and in the end walked out. Similar difficulties had occurred in three mills in nearby Barentin; laborers there had appeared on the road. The director had encountered a menacing group of them when bringing cash to the mill for pay that morning. All these spinners were insisting on pay at "1 centime per number." Faced with his own rebellious spinners that afternoon, the director finally capitulated to this demand.

"One centime per number" had apparently been the original "absurd" demand made on the twenty-eighth. A petition sent to Deschamps from Maromme dated 29 February and signed by both spinners and mill owners made the following demands: (1) a 12-hour day, (2) pay at "1 centime per number" for both warp- and weft-grade yarns, "no matter how many spindles the mule jenny may have," (3) all fines to be used to establish a fund for needy workers, (4) no discounts on pay in silver.[54] (Mill owners all over France were in the habit of discounting 1 percent of pay for each silver 5-franc coin used; silver specie had been in short supply under the First Empire, when the practice began, but was no longer.) A notice sent to Deschamps on 1 March from Pavilly also describes an agreement of mill owners there to pay 1 centime per number on mule jennies of whatever size, to pay 5 centimes below number for women who worked throstles, and 10 centimes an hour for preparations workers, and to put fines and silver discounts into a sick fund. This agreement was to hold provisionally until the government took further action.[55]

The significance of the term "1 centime per number" is not difficult to discover; it was a convenient way of specifying a whole piece-rate schedule, a *tarif des façons*, for the common grades of cotton yarn. Quite simply, No. 26 yarn was to be paid for at 26 centimes per kilogram, No. 30 yarn at 30 centimes, and so on. This rate of pay is in fact little different from rates commonly paid in the previous three decades. In this sense, the demand was highly conservative, merely for a rate of pay that corresponded to prevailing rates before the onset of the crisis in 1846, although it also eliminated the possibility of a *tâche* system. What made the director at Renard et F. Masson fils call the demand absurd was, no doubt, the added provision that this rate apply to all mule jennies no matter how many spindles they had. A moment's reflection reveals that this provision was not merely absurd, but revolutionary. During the forties, many mills had begun introducing larger mule jennies. The common size in the 1830s had been of 216 spindles. In the forties, mules of 300, 426, even 500 spindles had been introduced – very slowly, however, so that it was common for a mill to have machines of various sizes. Working these large mules required greater expertise, more effort, and more practiced piecers to assist; but it also made possible a much higher rate of output per spinner. On the largest mules, output could be easily doubled. Obviously, mill owners had lowered pay rates on these machines substantially to allow for the higher capacity. But the demand of 1 centime per number put a stop to such lowering of rates. This of course removed a great part of the incentive to invest in the larger machine. But it also meant that the larger machines already in operation would be extremely advantageous to the spinner, since he would reap most of the benefits of its higher productivity. The demand was "absurd" to Renard et F. Masson fils because under capitalism the ownership of productive capacity is said to go with ownership of the machine, not with operation of the machine. In this sense it was revolutionary, because it struck at the heart of capitalist notions of property. Yet its form was also conservative in the sense that it tended to preserve the fiction of independence, focusing as it did on a fixed price for yarn inside the mill, as if the mill were a marketplace for yarn. Obviously, from the laborers' point of view, it was neither conservative nor revolutionary exactly, but simply a demand that (like their opposition to the task system in 1830) arose out of a notion of fairness that focused on the pay procedure rather than on the work process. This is a notion of fairness that simply does not accept (or understand?) the capitalist concept of factor cost, or of labor as a commodity.

On 10 March Frédéric Deschamps accepted the 1-centime-per-number demand and gave it the force of law for the whole department.[56] He doubtless believed that he was merely establishing a minimum wage and thereby reducing the ravages of competition on the working class. It is clear, in any case, that he was no socialist. Six days before he had warned that "only respect for the rights of property and for the liberty of commerce" would ensure that grain would continue to come to market in sufficient amounts.[57] Everything about his actions in office suggests a moderate who wished to adjust, rather than to change, the present system. He had, in other words, no idea what he was doing to the cotton trade.

A petition from Lillebonne mill owners to Deschamps dated 18 March complains of the anomalous effects of the new piece rate where machines of larger sizes were in use.[58] Spinners on 500-spindle mules were earning up to 39 francs per week. (Twelve francs was considered a good income.) There were some eighty shops in the Rouen area where hand-cranked mules were still in use. Spinners in these shops were used to very low pay, but 1-centime-per-number on their 110-spindle machines meant income that was below the starvation level.[59] From Darnétal, from Fleury-sur-Andelle, Charleval, Fontaine-sur-Andelle, and other points came complaints to Deschamps of individual mill owners who had refused to follow the official rate or who were threatening to do so. From Pavilly came an anonymous letter, in a learned hand, whose author tried to explain to the commissioner what the inadvertent effects of his rate had been. The spinners had wished to prevent the introduction of larger machines, he explained, because they were much harder to operate but resulted in no gain for the spinners. Its effects were not equitable.[60]

From Fleury on 29 March came a spinners' petition complaining that a M. Penault had installed several 500-spindle self-acting mules in his shop and was not paying at the centime-per-number rate. He had hired children at 4 francs a day, when the official rate would have yielded over 12 francs a day on two such machines. M. Villeneuve, the petition continued, was threatening to do the same with mules that had 660 spindles. In other cases, spinners on larger mules continued to be paid at half the official rate or less, in defiance of the commissioner, whose authority and

208

time were insufficient to provide the necessary follow-up to his 10 March proclamation. Certain Rouen spinners, finally, complained of the use of irregular scales to weigh the yarn, begged Deschamps to issue rules to govern this matter and requested the abolition of all disciplinary fines in the mills "in view of the great disgrace this causes in the shops."

> We would prefer to establish a common fund ourselves [rather than have fines used to create a sick fund]. We assure you that the work would not suffer, that we would labor with zeal and exactitude, and protect if need be the holy government of the French Republic. This is why, citizen, we implore your clemency to render justice to us, for which, with good reason, you would enjoy our profound gratitude.[61]

What the spinners of the Rouen area tried to obtain in 1848 was not relief from subsistence-level wages set by the grim operation of the self-regulating market. Such an idea could not have been further from their minds or from the realities of their practical work experience. What they wanted was to be treated, as much as possible, as independent operators, equal in dignity to the owners, free of all but self-generated discipline, dealing with owners of the machines on terms set by the Republic, terms which allowed them to be the principal beneficiaries of any advance in the productivity of their labor. Here was their idea of the organization of work. Their brief success resulted only from the misapprehensions of a hard-pressed commissioner who saw the organization of work as the moderate alleviation of competitive pressures on labor and the reconciliation of all classes to a new republican order (but one in which property and free trade continued to determine economic activity).

How this situation in the mills might have evolved will never be known; the development of the movement in Rouen was cut short by the insurrection of 27–28 April and its vigorous suppression by the National Guard. Deschamps resigned on the thirtieth; all leaders and suspected leaders of the revolt – which meant all adherents to the Republic of even minor prominence among the poorer classes – were rounded up and taken off to Caen for trial.[62] From this time forward, Rouen-area mill owners were again in absolute control of their shops and sure of the enthusiastic support of the government and the police. Their nightmare was over.

In the Lille–Roubaix area, Ledru-Rollin's commissioner Charles Delescluze (later to win fame as head of the 1871 Paris Commune) collaborated closely with Alphonse Bianchi, editor of the opposition paper *Le Messager du Nord*, who like Courmeaux in Reims and local leaders in other towns brought together representatives of Lille's mutual aid societies shortly after the revolution.[63] The aim was to create local versions of Louis Blanc's grand Commission of Government for the Laborers, the so-called Luxembourg Commission, which was to propose sweeping reforms for French industry. Together Delescluze and Bianchi took steps quickly to reduce hours and increase wages in the local spinning mills. On 15 March, an agreement was signed by mill owners and spinners' delegates in Delescluze's presence reducing hours to nine per day and binding owners to do "everything within the limits of the possible" to ensure that spinners earned 12 francs per week at the minimum.[64] If the spinners' earnings fell short of this mark, the town government was to make up the difference. (Was this an echo of the 1839 wage-insurance scheme?) Delescluze had wasted no time imposing reforms on industry whose resemblance to the measures promoted by Deschamps in Rouen is doubtless no accident. Both commissioners were, in all probability, following the lead of the provisional government in Paris, that had responded to workers' demonstrations in the last week of February with decrees shortening hours throughout France to a maximum of 12 and calling for the establishment of minimum-wage levels. The provisional government had also outlawed *marchandage* in response to vigorous demands by Paris construction workers. This word referred to subcontracting by competitive bid, a practice whose elimination abolished at a stroke all free competition within the construction industry. Needless to say, the provisional government had no clear idea of this result. Its commissioners outside Paris were even less clear about the meaning of the word and, therefore, in following the Paris example, concentrated on those elements of the decree that they could understand, that is, those concerning wages and hours.[65] In this way, Deschamps inadvertently sanctioned measures in the Rouen cotton mills that were of equally revolutionary potential, by trying to decree a uniform piece rate. Delescluze had mollified mill owners in Lille by opening the public coffers to supplement their payrolls when necessary, an idea which prompted vigorous objections from the mayor of suburban Wazemmes a week later.[66] What the spinners of Lille thought of this new arrangement is not recorded. It is certain, however, that it had hardly touched the real problems of the trade as they saw them. In the ensuing months, with little regard for the rapidly evolving political situation, the spinners raised other, more vexing issues.

The charter of the Société républicaine des fileurs de Lille (Republican Society of the Spinners of Lille, formed probably as a branch of Bianchi's Société républicaine de Lille) was approved by the government on 24 April, as conservative victories were still being tallied from the previous day's election.[67] As was mentioned in the section entitled "Oil Lamps and Hidden Scales," the new charter was strongly reminiscent of the 1839 charter that had led to its signatories' trial and conviction for coalition. It provided for weekly meetings and dues, compensation to any spinner who found himself out of work either through no fault of his own or else as a result of having defended his rights, and elaborate regulations to ensure that members of the Society were always the first to be put forward for any job opening. Like the 1839 version, there is a flavor of mutual insurance to the provisions – no mention of strikes or other concerted action, no demands for closed-shop agreements with the owners, even though such provision would now have been perfectly legal.

Having formulated their charter during the conservative electoral victories of April, the spinners chose the closing weeks of June to put forward their list of demands for systematic changes in the workplace, just as the government in Paris was preparing its violent blows against the Luxembourg Commission and its supporters. Delescluze had already been replaced. These demands, and the response made to them by mill owners, are extremely revealing about the state of the trade at that time. Far from being concerned with hours or minimum wages, the spinners were utterly preoccupied with fixing the terms on which yarn was purchased from them by the owners.

They demanded to be paid solely on the basis of "weight, by kilogram or half kilogram," regardless of the machine on which they worked – the same demand as was raised in Rouen three months before. While most mule jennies were of 216 spindles, they commented, many spinners work mules of 324 or 380 spindles; some were asked to run two of these. "The owners pay these unfortunates 14 or 15 francs a week which would equal only about 3.75 francs for operating 216 spindles." Furthermore, the spinners wanted to receive the entirety of the amount per kilogram that they had earned. "We no longer wish to pay the steam-power fee nor the lighting fee."

> This is where the owners make a particularly good killing; and here is why: For a normal mule of 216 spindles, the laborer must pay 8 francs to the owner for steam-power costs plus 1 franc for lighting. For a mule of 324 spindles, the laborers must pay to the owner 10 francs for steam plus one fifth which the owner holds back from his pay because the machine provides one third more work. Hence the owner is the one who profits.

But meanwhile the spinner must pay a higher salary to his piecer, and he is left "with nothing but sweat for his profit [*bénéfice*]."[68]

Mill owners in Lille had managed the introduction of larger mules not by tampering with the piece rates, but instead by raising the steam fee or using other expedients to discount the rate paid on the 216-spindle mule. The spinners were demanding the abolition of all these discounts and fees (a measure that would have had the identical result as in Rouen), creating startling inequalities in the level of earnings of spinners on different size mules and eliminating most of the incentive for owners to

211

introduce larger mules. Finally, the spinners demanded that the piece rate, the reel, and the scale for weighing yarn be precisely the same in every mill; and they protested a number of cases in which their delegates, charged with representing them before the municipal government, had been fired.

The Lille Chamber of Commerce quickly issued public objections to these demands. Their implementation would put a stop to progress – or since that is impossible – would prove the ruin of French industry, the Chamber said. The steam-power fee had started when machines replaced the human arm as the source of power, making work easier, and therefore was perfectly fair.

> In any case, who does not know that the salary is itself a commodity whose amount rises or falls according to whether it is more or less in demand. The abolition of the steam-power fee would therefore necessarily bring an adjustment in the piece rate [*prix des façons*]; the salary would be paid in a different manner, but it would not be higher.

As for the five delegates of the Society who were fired, they had used their positions to conspire against the owners.[69]

In this peculiar way, the owners finally let the official truth be known: Who does not know, they told their spinners, that what we are paying you is a wage – itself a commodity bought by your labor – not a price for yarn. The only rule for determining what you earn is whether your labor is in demand or not; the number of spindles on a machine has no bearing. Yet if it had always been this obvious, one wonders why the owners had persisted for 20 years in maintaining a fixed, unchanging yarn price and adjusting for improvements in machinery by means of ever more complex fee and discount schemes.

The central problem, which both parties overlooked, was the problem of measuring the amount of labor that was exchanged. On identical machines under identical conditions, the answer is easy: Each unit of output is deemed to result from an equal amount of labor put in. But on machines of different size, how does one determine an equal amount of labor? The spinner wished to stick with the concrete truth of the weight of the yarn: More spindles, more yarn, therefore, more labor must have been expended in equal proportion. They complained that to earn the same for tending a larger machine is unjust. The owners went to the opposite extreme, increasing fees just in proportion to the increased capacity of the machines, so that the spinner's earnings remained roughly unchanged, although there can be no doubt that more spindles did entail much more effort to tend.

The form of pay in these mills had not yet become capitalist. Its form was still that of a price paid by weight for a finished good. It was impossible for its form to become capitalist – that is, to become explicitly a wage paid for a labor service – until there was agreement about how the amount of labor delivered was to be measured. Technical change and political revolution together forced this issue to the fore. The former brought changes in the tasks that workers performed, making measurement by means of weighing the product seem absurdly inequitable. And the brief freedom of the revolution allowed laborers to express their preference for product weight as a basis of pay, in spite of these new difficulties. The modicum of independence it provided was that precious. Faced with this problem, the mill owners finally resolved to reform pay procedures in line with the notion of a wage.

The solution that the mill owners adopted in the end was that suggested by the Chamber of Commerce's response of June 1848. In August the spinners' society organized a strike against all mills in which spinners tended more than one mule at a time; this was a first step toward achievement of their whole program. But within a week the strike failed.[70] By the end of the year, all the Lille mills had abolished the steam-power fee and introduced in its place a multiplicity of piece-rate schedules, one adapted to the capacity of each kind of machine.[71] This result was perhaps inevitable. In any case, it marked out the course that the whole textile industry would take for the remainder of the century. To measure the commodity of labor, it was necessary to adopt an indefinite number of piece rates, with one adapted precisely to each kind of task so that the effort expended was perfectly reflected in the price paid per unit of output. This metaphysic of effort was the industry's ultimate solution to the creation of a truly capitalist wage payment system.

The effects of collective actions in the wool-spinning centers of Roubaix and Tourcoing were much the same as in Lille. In October 1848 wool spinners in Roubaix went on strike for a uniform piece rate. (They referred to it as the "rate of Tourcoing," but there is no indication of what this meant.)[72] Sharp differences existed among the spinners' leaders as to the merits of the action. A spinner named Buisine, the president of the Société fraternelle des fileurs de Roubaix, who was also secretary of the Conseil des prudhommes – a body which had been opened up to laborer participation since the revolution – opposed the strike. On its second day, 26 October, he resigned his posts and returned to work. The following day he was replaced at a meeting at the Vache Grasse cafe by someone named Debuchy, whom police referred to as "a dangerous young man who speaks with facility and who is generally spoken of as an adversary of order." He was quoted as saying to the spinners assembled in the cafe, "Even if you were up to your necks in water, I would find a way to save you! So! Gnaw in silence your dry crusts of bread for three more weeks, and your position will notably improve!" He was seconded by a certain Leloir, secretary of the Tourcoing Prudhommes and a known associate of Bianchi in Lille. Leloire was admitted to be a worker although he was later charged with living in idleness off of the dues paid into the Tourcoing spinners' society. But Debuchy (like Bianchi or his other associate, the fiery Dr. Piscart of Tourcoing) was not a worker, according to police charges. They were of the educated classes, "and our poor workers, deprived of intelligence and of healthy reasoning powers, applauded these senseless words."[73]

The mill owners' response to the demands of the Roubaix spinners was obviously aimed at undermining the influence of these dangerous outsiders:

> A uniform rate, *for people who know nothing of spinning mills*, seems to lead naturally to the uniformity and regularity of salaries; whereas we all know, *owners and workers*, that with this sytem put into effect there would be nothing less regular than the salary, given the diverse operating conditions that exist in each mill. [Emphasis in original.]

These diverse operating conditions included:

> differences in the number of spindles of the mules;
> differences in the speed of the crank;
> differences in the number of rotations in the stretch;
> differences in the length of the stretch;
> differences between well or poorly prepared wool.
> And finally differences between a good yarn, regular and not stretched out and an over-twisted yarn, poor and irregular. This final consideration preoccupies the spinner throughout his week. For we all know, and it is incontestable, that no matter what the piece rate the spinner will never have a good week if the work is bad [*si l'ouvrage est mauvais*]. The uniform piece rate is unjust.

In its stead the owners proposed that a guaranteed minimum salary of 2.50 francs per day and a guaranteed average salary of 3 francs per day be used as the basis for calculating piece rates. Under such a system if spinners earned 2 francs a day on one job but 4 francs on another then "the piece rate for that mill has improper gradations or else the work [*ouvrage*] given to certain spinners is extremely bad."[74]

Everything that can be discovered about the art of operating a mule jenny in that period confirms the mill owners' observations; in all probability, those without experiences in the mills who were advising the spinners were not aware of the likely impact of a uniform piece-rate schedule. The mill owners' proposed solution to the problem indeed promised to even out differences in earnings in a manner that many spinners may have greeted as an improvement. But there are two knotty questions raised by the mill owners' comments: first of all, why did the spinners, familiar as they were with the work, agree to demand a uniform

214

piece rate if they knew uniform salaries would not result? Secondly, why did the mill owners only now, in 1848, come forward with a proposal to insulate spinners from variations in earnings that were beyond their control, resulting from bad wool or slow machine speeds or long stretches?

The answer to both questions is that until now, owners had benefited from allowing their spinners to carry some of the risks and some of the costs of production. The spinners, far from protesting this, had only demanded – through a uniform piece-rate schedule – to be allowed a greater share in the profits (so that, for example, if operating a larger machine or if working unusually good wool, the spinners' earnings would go up dramatically). Rather than give up a greater share of the windfalls that go with risk, however, the mill owners proposed a rate-fixing formula designed such that, given an equal amount of effort, no matter what the nature of the job he was assigned to, a spinner would receive equal pay. The idea necessitated a proliferation (and indeed a constant fine-tuning) of precisely calculated piece rates, just as in the case of the Lille cotton-spinning mills. Rather than paying for yarn, the idea was to pay for effort by taking the amount of yarn produced and certain other variables into account to arrive at effort-fair pay levels. Such a pay procedure was more in line with the idea of a wage because yarn measurement now became a vehicle for measuring another quantity, the quantity of effort expended. Accepting for the moment that effort can be measured, and that effort and labor are essentially the same thing, such a procedure satisfies all the requirements of wage labor, or a way of actually buying and selling labor. By the end of December 1848 this pay formula was adopted by the great majority of Roubaix mills; steam-power fees and lighting fees, as in Lille, were abolished.

Whether the spinners were entirely pleased with their new situation is difficult to say; signs of lively discontent continued in Roubaix and Tourcoing throughout 1849. The mill owners' charges, furthermore, had done nothing to shake the spinners' confidence in those outsiders who had promoted the idea of a strike the previous fall. Despite the new guarantees, spinners in both Roubaix and Tourcoing remained preoccupied with the exact manner in which their yarn was evaluated on pay day. In a letter to the prefect of 8 January 1849, Roubaix wool spinners complained that 11 of their fellows had been discharged after the October strike and that certain mill owners were violating their right of association by threatening to fire anyone who remained a member of the spinners' society. Their only reference to the new pay procedure was a bitter protest against mill owners gathering for secret meetings to discuss pay, without including any spinner delegates. Finally, they said, "the Prudhommes decided (which they should not have had to decide) that all scales and reels ought to be open to inspection by the workers. But nothing of the kind has been done; and when we go to complain to the owners, we are politely discharged."[75]

This same overriding concern with yarn-evaluation procedures is evident in the new regulations of the Société fraternelle des fileurs de Tourcoing, adopted on 22 April 1849. These regulations follow along lines already familiar from the Lille Society. Dues are to be gathered and used to compensate unemployment among the members. But the valid causes of unemployment are listed as follows:

> Article 4. The funds of the society shall be used to aid and compensate those who fulfill the following conditions:
>
> Cause to have an owner denounced for discount on the rate in effect; for trickery in the determination of the number [of the yarn]; or in the reel or the scale, or in the weighing up of the *levée*; for increase in the twist [a change in machine setting that would slow down the machine]; or for violation of the hours limitation decree.

Any spinner who did this would immediately receive an award of 5 francs and compensation of 40 percent of normal earnings for any time lost. Article 23 of the regulations made explicit provision for a strike, allowing compensation up to 30 percent of their total dues paid to date to any group of spinners who quit all at the same time for a valid reason. Nowhere in the regulations is there any reference to guaranteed minimums or to the proper calculation of piece rates, or to any of the features of the new rate-setting formula introduced the previous year. The fairness and proper accomplishment of the weighing of yarn remained uppermost in the spinners' minds.[76]

Likewise, it would be wrong to suppose that even now the strike had emerged unequivocally as the obvious form of collective action. Spinners at one of Tourcoing's 13 cotton mills, for example, tried to organize support for an increase in their piece-rate schedule in January. Meeting in their usual cafe, they were inspired by an older colleague (no longer dean of the mill, because he was now too sick to operate a mule), to draw up a new, higher rate schedule of their own. They decided to distribute copies of the schedule (written out by the wife of the cafe owner), to the deans of every cotton mill, so that they could present them to the owners. A fund was to be gathered to support deans in case the owners retaliated by firing them. No other plans were made. When a number of the deans were fired, they went to the local police chief for help in getting their jobs back. No strike was called, no further action taken. The owners (whose earlier meetings about rates had prompted the spinners' efforts), met and agreed to maintain rates at customary levels. This was in itself a small victory.[77] Tourcoing spinners even in 1849 continued to think in terms of insurance of individuals against unemployment, rather than in terms of what would today be called a strike fund. And again it appears that the spinners did not feel sure about how exactly to proceed.

Roubaix spinners, under the leadership of Debuchy, were meanwhile experimenting with tactics of an altogether different order. Twice in 1849 they carried out limited work stoppages aimed at winning concessions in a single mill. These stoppages were staged with all the care necessary to ensure that no legal pretext could be found for action against them. The aim was at once to isolate the mill owners and to concentrate their resources. The society could easily support out of its dues the spinners of one mill at a time. The first attempt came in early May at the small Defrenne mill; 13 out of 17 spinners asked for their *livrets* and retired from the mill demanding an increase in the piece rate. Police could find no reason to intervene; the mayor fulminated in his reports to the prefect against the cleverness of the spinners. But for reasons which cannot be discovered, the action was not pursued for more than three days.[78] In September, Debuchy in concert with *démocrate-socialiste* leaders Bianchi in Lille and Piscart in Tourcoing planned a banquet that would bring together members of the three spinners' societies of these towns in a suburban dance hall. Complaints from the mayor of Roubaix induced the prefect to forbid the banquet. But it appears that a banquet (perhaps of reduced size) was held anyway on 30 September.[79] In the meantime, spinners at another Roubaix mill had given notice in the proper manner and quit work on 1 October demanding higher piece rates. The mayor was sure Debuchy was behind it and that these spinners were receiving 12 francs a week from the society.

The strike was still underway when, in the third week of October, police and prosecutors began a systematic crackdown on the Roubaix and Tourcoing societies.[80] Against the Tourcoing Society the police used the new law prohibiting political clubs. Stationing themselves outside the Society's cafe on the night of 22 October, police agents overheard republicans songs and the cry of "*Vive la république démocratique et sociale!*" At this they broke into the cafe and demanded the names of all present. Those attending included many who were not spinners – locksmiths, wool combers, carpenters – and several workers from Roubaix. This in addition to the political chanting constituted proof that the society was not merely an occupational group but a political club (illegal since mid-summer). It was dissolved.[81] Debuchy and other members of the Roubaix Society were arrested on coalition charges. In November, Debuchy, "seeing that he was not even a worker" was sentenced to 10 months; four Roubaix spinners received sentences ranging from eight days to five months. The last collection of funds in Roubaix that year went to help their families.[82]

The Roubaix Society had in the end become to all intents and purposes a union, in the current sense of the term. Because of its suppression and the long silence that ensued, it is impossible to say whether its new mode of action emanated only from the leadership of Debuchy or whether it was something that the spinners themselves came to see as appropriate. The collaboration between the educated democrat Debuchy and the spinners of Roubaix and Tourcoing has left a record that is in this sense ambiguous. Did Debuchy fail to understand the significance of demanding a uniform piece rate in October 1848? Despite his sophisticated strategy, was it he who pushed for rate increases in 1849 when the spinners were more deeply concerned about the fairness of yarn-weighing practices? Even if the answer to both of these questions were yes, this brief experience of freedom of action (and of freedom to choose their leaders) in 1848–49 left an enduring mark on the textile laborers of the region, but not one that can be gauged in terms of institutional or tactical achievement. Eighteen years passed before a recognizable strike occurred again in the town of Roubaix; and it was not until 1872 that a *Chambre syndicale* was formed there, the first of a great array of unions that would flourish in the region under the Third Republic.

LIMITING CASES

Throughout Normandy and the Lille–Roubaix area spinners in 1848 challenged the employers' right to control the fruits of enhanced productivity, by insisting on flat-rate prices for all yarn. Following the defeat of the popular forces in Rouen in April, mill owners regained the upper hand, reintroduced the *tâche* system on a broad scale, and continued increasing the size of their mules. In Lille and Roubaix, mill owners thoroughly revamped the whole pay system, abandoning the pretense of charging fees for heat, light, and steam, elaborating new piece-rate scales that attempted to measure effort. In terms of workplace practice, wage labor may be said to have finally begun.

In both areas, spinners were helped by government officials and educated activists who more or less misunderstood their grievances, failed to appreciate the implications of specific demands, and applied stereotypical views of the workers' plight in an uncritical manner. The goal for them was to reduce hours and shore up wages by means of government-sponsored accords or carefully planned strikes. The miscues would surely have been discovered sooner or later had not the tide of reaction swept away all these efforts at collaboration between laborer and middle-class visionary before they got very far.

In other northern textile centers the story of the revolutionary period does not fall into the same pattern. In both Mulhouse and Reims, for example, there are records of considerable activity among textile laborers, but none of it can be linked to significant technical or managerial changes in the mills. It may simply be that such changes were not occurring at that time in mills of either of the two towns so that methods of payment and control of machinery did not come up.

Mulhouse mill owners cut back to eight-hour days at the beginning of the revolution, anticipating a severe slump in demand.[83] Spinners were offered an indemnification for the short time equal to one-and-a-half hour's pay. In other words, once the price for their yarn was tallied on pay day, they received an extra payment equal to three-sixteenths of the price (one-and-a-half divided by eight). Mulhouse spinners were used to this sort of complicated calculation; at Koechlin Dolfuss frère, for example, there was a three-level premium system and apparently complicated formulas for figuring the pay of piecers.[84] The piece-rate system was therefore already huge and complex before the indemnity payment was added on. It appears that Mulhouse had long passed the transition to effort-based pay that was causing so much opposition in Normandy and the Nord. Mulhouse spinners attempted a series of strikes (the word appears in the reports) – without any organization or central planning – in late July and August when several mills stopped paying the indemnity. These were minor affairs but caused much anxiety for the local police; a left wing group (including "some foremen and even workers") had just won the municipal elections.[85] Members of the National Guard had been heard to declare that they would not protect the mills. But the trouble blew over by the end of August.

In Reims the remarkable Association rémoise flourished for over two years and attracted the participation of a large number of wool weavers and mule spinners.[86] But there are no records of workplace change having any impact on its activities. The Association was born out of the attempt of local Icarians to ward off violence in the days following the February insurrection. Under the leadership of a librarian, Eugène Courmeaux, they called a meeting of all the presidents and secretaries of mutual aid societies in the town on the night of 25 February, as crowds of laborers and National Guard skirmished in the streets. Courmeaux was sure that "the mass of the laboring population" could be easily returned to a stance of calm vigilance if called on by those who had its confidence. Those present at the meeting took up his suggestion and "plunged into the middle of the crowd" to urge their fellows to go home. The fighting was stopped. One mill, which had recently installed the first steam-powered looms in the region, was burned down on the twenty-sixth; but following this incident the subsequent months and years at Reims were free of violence. Gustave Laurent has attributed this fact to the Icarians' commitment to peaceful change, and the strength of their influence in the town.[87]

From calming the crowds it was but a short step to the establishment of a permanent organization, first as a campaign organ under the name of the Comité électoral de la Démocratie rémoise, and later as a comprehensive working-class institution, the Association rémoise. Courmeaux was made subcommissioner for the Reims area; another Icarian, a wool weaver, was given a seat on the new municipal council. Nowhere in 1848 did the working class seem more self-conscious, more well organized, or more successful than in Reims. Of course they suffered from the familiar weaknesses – the failure to gain control of the unemployment relief effort, and a naiveté about electoral politics that led to crushing defeat at the polls in April.

The Association rémoise, like the Luxembourg Commission, was a comprehensive grouping of *corporations* of laborers, one for each trade, each *corporation* having a democratically elected council. It is difficult to say what the real extent of participation in the Association was, but at least twenty-one such *corporations* were created by January 1849, and 13 still existed at the time of its dissolution two years later. Prominent among them were the *corporations* of weavers, of combed-wool spinners and of carded-wool spinners, of wool finishers (*tondeurs*), as well as of numerous artisanal trades: shoemakers, masons, carpenters, tailors, and others.[88] The Association promised relief to its members in case of *chômage ordonné* (sanctioned unemployment), which explicitly included nonremunerative duties in public office or electioneering; but no mention was made of disputes with employers. According to one of its inspirers, an eye doctor formerly of Lyon named Agathon Bressy, the ultimate goal of the Association was the "exploitation of labor by the proletariat itself" – associative production. It is not known whether experiments in this line were carried out.

One gains the impression that Reims authorities felt no anxiety about the actions that the Association sponsored, even in cases where workplace confrontations were involved. An agreement in one wool spinning mill was negotiated in February 1849 establishing a 10-hour day and a compensatory raise in rates of 5 centimes per hundred spindles – without the need for a work stoppage. When the spinners found that the pay increase did not compensate for the shortened day, they quietly returned to the former system. In October and November 1849 there was a general strike in all the spinning mills of the town, carried out in perfect calm and extending over four weeks, in protest against a rate cut introduced that fall. But the police reports on the incident are laconic, summary, unconcerned; a lieutenant of the Gendarmerie blithely commented in the third week of the strike that there was no reason for the authorities to concern themselves over the affair. There is no record of the outcome of the strike.[89] This is a startling contrast with police reports on other laborers' actions of that same period. In this and one or two other incidents, Reims spinners demonstrated, even in apparent defeat, calm self-confidence. And their demands were in every case perfectly in line with the expectations of middle-class reformers.

With the exception of the one power-loom mill burned down in February, weavers in Reims apparently engaged in no collective action during the revolution, despite the prominence of some of their number in the Association. Weavers throughout the north were notably quiescent in 1848 and 1849, considering their activism earlier in the 1840s.[90] It may be that conditions in the trade were so depressed that action seemed irrelevant. The famous industrial inquiry carried out by the Republic during 1848 collected evidence that rates being offered to rural weavers were extremely low; indications are that many had temporarily abandoned the trade.[91]

UNCERTAIN HARVEST

The consequences of the revolution and the forms of action and organization it threw up thus varied considerably from place to place. A high level of political involvement and the coordinated planning of strikes in Reims coincided with little apparent change in workplace practice. Normandy and Lille–Roubaix, where political organization was visibly less elaborate and more vigorously repressed, saw rather profound changes in the relationship between owner and laborer associated with significant technical alterations. In Mulhouse, where this transition seems already to have been accomplished, laborers participated in a successful electoral organization but were left to their own devices as far as work was concerned, their principal recorded grievance being resistance to the end of a relief measure. Rural weavers, finally, have left very little impression at all on the extant documents; political organization in any case remained difficult in the countryside throughout this period and the trade was severely depressed.

It can be said with some confidence, however, that textile laborers, briefly enjoying complete freedom to act, did not immediately set out to form unions and launch strike efforts to better their market position. Their most noteworthy grievances concerned an on-going defense of every fragment of independence that remained to them in workplace practice. Mutual insurance schemes continued in favor; calls for fair and open procedures in the weighing-up of yarn remained common. But the demand for flat-rate yarn prices regardless of the size of the machine turned out to be a hopeless one. Whether the spinners knew it or not, it struck against the core of entrepreneurial control of the workplace, a control that mill owners had to exercise if they were to survive in a competitive yarn market. Larger mules had to be introduced and rates paid for yarn cut back in proportion so that productivity advances could be translated into profits and competitive prices. In response to the impracticable demand, the vestiges of subcontracting (so useful in Lille and Roubaix in the previous two decades) were now jettisoned forthwith. Piece-rate scales became more complex in order to isolate an abstract feature of laborer behavior – effort.

None of the political helpmates who offered themselves to textile laborers in this period appear to have appreciated what was going on. Codron, Deschamps, Delescluze, Bianchi, and Debuchy led without giving much attention to the specificities of their followers' existence. They were workers; their problems could be deduced from this fact. Spinners and weavers were happy to follow. Despite the confusions that resulted, their experience of solicitude and leadership of this kind had a profound impact.[92] Somewhere between the abstractions of learned discourse and the realities of their lives, laborers, between 1848 and 1850, went through formative experiences. The idea that they were members of an oppressed working class seems to inform every subsequent collective action. The idea of the strike (and the word for it) gained wide currency, although other forms of action, as in Tourcoing in 1849, were not ruled out (and the word continued for some time to mean other things). Finally, by the end of the Republic a deep bitterness and sense of loss had descended over the mill towns of northern France that would color everything which came afterward.

A sense of loss, a feeling of membership in the working class, a set of possible conventions to follow in organizing and protesting – these are sizable acquisitions for two-and-a-half years of at first bright, then waning freedom. The kind of ambiguity so evident in the incidents at Lille and Radepont in 1839 will not be seen in that precise form again. The new machines and pay procedures inside the mills would do their part, as well, to alter the context of conflict and the laborer's notion of who he was. But it should not be imagined that all problems had been cleared up, nor that the old attachment to elements of independence had disappeared. Textile laborers had reaped a variety of new ideas and practical experiences, but it was not at all obvious what sort of harvest this was. After all, as long as they were not properly armed against the tendentious terms of market culture, could they ever hope to create a collective identity that took their whole social predicament into account?

After all, was not their desire for independence at base a longing to break free of the reign of market categories over their lives? Mule spinners wanted to be left completely to themselves during the week. Assigned to a particular machine, in control of their own discipline and of whatever fines they might choose to impose on themselves, they would be free to weigh all the different criteria for guiding action that arise in the normal course of human life. Instead of being subjected to the single criterion of maximizing production, they would be free to act on the assumption that work was more than just producing, it was also living; they would be free to take breaks as they pleased, to speak with a friend for a moment, to arrive late if they chose, to spend an extra moment checking the spindles for wear, to stare out the window at the blue sky. The owner would have nothing to say about it. His influence would be limited to setting a single price for each grade of yarn and paying that price on pay day, providing a firm basis for the calculations spinners made about how to spend their time. His larger, more productive mules would reward the spinner generously for the extra attention and anxiety they caused. This was the ideal that the spinners glimpsed on the day after the revolution. But 1848 in the end did not offer them a coherent public language for expressing or defending this ideal.

PART THREE

Unquestioned assumptions, 1852–1904

> The relations of capital and labor have, up to the present remained in [a] state of juridical indetermination. A contract for the hire of services occupies a very small place in our Codes, particularly when one thinks of the diversity and complexity of the relations which it is called upon to regulate. But it is not necessary to insist upon a gap which is keenly felt by all and which everybody seeks to fill.
> —Emile Durkheim *The Division of Labor in Society* (1893)

Thanks to the recent flurry of new research, the revolution of 1848 is emerging as a period of ferment among French laborers in some ways more creative than anything that has occurred since. For a while they felt self-confident; they thought they had won and that the struggle was over. Without much central leadership or planning they set about rebuilding the world of labor as they wanted it, ignoring the warning signs of impending reaction until it was too late. Never again would they be so naive; but at the same time never again would their aims be formulated with such a slim admixture of market language. In the future, escaping from the reign of the market would be relegated to the status of a dim hope. Action would be increasingly planned with an eye to manipulating market forces. Many of the socialist and union organizations that later grew up under the Third Republic encouraged such manipulation. The state accommodated it. Laws allowing for strikes and unions and facilitating collective bargaining were slowly pushed through, at first by a liberalizing Empire, later by the working class' own elected Radical and socialist representatives.

But market language remained so ill-adapted to the reality of textile laborers' relations with employers and with each other that the formal structures of unions and strikes could hardly contain all the complex forms of grievance that moved them to act. In this they were hardly different from French laborers in many other trades. The new conventional structure of protest was pressed into service as a means of expressing a whole array of dissatisfactions that could never be resolved by a negotiating session. Michelle Perrot has brilliantly described the strange amalgam that resulted.[1] The strike took on the character of an insurrection against constituted authority, of a holiday from the daily calculus of work, of a collective celebration, of a subsistence emergency that brought the pooling of meager resources. The idea of the general strike as a means to revolution fed upon and in turn encouraged this development. Local strikes were felt to give a foretaste of post-revolutionary society; the power of bosses was in abeyance; street demonstrations angrily announced its defeat; the strike kitchen was always a *soupe communiste* that foreshadowed the end of private property. A great many things occurred that had very little to do with winning demands; often enough the multiplex purposes that strikes served ensured that they would fail as market maneuvers. Above all the bosses, for reasons which only partially involved maximizing profits, put up a stone wall of resistance against any form of collective treating with their employees.

As a result, mere market maneuvers continued to make little sense to laborers. It has been common to see all these aspects of strike activity in the second half of the century as irrational and immature. But this is true only if one assumes that open–market exchange was the defining element of the wage relationship. As soon as one questions this assumption, then the evidence of supposedly irrational strike behavior can be used to help discover what the wage relationship was really like. For the textile trade, the evidence is in fact overwhelming that nonmarket factors – family survival, political and patriarchal authority, control of the workplace, the desire for independence – continued to play a determining role. Unfortunately as time passed, the possibility of finding a theoretical and political language adequate for the defense of nonmarket grievances became dimmer. The terms of market culture took on the status of unquestioned assumptions for all concerned. The real market forces that reigned in product distribution, the unending technical advances that these forces dictated, the deceptive interpretive flexibility of market language, and its continued hold on the literate and the articulate made this an almost inevitable trend. Marxism in the simplified form popularized by French socialists after 1880 only reinforced it.

As individuals, as families, as communities, textile laborers had diverse and complex characters; like any large group of human beings they faced great difficulties coming to an understanding of each other, agreeing on conventional notions of who they were as a group and how they should normally act. The abundant dialect literature from textile laborers of the Nord that has recently attracted several historians' attention shows how these people worked with the ideas, images, habits, and economic possibilities at hand to create a coherent way of life. But in the public realm, the language of market culture, by oversimplifying their situation and the problems of collective unity, handicapped their efforts.

8 The clock time of the Second Empire

Under the Second Empire textile laborers learned arithmetic. They had little choice in the matter. On the one hand a prolonged and unprecedented boom stimulated a series of technical changes in the industry that entailed continuous reorganization of tasks and recalculation of pay rates. On the other hand, the regime barred all forms of public protest during its first 12 years and, while legalizing strikes after 1864, continued to forbid trade organizations of any kind and even assemblies of over 20 persons. It remained impossible to meet, to plan, to picket, to demonstrate, to delegate. Opportunities for the expression of fundamental dissatisfaction with the regime or the social order were nonexistent. Laborers found that resistance was most successful when confined to narrow, local, detailed concerns. The boom meant that owners had room to make concessions on pay, and laborers found that they did make concessions when pressed hard enough, provided that the demands were formulated strictly with reference to the specific pay conditions involved. Laborers learned to use the notions of time and effort to advantage, to bargain for the first time over the terms of sale of labor, instead of yarn and cloth. But this new facility did not blot out the old yearnings.

LIBERALISM BY DECREE

The government found it necessary to arrest over twenty-seven thousand individuals when Napoleon seized power in December 1851. Resistance had been fierce, if sporadic. The new regime was under no illusions as to its survivability without the use of force and, with disturbing rapidity, instituted a thoroughgoing police state.[1] At the same time, however, Napoleon III felt he had to live up to the Napoleonic myth (something his uncle would never have done). He had to appear as protector of the people, as embodiment of the popular will, as defender of progress and

227

industry. Therefore from the beginning, he instituted a kind of imperious liberalism. There were elections, but each elector was scrutinized by police or mayor as he placed his ballot in the urn. Opposition parties were not allowed, but opposition candidates might run for office if they requested permission to do so and did not appear dangerous. There was a privately owned press, but it was made dependent on government favor for survival. Napoleon III had all the reins of power in his hand, but on election day he still felt like a candidate; and if his majority fell from 95 to 85 percent it was enough to sow panic among his followers. Such a dip in 1857 pushed him toward his imperialistic experiment at liberating Italy; another in 1863 toward successive liberalizations that had all but created a real parliamentary government by the time of the regime's fall in 1870. In the search for a more enduring popularity, he had given up almost all his personal power by the time he was captured by the Prussians at Sedan.[2] He had warded off the twin dangers of socialism and monarchism by commanding France to be liberal and then belatedly and fearfully giving France some of the substance of a liberal regime.

Even this cynical form of political stability was enough to prompt a stunning revival of commerce. Soon after Napoleon's coup, cash came flowing out from hidden coffers and from under mattresses to irrigate a remarkable growth of credit. Capital investment hit record levels in the early 1850s; textile firms were among the leading beneficiaries of the return of confidence. Machine builders were swamped with orders, with 15- to 18-month delays in delivery of new spinning equipment. Nor was consumer demand lacking. Some spinning mills in Normandy by the fall of 1852 had back orders for two years of full production.[3] In return for acquiescence the working class got higher wages. Some of it was eaten up by higher prices, but not all.[4] This was the period when even simple workers began to have a cheap suit in the closet for wearing to funerals and weddings, when even working-class girls might be seen on the streets in machine lace and crinoline on Sundays. Potato vendors began to fry their potatoes in oil instead of boiling them. Paris masons in Haussmann's heyday lined their apartments with silk brocade, bought inlaid Chinese chests and bric-a-brac for the mantle. Huge new department stores catered to their tastes.[5] Such pretensions were well beyond the means of textile laborers, but even they made significant wage advances. Like the rest of the urban working class, even in the most repressive years of the 1850s, they refused to vote for official candidates.[6] Napoleon was never left in doubt about their attitude. But prosperity, police surveillance, the departure for prison or exile of their former leaders, and the frequent success of clandestine efforts to win wage concessions were enough to keep them in line.

The clock time of the Second Empire

One did not argue with this kind of success. Public discussion continued, at least among the notables, but it was discussion of a highly circumspect nature. Even public inquiry was allowed to continue. Public inquiry is, after all, a characteristic of liberal regimes. Hearings and investigations were carried out in due form according to models laid down under the July Monarchy. But the proper conclusions were known in advance; the evidence gathered was made, in effect, to march forward like the obedient citizen and cast its ballot for official doctrines. The major published sources on the textile trade from this period, as a result, often look like spiritless, almost comical imitations of July–Monarchy originals. The government inquiry into import prohibitions in 1860 or the inquiry into child labor of 1867, for example, follow exactly the same format as their respective predecessors of 1834 and 1837.[7] Even the investigative tradition of Villermé and Blanqui was carried on by new practitioners who published more voluminous tables of average daily wages and family budgets and more poetic breakthrough passages on the shocking conditions of working-class neighborhoods. But political considerations impinged at every step. The shadow of 1848 and the watchful eye of Bonapartist officialdom influenced the composition of every sentence.

Typical of the regime's style was the fiasco made of the inquiry into import prohibitions in 1860. Months before it was due to begin, Napoleon III had surprised the nation with a new free-trade treaty with England.[8] Obviously, he was hardly likely to go back on this decision any time soon; the inquiry had therefore become irrelevant. Nonetheless, a responsive regime consults with its citizens. On the appointed days, the mill owners dutifully came forward to read their evidence and express their support for continued prohibitions before a sleepy board of inquiry, stopping only occasionally to mention their dismay at the suddenness of the recent treaty's conclusion. Four volumes of testimony were duly published. England had free trade and published a continual flow of government inquiries; France would do the same.

That same year, 1860, saw the publication of the second, enlarged edition of Armand Audiganne's *The Working Populations and the Industries of France* as well as the delivery of the first installments of Louis Reybaud's inquiry into the "moral, intellectual, and material condition" of workers in the cotton industry.[9] Each of these in its own way was a masterpiece of political accommodation. Both investigators explicitly and repeatedly acknowledged their intention of carrying on where Villermé left off, bringing up to date the picture he had so masterfully drawn. The differences in emphasis and in treatment of evidence speak volumes, as a result, about the altered political atmosphere brought about by a failed revolution and the imposition of the Empire's liberal straitjacket.

Mulhouse, for example, as these two studies describe it, is hardly recognizable as the same town that Villermé visited in the 1830s or whose misery had been described as recently as the industrial inquiry of 1848.[10] What had moved earlier observers had been the irony that so much industrial prosperity, such evident progress and proficiency should be the cause of painful overcrowding, deprivation, and moral degeneracy among the laboring population. Investigators broke with their otherwise prosaic tone to inject lovingly constructed, rhapsodic passages of vivid (if quickly stereotyped) description in order to bring this irony home to the reader. But in Audiganne's discussion it is almost as if this contradiction had never been an issue. Yes, the town of Mulhouse is a great industrial hub, an exemplary community. But nothing unsettling flows from this for Audiganne. The laborers and their conditions are merely an unfortunate side effect of the town's success: "The mass of the population is, in effect, composed of very mixed elements that the wind of misery blows toward Mulhouse from every point on the horizon."[11] It is almost out of envy that the poor workers come, in other words; their misery antedates their arrival (and therefore cannot be attributed to their salaries or their masters).

Audiganne explicitly takes to task those who have overstated the immorality engendered in the town. That overcrowding increases the likelihood of vice – this, he admits, is well known; but "the prospect of Mulhouse's morality is far from being as dismal as is generally imagined."[12] *Concubinage* (cohabitation), which is common there, results most often because foreigners who come to work in Mulhouse from nearby Swiss and German territory cannot obtain the necessary papers to celebrate a legal marriage. This disorder "does not arise from a systematic and willful opposition to the rule."[13] And, therefore, by implication, it is not very bad. Of course this very inability to obtain papers had been viewed by Villermé as yet another manner in which poverty pushed laborers into lives of immorality. But now the evidence is turned on its head and seems to prove the opposite.

As for the oft-invoked rag-covered children straggling in from the countryside, they do not appear. This figure had been banished by Penot in 1843 – a banishment which was by now, it seems, permanent. The reader is told that spinners live as close to their mills as possible because work often starts before dawn in the winter. The reader is treated to the prospect of 2,000 workers' children marching off – "nicely dressed," Audiganne notes – to the town school; and he remarks as well the large-scale housing projects that have been built thanks to the generous investment of local industrialists. Housewives, finally, are found to keep their homes remarkably clean and neat.[14]

Audiganne mentions that foreign workers have no right to poor relief and remain subject to summary ejection from town at any time that they become unemployed. But even this harsh detail is presented in a comforting form. These workers, according to Audiganne, are the most disorderly of all in their personal lives. "Voyagers of a day on a soil that is ready to reject them," he adds, "they respect no one, except perhaps the gendarme."[15] It is, in other words, a moral flaw in them to remain in Mulhouse at all in the face of such a threat. The fact that they are subject to ejection means that they deserve ejection. Moreover it is not people but "the soil" that rejects them.

Reybaud is even more insistent in his praise of Mulhouse and its forward-looking entrepreneurs than Audiganne. He cannot find words enough to recount all the virtues of the Industrial Society of Mulhouse (of which he gives a complete history, highlighting its social reform efforts), or to describe all of the advantages that the town's mill owners offer to their employees. Unfortunately, however, "unqualified workers abound just beyond the frontier" in Switzerland and the Rhineland and these are attracted to Mulhouse "by the certainty of a salary and the similarity of the language."[16] Precisely as in Audiganne, the character of the working population is made to appear as an accidental feature of geography. *Concubinage* likewise appears as a matter of formalities. Those who fall into "open prostitution," Reybaud finds to be rare; they are "exceptions of the kind one finds everywhere."[17] Reybaud further shows that army recruits from Mulhouse are in just as good health as those from the surrounding countryside, that crime has not increased with the growth of the town; and his long tables of wages and budgets strongly suggest that a comfortable sufficiency is easily available to working-class families. As with Audiganne, in Reybaud's report every hint of a problem is simply conjured away.

In their treatment of Lille, the two investigators diverge significantly, however. Audiganne persists with his strategy of turning once damning bits of evidence on their head. He describes, for example, the unusual custom of Lille mutual aid societies that spend their reserve funds every spring on the celebration of the feast day of Saint Nicolas, the patron saint of spinners. Villermé had remarked the same practice, finding in it a most extraordinary perversity.[18] That the laborers' meager funds, the only resource that they had set aside for a rainy day, should be dissipated regularly on food and drink was for him the ultimate viciousness. Audiganne finds it quaint. The practice was blessed by tradition; the old guilds had followed it before the Revolution of 1789. Being centuries old, religious in origin, and thoroughly implanted in local mores, these festivities were above suspicion. Audiganne is anxious to recall that, unlike certain other practices of mutual aid societies, these in no way result from socialist inspiration.[19]

As for Lille's infamous cellars, they, too, appear to Audiganne in an altered light. Those unhealthy ones that Blanqui had described in his 1848 study – or most of them – the reader is assured have been closed up by the municipal government. In any case, given the inveterate habits of the laborers of Lille, their habitations do not have any great influence on their character. This is because "no one stays at home." Even the owner of a palace in Lille would not stay there long without company. They go out to their little clubs, "*des especes de cercles*," Audiganne calls them, which meet each in one of Lille's numerous cafés, "whose green shutters have a much more agreeable appearance than the reddish front-ages of Paris dance halls."[20] These cozy, green-shuttered meeting spots are, of course, identical with the hideous ant hills smelling of gin and tobacco that had so repulsed Villermé. Beauty is in the eye of the beholder.

Before leaving the subject of Lille's cellars, Audiganne insists that the laborers actually like them anyway and quotes approvingly from a song written by "a worker" called *M'cave et min guernier* ("My Cellar and My Garret"). In the song an inhabitant of Saint-Sauveur says that he had read in the paper about a "whole lot of long speeches" on cellars and alleyways:

J'ai bien compris à m'manière	In my own way I caught the drift
Qu'on nous f'rot aller,	That we were supposed to go
Pour respirer la bonne air	And breathe good air
In haut d'un guernier...	Way up in some garret...
Y m'ont dit, ches gins habiles:	They told me, these clever fellows,
"Vo cave est malsain."	"Your cellar is unhealthy."
J'y vivos avé m'famille	Well I've lived there with my family
Sans besoin d'médecin...	Without any doctor's help...
Allons, y n'y a point d'répliques,	Oh well, there's no possible reply,
A moins qu' j'intindrai	That is unless I hear
Les anches canter des cantiques	Angels singing songs
Pa d'sus d'min guernier.	Up there above my garret.

"The feeling expressed in this song," says Audiganne, "is really that of the masses themselves."[21] They actually prefer these cellars that have been so widely denounced.

Reybaud takes a slightly different tack with Lille. He rehearses in condensed form the spine-chilling descriptions from Villermé and Blanqui of the cellars of the Saint-Sauveur district. He, too, notes that the city has closed many of them up, but the tenement and row houses that are replacing them, he says, are hardly better. Throughout both Lille and Roubaix (he sees no distinction), Reybaud finds "a misery that is cynically displayed and exaggerated [by the inhabitants] more readily than combatted."[22] A few spots are reasonably cared for, showing what could be accomplished if the will were there. Following Villermé's revelations there had been a spate of charitable efforts to right the worst symptoms. "A profusion of bed linens was distributed to poor families; in Lille alone 4,000 iron beds were given out within the space of a few years; mattresses, curtains, blankets rounded out the flood of giving." But often enough these charitable gifts were pawned or sold. "If these classes have reached this level of depravity, one cannot blame it on their salary."[23] In Reybaud's version, the deprivation of Lille laborers is frankly recognized but becomes an extra-economic fact, a consequence of moral decay that perverts any attempt to bring material aid. Their misery is "cynically displayed." Reybaud too wants to say that they like it this way, in other words; but unlike Audiganne who presents this as an innocent matter, a quirk of local custom, Reybaud is repulsed. Either way, of course, society and its economic system are completely exonerated. The dilemma that galvanized public opinion 20 years before is simply nonexistent. It has been cleaned up; it is merely a local tradition; it is an accident of geography; it is the consequence of an inherent immorality.[24]

Everyone had heard enough of working-class suffering in 1848 when socialists had rehearsed the dire exposes of the investigative literature in local town meetings and before the National Assembly. The shock effect of the breakthrough passage had been put to unexpected uses. The mason Nadaud tells of being horrified when he first read Villermé (although he had certainly lived in equally bad conditions in *garnis* around the Place de Grève in Paris). Later he was shouted down in the National Assembly when he tried to talk about it. Hugo was preparing yet another speech on the problem of poverty for the National Assembly when he was forced into exile.[25] The new generation of investigators frankly appealed to a widespread distaste for any further wringing of hands over the plight of the proletariat.

The problem that they faced and that had been unknown to Villermé, however, was precisely that everywhere they turned something new and terrifying called socialism had won working-class support under the Second Republic. What aroused interest in investigators' findings now, what shocked respectable people, was no longer the sharing of beds as in Villermé, but politics. Audiganne and Reybaud served up to their readers the spectre not of incest but of political alienation. Reybaud's favorable opinion of the workers of Alsace is couched in terms of their political, not their moral, orientation. "In the troubled days there were indeed some storms [in Alsace]; these storms did not last; they were more visible in the results of elections than in the shops or the streets."[26] Since that time they have been tranquil and hardworking.

Likewise, Audiganne's one unfavorable impression of Lille textile workers concerns the legacy of 1848: "Nowhere in France is there a larger distance between the two great elements who cooperate in production [capital and labor]. The separation is absolute. Defiance, mute but still active, has taken hold in the depths of the workers' soul."[27] Concerning Rouen he observes:

> One preoccupation torments our workers more even than questions of salary; it is the need for a certain respect, for a certain protocol in the exercise of authority...Unfortunately, it has been gradually mixed with an extreme mistrust of the manufacturers. Quick to suspect, the workers constantly fear being fooled. The idea that they are the victims of an organized exploitation has penetrated their hearts like a poison.[28]

Hope for a solution to this terrible state of affairs, Audiganne constantly reiterated, came from only two directions, from improvements in the condition of workers and from instruction. "Ignorance is perhaps a means of domination, a hardly honorable means, to be sure; but once aggregates of men begin to reflect on their social state, the development of intelligence united to development of the moral faculty is the only way to insure social peace."[29] The revolution of 1848 had occurred because ignorant but thoughtful workers had been duped by the plausible theories of political adventurers. This was the prospect (rather than Villermé's visions of physical deprivation and systematic vice) that Audiganne used to convince his reader of the need for a moderate kind of reform to counter the danger of recurrent revolution.

Audiganne was prepared to approve of the laborer's "need for a certain respect," of his desire for political self-consciousness and participation. The dilemma of the Second Empire was that it could not simply rule such aspirations out of order; Napoleon III had achieved power by appealing to them. Audiganne tried to walk a tightrope on this issue, as did the regime as a whole. He admitted that some of the social experiments of the revolution had much virtue. There was the consumer's cooperative called l'Humanité that had flourished in Lille from 1848 to 1851 when it was suppressed by the police. Fourteen hundred families had bought bread, meat, clothes, and coal at discounted prices through the cooperative. Lille butchers had had to reform their pricing practices due to its competition. It was open to all and voluntary, therefore in Audiganne's mind, free of the taint of socialism. All of this Audiganne approved of enthusiastically. "But," he intoned, "L'Humanité should have feared above all to allow politics any place in its ranks."

> In its halls where the executive commission met, in the kitchen where cooked meats were given out, anywhere, in a word, where members might meet together, prohibitions against political discussion were posted in big letters...Nonetheless the fears that many persons entertained at the time of the danger which politics represented to this association, were justified in the event: the institution was closed by the government.[30]

The fact that it was closed, in effect, proved that it had failed to be apolitical. Was not being closed in itself a political involvement? "Nonetheless," he concluded, "the application of a principle, accidentally defective, does not prevent this principle from producing advantages in more propitious surroundings."[31] That the cooperative had in fact been political was even itself, then, an accidental defect.

The interpretations of July–Monarchy investigators had been capricious in the extreme, those of their Second–Empire counterparts were no less so. Where Villermé found ant hills, Audiganne saw neat green shutters; where Villermé saw a strong contrast between Lille and Roubaix, Reybaud saw none; where Villermé saw the immorality of open and prolonged cohabitation, Audiganne and Reybaud saw merely a bureaucratic detail. Where Villermé saw drunken debauchery, Audiganne perceived a quaint local custom, and Reybaud found misery that was "cynically displayed."

The great difference between Villermé's judgments and those of his successors lay in the uses to which they were put. Villermé's observations were given coherence by the doctrines of political economy, in particular the belief that the labor market determined the condition of laborers. He wished to show that its power had certain limits, that the laborer still retained a restricted realm of self-determination (and therefore of moral responsibility). Further, he found that limited reforms might enlarge that realm. Reybaud's and Audiganne's judgments were given coherence by Napoleon III's coup d'état. Having debunked the now politically dangerous idea that market forces were in any way damaging, they concluded that the victims of poverty and repression were themselves responsible. That they were victims proved that they deserved to be victims. If Alsatian towns exercised the right of expulsion over immigrants, it only showed how indifferent the immigrants were about where they lived. If the government closed up a useful cooperative, it only proved how dangerous it was to dabble in politics. Arbitrary thought justified the use of arbitrary power. It is significant that the same methods of inquiry, the same rules of evidence, the same canons of proof could be used to arrive at such vastly different, but in each case politically correct, conclusions. The economic doctrines that were applied in one case were as arbitrary as the power that was exonerated in the other. But then, salvaging those doctrines from a mortal threat was the task that had required Napoleon's dictatorship in the first place.

GRADGRIND IN THE FACTORY

The arbitrary power of the state found its way not only into published documents about the textile trade but also into the mills themselves. Certainly its greatest impact was indirect, by limiting the ability of laborers to act, and doing so more effectively than previous regimes had been able to. But direct influence was also present, as demonstrated by the activities of F. Dupont in the department of the Nord between 1852 and 1867.

F. Dupont served for years as the only salaried factory inspector in the country; he was hired in 1852 by the prefect of the Nord, who alone among his colleagues felt sufficient pangs of conscience to take seriously the enforcement of the 1841 child labor law. Dupont's task was herculean: to watch over several thousand workplaces scattered over the space of the whole department and to make sure somehow that no child under eight was admitted to work in them, that any child between eight and twelve worked no more than eight hours a day and attended classes for primary instruction during the noon lunch hour, and that children from 12 to 16 worked only 12 hours a day and only if they had a certificate of instruction.[32] These provisions of the 1841 law had never had even a beginning of enforcement. A number of Alsatian mills had voluntarily complied with some provisions and, as Audiganne mentioned, lunchtime schools had been established at least in Mulhouse. In the Nord, nothing had been done.

Dupont first worked to induce the major industrial towns – Lille, Roubaix, Tourcoing, Armentières – to establish noon classes and find a place for them in the municipal budget, so that it was at least hypothetically possible for mill owners to comply with the law. By 1860 or so, he had in fact single-handedly shamed these town governments into taking the necessary steps. But having gotten this far he was faced with an even greater difficulty created by the widespread indifference to clock time that he found prevailing in the Nord's spinning mills and weaving shops. How could he discover if eight- to twelve-year-olds worked more than eight hours if all the mills in a particular town started work at different times, changing those times from one season to the next, and if no one could tell him exactly what those times were since every mill had a clock that followed its own idea of the hour? Worse still, how could he ensure that the children reached noon classes on time if every mill had a different idea of when noon was? Dupont reported such conditions in every one of the larger towns. It was not that the work itself was not timed by the clock in the mill; it was. Work ended thirteen and a half hours after it began, with an hour and a half off in between for lunch and breaks. (At least this was the case in steam-powered shops; Dupont reported that in some weaving shops, weavers seemed to come and go at will).[33] But the end of work was measured strictly only vis-à-vis the beginning in most cases. The beginning of work often depended on the time at which sufficient daylight was deemed to be available for work; the clock was then set at 5:30 (or 7:00 in winter) and the steam engines ran until the clock read 7:00 in the evening (or 8:30 in winter). In most mills, it seems, even though the posted work rules stipulated break and lunch periods, laborers were free to take these times off whenever they wished. Most arranged things so that the machines could run all day, while spelling each other for rest periods when convenient. In Dupont's report on Roubaix of 13 February 1858, he admitted resignedly that posted work rules that specified the hours of operation mean nothing. "These documents are usually copied from that of a neighboring mill and are put up purely for form's sake. They serve as legal protection in case of complaints made to the Prudhommes."[34] Spinners and piecers "generally" did stop for lunch, but women and girls in preparations were arranging to spell each other all through the day and everyone contrived to do so for breaks morning and evening.[35]

Dupont's reports do not imply the machines were working steadily thirteen-and-a-half hours per day. Evidence from the 1860 inquiry into import prohibitions shows that managerial style had not changed all that much since 1834. There was no revealing controversy in 1860 (since the import prohibitions had already been lifted). But one finds the same unexplained discrepancies in output figures; for No. 15 cotton yarn, for example, reported output per spindle per year ranged from a high of 37.8 kilograms to a low of 15.8 kilograms. The low figure was reported, significantly, by Joly of Saint-Quentin, an old and competent firm; they explained that their figure took Monday absenteeism and other causes of down time into account.[36] Octave Fouquet of Rouen reporting on the family's latest mill provided a whole range of figures on size, capacity, and costs, including average daily wages – mentioning as an afterthought that the mill was still under construction.[37] In short, old habits remained in force. What Dupont's reports do suggest is that when the machines were running well, laborers were reluctant to stop them. They enjoyed their down time when it was convenient; the bobbins got full, a roller jammed, or the roving ran out, and then it would be time to see how friend Auguste was doing at the other end of the shop. Official break periods were ignored. Dupont himself remarked that laborers were much more respectful of official lunch hours and much less inclined to relay each other at the machine during off-season when business was slack.

This rhythm of work particularly annoyed Dupont, although he does not come out and say it. The disorderliness of the real social world exasperated him. The scandal of child labor was frustratingly different from what he supposed it to be. There was no strictly measured exploitation of the child by capital upon which he could conveniently impose his own state discipline. Instead, he found a series of informal arrangements and encountered great difficulty measuring anything. Mill owners smilingly told him that they did not know the ages of the children in their shops; they were the employees of the adults. Repeatedly they assured him that the children did not work more than four hours a day anyway; they took naps behind the machines; they played with friends in the courtyard.[38] Dupont grudgingly acknowledged the truth of this but insisted that the law was blind to such matters.

He found, in fact, that he often had to disregard completely the well-being of the laborers in order to enforce his law. He forced a mill owner in Lille to dismiss three children in 1858 because they were under 12 and were not listed in the mill's register. (These registers were another requirement he had invented.) By chance, a police report on the same case has been preserved in Dupont's files, revealing that the three children had been working with their mother, a young widow recently arrived from a village near Ghent. She had no money to pay for baby sitting and no local network of friends to turn to for help. She had already been fired at one mill because her youngest could not possibly pass for 12. Now she was fired again. Dupont had turned them out on the street without resources, yet he breathed not a word of this in his own report. Even the police agent who reported the whole truth remarked on the cynical willingness of parents to exploit their own children.[39]

Dupont was not to be deterred by an intractable reality. True to the tenor of the regime that employed him, he aimed to force expectations decreed by principle on the reality that confronted him. If the scandal of child labor did not appear in the form that the law had envisioned, then the mills would first be reformed so that they could be scandalous in the proper way and then be forced to comply with the law. The mill towns would have to accept the idea of a communal clock. With an official time told by a clock at the town hall and with a bell or a whistle to announce it, it would at least be possible to coordinate lunch hours, to get all the children to class at roughly the same time, and to know just how long they were being exploited each day. But this idea was strenuously resisted by the mill owners. Where in the law did it say how they should set their clocks? Dupont was trespassing in an area where government had no competence. The Lille Chamber of Commerce was particularly piqued, as their response to an 1867 questionnaire shows.[40] It appears that at least Roubaix and Armentières, however, were induced in the end to establish a town clock.[41] In this way, some factories were at last made to run with a bit of that regularity appropriate to the accepted image of a factory.

Irregularities persisted throughout Dupont's 15-year tenure, of course. Massive absenteeism and indiscipline plagued the noon classes; Dupont found parents who were willing to pay the necessary fine in order to keep their children working with them during lunch. Dupont never solved the problem of determining which children had worked more than eight hours. Piecers had soon been taught to lie to him when questioned about this matter, he complained.[42] There was the annoying habit Tourcoing children developed of switching mills whenever he came to town to inspect. After working eight hours with their usual spinner the piecers would leave work as required by law but then run across town to work the rest of the day with another spinner. Meanwhile *his* piecers would arrive at the first mill to "start" work, relaying the ones who had just "quit." As Dupont examined each mill in turn, he would see what appeared to be an admirable and orderly conformity to the law. And in fact no one could be charged since each individual mill did not work a piecer under 12 for more than eight hours – as long as Dupont was in town.[43] Children were in short supply, particularly during peak periods; it was impossible to have a real second shift. Spinners had enough trouble as it was hiring all they needed. But this marvelous scheme carried out by the Tourcoing laboring community reveals as well the extent to which informality – that is, the community's own chosen order – still reigned in work arrangements in the mills.

Dupont did make some headway against it all. Here is where his peculiar form of blindness had a real impact on practice. By dint of single-minded persistence Dupont had, by 1866, overseen the establishment of numerous classes, straightened out the time schedules of hundreds of mills, induced a good number of them to do away entirely with children under 12 in the shops, and actually imposed a grudging, halfway conformity to the law in the department. Modest success had brought imitation; by 1867 there were similar salaried inspectors in six other departments, most active only since 1865.[44] The real significance of the changes Dupont and company were carrying out concerned not so much compliance with the law, as those subtle shifts in practice which made enforcement possible. Dupont's impact resulted from his blindness, from his sublime indifference to how factories actually worked. It was already known how they worked and what they were; therefore, they were forced to conform more closely to what was known of them.

True to form, the regime fired him and his colleagues without notice or pension in 1867 at the conclusion of a new inquiry into child labor. The job of enforcing the 1841 law was turned over to the already over-burdened mining inspectors, which meant in practice that all enforce-ment was suspended.[45] Doubtless the complaints of the Lille Chamber of Commerce against this officious individual had had their effect.

THE PLASTICITY OF LABOR

But time was on Dupont's side. Market forces, given free play on the product-distribution side under this economically orthodox government, were pushing shop-floor practice in a similar direction. The clock became a growing preoccupation of all parties, as technical change forced re-organizations of work and pay.

The boom was an imperious one. Raw cotton imports expanded to 64 million kilograms in 1854, to 114 million in 1860.[46] Wool and linen grew less rapidly until the American Civil War caused a disastrous drop off in cotton imports and the two traditional fibers moved in to pick up the slack.[47] The sustained intensity of demand ensured that even poorly equipped firms could turn a profit, but it also eliminated fears about investing in new equipment. And new kinds of equipment were constantly being brought out.

In spinning, the new generation of larger mule jennies that had come in the mid-1840s and been such a contentious issue during 1848 turned out to be only the first round in a series of major improvements. By 1855 self-acting mules were available at affordable prices, offering varying degrees of automation. Most common were those self-actors that were capable only of driving the mule through the stretch, still requiring the spinners' attentive assistance for the winding on. Those that offered com-pletely automatic operation were rather rough on yarn, useful only for the coarser numbers, and in practice often plagued with problems of gearing and tension adjustment. For the finest numbers, no self-acting mechanism proved sufficiently sensitive to be competitive with the simpler machinery.[48] Nonetheless, the introduction of this equipment in many mills meant a major change in work routines for spinners. The only way mill owners could save on labor costs (and thus pay for their investments) was by inducing spinners to tend even greater numbers of spindles and by hammering out new lower prices for the yarn they produced. All of the issues so passionately disputed in 1848 were thereby insured contin-uous relevance, only now it was in a political climate that discouraged thought and suppressed attempts at organization or protest.

In weaving as well, power looms were available by the mid-1850s capable of handling simultaneously up to six different colors of yarn, so that the weaving of fancy plaids, checks, and eventually even herringbone and similar patterns could be moved out of the cottage and into the factory. Most of these machines were slow, however, offering only limited improvements in productivity in return for heavy investment, so the transition was a prolonged one.[49] (One finds a flurry of reports from as late as 1878, for example, on the final dying out of handloom weaving of fine linens and muslins in the Saint-Quentin and Cambrai areas.)[50] At the same time, looms used on common numbers got better; breaks in the yarn became rarer, operation smoother. The weaving of cotton became almost entirely a female profession, as owners sought to employ the cheapest labor possible on a task no longer deemed difficult. To realize real savings on labor costs from these improvements, owners tried to get their weavers to double up, tending two looms at a time, while accepting substantial cuts in piece rates.

During the cotton famine of the early 1860s, caused by the American Civil War, towns like Roubaix and Reims that specialized in cheap woolens and other cotton substitutes, used their profits to hasten in the age of steam-powered looms. With the return of U.S. cotton to the market after 1867, they in their turn faced shrinking demand and difficult readjustments.

Change was therefore the order of the day, and every one of these changes required owners to interfere directly in the work process, to induce their laborers to alter their habits, apply themselves more assiduously, and accept dramatic price cuts. What had occurred once or twice between 1820 and 1850, inducing owners for the first time to actually attempt labor management, now became almost a routine. Laborers did the best they could with the only weapon at hand – mute, informal resistance. The record suggests that they were successful at least in winning some monetary compensation for all the changes.

Typical of what must have occurred in hundreds of mills is an 1856 dispute in Lille reported on by an overzealous police informer. (Had he not been in danger of losing his job, this minor fracas would never have attracted any attention.)[51] The mill owner Charvet announced a 25 percent pay cut to his spinners on 30 September, citing as the cause a recent scare in the markets that had sent prices momentarily plummeting. But this was a ruse, for after half of his spinners had quit in protest he took no steps to replace them. Instead, during the following week he began having new long handles installed on the drive gears of the mules. He was making the handles easier to reach from a distance in order to begin assigning each spinner two mules to tend instead of one.

Jean-Baptiste Cambier, married with two children, one of the spinners who had remained at work, was involved in a street fight with a fellow spinner during the morning break following the walkout. Vernier, a younger spinner who had quit, approached Cambier and a friend, be-

241

rating them for staying on with Charvet. They were cowards, he said; the cotton spinners of Lille ought never to work at such a price. A scuffle began; Cambier pushed Vernier who fell on his hand on the pavement and broke his wrist. Vernier pressed charges and Cambier and his friend were arrested at the mill that morning and charged with assault. But they were freed later on. (Did Charvet intervene in their favor?)

After resisting this kind of pressure from their fellows, the spinners who stayed on with Charvet were particularly angered two weeks later when further double-dealing from Charvet again threatened their wages. Having switched them over to two-mule work, Charvet revealed to them that he was only going to pay them half as much as before. After all, he argued, they were being paid for the yarn from twice as many spindles. By this time they had already done a week's work on the new system. By this reckoning Cambier, who normally earned 20 francs a week, was to receive only 14 francs, his fellows even less. A bitter argument erupted between Charvet and his remaining spinners; they refused to accept pay reckoned in this way. In the end Charvet agreed to pay Cambier 22 francs and the other spinners 20 each and to continue paying them these fixed amounts for a three-week test period. On the basis of output during this period they would then hammer out a new piece-rate schedule for two-mule work. Here the reports break off.

Charvet faced a common problem, trying to translate machinery improvements into lower labor costs, which required altering the work patterns of the shop. Laborers must tend more spindles or more looms. Piece rates must be lowered to reflect the greater output possible under the new arrangement. But lowered how far? To what extent did tending increased capacity entail greater effort? To what extent did the new arrangement require a learning period before new rates were set? Uncertainty about these matters usually resolved itself into a struggle of wills between laborer and owner. Given the political climate, laborers did better if they struggled on the owner's terms, appealing to his sense of fairness, countering with their own calculations of proper pay. Charvet's initial assumption that twice as many spindles justified halving the piece rate was so patently unfair that eventually he was made to back down. Having docilely accepted a 25 percent pay cut weeks earlier, his remaining spinners now argued bitterly and successfully against him. He saw they would leave the shop: Good, he must have thought, this is as far as I can push them. Such limits were difficult to identify. As soon as the test period began, doubtless the struggle only moved into a new phase. Charvet's foremen would have to make sure the spinners did not go slow hoping to falsify the test results. Control took one step forward.

Numerous conflicts of this kind have left traces behind, if one is alerted to look for them. In a hemp spinning mill in Dornach (Haut Rhin) in

1854, for example, the owner knocked his rate down from 12 to 8 centimes per kilogram citing a "new system" he had installed in the mill. One hundred fifty laborers walked out en masse, attracting police attention. The police made the laborers go back for the duration of the legal notice period. Hartmann, the owner, insisted that "at the end of a couple of weeks they would be earning just as much as before."[52] At Birshcenbach (Haut Rhin) in 1860, after making certain improvements to their looms, Gros Roman et Odier began installing warps on the machines that were 5 meters longer, but without increasing the rate of pay per warp. One hundred sixteen women cotton weavers left work. They refused, said the local *procureur*, to recognize the advantage that accrued to them from "the new system employed" which ought to profit "the owner alone."[53] Hofer et Schlumburger of Ribeauvillé in 1860 gave their spinners the option of tending two mules at once, but lowered all piece rates in the shop simultaneously for both one-mule and two-mule work. Fifty-two spinners left work, but agreed to return at least for a notice period, while remarking that Hofer et Schlumberger's mules were not as good as those in other shops where spinners tended two at a time, and that two months of this kind of work would be enough to "ruin their health."[54] Wool weavers in the new power loom mills of Roubaix fiercely resisted tending two looms under any conditions of pay for a period of seven years until they lost a decisive struggle in 1867.[55]

This kind of conflict forced textile laborers to measure time with greater acuity. Time was the reference point against which to measure any new work and pay arrangement. Did it allow one to earn equal money in equal time? By 1862 women power-loom weavers in a Rouen mill were calculating the answer down to the last centime. The mill owner had initially responded to the onset of the cotton famine by cutting back hours from twelve to eight per day, but now he wished to cut pay from 3 1/4 centimes to 3 centimes per meter. The women objected. The hours reduction had cut back average output from 70 to 47 meters per day, they claimed; their salary was down from 2.27 francs to 1.53 francs a day (70 × 3 1/4 versus 47 × 3 1/4). If the price is dropped to three centimes, they charged, it will never be raised back up. They proposed instead further hours reductions, but rearranged in the form of a four-day week of full 12-hour workdays, instead of a full week of eight-hour days. This would give them all more time to do their housework and watch out for their children.[56]

In the early sixties 260 Elbeuf weavers signed a petition complaining of recent rate reductions. The text of the petition carefully spelled out all the ancillary expenses (bobbin winding, light, sizing), all the secondary tasks, all the possible causes of delay, and carefully calculated their effects on the weaver's average daily wage. They asked for a floor to be set under their average daily wage; if any warp they worked up did not yield this minimum, they wanted compensation.[57]

In both these incidents, laborers had begun, in effect, to talk Villermé's language. It is difficult to tell whether they were beginning to accept these terms themselves or only searching for the most persuasive way possible of phrasing their demands for the owners. But the contrast with the July Monarchy is immediately recognizable. Laborers had learned to think of time and effort as underlying variables in relating work to pay, instead of concentrating all their attention on the tangible product.

Laborers were also brought into contention over the structure of the working day, and in some cases, with results that were remarkably compatible with the aims of factory inspector Dupont and his colleagues. Two strikes of considerable amplitude carried out by women cotton weavers in mills in the Fleury-sur-Andelle region in 1860 and 1863 had as their object suppression of a system called *doublage*. This was nothing more than a formalized arrangement for weavers to spell each other on their machines, so that they could have their rest breaks while the machines ran all day long, for 14 hours straight. At some point mill owners in the area must have noticed their employees engaged in such activities and decided that spelling was, after all, a worthwhile idea. The usual breaks, for breakfast, lunch, and *goutter*, were abolished. Instead, when a woman went for her morning break or her lunch hour, the owner designated another woman who was to tend her machine for her. A report of 1860 speaks of this system of *doublage* having been in effect in many mills in the Andelle valley for 10 years.

By 1860 however, each individual woman was now tending two looms of her own and, during *doublage*, was therefore expected to tend four. On 25 January 1860, weavers in the Pouyer mill in Fleury announced that they would no longer spell each other. Too many fines were resulting, they claimed, from flaws in the cloth that occurred during *doublage*. (Obviously, to avoid fines, a woman would care for her own looms more closely than for those of the absent woman, who might return to find flaws she had no responsibility for.) Pouyer offered to abolish fines during *doublage*, but the women persisted in refusing. Two other mills soon joined in the walkout. But the action collapsed after one woman was arrested.[58] The eventual solution was to abolish all fines and institute a system of bonuses for high quality work. That system was, however, according to local reports, more arbitrary than the fines had been, leaving too much discretion to the clerk who inspected the cloth.

The women closed down four mills again in 1863, when the cotton famine had forced owners to switch over to Indian instead of U.S. cotton. Yarn breakage was up dramatically; *doublage* had become an unendurable burden, and this time, after the women had held out for ten days, the mill owners gave in, abolishing the system until such time as U.S. cotton should again become available.[59] The progressive increase in the intensity of their labor, made possible by continuous technical advances, had brought these women to demand vociferously exactly the same arrangements that Dupont was working to achieve in the Nord – regular breaks at the appointed times.

Concomitantly laborers lost all patience with fees of any kind. Even in Lille, where mule spinners had peacefully paid steam-power fees for 20 years, 900 *filtiers* (sewing thread makers) signed a petition in 1855 against the continued withholding of light and heating fees from their pay.[60] In the same year, Roubaix spinners complained to the government of lighting fees still being charged against their salary and even expressed dissatisfaction that they received no compensation for down time when their mules were out of order.[61] Complaints against such practices had never been heard of before. The old concerns were still alive, however, as Roubaix spinners two years later were complaining again to local police that they were not allowed to observe the weighing up of their yarn.[62]

Clock time seemed to be on everyone's mind, and not just because of the constant alterations in machinery and piece rates. The 1848 law limiting the workday to 12 hours had never been repealed; by the time the Second Republic had fallen, mill owners had recognized that fewer hours did not necessarily mean less work. Output had not dropped, or else it was "almost equal in quantity and superior in quality," according to the Chamber of Commerce of Rouen.[63] This claim had been made before but few believed it. Now it became a commonplace of industrial management: Exactly how time was spent was often more important than how much. As Dupont pressured mill owners to regularize their hours and get their children to school at noon, owners campaigned on their own for greater punctuality from their workers. A group of Halluin weavers struck in 1860 demanding to be allowed to go home at least at 4 P.M. on Mondays, in return for which they were willing to work an extra half hour the rest of the week.[64] By the first decades of the Third Republic, it was standard practice to close mills a half hour early on Mondays but this was all that remained of *le bon lundi*.

The hours law, the child-labor law, the continual improvements in machinery, the sustained boom allowing more confident calculation of prices and profits, the laborers' new facility with arithmetic – all these factors stimulated heightened awareness of the plasticity of labor. It could be expanded to cover more spindles and looms, it could be compressed into shorter time and still yield equal output. It needed to be measured; the clock and the careful refinement of piece rates were the answer.

THE STRIKE'S NEW FORM

One of the gestures with which Napoleon III in the 1860s tried to court popular favor was to repeal the anticoalition statutes in 1864. Coalitions amongst laborers of a single occupation to obtain redress of grievances from employers or to improve their bargaining position, outlawed since 1791, were made legal. But strict limits on this new freedom remained in place: (1) No change was made in laws forbidding meetings of more than 20 persons; hence exercising the freedom to combine might be quite difficult. One would have to coordinate action without holding meetings. (2) Coalitions imposed by violence, threat, or "fraudulent maneuver" – which was acknowledged to be a phrase giving the police wide latitude – remained illegal.[65] Public discussion of this new law treated it as a law legalizing "strikes"; historians speak of it as having legalized "strikes" but not "unions." In fact, the word *grève* appeared nowhere in the text of the law; but obviously strikes, collective bargaining, the choosing of delegates (under certain circumstances) – but emphatically not strike committees or picket lines or anything that smelled of coercion or formal organization among laborers – were made legal by this reform.

Michelle Perrot has described how French laborers quickly took advantage of these new freedoms in the closing years of the Empire, and how newspapers, exploiting new press freedoms granted to them, began offering dramatic, circumstantial accounts of the larger strikes – accounts wired in by special correspondents on the scene and read by a national audience.[66] By the time that textile laborers began to share in the new combativeness of the working class in 1867, they had already for several years been reading or hearing of strikes, referred to as such, from a new crop of newspapers aimed especially at them.[67] Legal sanction, models ready to hand, and the eager audience of the press all encouraged textile laborers to see the strike as *the* form of laborer protest. Seconding these public and general shifts were all those changes in the workplace currently under way, which meant that grievances increasingly centered around the notions of time and effort. The idea of withholding that time and effort from the owner during a dispute seemed therefore doubly appropriate. Difficulties in the textile industry of the years 1867–1870, associated with the return of abundant cotton to the international market, therefore touched off a good number of conflicts. Of the strikes which Perrot has catalogued for these four years, over 30 percent occurred in branches of the textile industry.[68]

The bitter wool-weavers' dispute of 1867 in Roubaix signaled the emergence of this new style of conflict. Having prospered during the cotton shortages of 1862 through 1865, producers of cheap wool found themselves hard pressed in their turn once U.S. cotton began returning to the world market after 1866. Roubaix by this time had become a principal center of power-loom production of cheap woolens, with over fifty mills established since 1860, employing about 6,600 power-loom weavers. Under pressure to cut costs and preserve some of their market, Roubaix mill operators launched a concerted campaign in the spring of 1867 to cajole or coerce the weavers into tending two looms at a time. Half-hearted efforts in this direction had been made before from time to time since 1860 but had met with fierce resistance from the weavers. The owners were perfectly aware that resistance was likely to be renewed.

These looms did not yet have yarn-monitoring devices; in other words they did not shut down automatically whenever a yarn broke (as all modern looms do). Operating the machine therefore required that one keep a careful watch for yarn breakage and act quickly to disengage the loom from its drive mechanism whenever a yarn broke. Failure to act quickly could result in a run in the cloth; runs were fined against the weaver's pay. Broken yarn ends had to be tied together; messy knots were also fined. Crucial to the difficulty of the task, therefore, was the dependability of the yarn. Males had been retained in wool weaving (where cotton looms were usually tended by women) because wool yarn was much less dependable than cotton, and wool weaving therefore involved continuous effort as weavers jumped for the drive lever, tied off breaks, and restarted the looms as quickly as possible. One had to minimize down time without sacrificing quality. To add a second loom was therefore to complicate the task considerably; weavers now had to keep an eye out for breaks on two sides of them, and repair yarn on one loom while continuing to monitor the other. The looms shot the shuttle about 110 times per minute; it was therefore essential to remain alert.[69] Mill owners in Roubaix paid 9 centimes per meter for single-loom work, and in the spring of 1867 they offered to pay two-loom work at 6 centimes per meter, considerably more than half the single-loom rate. Hence allowance was made for considerable extra down time. But the weavers maintained that this hardly compensated for the increased difficulty of the work, or the increased number of fines incurred for runs and bad knots.[70]

The weavers' grievance reflected the common problem of the period, how to evaluate the worth of labor on a rearranged task. The weavers were in effect insisting that even if they earned the same amount per day on average tending two looms as they had tending one, they were not being fairly compensated since two looms required a marked increase in

247

the intensity of effort. In fact they announced their utter opposition to two-loom work at any rate of pay. This labor was not worth doing; and it was quite explicitly their labor and not the price of the cloth that was at issue since they simply refused to do this rearranged task. In similar circumstances in 1848, mule spinners had demanded payment at the old full rate for mules of double the old capacity – a demand concerning the price of the yarn. In 1867 the power-loom weavers' grievance was instead focused on the nature of the new task.

From the way the conflict unfolded in the initial weeks, one senses that the weavers were experimenting with their new legal freedoms as well. As laborers disputing the use of their labor, they attempted to strike within the bounds of legality and the Roubaix police attempted to over-see, without interfering in, their actions.[71] Neither side felt entirely sure of its proper role.

One weaver at the Delattre mill had agreed on 13 February to tend two looms; but that evening after work he was assaulted in a back street on his way home and reported sick the next day. Five days later all 443 weavers at Delattre quit when Delattre announced a general shift to two-loom work for most of his weavers in the near future. The following day, Saturday, 20 February, 53 weavers returned to work (to tend single looms). But they did not come back after lunch. On Monday, 22 February, 160 weavers returned to work at Delattre but when one weaver was set to two-loom work shortly after work began, all again walked off the job. One senses from these fits and starts that the weavers were in some confusion as to what precisely to do. Over the next two weeks weavers slowly trickled back to work at Delattre and were set to tending two looms; there were 12 at work on the twenty-third, 55 by the twenty-eighth; 138 by 4 March. In the meantime, 500 weavers had quit at Dillies Frères on 26 February over a rate cut of one-half centime per meter; 200 of them were back at work the next day. There, too, it appears, the weavers experienced difficulties coordinating their actions or maintaining unity without holding meetings or forming an organization. It is impossible to know (and it may have been for them, too) whether there was real agreement among them on their aims or on actions to be taken. The exercise of their highly circumscribed new freedom was proving less than easy.

During all of this, the police tried to supervise the strike at Delattre instead of breaking it – a job for which they had little practical experience. Agents were posted at the Delattre mill entrance to guard against disruptions. On Saturday, 20 February, the local *commissaire de police* had personally overseen the disbursement of pay to the 400 striking Delattre weavers who had turned out to collect their wages that afternoon. He let them into the pay room in groups of 30 at a time and gave each group

248

a "stern yet conciliatory" lecture on their freedoms and their duties. He described the procedure in detail in his report as if this were quite an unusual operation, carefully thought out in advance.[72]

The atmosphere in Roubaix grew increasingly tense during these hesitant strike efforts. On 21 February, the Roubaix Consultative Chamber of Commerce posted an announcement in town to the effect that two-loom work was essential to the survival of the industry. Obviously the hope was that the weavers could be won over gradually in advance of actual implementation of the new policy. But the poster seems to have had the opposite effect. On 23 February, police found a counter-declaration in the streets that went as follows: "Notice to the mill owners and shit for Henry Delattre. Signed le bon Louis, [guitar] player of Roubaix and decorated for his acts in 1848. The Consultative Chamber of Workers says two-loom weaving is suppressed and no wage cuts. Courage my brothers."[73]

The announcement had been handwritten in red and blue ink. The bitter reference to 1848, and the open rejection of the present order – even to the point of mockery, since no consultative chamber of workers, of course, existed – suggest that some weavers were under no illusions about the very limited nature of the new freedom they enjoyed and were far from seeing any justice in the present regime, connecting it, indeed, with their current grievances.

Scattered walkouts continued in the first two weeks of March; 40 weavers quit at Scamps on 5 March, all but five returned the next day; 347 quit at Mazure-Mazure on the fifteenth. One hundred seventy walked out of the Desrousseaux mill and 120 quit at Roussel early on the morning of 16 March. Shortly after lunch that same day, further walkouts occurred at Gaube-Tiberghien, Eugène Grimonprez, Screpel, and Rousseau. (Apparently a good number of mill owners had posted a Conseil des prud-hommes ruling in favor of two-loom work made the previous day.)[74] No longer happy with trying to work within the law, the striking weavers gathered in the streets in large crowds and began stoning factory entrances. Police tried to hold them off, but were too few in number; at 5:45 P.M. the police chief wired the prefect to send troops, adding the phrase "they are smashing the shops." Before the night was out, the Scamps mill was burned down, and those of Roussel, Desrousseaux, and Delattre all sacked. Scamps' personal residence and the concierge's quarters at Delattre had also been damaged extensively. The riot created a sensation; Roubaix suddenly leaped into the national limelight, as so many other towns in the grip of labor strife would do one after the other in succeeding decades. (The pattern, of course, became a regular feature of French national life over the next century.)

During the following three days, all mills in town remained closed; a few reopened on 20 March, but hardly any weavers returned to work. In view of the serious breach of public order, the prefect rushed to Roubaix hoping to settle the matter before it became a political liability. He sponsored a series of meetings between owners and weaver delegates who at first merely engaged in a shouting match at each other; eventually, however, it was agreed in principle that no weaver would be forced to work two looms against his will.[75]

On the twenty-first there were several street incidents as weavers expressed their dissatisfaction with this accord. One weaver was arrested while tearing down posters on which the accord had been announced. Others were arrested while spitting curses and threats at weavers who had returned to work. Still others ran afoul of police when a crowd of 200 came through the streets crying "Vive Garibaldi!" This reference to a renegade republican who had succeeded in uniting Italy (after Napoleon III had ostentatiously failed in the same task) linked mill owners, Napoleon's prefect, and the whole regime in a general condemnation.

But in subsequent days, there was a gradual return to work. By 24 March, virtually all mills (except the damaged ones) were back in operation. Owners, however, with both relentlessness and patience, continued to push for the extension of two-loom work wherever possible in subsequent months. In April, the owners approved a mass resignation of their delegates on the Roubaix Conseil des prudhommes, charging that certain worker delegates were not workers but barkeepers who were sabotaging the work of the Conseil. This is the only hint in the record of the emergence of yet another common future pattern: the habit of blacklisted working-class leaders finding refuge in the profession of bartending.

The contrast between this incident and the conflicts that have been examined so far is quite remarkable. Where before laborers had appealed to the concept of popular sovereignty or to their social betters' own sense of justice, where before their grievances centered on getting a fair price for the product of their labor, now laborers purposefully withdrew their services from sale and their grievance concerned the use of the labor they sold, and the reckoning of its value. Several other major confrontations of the Empire's final years shared these new characteristics; both Mulhouse and Rouen, for example, saw significant strike movements in 1870 and 1871. The massive strikes among spinners of the Mulhouse region in June and July of 1870 – cut short by the outbreak of war – came in support of the following list of demands: (1) the 10-hour day, (2) wage increases for certain day laborers, (3) abolition of fines, (4) abolition of fees for lighting, (5) transmission of mutual aid funds to worker control, (6) employer liability for work accidents, (7) one mule per spinner.[76] This list, from a committee of Mulhouse spinners, although it is difficult to say to what extent it represented the fundamental grievances of the various walkouts under way, nonetheless reflects a new orientation to the employer–employee relationship. The focus had widened from pay procedures to include the work itself; the amount of time spent there, the danger of accidents there, the arrangement of tasks are now of paramount importance. Fees for lighting, employer control of sick funds, once matters of indifference, are no longer to be tolerated. Laborers were now concerned with the terms of sale, and manner of use, of a service they provided, which was work.

No industrial system that constantly brings into practice new ways of applying labor to production can fail to impress upon all involved some idea of labor as a potential, as something without particular form, whose control and application are of the utmost importance. That this abstract notion of labor, so powerful in its implications, should have come in the particular form of labor as a service, as a commodity delivered for consumption at a particular price was, in the West, an historical consequence of the fact that labor was discovered, so to speak, through the development of a worldwide system of commodity exchange. That French textile laborers became familiar with this particular capitalist notion of labor only under the Second Empire and only after 1848 was a result of the particular convergence of circumstances (which was itself no accident) under consideration here.

It was as if the revolution of 1848 and the repression of the Second Empire had served as a great political drama that inculcated in the laborers a new sense of their position in the world, one which finally corresponded *grosso modo* to that which had been so long attributed to them by their literate betters. In 1848 socialists had pushed them to plan strikes and to negotiate for better wages and shorter hours, even though their inclination had been to concern themselves with quite different grievances. Louis Napoleon had then stepped in and violently deprived them of their socialist collaborators and stripped them of the freedom to act collectively. Under his repressive rule, a sustained boom and a long series of technical changes transformed the shop. Constantly changing work requirements forced the attention of textile laborers on work itself in the abstract as something which they provided to the owners.

From these experiences emerged the strike in a new form in the last years of the Empire. Seeking redress of a specific grievance as wage laborers, textile workers went on strike and withheld their labor from sale in order to bring the owner to terms. Explicitly, this was taken by all as a form of bargaining maneuver. The problem was that, although the laborers could now quit en masse, they really had nowhere else to go, no competing alternative, no easy access to some form of labor market that could make bargaining into something more than an artificial ab-

251

straction. They and the owners were there, for good or ill, as long-term members of the same community, a community over which the owners claimed great authority, to which the laborers had much more to give than a mere service, from which they all needed much more than money.

As a result, Roubaix weavers in 1867 were unable to sustain the fiction of the newly legalized form of protest. The police were barely able to contain their urge to treat the weavers like wayward children. Mill owners were only brought to a bargaining table by the authority of the prefect's personal presence; even then they made only backhanded concessions. In the streets, the weavers gave in to their strong sense that, far from doing something normal and allowable within the rules of the market game, they were engaging in a dangerous rebellion against constituted authority in all the guises it had taken on since 1851 – Napoleon's fumbled imperialism, his ever-watchful police, the owners, their mills, and their new machines.

9 The moral sense of farce

A life lived in ugly surroundings is also ugly. The social investigators of nineteenth-century France found nothing in their research that contradicted this proposition and plenty that appeared to confirm it. They were even able to come up with corroborating evidence from the laborers' own mouths. Audiganne discovered a local dialect poem that proved Lille inhabitants preferred the cellars of the rue des Etaques to lighter, drier dwellings. Reybaud, too, claimed to have heard this repeatedly from the laborers themselves while in Lille. Villermé had seen with his own eyes the relish that they took in their gin- and tobacco-ridden dens.

Audiganne could have used other dialect songs to help prove the inherent grossness and meanness of Lille's laboring poor. There is an undated song from mid-century called "Le Branle-Bas" ("The Big Commotion"), for example, which can be used to show the immoral atmosphere surrounding family life.[1] It is undoubtedly a genuine piece written by an illiterate or semiliterate factory laborer. It tells the tale of a widower with two older children who is looking for a wife "just to warm his feet" at night. He marries a woman who owns an abundance of furniture. He is thrilled by the extent of his windfall. But his children treat the woman badly. As soon as the father leaves the house, the children begin "to make trouble, making all kinds of demands; the woman was so frightened she froze to the spot. The boy and girl, as furious as wolves, spitting in her face said 'You should have come with a cord around your neck.'" Soon the woman leaves, taking her furniture with her. The daughter tells her father on his return, "'You'll have to sleep in your little boy's bed; and every evening we'll put a hot water bottle in to warm your feet if you're cold at night.'"[2] The song was intended as a piece of amusing commentary on contemporary life, for performance in one of those ubiquitous cafes. Here, surely, is marital disorder cynically displayed; here is deprivation causing venality to rule over love and trust, the whole callously treated as an occasion for humor.

Or there is another, untitled song written in the Lille dialect for Carnival time, 1868, which tells of a young factory girl who got pregnant but did not understand what was the cause of her morning sickness.[3] She told her mother that she thought she had an "inflamed finger"; but her mother knew what was wrong and kicked her out of the house. She went crying to her lover, who got angry and told her it was not his fault she had an inflamed finger; anyway it would heal up in a day or two. But, the song concludes, "If you take a woman who has an inflamed finger, it is not at the end of nine days that it can be healed."[4] The refrain goes as follows:

Et vous junn'homme, acheteur,	Oh young man, at such a time
Plutôt qu'à marier	Rather than marry
Vaut mieux dans la Mobile	Better sign up with the army
Aller faire un congé.	And take a vacation.

Here is rough-and-ready advice that frankly condones extramarital adventures and rather cynically disregards the suffering and vulnerability of a young working woman.

Both of these songs are poorly written. The rhyme scheme and meter are disorderly, many of the lines are awkward to pronounce and unequal in length. They were both printed cheaply on broadsheets; typos, missing punctuation, inconsistent spelling abound. And there are numerous others available of more or less the same kind. It is easy to see meanness of spirit coupled with physical deprivation in them if one chooses. And therefore, it is also easy to imagine that even a reasonably skeptical observer confronted face-to-face with members of the community that produced these songs, living in what was no doubt an intolerable slum, could have come away with impressions of a cynically displayed misery and immorality that he would personally find to be irresistibly concrete and convincing.

Under the Second Empire, it was easy to turn such impressions to new uses. When, for example, Roubaix weavers, also inhabitants of a disorderly slum, failed in their first attempt at a town-wide strike in 1867 and quickly turned to riot, burning, and looting several mills, the shock of respectable people was tempered by foreknowledge. They had been prepared by the testimony of investigators, and by the tenor of conservative judgment on 1848 in general, to expect no better of the poor.

Questions have been raised in this study and elsewhere about the validity of such an outlook, but in reality little has yet been done to shake the hold that it still has on modern civilization. The experience of Villermé is, after all, still a familiar one. Every town has its rue des Etaques. Who has not witnessed misery, both moral and physical, "cynically displayed" in places like Times Square in New York, the Boulevard Rochechouart in Paris, in Marseille, Naples, or Los Angeles? In Lille the Saint-Sauveur district has been razed and rebuilt by a socialist municipality; but misery has not moved very far. It may now be found in Wazemme along the rue d'Iena, or in old Lille along the canal. When rioting and looting rage through such areas in Miami or London, one may be disturbed but not really surprised. Most agree that the laboring poor either in the nineteenth century or today are likely to be rough-and-ready sorts of individuals, unreflective, prepared to follow violent impulses under the proper circumstances. Some admire this style, others deplore it. But it is usually seen, in either case, as a natural result of the experience of poverty.

Such a view of the poor, however deeply rooted or carefully worked out, still has the status of an interpretation, and a dubious one at that, above all because it treats the communities of the poor as fully realized entities with a single character. The poor have been endlessly examined and dissected in order to see what they are like, but seldom in order to see how or why they struggle to become something.

Individual personalities are constructed within concrete relationships. An individual may see himself as a saint or a prince, but these images only have meaning as imagined forms of relationships to other human beings. They cannot be realized unless the individual can bring his fellows to agree on them; the most fundamental limiting condition on individual identity is the range of possibilities made available to an individual by those around him. The same goes for a community within a larger society, with the added complexity that the community's identity arises out of the search of its individual members for identity vis-à-vis each other as well as society at large. In this sense, no community has a stable identity; this identity can exist only in the form of a number of more or less well focused interpretations of it that have gained more or less wide currency. The scope for contradiction, or for sheer incoherence, is large (so is the scope for great precision, as in the officer corps of an army, for example). Political conflict and economic change may bring specific contradictions to the fore or push people to search for greater coherence – enough to allow collective action, for example, or organization.

Community among the poor, just as among any other group of individuals, where it exists, is constantly being produced and reproduced by communicative acts that are more or less successful. These communicative acts themselves consist of interpretations, approximations, aimed at persuasively revealing to the community what it is and what the individual actor is within it. According to the success of these acts and their content, the sense of community takes on a certain shape and undergoes a certain history. And of course these cannot be understood in vacuo, apart from the larger social (or economic) context in which they occur.

255

But nineteenth-century social thought took none of these problems into account and its legacy is still strong. Interpretations of social class are still confidently put forward that are utterly mythical in form.[5] Groups are characterized by describing the outlook or mentality of a typical member of the group; all evidence is used to construct the image of that typical individual, as if such a thing could exist. All signs of rhetorical efforts to make, mold, or alter community identities are systematically ignored. Economic doctrine has supported this approach by oversimplifying the question of motives. It is easy to treat great masses of individuals as all alike when one believes that basic human motives are a simple matter of comparative net advantage (a code word for money).

An entirely different view of working-class identity is possible, however, as soon as one begins to treat records of working-class expression as instances of a continuous effort to create identity, as interpretations, as tentative proposals about self and others, with no particular authority or finality and formulated in the difficult material and political context that surrounded laborers in the nineteenth century.

The existence of a large body of nineteenth-century dialect songs and poems from the mill towns of the Lille area provides an unsurpassable opportunity to explore these issues. Some of this material has recently been surveyed and catalogued, making it readily accessible. Pierre Pierrard has found over eight hundred songs and poems in Lille dialect and gathered biographical information on 30 authors for the two decades of the Second Empire alone.[6] Laurent Marty has located over four hundred pieces from Roubaix for the period 1850 to 1914.[7] The better known authors have continued to enjoy new editions of their works; and it is not difficult to locate additional songs from other towns in the region.[8] There can be no doubt that much of the material was written by mill workers in their own everyday language, nor that local interest in the dialect reached a peak of intensity under the Second Empire.[9] It is, therefore, an incomparable source of information for supplementing what has already been discovered through examination of conflict and critical evaluation of social investigations.

DESROUSSEAUX'S DELIVERY

Audiganne would doubtless have found no dialect poem to quote from about the cellars of Lille had it not been for the transforming experience of 1848. A whole new array of messages had come in from the outside about who laborers were and what place they held in society. Textile mill workers in Lille had only begun to respond to it before repression returned. How this resulted in a revived interest in dialect poetry is not difficult to trace, but it immediately involves one in the story of a specific individual's efforts to find both a stable identity and a stable income. The two often come together in Western industrial societies. But this does not mean one must give in to the temptation to equate the search for identity with a mere search for gain. (Nor should the search for income be ignored.) In fact, in the case of Alexandre Desrousseaux, it would be fair to say that his greatest difficulty arose from his refusal to seek gain in certain ways.

Desrousseaux was highly literate and also without property.[10] In late adolescence he had joined a singing club in Lille that performed and wrote songs in the Béranger style (in perfect French). Alphonse Bianchi, later a journalist and *démoc-soc* leader under the Second Republic, was its organizer. But in 1841, Desrousseaux was drafted and served seven years in the army, a long and painful absence, to judge by his later works.[11] He returned to pick up the threads of his life just as the Revolution was breaking out.

Apparently he did not do very well. As Pierrard has reconstructed the story, the great change in his life came in November 1848 as he sat, destitute and in poor health, in a Lille garret – doubtless in the Saint-Sauveur neighborhood where he was born. He thought desperately of going to Paris to make a new start. Outside his window the spinners, lacemakers, *filtiers*, street vendors, and market women of the neighborhood where he had grown up were little better off. The hopes of February had been dashed; the spinners' organization had been broken up, their August strike had failed. Bianchi and his circle carried on, but confidence had drained away. Thousands were out of work, the municipal workshops were short of funds and had recently switched to payment by the piece, a change that had been bitterly opposed. The mayor had been spat on and insulted when he tried to explain the necessity of the change.[12] At least bread and potato prices were coming down. (But still, 42 percent of the Saint-Sauveur neighborhood's residents were listed as indigent in early 1849.)[13]

At that moment, he dreamed of leaving for good, yet Desrousseaux obviously loved this desolate neighborhood. Years later, with a secure job and a wife and family comfortably lodged elsewhere, Desrousseaux's mind remained full of Saint-Sauveur. It "held the greatest place in his heart," said his son, whom he eventually sent off to study Greek at the Ecole normale supérieure (and who later became a professor at the Ecole des Haute Etudes in Paris). Before leaving home, the boy was taken on frequent excursions to his father's old neighborhood. Desrousseaux's preferred promenade always took him back to the dirty alleys and the sad little square – the so-called *jardin du Reduit* – where he had played as a child, to show his son the crumbling old three- and four-story houses "where misery and love lived together in spite of all, where lived an industrious population who were never sure of tomorrow" (again his son's words).[14] They would stop at a corner cafe to have a beer and enjoy the company of workers.

Only a stroke of luck had made it possible for Desrousseaux to stay on in Lille after all. On one day during that dark November, a man named Danis came to visit Desrousseaux. Danis knew something of his past, knew that he had formed part of Alphonse Bianchi's singing club, and had written songs for it. What interested Danis, however, was a song Desrousseaux wrote at the age of 17 in the Lille dialect called the "Spectacle Gratis" ("Free Show"). In mid-1848 Danis and his local Société lyrique had decided to encourage the writing and singing of dialect songs, something which had been a passion in Lille in the eighteenth century but had apparently lost ground after 1800. Desrousseaux's forgotten composition seemed promising to them, and Danis had come to urge him to write more.

Within eight days Desrousseaux prepared 20 songs for publication, among them some of the best he ever wrote, including "L'Garchon Girotte" – locally his most popular song – or the Rabelaisian "Ro Bot!" ("The King Drinks!"), or the nostalgic "Retour de Nicaise" ("The Return of Nicaise"). The rapid success of these pieces put an end to his money worries for a time. They were printed in little booklets and on broadsheets; he performed them personally at first in cafes and in the town square on market days, selling copies of the songs at 10 centimes a piece.

The contents of Desrousseaux's third collection of 1849 gives an idea of the range and flavor of his early pieces.[15] It includes "Le Lundi de Paques," a story about celebrating on the Monday after Easter; "Le Crieur de la Ville," facetious announcements and scandalous gossip from the town cryer; "Minique l'Arlequin," the adventures of a man who left his clothes as security when renting a Carnival costume; and "Jacquo l'Balou," a henpecked husband who does all the housework. None of this subject matter is original; it is all from age-old themes of European popular literature. In each piece, however, the setting is explicitly and carefully specified as Lille; events are presented as facets of life here and now in that town.

One poem in particular stands out (and all Desrousseaux's early collections had one or two like this), because it is a moralizing tale intended to be moving and uplifting – without ruling out farcical elements – and because it is deeply rooted in the circumstances of local life. The poem is called "Casse-Bras." Casse-Bras is the nickname of an old man, laid off from his factory job due to age, who has decided to retire to the *hospice* for his last days, as he cannot support himself any more. His relatives and friends come to see him off; a good deal of coffee is drunk, much of it laced, as was the custom, with *eau-de-vie*. Casse-Bras decides he had better leave for the hospice before everyone is too drunk to come along. He takes his wife by the arm and starts off, the others follow. Unwittingly they form a procession; one of them grabs an old soap box and begins beating a martial rhythm on it. People run from all around to see what is going on:

In s' dijant comm' cha l'un à l'aute	Saying to each other something like this:
"Ch'est-i des gins qui faitt'nt ribote?	"Are those guys all completely pissed?
U bien, s'in vont-i pou' plinter Incore un arbre d'liberté?	Or maybe we're going to see Them plant another liberty tree?"
– Non, dijot l'aut', ch'est un mariache!	"No, it's a marriage!" says another, annoyed.
– Bah! ch'est d's ouveriers sans ouvrache!	"Bah! It's workers who are unemployed!"
– Ch'est peut-ête eun révolution?	"Maybe it's a revolution?"
– Mais non, puis qu'i n'ont point d'baton!"	"But, no, they have no sticks, not a one!"
Su'vingt raisons, n'y-avot personne In état d'mette l'nez su' l'bonne,	Out of twenty reasons, not a person Was able to put a finger on the right one.
Et nous aute', in cantan' un r'frain, Nous allîm's no' bon-homm' de q'min.	And us, we just kept up a song, And kept on marching right along.

Casse-Bras and his companions decide to stop for further refreshment along the way. They stop in at the bar known as the Cat-Barré, or "Cat Barred" – a pun on the word *cabaret* – which really existed in Lille, having on its sign a picture of a cat and a metal bar. After further libations Casse-Bras ("who had some schooling") stands up on his chair to make a speech. He complains of being laid off after working 30 years at the same mill and faithfully raising his family. "You cannot say that I was ruled by vice." But his virtue and fidelity carried no weight.

Et v'la comme je m' trouv' su'l'pavé!	And that's how I ended up on the streets!
Ah! si dins l'temps qu' j'étos soldat Un boulet m'avot cassé l'bras, J'aros dro' à les *Invalides*!	Ah! If only when I was a soldier A bullet had hit me in the shoulder, Then I would have a right to the Invalides! [The Paris rest home for disabled veterans]
Comm' mes gamb's sont incor solides, Là, du moins, j'aros l'contint'mint	Since my legs are still quite solid, There at least I would have had the pleasure

De m'in aller, avé m' viell' gra-mère.	Of taking my old woman out for a walk
Bras, d'sus et bras d'zous, à l'barrière,	Arm in arm to the gates of the city wall
Boir' du vin, quand j'aros quéq's sous!	To drink a little wine if we had the money!
Bah! ch'bonheur n'est point fait pour nous!	Bah! For us this was not to be!

At this Casse-Bras' wife interrupts in anger: What, a good Lillois would drink wine instead of beer? Leave Lille and your family? She wouldn't do it, not for her weight in gold, she exclaims. She tells Casse-Bras to take courage, reminds him of his good fortune in having a roof and a bed and a little food at the *hospice* for his declining days. Soon she will join him there. At this, he cries out what a good wife he has had through all the hard years. The party takes up its journey again. At the end of the poem they break into a song, "Lillos-Trompette," another of Desrousseaux's pieces, about a soldier in Algeria who is homesick for Lille. (This is an obvious cue for those listening to begin singing the song themselves.)

In most collections of Desrousseaux, "Lillos-Trompette" is printed directly after "Casse-Bras," as it was in the original publication in 1849. It is very likely that "Lillos-Trompette" is more than a little autobiographical, and therefore one may suspect that the two poems together had a special significance for Desrousseaux. Military service in a distant land and being laid off due to old age: the pieces treat two difficult moments when the outside world impinges on a poor man in Lille, one at the beginning of life, one at the end. But they also provide strong recommendations about how to face these ordeals. For military service, the answer is loyalty to Lille, a loyalty which is transferred to the larger entity of France, but which also makes homesickness all the more moving. All of Desrousseaux's pieces dealing with military service handle it in this way, including his first great success, the song "L'Garchon Girotte," which celebrates the plucky young Lille native in his snappy army uniform. (Desrousseaux performed it himself in costume on the town square to admiring audiences early in 1849.)

In Casse-Bras' case, the recommended solution is more subtly stated. Casse-Bras and his entourage march through the street beating a drum. At the Cat-Barré, he gives a speech bitterly protesting his treatment at the hands of his long-time employer. These are conventional forms of political action. But the march through the streets is turned into a delightful trick played on the rest of the town. And Casse-Bras' desire to speak is treated ironically. It is excused on two accounts, first because they have all had a lot to drink by that time, second because the poor fellow "had a little schooling" and by implication was therefore unfortunately prone to this sort of thing. Casse-Bras is brought to order by his wife, however, who proudly sounds the note of loyalty to Lille, but recommends as well that Casse-Bras look on the bright side and refuse to give in to bitterness. In the context of her scolding, the elements of farce in the piece (the name of the Cat-Barré, the fooling of the town) take on a moral significance. The proper manner to deal with this somber event, with this signal injustice perpetrated on an old man, Desrousseaux seems to be saying, is to respond with irony and good humor. Giving in to bitterness would only mark the final defeat. The pretenses of politicians and the solemnity of revolutionary demonstrations are gently mocked, even though the injustice of the status quo is openly admitted. Even political action, if it is taken, ought to come in the form of a good trick, the song seems to say.

This message could hardly have been lost on anyone in the context of 1849. The different suggestions that are made about the march (Are they going to plant another liberty tree? Is it a march of the unemployed?) may have gotten some knowing laughs from Desrousseaux's audiences. Doubtless they had been doing this sort of thing themselves for the first time in their lives over the previous year and a half, all in the end to no avail. Desrousseaux and his traditional Carnivalesque dialect poetry, bursting on the scene at just this moment, offered a way out. The old farcical spirit that stretches back into time immemorial in popular literature was now being offered as an alternative to hope for justice, as a means of coping with failure, as a safe form for preserving the new self-consciousness stimulated by the revolution. Loyalty to Lille in this context means loyalty to this old popular spirit. Desrousseaux must have even played the soldierly Girotte a bit overbroad, the martial tempo contrasting ludicrously with the whimsical self-description. The last stanza of "L'Garchon Girotte" reiterates the Desrousseaux doctrine:

Quoiq' point riche, l'joyeux cadet	Although not rich, the happy cadet
N'aïant jamais connu l'einvie,	Never having known envy,
Espèr' bien, comm' dit ch'vieux couplet,	Hopes indeed, as the old couplet says,
"Passer gaimint l'fleuv' de la vie."	"To pass through life's river gaily."

Did the working people of Lille appreciate Desrousseaux's message? For a time, in any case, their response was sufficient to allow Desrousseaux to get by. At his peak, on or about Carnival time in 1851, Desrousseaux managed to sell 2,000 broadsheets in a single day.

But the selling of broadsheets could not yield enough to live on over the long run. With the return of prosperity in 1852, Desrousseaux could certainly have found any number of jobs as clerk, foreman, or salesman, trading on his literacy in a time when such skill was in short supply. Instead it appears that he stuck to writing, casting about for ways to make it pay better. He began selling songs through bookstores or by subscription in small five- to ten-page *livraisons*.[16] These were also bound into book form and sold as such. This scheme involved appealing to a more wealthy, more literate clientele, and a subtle shift in his writing is apparent from this period. The two-volume 1855 edition of his songs significantly included a glossary of dialect terms at the end.

The change in tone may be illustrated by a look at two of Desrousseaux's most famous songs from the early 1850s, "Le Canchon Dormoir" ("The Lullabye") and "Marie Claire."

"Le Canchon Dormoir" is a simple, sentimental evocation of motherly love bearing up in the face of poverty and hardship. The chorus is a piling up of endearments commonly used in the dialect:

Dors min p'tit quinquin,	Sleep my little one,
Min p'tit pouchin,	My little chick,
Min gros rogin;	My big grape;
Te me f'ras du chagrin	You'll make me sad
Si te n'dors point qu'à d'main.	If you don't sleep until tomorrow.

Most of the verses depict the mother promising her child little luxuries and treats she can ill afford, as in the following verse two:

Et si te m' laich' faire eun' bonn' semaine,	And if you let me do a good week [that is, work well and long].
J'irai dégager tin biau sarrau,	I'll go redeem your pretty smock [from the pawn shop],
Tin patalon d'drap, tin giliet d'laine.	Your woolen pants and jacket.
Comme un p'tit milord t s'ras farau!	Oh, you'll be turned out like a little lord!
J' t'acatrai, l'jour de l'ducasse,	I'll buy you on festival day
Un porichinell' cocasse,	A little Punch puppet all decked out,
Un terlututu	A reed-pipe
Pour juer l'air de *Capiau pointu*.	To play the *Pointed-hat* song with.[17]

The sufferings of poverty and of long hours of work (the woman who sings is identified as a lacemaker) add poignancy to motherly love; and the reader is invited to share in the sharp, simple pleasures that poverty engenders. This song is not really aimed at poor people. It is more likely to appeal to those who, having begun life with nothing, are now well-off. The *p'tit quinquin* is the self-made man in his early days, or rather his early days as he now remembers them, rich with lost simplicity and sharply etched fantasy.

Desrousseaux's "Marie Claire" is even more obviously a celebration of the simplicity of the poor, of the clarity of motive and of self-concept that deprivation engenders. And it is, therefore, equally clearly a romanticized view of poverty, available only to those on the outside looking in. Marie Claire is a beautiful young girl seduced by an army officer who leaves her pregnant. After she bears a son, the officer returns in secret and steals the beautiful boy away. Marie Claire goes mad and spends the rest of her life wandering the streets of Lille in a distracted state, singing songs in return for coins, becoming known to all.[18] (Whether a specific figure served as a basis for the song is not clear; there were many perennial mendicants in the town.) The song invites the listener to pity and implicitly counsels generosity in alms giving. It is a lesson for the comfortable of the world, to the effect that poverty is not always deserved.

These two pieces defend and sentimentalize the poor of Lille before the gaze of outsiders. There is not a hint of irony in either; the moralizing is all aimed implicitly at those who are better off than the subjects of the pieces, instead of at those who share their fate as in "Casse-Bras." It seems highly likely that this difference represented a conscious choice on Desrousseaux's part to appeal to a middle-class audience as he switched to the *livraison* format.

Even the monthly *livraisons* and the new sentimental tone did not bring in enough regular money, however. In 1854, Desrousseaux took a job as a clerk of the Etat civil (birth and marriage register) at town hall. By this time his fame was such that the job was almost honorific in nature; and it suited him doubtless because it put him in direct contact with the town's people at moments when they were beginning one of those ceremonies he had so often written about in colorful unforgettable lines.[19] He stuck with the job and moved his family into a nicer neighborhood, satisfying himself with occasional walks through Saint-Sauveur. He continued writing into the 1880s. In 1884 at age 63, he was made a member of the Legion of Honor. By unremitting effort he had found, in the end, a way of making his talent and his need for money cohere in a stable way of life.

His troubles show that textile laborers' resources did not allow them to support their own communities' communication specialists. Many other examples demonstrate this. There are no cases known of songwriters supporting themselves on writing alone. Those that did emerge after 1848 had to make do by various expedients like Desrousseaux, all the more so in that no one ever matched his fame or his output. Most often they set up cafes where they would preside over the singing clubs that favored their songs. This provided the establishment with a ready-made clientele and the songwriter with a source of income.[20] The works of such specialists constitute a large proportion of the dialect pieces that have survived, as much as a third, although it is impossible to say what proportion of all songs sung or poems recited they made up. With some of them it is easy to tell merely on internal grounds when one is confronted with one of their pieces. Certain literary standards come into play, certain devices and subjects appear that are absent from the occasional pieces of amateurs. This division within the dialect literature presents a difficult problem. It is a trace of the influence of economic necessity on the way the literature was produced and reflects as well the more determined, more conscious activities of certain individuals who were trying to establish their social identity as that of songwriter. It is impossible to ignore this problem if one wants to use the literature as a historical source about community identity. Would-be songwriters were bound to depict the community in a way that put their activities at the center of things and made the community appear eminently worthy of depiction. But then, insofar as any community existed at all, it had to be the offshoot of just such tentative, searching individual purpose.

The problem is therefore twofold, first to determine to what extent the individual purposes of all those who contributed to the literature, amateur and expert, managed to converge on a single coherent vision. Equally important is to inquire into the relation between this (or these) literary vision(s) and the other forms of expression (often not recorded) that went to make up the laboring community's conscious life. Armed with answers to both these questions, one might begin to provide an informed alternative to the interpretations of those who insist on seeing everything as emanating from a single, mythical, fully realized communal identity.

THEMES OF THE DIALECT LITERATURE

The simplest approach is to begin with a point-for-point comparison of the large corpus of Desrousseaux's songs and poems with pieces by nonspecialists. Significant divergences will indicate something about the nature and limits of the famous songwriter's special role.

This approach suggests itself because the overall similarity between Desrousseaux's work and the rest of the dialect literature is evident. Whether in imitation of Desrousseaux or because he was only following an established trend, the self-conscious effort to provide colorful pictures of local life dominates this whole literature. This was a sharp change from the Brûle-Maison tradition of eighteenth-century Lille that consisted entirely of tales about the hapless inhabitants of Tourcoing. Of course,

Lille had always been the real subject, the implicit point of comparison. But now in Lille and in the other towns of the area that took up the fashion of dialect song writing, self-consciousness became explicit. There is not a single song from mid-century Lille about Tourcoing, even though the Brûle-Maison literature continued to be widely read and admired. Desrousseaux's second collection included a poem in honor of Brûle-Maison. Other songwriters followed his example. Charles Descottignies claimed to be his descendant. Louis Catrice of Roubaix said Desrousseaux was his father and Brûle-Maison his grandfather.[21] But no one diverged from the now accepted pattern of concentrating on local life. That this was a reaction to political change can hardly be doubted. Before and especially during 1848 self-consciousness was thrust upon the poor.

With equal uniformity the literature divides itself into themes. A song or poem had to be written about one of a series of preordained topics: young love, married life, old age, street vendors and shopkeepers, drinking, women, the town and its landmarks. How does Desrousseaux's treatment of these themes differ from that of others?

Love, marriage, and women were almost always treated negatively. These songs were all written by males for performance in singing clubs of married men meeting in neighborhood cafes. Male cameraderie dictated that women and children be made the objects of complaint. The very broad humor and highly conventional nature of the complaints, moreover, suggests that the contents of these songs did not represent personal feeling in any simple way. Women are beautiful when one marries, the songs lament, but slovenly afterward. They neglect the housework, drink coffee all day ruining the family budget, gossip, and forget to make dinner.

In "L'Homme Marié" ("The Married Man"), Desrousseaux brought together the usual catalog of complaints, adding a few twists of his own to make the effect even broader.[22] She was beautiful before I married her, cries the married man, but now she never washes. She is so sticky you could glue her to the wall. When she is working at her lace she is irritable. I bring her food, I wait on her hand and foot, but then she stops for hours to talk to her neighbor, drinking coffee and getting nothing done. She gives me another baby every year. When we had 12 I prayed God to stop it there; the next year she had twins. And I am the one who ends up taking care of them when I come home from work at night. Desrousseaux's contribution on this theme was almost a spoof of the conventional treatment.

When crinoline petticoats became fashionable in the 1860s, they also became a regular target of male complaint, as in an Armentières song which charges that women

Pou' nous infiler tous, mettent	To entice us all, they even wear
Des crinolines pour eus aller ouvrer.	Crinoline when they are going off to work.

But after marriage, the song goes on, they only wash once a week, dally in the square drinking coffee on market days, forget to make dinner then make lame excuses, and so on.[23] The list is remarkably invariant. In one variation, however, they are charged additionally with being superstitious. They go to have their futures read in cards or in the grounds at the bottom of the coffee cup – which is a scandal *"dins l'siècle qu'nous somm's"* ("in the present century"), says one songwriter.[24] (The literature as a whole is adamantly secular, if not to say irreligious, in outlook.) Desrousseaux with his usual virtuosity manages to tie this complaint in with the others in a song called "Les Deux Commères" ("The Two Women-Friends") in which two women try to discover from reading coffee grounds what moods their husbands will be in that night. But in doing so they forget to make the soup, which ensures, of course, that the two men will be profoundly irritated.[25]

It is probably no accident that the complaint about unmade soup is the most frequently heard of all. These songs reflect more than an in-grained male chauvinism (which is unmistakable); they also speak of the hardships of running a household on a very small income brought in at the cost of very long hours on the job. The working male envies his wife's idleness because of his own prolonged absences from the comforts of home. The crowning irony, then, arises when her domestic enjoyments lead her to forget her husband's need for a share of the same. The popularity of the unmade-soup lament derived in part, doubtless, from a concealed unhappiness with the work routine of the factory. Here a piece of genuine popular experience – the exhaustion and the high expectation of relaxation that were felt by men coming home from the mill – influenced the choice of clichés. Women who worked also felt this exhaustion, to judge from a song glorifying coffee, "Le Plaisir des Femmes" ("Women's Pleasure"):

Les femm's qui vont in fabrique	Women who go to the mill
Et donn'nt leus infants à soigner	And leave their kids with others,
L'soir sorties d'leus boutiques,	In the evening on leaving work
I faitt'nt bien vit' du café.	Make that coffee right away.

They make it, the song implies, before even picking up their children.[26]

It is indicative of the way in which normal experience was deformed to make it fit the literary conventions that this sense of exhaustion and desire must be displaced and expressed indirectly in stylized complaints against the women at home and in fantasies about her idleness, or else in a song in praise of coffee – an equally conventional theme.

Such literary transfigurations of everyday experience were, of course, what these songs and poems were all about; for writers and listeners this was their principal charm. Briefly they could contemplate themselves as dressed-up inhabitants of the picturesque world of Lille. Desrousseaux was not, therefore, qualitatively different in his treatment of this theme so much as simply more resourceful than the others; he called upon a wider repertoire of formulae and used them with greater skill. In the case of husbands' laments, he followed closely the conventions prevailing among unschooled and less self-conscious writers, improving on them rather than seeking forms from outside.

Within the whole sphere of sexual relationships, Desrousseaux nonetheless stands out in that he alone wrote songs glorifying and romanticizing young love, which was treated as an occasion of deception and disappointment by other writers (as well as frequently by Desrousseaux). In other words, in his treatment of this sort of subject matter, he chose sometimes to instill poverty with that sweetness and nostalgia previously encountered in "Le Canchon Dormoir" or "Marie Claire." In several pieces he shows love transcending the difficulties of privation (as in "Le Bonheur du Ménage" ["The Happiness of the Home"], "Patrice," or "Le Faux Conscrit" ["The False Conscript"]).[27] But when he did treat the disappointments of courtship, he was quite faithful to the accepted formulae.

There was in this literature a great preoccupation with specific geographical features of Lille (or of the other towns the songs came from). Expressions of local pride and descriptions of local color went well with the sense of quaintness and originality the literature bathed in. But this confronted the songwriter with a problem. The grimness of the working-class environment was too salient to escape commentary. Writers did not shrink from dealing with the ugliest features of the landscape; yet they struggled to maintain the innocent, admiring tone they felt to be essential to their literary idiom. The result in most cases was a satirical rehearsal of woes. Even in the best of cases, admiration was tinged with irony.

Jules Fouque's description of the "jardin du Reduit," for example, succeeds in being thoroughly positive in tone:

Au soir à l'sortie des boutiques,	At night when people leave the mills,
On vot tous ches p'tits ouveuriers	You see all those little workers
Qui vont respirer l'bonn' odeur	Go to breathe the sweet smells
Dins ch'biau gardin su Saint-Sauveur.	In that pretty garden in Saint-Sauveur.

On vot ches p'tites mères de familles	You see those little mothers of families
Accourir avec leus infants.	Hurrying there with their children.
In attendant d'aller dormir	While waiting to go home to sleep
Pou' tâcher d' s'assir sur un banc	Trying to get a seat on a bench
Tout criant: J'aime bien l'bonn' odeur	While crying: I like the lovely odor
De ch'biau gardin su Saint-Sauveur!	Of this pretty garden in Saint-Sauveur.[28]

Despite the positive tone of Fouque's song, anyone who knew the area would have sensed the irony of these references to the sweet odors of the park. The rest of Saint-Sauveur stank to high heaven. As another commentary put it

Là passint fallot serrer s'bouque.	Passing through you'd better cover your mouth.
L'ordure pourichant dins le coins...	Garbage [is] stinking in every corner.[29]

The little park provided a rare refuge from the prevailing stench. This was more important than the fact that it had a few trees and some grass; it dominated local experience of the place. How sweet it smelled (not to smell anything)!

Other attempts to be simply celebratory about local landmarks ran into similar difficulties: Irony was almost unavoidable and the success of these songs as literary pieces depended largely on the writer's willingness to accept the ironic implications. An 1862 song from Roubaix, for example, sings the praises of the town's newly established slaughterhouse. Now meat will not have to be carted in from outside; freshness will be assured. The writer in one stanza, however, provides a vivid description of the rotten meats that Roubaix butchers had been in the habit of selling before. The sickening details dominate the song. The whole thing is presented in a flat tone with no hint of irony.[30] One does not know whether to see the piece as a failed work or as doubly subtle in its handling of the ironic possibilities. Ironic intention is obvious and entertaining, on the other hand, in an Armentières song of 1869 that rhapsodizes about the new breweries in town that are equipped with steam engines. This is marvelous, indeed; the supply of beer is not in danger.[31]

Specific cafes were frequently made the subject of admiring songs; Desrousseaux wrote a good number of such pieces. His interest in this kind of song seems to have been inspired partly by entrepreneurial calculation; he often accepted commissions from particular clubs to write about the cafe where they met, evoking its charms and its atmosphere in a flattering way.[32]

Slum-clearance and street-construction projects, launched in imitation of Paris, were common in most French towns of any size during the Second Empire; and these became favorite topics of celebratory songs in which the element of irony shone with full force. Desrousseaux constitutes a telling exception here. When a well-known bell tower was slated for demolition in 1857, for example, Desrousseaux lamented its passing in a poem called "L'Ascencion au Befroi" ("The Ascension of the Bell-Tower"), which includes an account of all the things one can see from this vantage point. As Desrousseaux's eyes roam, he recalls significant moments of his youth: There is the square where he first courted his wife; yonder in the distance is Saint-Sauveur church where he was an altar boy.[33] The passage of a landmark provides another opportunity for the evocation of simple nostalgia – a major theme for Desrousseaux and therefore, one must imagine, for his audience.

But nostalgia plays no role whatever in most songs of the period that deal with the urban improvement projects. Instead, there is a great out-pouring of tongue-in-cheek admiration. Gustave Bizard's "Rue de la Gare," for instance, was written in 1870 in honor of a new broad avenue that was pushed through a poor neighborhood in order to connect Lille's train station with the town's main square.[34] The song has two refrains that go in opposite directions. There is no indication about which to sing when. The first is admiring.

Cheull' rue d' la Gare	That rue de la Gare
Vous pouvez m' croire	You can believe me
S'ra l' p'us bielle rue	Will be the most beautiful street
Qu'on n'ara jamais vu:	Anyone ever did see:
Lillo's mes frères,	Lillois, my brothers,
Soyons fiers,	Be proud.
L'agrandich'mint	Our rebuilding project
Nous met au premier ring.	Puts us in the very first rank.

The other a cry of distress:

Cheull' rue d' la Gare	That rue de la Gare
Que désespoir	What despair
Qu'elle va donner	It will give
Aux vieux du temps passé.	To old people of the good old days.
A tort quand même	Mistaken, even so,
Les hommes les femmes	Men and women

| Toudis r'grett'rons | Always will regret |
| Ch'vieux marqué au pichon. | That old fish market [which was being torn down]. |

As the translation suggests, this second refrain is not very good verse and the syntax is unclear. Does Bizard mean to suggest that people who do regret the demolition project ought not to, or that the demolition itself is a mistake? At any rate the rest of the song puts the emphasis on regret, and reveals that much more than nostalgia is involved. Bizard evokes the prospect of carts and worn out furniture cluttering the old streets where people are moving out of condemned buildings: *"Ch'étot l'pillage dins l'rue d'un bout à l'autre."* ("The street was a wreck from one end to the other.") He says he saw clearance-project officials trying to lead away an old woman who was in tears having lost her cat. (As for the officials: *"Ch'est des graingniards, ch'est un métier pour ça."* ["They have permanent frowns, the job requires it."]). On the fish market that was being destroyed, Bizard remarks

Ch'est malheureux pour ches vielles pichonières	It's too bad for those old women fishmongers
Dans leu's vieux jours qui faut quitter ch'l'état	To have to leave that trade in their later years.
N'y-en-a gramint qui vont faire leu' affaire	A good many are arranging their affairs
Pour euss' aller morir à l'hôpita.	So they can go die at the *hospice*.

Quite clearly urban improvements were personal disasters for hundreds of working-class people, and no mention of these projects could help but bring this out, even though convention may have required the expression of simple local pride. The only solution was to offer an equally simple, understated (but crushingly obvious) ironic treatment of the subject. Another song on the rue de la Gare (by Louis Longret) carries the same message. The grandness of the project is contrasted with the private sufferings of persons affected, especially the aged who have lived there for many years and who find leaving difficult.[35] An Armentières song likewise praises recent enlargements in the state insane asylum there (at the expense of an adjacent poor neighborhood): *"Ché si biau qu'sans malice / On vodrot dev'nir sot."* ("It's so lovely that – honestly – it would be really nice to be nuts.")[36]

It is characteristic of all these songs on the urban renewal projects that one occasionally must stop to ask oneself whether the ironies are really intended. The careful avoidance of explicit condemnation is eventually disturbing. Were police censors forcing the songwriters to walk a tightrope? Even if they were, it is extremely significant that outcries against the projects were so worded that one is occasionally brought to wonder if they are protests at all. The tone is always straightforward and understated. Was the effect due to a lack of skill or was it intentional? In any case Desrousseaux never wrote one of these pieces.

Another group of songs in this same genre deals with living conditions in the working-class neighborhoods. The experience of moving holds a great place in these songs, just as in those dealing with rebuilding projects, only the reason is different. People moved frequently because it was so hard to find a place one could tolerate. As an anonymous song of 1859 puts it:

Les dimanches d'dins Lille	Sundays in Lille
On vot d' tous les cotés	One sees on every side
Des gins canger d'asile	People changing homes
Et tout déménager;	And moving everything out;
Dins les rues d' Saint-Sauveur,	In the streets of Saint-Sauveur
Ch'est comme eun' procession,	It's like a procession
Car tout l'monde, d'un bon coeur	One and all with a good heart
Déménage de s'mason.	Move right out of their houses.[37]

Pests were highest on the long list of reasons for moving out: cockroaches, lice, bedbugs, and mice. Usually songs on this subject took the form of a light-hearted recounting of a succession of frustrations. The first place I lived in had cockroaches, says a song of 1855; in the next I woke up in the middle of the night to find bedbugs parading across my nose. I moved again, but the fireplace did not work. My next place was sold by the landlord and I had to move.[38] Also frequently complained of were leaky roofs, mildew ruining clothes, landlords who didn't like children, insufficient light.

The complaints are both more circumstantial than the descriptions of dwellings found in the investigative literature and starkly different in tone. Villermé imposes a moral calculus on the details he selects for his description of a Lille cellar dwelling: from each feature a moral consequence flows, the sum of features equals utter demoralization. The single bed means incest; the dirt floor means a dirty life; the absence of furnishings means a spiritual deprivation. For the workers, the drawbacks of these places are experienced as annoyances and inconveniences. They are sorely tried by dirt, cold, dampness, and vermin, but they try to bear up in the face of them; they write songs about them, and in doing so they create the same light, ironic tone found in their descriptions of slum clearance. If anything, because their homes offer another occasion for

271

them to display their tolerant cheerfulness before life, they gain morally in their own view by being forced to live in such places.

Money was an inexhaustible theme for these laborer–songwriters. The meaning of having little money in life was dealt with at least by implication in almost every song, and it received a great deal of explicit treatment. Buying and selling with it, borrowing it, getting by without it, earning and losing it: every kind of experience with it drew songwriters' attention. They felt a particular fascination for the market vendors and shopkeepers who provided them with their daily needs. Some were poor themselves and were the object of deep affection. In the songs they are found walking the streets, filling them with color and with the sound of their clever cries. One fishmonger calls out to all the women by profession; she has eels for all the "*dévideusses, ratacheusses, faigeusses de sariaux, fileusses, bobineusses, couseusses de piqieaux, modisses, soigneusses, éplugueusses, brodeusses au crochet, gazeusses, faigeusses de dint'let*" ("reelers, piecers, smock makers, spinners, bobbin winders, quilt sewers, dressmakers, machine tenders, cotton cleaners, needle knitters, gauze makers, and lace makers").[39] They all need her eels. The feeling of intimacy with and affection for the workers implicit in this call reflected the simple fact that most street vendors had started as laborers themselves and that most laborers dreamed of becoming vendors and escaping the factory. A hundred francs or so was enough to get started as a coal hauler or fishmonger; such trades were therefore a realistic alternative to the mill. But the danger of foundering was great.[40]

One of Desrousseaux's early songs concerned a potato vendor. They had begun to appear in Lille markets in the 1820s with their kettles of boiling water and hot potatoes ready to eat. Desrousseaux's potato vendor had been laid off:

Comme l'commerce est à l'baleine	Since trade is turning cold
Min maît' m'a donné min livret;	My boss has turned me out.
Mais j' vas tâcher de m'tirer d' peine,	But I aim to get out of the hole
In essayant d'un aut' métier.	By trying another route.
J'irai d'main, avec eun' cayère,	I'm going tomorrow with a chair
Avec eun' marmite d' puns-d'-tierre,	And with a pot full of potatoes
Sus l'Grand' Plach' tout le long du jour,	To spend all day on the Grand Square
Crier de bon coeur et comme un sourd:	To yell with a will like someone deaf:
Tout boulants! Tout boulants!	Boiling hot! Boiling hot!
V' là des puns-d'-tierres charmants.	Charming potatoes in the pot![41]

Desrousseaux's potato vendor takes special pains to provide just what the laborers like when they get out of work:

272

L's ouveriers sortant d'leu fabrique,	Workers when they leave the mill
Dirons "Courons vite à Gustin.	Will say "Let's head for Augustine's.
A s'boutique, suivant l'vieux principe,	At his stall you'll find your fill
Pour un doupe, on alleume s'pipe,	Of pipe tobacco for one sou.
On a des puns-d'-tierre et du sé,	He's got potatoes and he's got salt
Meme eun' vaclett' pou s'récauffer."	And a stove to warm up with too."

Another song (not by Desrousseaux) describes the same scenario, a factory laborer trying to establish himself as a street vendor, in this case not of potatoes but of other favorite lunch and dinner foods. This vendor counted on his old workmates to provide the core of his clientele (and apparently walked freely through the mill selling his wares):

J'ai quitté m'boutique	I left my factory job
Pour mi m'établir marchand d'lait;	To set up as a milk vendor;
Au matin j'vind des poires cuites	In the morning I sell cooked pears
Pour faire plaisi à l'z'ouveriers…	For the pleasure of all the workers.
J'vas toudis dins m'n ancienne boutique	I always go into my old factory
In leu vindint m'bonne chicorée…	To sell them my good hot chickory.
Au dinné j'vind de l'bonne soupe	At lunch I sell good soup
Acompagnée de bielles portions…	Each serving with a morsel of meat.
Faut jamais avoir peur de faire credit.	Never fear of extending credit.
Et vind toudis à payer à s'maine.	Sell everything on weekly account
Y a qu'comme cha qu'on s'inrichit.	That's the only way you'll ever get rich.[42]

These lines do not have the sparkle of Desrousseaux's; rhyme and meter are less carefully worked out. But the joy taken in the *menus détails* of the street vendor's art is very much the same.

More substantial merchants like butchers and sausage makers whose products were expensive but greatly desired, were treated with suspicion and envy in the laborers' songs. They cheated on the weight or slipped horse meat into the *saucisses*, the songs allege. But any vendor who was obviously poor and whose status might be reached by the laborer was viewed with unambiguous favor.

Street vending obviously appealed because it meant liberation from the factory routine. But this was not its sole attraction: despite the precariousness of these professions, they seemed more stable than the factory. The singer of one song complains that he passed *"m'maudite carrière / Pindint trinte ans in boutique"* ("my accursed career / For thirty years in the mill"). But now he is making money hand over fist selling fried

273

potatoes.[43] Pierrard explains that factory wages made the laborers uneasy; the income seemed undependable, liable to unpredictable fluctuations. Many who did work in the mills were constantly on the lookout for odd jobs by which to make money on the side: fixing furniture, repairing shoes, buying and selling used household utensils in the Sunday market. The dialect even had a special word for those who were always looking for odd jobs on the side: they were *manoqueux* and doing such jobs was to *faire le manoqueux*.[44] The practice may account for the popularity of the rummage sale festival every fall (which is still celebrated today in Lille with considerable enthusiasm).

This is the opposite of the attitude toward factory labor common today. The drudgery of such work is now supposed to be balanced against stability and predictability: The small farmer who cannot make ends meet in this century sends sons or daughters, or goes himself, to the factory to tide himself over a bad harvest. But the image was the reverse for nineteenth-century French textile laborers. A multitude of factors might cause weekly earnings to vary – from trade cycles to faulty machines. Signs that the laborers saw their income as volatile only confirm earlier evidence, underscoring the irrelevance of those exact daily averages so dear to social investigators.

In the face of the real insecurity that factory work represented, Lille–area laborer–songwriters followed their usual strategy of indirection. Their songs were not to be vehicles for complaint, but a means of seeing themselves as the colorful and stalwart, simple yet knowing people that the literature depicted. Therefore, rather than rehearsing their own insecurity, they turned their eye toward the enchanting figure of the street vendor, concentrating their attention on his produce, his cry, his routine, his worries. He was the first thing they saw on leaving work, the harbinger of leisure and freedom. This stock figure in their literature, like the stock image of the wife whose soup is late, speaks by implication again, of that experience which was almost never directly mentioned, the life of work at the shop.

For work itself was a taboo subject to these songwriters. There are perhaps three songs that discuss work in the mills directly, two of them were definitely written by persons who never set foot in a mill, the other by a successful songwriter who, like Desrousseaux, had moved up in the world.[45] But further indirect commentary on factory work comes from a variety of directions. There is a song about a military conscript who is happy to be getting more food more regularly than when he worked in the mill (echoing "Casse-Bras": even common soldiers are better off).[46] Louis Longret's lullaby "Le Jour de Bonheur" ("The Day of Happiness") laments that the little girl will end up as a bobbin winder sooner or later.[47] Mill work, in other words, is inevitable, a trap, a fate unavoidable for the poor.

Bonnart's "Le Chômage du Lundi" ("Taking Mondays Off") is a drinking song turned into a defiant celebration of Monday absenteeism. The first verse and refrain are particularly revealing:

Mais quo vous êtes acore à l'brunne	But while you are still in twilight
Epu l'machine est arreté,	And the machines are still at rest,
Tous les lundis ché toudie l'même	Every Monday it is the same
Vous n'avez jamais bu assez;	A bit more to drink would be best.
Apré in fait carnage,	Later you are in for it,
Parce qu'i n'a pu d'argint,	The money has run out,
L'diable est d'vint l'minnage.	The devil is at the door.
Vous êtes des droles de gins.	You are peculiar louts.
Refrain:	*Refrain:*
Mes amis acouté chi	My friends, listen here,
In boen consel que j'vous donne.	I'm giving you good advice.
Grâce! et pour l'amour de Di	Grace! and for the love of God
N'faites jamais pu l'Lundi.	Don't do Monday any more.
Réponse des buveurs:	*Response of drinkers:*
In acoute poent chin te di	We won't listen to what you say,
Nous ferons toudi l'Lundi	We will always do our Monday.[48]

The song depicts the laborers arriving at the mill before sunrise, waiting for light to work by, but giving in to the call of the cafe before the machines can be started. What hurts them later is not the foreman's discipline (which is not even mentioned) but exhaustion of Saturday's pay before the week is out. The remaining stanzas of the song concentrate on the long week without money and on the drinker's neglect of home and family. We care not, say the drinkers, we will always do our Monday. The defiant tone may well reflect the fact, as other evidence shows, that Monday absenteeism was under attack during the Second Empire for the first time.

In another song called "Un Dur Méti" ("A Very Hard Trade"), dyers are depicted going to work in the morning, lighting the fires under their vats, and then retiring across the street to a cafe to plan out their colors.[49] Yes, indeed, the songwriter laughs, now there's a hard trade. All these references demonstrate how sharply the laborers regretted being tied to their machines, how persistently they sought occasions for escape, how strongly they envied those who appeared to them to be free of this

275

bondage. However loose discipline may have been by today's standards, laborers nonetheless had to be in the mills most of the time; like Truquin, they found this to be the one part of life they could least tolerate. But still, all commentary on this grievance was achieved by indirection.

THE FARCICAL IN PRACTICE

One prominent divergence emerges from comparison of Desrousseaux's pieces with those of nonspecialists. The nonspecialists never take themselves or their subject matter seriously. Apart from work itself, they shy away from nothing in their environment, however unpleasant, yet they resolutely transform it all into matter for parody, posturing, light-hearted ridicule, highly conventional in form and tone. Desrousseaux repeatedly showed himself to be master of this style, although he did not apply it to certain subjects: slum clearance, living conditions, cheating shopkeepers. At the same time he had another style almost all to himself, the evocation of sentiment, nostalgia, and pity for the lives of the poor.[50] The likelihood that Desrousseaux was carefully cultivating an audience of both middle- and working-class townspeople seems therefore very high. He could not afford to ridicule slum-clearance officials because they worked in the same building as he did, nor cheating shopkeepers, as they were highly likely to be both versed in the local dialect and prosperous enough to afford the more expensive books he sold increasingly after 1852. He felt the need to defend the humanity of the poor and to elicit sympathy for their plight from this larger audience, and to do so he adapted themes not at all indigenous to the local literature: He wrote lullabies, he wrote about madness, about the distant years of boyhood, about the intense joy of young love.

Desrousseaux alone of all these writers also dealt with local festivities, holidays, and celebrations. He often set his tales against the backdrop of Carnival time, of a christening or a parish feast day. He wrote a string of songs describing such celebrations. And in later life he published a two-volume work on Lille folklore.[51] Other songs often announce that they were intended for use at Carnival time, but it is very rare to find a piece that actually deals with collective ceremony. Desrousseaux had a scholarly proclivity completely missing from other writers. But his works can help to reconstruct some of the collective practices of the community that produced these songs.

Desrousseaux laments that the traditional round of annual holidays was no longer followed with the same enthusiasm as in his youth.[52] The catalog, even for the Second Empire, is nonetheless impressive.[53] The principal festivals were Carnival and the Fête du Broquelet (Lace-Needle Day, celebrated on Saint Nicolas' feast day, 9 May, the holiday for which

276

spinners' aid societies spent their reserve funds). Each of these took two to three days. Next in order of importance was the feast day of each parish's patron saint, the *Ducasse*. Of secondary importance was the Braderie (a citywide rummage sale each fall), Lundi de Pâques (the day after Easter), a festival for little boys and one for little girls in early winter, and a certain number of professions' saints' days. In all, perhaps 20 workdays a year over and above the great Catholic feast days of Christmas, All Souls' Day, the Assumption, and so on.

As for what was done to celebrate these occasions, much of it was reminiscent of the tone of the dialect literature. At Carnival time the songs themselves played a central role. Each singing club put on costumes or organized a float to illustrate or act out the subject of their Carnival song. At each corner along the way, they sold the words on broadsheets and encouraged onlookers to join in singing it with them. (At least Laurent Marty has shown that this was done in Roubaix; it seems likely to have been the common practice of the region.)[54] The humorous self-mockery of the songs is therefore related to a very public ritual practice.

Desrousseaux's "Broquelet d'Autrefois" ("The Lace-Needle of the Past"), describes the traditional mode of celebrating St. Nicolas' feast day (no longer followed by the 1850s): a great procession filed through town led by a man dressed up as the Saint. The procession came to its end at a square next to the canal and, as the Saint turned to begin preaching to the crowd, he was picked up by two attendants and thrown into the water, to the cheers of the assembled people. Likewise in the song "Ro Bot!" ("The King Drinks!"), Desrousseaux describes a traditional banquet on the feast of the Epiphany (celebrating the visit of the three kings to the newborn savior). In this song's account, a great deal of alcohol is consumed during the meal. Once the banquet is completed, a hat is passed with slips of paper in it; on one slip the word *sot* (fool) is written. The person who picks this slip out of the hat (keeping the fact a secret) is then required to *faire des farces* – to play tricks on the others and act the fool.[55]

There are countless traces of ritualized farce of this kind in Desrousseaux's work. In an appendix to the 1855 edition of his songs he defines the word *ban* as follows:

> Applause in rhythm imitating a military drum. This is done everywhere. But in Lille we make many variations. There is the *ban* simple, the *ban* of cats, the *ban* of ducks; that is, while clapping one imitates the calls of these animals. It's quite a delightful spectacle to see how seriously this exercise is taken. The commander has in his demeanor something of a sergeant-major, which he is, in effect. All eyes are on his to see the signal of the cessation of the ban. If all hands stop clapping in perfect unison according to the rule, then he announces triumphantly,

"Okay, there are no conscripts!" But if there is a conscript, the punishment follows immediately. The conscript, or the convict if you like, climbs up on a table, and must drink a glass of water very slowly while his friends sing in unison:

I va passer par l'trouglouglou	He must pass through the trouglouglou
De ma tanturlurette;	Of my tanturlurette
I va passer par l'trouglouglou	He must pass through the trouglouglou
De ma tanturlourou.	Of my tanturlourou.[56]

Even if many of the traditional farcical elements of public ceremony had fallen away by the Second Empire, there is evidence that other practices had replaced them. Several songs (and other sources) speak of a form of puppet theatre that was popular with Lille-area laborers.[57] Puppet shows were put on occasionally by laborers who had learned the skill (doubtless they were *manoqueux* looking for extra income). They rented a cellar, charged a sou admission, and put on a puppet play chosen from among a highly restricted repertoire, portraying biblical or well-known historical persons and events. Not children but adults made up the audience; and they bought beer and food to consume in their cramped seats. Everyone knew the plays by heart, and the crowd heckled and harassed the puppets all through the play. Making puns on the lines was particularly popular and everyone waited for their favorite moments to start up the teasing. Here is a passage reproduced by Pierrard from Descottignies' 1858 song, "Le Théâtre de César" ("Caesar's Theatre"), describing a performance of *Joseph vendu par ses frères (Joseph Sold By His Brothers)* – the story of Jacob's son Joseph from the Bible. Included in the account is a description of the usual points at which the crowd intervened:

L'rideau s'lève et pou qu'mincher	The curtain goes up and there we find
Les garchons d'Jacob sont in route	Jacob's sons on the road;
Et faitt'nt l'complot que pindint l'nuit	They are plotting to throw Joseph
On j'ttra Joseph dins l'fond d'un puits.	Into a well during the night.
A l'plache de l'tuer, fort heureus'mint,	Instead of killing him, thank goodness,
Ruben, l'ainé des frères, décide	Ruben the eldest brother decides
Qui fait l'vinde un bon prix d'argint.	To sell him at a good price.
L'marchand arrive et dit tout d'suite:	The merchant arrives and asks at once:
Combien ch'qu'on vind ch'petit capon?	"How much for that little squirt?"
– Deux doupe', un spectateur répond.	"Two cents," a spectator replies.
...Au 2ᵉ aque, on vot ch'garchon	...In the second act, we see the boy
Chez Putiphar tout près de s'femme:	At Putiphar's quite close to his wife

Ell' li caressot sin minton;	Who caresses his chin;
Mais ch'benêt l'repoussot quand même.	But that simpleton rejects her anyway.
Din l'caf' tout l'monde in veyant cha	In the cafe everyone, seeing this,
Crie: "Ell' l'ara point...Ell' l'ara!"	Cries out: "She won't get him...Yes she will!"
Pindant qu'Joseph chez Pharaon	While Joseph is with the Pharaoh
Est in train d'li conter ses rèfes	Trying to explain his dreams
On intind dir' par un garchon	We hear a boy who says
"Te trann', comm' si t'avos les fièfes!"	"You look as though you've got a fever!"
Et crac, i jett' su s'tiète d'bos	And pow, he throws on his wooden head
Eunn' poir' cuit' qui l'retint su l'dos.	A cooked pear which sticks to his back.
...Au 4ᵉ aque, Benjamin	...In the fourth act, Benjamin
Veut s'in aller s'trouver ses frères	Wants to go find his brothers
Et l'père Jacob, qui s'crot malin,	And father Jacob, who thinks he is clever,
Repond chez perol's singulières:	Responds with these singular words:
"Allons, mon fils, allons ver eux."	"Let us go, my son; Let us go toward them."
Là-dessus chacun crie: "Eh! vereux!"	Thereupon all cry out "Huh! Wormy!" [The pun is on *vers eux*, toward them, and *vereux*, wormy.]
...L'dernier aque n'a point pu s'finir	...The last act is impossible to finish
Tell'mint qui s'faijot du tapache;	So loud was the ruckus that they made;
Veyant cha, César a du v'nir	Seeing this, Caesar had to come out
Pinsint l'calmer par sin partache.	Hoping to calm them down with an appearance.
Mais l'voix de Joseph qu'il a guardé	But he still spoke with Joseph's voice
Est caus' que l'tapache a r'doublé.	Which caused the noise to redouble.[58]

There is another account of 1855 (not in song form) of a performance of *Joseph vendu* in which, with slight variations, the same scenario of crowd interference unfolds, culminating in an appearance of the puppeteer from behind the stage when the animal noises and laughter have become too loud for the play to continue. In this case, the audience does not feign astonishment when he speaks with the same voice as Joseph, but the puppeteer's mock harangue is deflected in an equally silly direction when someone in the crowd cries out, "No smoking here!" The puppeteer picks this up at once: "Yes, that's right, no smoking here, no smoking, please!" All busily put out their pipes. But of course there is no such

279

rule. Then the puppeteer makes a long speech to the crowd about their bad manners. (They are called, among other epithets, *méchants bougres* – "dirty buggers.") Finally the play resumes.[59]

Plays mentioned in other songs include *Robinson Crusoe, Richard Sans Peur* (*Richard the Lion-Hearted*), *Jeanne d'Arc*, and *Phinard et Lydéric* (two giants who lived in Flanders in a mythical past). Not only are audience interventions integral to accounts of these others plays, but there are indications that the puppeteers took considerable liberties with their scripts, embellishing their stories with delightful and ridiculous asides and puns.[60]

Farce, then, as an organized part of the community's life was still very much alive in the Second Empire, even if its form may have changed. These collective, ritualized occasions of farce modeled in a pure form the attitude toward life that pervades the whole dialect literature. It is important not to make the mistake of seeing these puppet plays or the throwing of St. Nicolas into the canal or rhythmic applause with animal noises as merely a number of amusing leisure-time customs of some poorly educated workers. What must be held in mind is the organic relationship between these kinds of collective practices and the preference for light-hearted irony and indirection that laborer-songwriters displayed in dealing with the most troubling and bleak elements of their lives. The evidence on practice demonstrates that the dialect literature was not a peculiar, idiosyncratic sideline of a few isolated groups. Instead, it arose out of and shared in the central elements of the community's public celebrations.

Desrousseaux's early poem "Casse-Bras" appears on reflection as a key to all this material. Appearing when it did in 1849 it announced the new meaning that dialect poetry would have in the coming period of repression. Desrousseaux, in many of his early pieces but most explicitly in "Casse-Bras," showed that the old farcical tradition could be given a new moral function. It would be possible now to look directly at those features of their lives that politics had taught them to be aware of, which marked them as members of the lowest class in society, the proletariat, the baseline of comparison, the exploited par excellence. It would be possible to contemplate them and to retain one's balance by applying the old farcical, carnivalesque idiom to them. Refusing the twin hazards of helpless bitterness and studied unconsciousness, one could find a kind of wisdom and self-respect in the understated ironies of the new dialect song.

FROM FARCE TO POLITICS

It should not be supposed that this moral choice entailed turning away from politics or from direct efforts on the laborers' part to take political action on their own behalf. There is evidence of at least one episode of conflict in which laborers brought the spirit of farce into the workplace and turned it on their employers. In the case in question, laborers at several mills made repeated complaints that the work they had been set to was too hard. The piece rate would have to be raised. It was during the boom of the early 1850s and the laborers had some easy successes. At one mill, laborers all pretended to go on strike and then returned, on two successive occasions. In another, half the laborers quit work and the other half stayed on; under the direction of one of their fellows they feigned a series of difficulties with the work, quitting in their turn, one at a time. In yet another mill, laborers played at lighting their pipes in air that was filled with explosive cotton dust. On two of these occasions, they successfully provoked clerks and owners into giving them angry lectures on their behavior. Even the standard puppeteer harangue, in other words, was reproduced in the mill. How many other campaigns of this kind may have been waged in Lille-area mills is impossible to know; in this case, luck has preserved some fragmentary reports.[61]

When the Empire was proclaimed in 1852, one songwriter recounts, the prefect mounted a stand in the square and read the news out *"d'un bon coeur"* ("with a good heart"); a banquet followed described in the song as "un diner à l'fourchette" ("a dinner with forks"). The songwriter's judgment on this affair is summed up in a single phrase: *"D'parler politique / L'saison est passée."* ("For talk of politics / The season has now ended.")[62] Yet another mild cut, passed by the police censors unnoticed, speaks of a lively interest in political affairs.

Once the Empire had fallen and freedom of speech was gradually reestablished under a republican government, politics in fact became a favorite topic for songwriters. One may trace the laborers as they test the waters, so to speak, to see if they are safe in the early 1870s. Their attitude toward the new Republic was far from unreservedly positive, to judge from a number of songs which deal with the end of excise taxes in 1873. These taxes had been instituted on coffee, chicory, and other items of common consumption to help pay off the indemnity owed to the Prussians following the war. The lifting of these taxes was a cause of celebration, as explained in Louis Longret's "Le Dégrèvement de la Chicorée" ("The Abolition of the Chicory Tax"):

In buvant de l'bonne chique	Drinking good old chicory
Assis au coin d'min fu	Sitting in the corner by the fire
J'crie: viv' la République!	I yell, Long Live the Republic!
L'impôt est disparu.	The tax has finally expired.[63]

Censor or no censor, the songwriters of Lille still prefer the light touch, so light one wonders if it is really there.

After the consolidation of the Republican government and the repulsing of the monarchists late in the 1870s, the laborers' attitude became for a time frankly positive – to judge from an 1879 Tourcoing song called "La République." The decline of the monarchist parties is openly applauded:

T'cheu bonheur	Happiness is here
Pour ach'teur	For as of now
Pu d'bétisse	No more mischief
Eu d'royalisse	No more monarchism
Ché compris	It's understood
Din l'esprit	In the minds of all
Qu'in s'ra Républit'chin sa vie.	We are republicans for life.

This song reveals particular appreciation for the free flow of information and freedom of expression that the Republic brought with it, and calls on workers to open their eyes to the world:

In République, in a de l'chance	Under a Republic, we have the chance
Eu d'savoir chin qui s'pass in France	To know what's going on in France
Pour vir claire, y n'faut pu d'ékance...	To see clearly, you no longer need an *écang* [Tool for separating linen fiber from the stem of the flax]...
Eu j'vous d'mande à quo qu'cha sert	I ask you what good is it
Eu d'dormir eu d'su l'ouvrage	To sleep, bent over your work
Y vaut mi les zis ouverts...	Better to keep your eyes open...[64]

But in the Lille area as elsewhere, the disillusionments of the 1880s and the failure of Boulangism led to a massive turn toward the socialist parties in the 1890s. This too is reflected in dialect songs. Indeed, the rise of socialism may be considered the most significant challenge that the dialect songwriters had faced since the earlier outburst of enthusiasm for songwriting in 1848. For the first time, socialism called on the laborers to forgo their removed, ironic stance and to speak openly of their sufferings, their political feelings, and their aspirations. Laurent Marty's recent work on Roubaix dialect songs has begun to explore the consequent changes in the tradition.

First of all, Desrousseaux's style was kept alive for the new generation by younger prominent songwriters, the best known of these being Catrice of Roubaix and Jules Watteeux of Tourcoing, known as Le Broutteux.[65] Le Broutteux's themes remained the classic ones, coffee, marriage troubles, memories of childhood. At the same time, numerous anonymous writers carried on the carnival- and cafe-song tradition; the contrast between their style and Le Broutteux's remaining much the same as that between their predecessors and the nostalgic tone of Desrousseaux. Finally, a group of songwriters, including Louis Catrice, began composing on socialist-inspired themes. There can be no doubt that they had the hardest row to hoe. The tradition offered them no hint as to how to proceed; subtle irony had little place in the tough, intransigent style of Jules Guesde whose socialist Parti ouvrier français had won widespread support in the Nord's mill towns by the early 1890s. The very popularity of this blunt, passionate orator signals a significant shift in the laborers' outlook. His lieutenant, Gustave Delory, elected mayor of Lille in 1896, among his many other activities, operated the "Workers' Press" that printed a large number of dialect songs. Among its products one finds numerous pieces on socialist themes. Many, perhaps most of them, deal with current affairs – elections, poor relief, military service – and were, therefore, only of temporary interest. Several of these songs are significantly not in dialect at all, but written in perfect French, such as "Pour la Patrie" ("For the Fatherland"), an 1895 composition written about the plight of working-class conscripts. *"Tu dois partir . . . pour servir la France"* ("You must leave...to serve France"), the song remarks,

Pendant ce temps ton père dans les fabriques	During this time your father in the factories
Souffrant la faim, se meurt en travaillant	Suffering from hunger, dies on the job
En maudissant ces hommes politiques	While cursing those men of politics
Qui lui ravirent son soutien, son enfant.	Who have stolen his support, his child.[66]

Socialist dialect songs never involve such combinations of sentiment and political analysis as the French productions that sometimes came out of Delory's press. When the same subject of military service was taken up in a dialect song, for example, the treatment was more direct, based on an uncomplicated moral egalitarianism, as in "L'Actualité Roubaisenne" ("Now in Roubaix"):

J'veurro bin connaîte in patron	I would like to know one boss
Qui a été blessé à la j'jerre,	Who's been wounded in a war,
O bin qui a perdu sin garchon	Or else who has lost his boy
Pindint sin service militaire,	Doing his military service,
Dit's inne fo l'nom d'vos calotins	Just for once tell me the names of you churchgoers
Qui sont morts sur in champs d'bataille?	Who have died on a field of battle.

Comme mi vous nin connichi nin	Like me, you can't think of one,
Vous êt's inn' vrait bind' de canailles.	You're nothing but a bunch of rascals.[67]

This is bitter in tone, and the dialect becomes more thick at just the point where the bitterness is most extreme: "*Comme mi vous nin connichi nin.*" ("Like me, you can't think of one.") But if one compares such a piece with the products of the repressive days of the Second Empire, it is clear that the literature has paid a price in cutting itself loose from its disingenuous irony. Having lost those moorings it had not by 1900 found new ones.

Louis Catrice came the closest to bridging the gap between the old and the new styles. Blacklisted for union activities, he ran a cafe in Roubaix, partly as songwriter, partly as militant for the Parti ouvrier. He helped Carette get elected mayor in 1892 but refused to seek office himself. He enjoyed broad practical jokes. He disguised himself at Carnival time one year to sneak up on his singing club and harass them as they performed their song. Finally they recognized who it was, and laughed as hard as he. He could write explicitly on political doctrines with something of the old understated tone, as in a long poem denouncing Christianity that takes the form of a telephone call to God.[68] At the same time he could write about cafe owners in the conventional manner.

Ch'est un bon commerce	It's a good trade
D'êtt cabareti,	Running a cafe,
Surtout tchand qu'in verse	Especially when you pour
Des verr's à monti.	Half-full glasses.[69]

One of Catrice's admirers after his death spoke of the "healing" effect that his "indefatigable verve" had on the working-class spirit.[70] The comment might well be applied to the whole dialect tradition.

Third–Republic material, in short, shows the dialect songwriter prepared, even anxious, to deal with political issues, to wrestle with the problems of working-class life in a political context (once some conventions had been created for doing so), to reach out for a wider point of view once freedom of speech was restored. In the process, there are traces of an attempt to rework the farcical wisdom of the past; but this only underscores that this brand of wisdom had nothing to do with escapism or willful blindness to the oppressive conditions of working-class life.

WHAT PEOPLE MAKE OF WORDS

Every working-class inhabitant of the mill towns of the Lille area was regularly exposed to dialect literature and popular ceremonial in the second half of the century. Up until 1880, furthermore, it had few rivals. There was little in the way of a popular press or of a specifically working-class political leadership or of religious or artistic forms of communication available. True, the Catholic Church and wealthy supporters began working in this period to revivify popular devotion, to attract the poor to its liturgy, to assuage suffering, and win loyalty.[71] The church was increasingly seen as a necessary arm in the fight against socialism. It is also true that Tourcoing rightly had a reputation for its high proportion of practicing Catholics.[72] In view of the efforts made by Catholics, however, the fruits over the long run were very meager. What relation may have existed between Catholicism and the dialect literature is difficult to say. The potential for points of contact was obviously great, not only because so much popular ceremonial was Catholic in origin, but also because the ethical tenor of the literature was partially compatible with Christian moral teaching. But it is unlikely that this potential was recognized. The songwriters' disdain for all superstition, their frank acceptance of drinking, and humorous treatment of the serious matters of life were bound to alienate them from the missionary spirit of the church's supporters. The question how far the church became a preserve of female activities just as songwriting was monopolized by males must be left to others to answer. It is certain, in any case, that even among women churchgoing was far from being a universal habit.

The dialect tradition, then, was not only ubiquitous but also practically unchallenged as a mode of expression in working-class neighborhoods until socialism appeared and developed its uneasy, or perhaps one should say unfinished, relationship to it. Virtually everyone in these communities was familiar with dialect song and ceremony and experienced at least some parts of life in terms of its special language. At the same time, there is evidence of many levels of participation. There were songwriters who worked at it all the time, others who wrote a good number of pieces, still others who are known from only one or two, and of course a great number who wrote no published songs.

Something of the significance of these different levels of participation may be gleaned from a reconsideration of the two songs mentioned at the beginning of this chapter. Once familiar with the conventions of the dialect literature it is possible to discern what the two songwriters were trying to achieve. Both were occasional participants at best, and their compositions clearly reflect their lack of practice. The song about the young woman with the inflamed finger was supposed to be a contribution to the genre dealing with the tribulations of courtship. Its refrain contains the conventional warning against marriage. But the story is told in a way that makes the listener identify too closely with the woman's situation. The writer seems to have had some personal acquaintance in mind. In the first stanza, he says he saw the woman and her man (a spinner) one Sunday night. He said hello but she did not respond, afraid to be recognized. The second and third stanzas continue:

Arrivant sur la place	Coming to the square
In face du boulanger	Across from the bakery
Là à l'clarté du gaz	There in the light of the lamp
J' l'ai bien distingué;	I saw her distinctly;
J' cros bien qu'ell' a eu peur,	I think she was afraid
Car depuis ch' momint-là,	Because since that moment
Elle a eu des battmints d'coeur,	She has had palpitations of the heart,
Et des mas d'estomac.	And aches in her stomach.
Et l'lundi au matin,	Monday in the morning,
Euss' mère elle cri après,	Her mother called out to her
Elle li dit dépêch' te vite	Saying, Get moving,
La cloche elle va sonner.	The factory bell is about to ring.
Elle dit aoui ma mère	She says, Oh yes, my mother,
J'n'ai point dormi de l'nuit	I haven't slept all night
J'ai du ma à min doie	I have a pain in my finger
Ech'cros bien j'ai l'panari.	And I think it is inflamed.

The problem with the song is that these details are too vivid and too touching to sustain the conventional warning against marriage, which becomes callous in appearance as the song tells how the girl's mother saw what was wrong and forced her, crying and confused, out of the house. The experience behind the song is only half-digested and not really very appropriate to the prevailing literary conventions. Mother's warning about the factory bell on a Monday morning, the infection in the finger – the dialect even had a special word for this common ailment of textile workers – these touches breathe with a kind of authenticity that the conventions could not accommodate. As a song, it is a failure. Likewise one may guess that its writer neither fully understood nor applied to his life the farcical wisdom developed with such intensity and dedication by Desrousseaux and others. He did not have the same need, either, to make his meaning so precisely and richly clear as a songwriter specialist. His social identity did not depend so heavily on how people interpreted his verse.

The same can be said for the other song, about the widower who marries a woman with a lot of furniture. The major problem with that song, an attempt in the genre dealing with the woes of married life, is

286

that the woman has the sense and self-reliance to move out. Convention dictates that women be either domineering or else lazy and prone to gossip, or both. This woman had evident strength, ends the bad marriage on her own account, and does not even lose her furniture. The man suffers nothing at all from the liaison, except the loss of the desirable new possessions. Doubtless, the song was based on another undigested bit of personal knowledge.

The coarseness and depravity that appear at first glance in these songs (especially if one is looking for signs of it) actually resulted from the fact that they were not fully realized literary pieces. They were composed by unpracticed writers and based on bits of personal experience that only poorly fit into available conventions. The problem lay, in particular, in the inability of the writers to assimilate their knowledge of women to the accepted stereotypes of the literature. Their indifference to convention, as nonspecialists, may have been the reason why they were satisfied with these unrealized pieces.

The song Audiganne quoted from, "M'Cave et M'Guernier," was written by Louis Dubuire Dubuc, identified by Pierrard as a middle-class man who liked to *"faire peuple."*[73] Knowledgeable about the dialect literature and the local laboring community, he was trying to express a sentiment he sensed in them toward the municipality's efforts to close up cellar dwellings. But his aim fell wide of the mark. Other songs show how little textile laborers liked living in those dank spots. What they did not like about the municipality's program was being forced to move; they had to move often enough as it was.

In view of the richness and diversity of the material that has been examined, it is strange that Provençal peasants still have a monopoly on the reputation for sociability. Partly this is due to the sources, no doubt. To nineteenth-century observers, peasants in sunny climes who went into bars to sing and joke were being folkloric, but mill operatives who did so were depraved proletarians. So heavily has this weight of expectations impressed itself on the records that social historians can only break free of it by means of the most persistent effort. Once one has done so, however, how odd the old assumptions look. The sun that shone inside bars throughout the Nord, however somber the clouds and the streets outside, was every bit as bright as that of the Mediterranean coast.

This is not to say that, were one able to walk the streets of Saint-Sauveur again, one would find no bitterness, no fear or depression, no loneliness or failed relationships. Such breakdowns of connectedness occur everywhere; poverty can make them more difficult to tolerate. Much of the energy of writing dialect songs was aimed, after all, at assuaging the pain of such things; and there is internal evidence that they often did not work very well. The very negative interpretations of outside observers like Villermé or Reybaud were perfectly plausible; certainly there was evidence to back them up. Where they went wrong was in supposing that all the evidence before them arose out of a perfect coherence, that the singing and drinking, the cellars with one bed, the *concubinage*, the children begging in the streets were all emanations of a single identity, were all enjoyed with equal relish by all members of the laboring community. Once one strips this assumption away, the signs of striving and suffering, of discord and persuasion, of happiness and unhappiness suddenly take on the appearance of contingency and incompleteness that are the hallmarks of the human condition.

It is important to remember that interpreting is not an activity confined to observers or historians. It is the means by which human beings make sense of the messages they receive from the world. The limits of interpretation therefore constitute limits to the creation of community. Dialect literature in the Nord's mill towns offered, to a greater or lesser extent depending on the piece, an interpretation of the working-class community's character that offered at once to save it from the larger world's shallow judgments and to arm it with a kind of light irony perfectly attuned to the repressive atmosphere of the time. But its conventions were also limited, its stereotypes often brittle. It hardly satisfied every need, particularly after republican freedoms made it possible for laborers to stand up and speak publicly for themselves again. Laurent Marty has dated the years of the literature's decline as roughly between 1900 and 1930 when the outside world began delivering not just printed but also visible and audible messages on a massive scale via cinema and radio to local communities.[74] It would be proper to lament this decline only if the literature itself was completely forgotten, which does not now seem likely. What human beings need is not located in particular arrangements of words, in any case, but in what groups of individuals, with more or less accord, make of them. It is not possible to know what textile laborers in the Nord were or what they wanted, but it is possible to gain an understanding of some of the things they tried, in protest, in leisure, and at work, to become for each other.

10 Little insurrections

Under the Second Empire a new consensus was achieved among laborers and mill owners to the effect that equal effort and equal time ought to receive equal pay. This consensus provided a guide for the introduction of new spinning and weaving technology during the long mid-century boom. It amounted to a proper conceptualization of labor as a commodity in that the justice of a pay rate was now firmly linked to abstract features of the laborer's behavior instead of to tangible amounts of product – although the product continued to be the immediate thing that was paid for. Strikes were legalized, defined in law as the withholding of a commodity from sale; and textile laborers had by 1871 made several experiments with this new form of action.

Under the Third Republic there were further reforms in the same direction. Unions were legalized in 1884; an optional state arbitration and conciliation procedure was set up in the early 1890s. The state threw its weight firmly behind the idea that labor conflict represented a normal facet of bargaining between freely contracting parties.

But these changes in the end did little to alter the social position of textile laborers. Even if there was a consensus available now for bargaining about pay rates under certain circumstances, there was still no firm consensus about the form that bargaining ought to take. And very little in the way of formal bargaining occurred; owners simply refused to engage in it. Competitive pressures remained restrained and indirect in their impact on the distribution of labor. Nonquantifiable factors in the organization of work and in the structure of local communities continued to determine laborer choices as greatly as ever.

The state's enlarged sphere of activities did, however, generate a much vaster range of documentation on industry and industrial conflict. Parliamentary and ministerial inquiries multiplied; systematic statistics on strike activity began to be gathered in 1891.[1] Social historians in a number of pioneering efforts have surveyed part of this vast mass of material and have mapped out the topography of social conflict under the Third Re-

289

public.[2] In their work the textile industry of the last third of the nineteenth century has emerged as representing the impact of industrialization on social life in an exemplary way. Fully mechanized, concentrated in a string of mill towns that stretched across northern France in a great crescent, employing unskilled or semiskilled machine tenders in large numbers – who were frequently involved in conflict – textiles have been seen as emblematic of the new industrial France.

A DETAIL AND ITS MEANING

"France on strike," remarks Michelle Perrot in her intensive study of industrial conflict in the period of 1870–90, "is the France of the textile industry, capital Roubaix."[3] In Perrot's view the characteristics of textile–industry strikes and those of industrial conflict for France as a whole in the period were the same: The typical strike was "rough and sudden, exploding brutally under the effect of emotion, anger, or desire. . ."[4] Her figures show, moreover, that textile strikes bulk inordinately large within the sum of industrial conflicts.

Between the years 1871 and 1890, she finds workers in spinning and weaving mills in France engaged in 857 known strikes involving a total of 325,515 strikers, accounting for 29 percent of all recorded strikes and 37 percent of all strikers in this period. Their propensity to strike was over twice that of the average French worker and second only to miners among industrial workers. Like the miners, according to Perrot, they tended to strike spontaneously, without giving advanced warning or engaging in preliminary negotiations. Unpremeditated strikes, Perrot judges, accounted for 71 percent of all conflicts in mining, and 64 percent in textiles. Unlike the miners, however, textile workers seldom formed unions or turned to unions for help once a strike had begun. Perrot's tabulations show further that textile workers, unlike miners, seldom coordinated their strikes with periods of prosperity when owners were more likely to give in. Their strikes were more often defensive than offensive, were shorter than the average, and more often ended in failure than the average.[5]

Government statistics for the period after 1890 reveal much the same picture. Aggregate figures show that textiles as a whole accounted for 24 percent of all strikes in the period 1890–1914, while participation in unions remained unusually low.[6] Propensity to strike peaked shortly after 1900; 7 percent of all textile workers were involved in strikes in the average year between 1901 and 1905, again second only to miners (whose general strike of 1902 raised their equivalent average to 19.2 percent).[7] By 1910–14, however, this high propensity appears to have begun dropping off, beginning a decades-long slide toward very low levels in the mid-twentieth century, a slide which was not, however, accompanied by any effective unionization.[8]

These figures create at first glance a picture of social disorganization. Historians have found it relatively easy to accept this picture because demographic data from textile towns and information on technical conditions in the industry also seem at first glance to confirm it. The labor force of spinning and weaving mills – made up of men, women, and adolescents in about equal proportions, recently arrived in rapidly growing factory towns, working as poorly paid machine tenders – was new to industry and therefore, it is easily believed, uprooted, disoriented, uncertain of its social identity, demoralized. Hence collective actions were not rational; seized by anger, textile laborers struck out at random at the capitalist order that now embraced them. If their strike patterns were characteristic of the period, it only underscores the immaturity of France's whole industrial work force in that era.

One historian after another has echoed this verdict, or some version of it. For Michelle Perrot, the textile mills of the *belle époque* were "the world of the O.S. [that is, the *ouvrier spécialisé*, the semiskilled machine tender] that the recent mechanization of weaving, still incomplete, had just created, the 'prisoner' of the 'industrial penitentiary.' "[9] The social environment was one of "migrations, or rural exodus, of mixed populations in ferment, uprooted, traumatized, thrown into the factory and confronted with the machine for the first time." Strikes in this environment were "impulsive, angry, truly wildcat" and "prone to extension," that is, to spreading from one mill to another "not by plan but by imitation, by contagion. . ."[10] This propensity to extension she explains as follows: "The geographical concentration of the factories, the homogeneity of the work force, the importance of women and youths, permeable to waves and rumors, finally the absence of organization constitute factors favorable to epidemics." However, "The fever quickly subsides."[11]

Daniel Vasseur, in a study of strikes and union organization in the Belfort-Montbéliard region at the turn of the century – in which textile strikes were a principal ingredient – characterized industrial conflict of the period in almost identical terms as "instinctive, brutal, and disorganized."[12] According to Peter Stearns, textile workers in this period "struck frequently, but in disorganized fashion and for very limited goals," while in contrast they cherished unrealistic visions of a "socialist utopia perhaps more fervently than did any other large group of workers." Overall their efforts at self-defense were "feeble."[13]

Edward Shorter and Charles Tilly consider textile workers to be "semiskilled proletarians" in a "new industry" and therefore "organized, if at all, only loosely by politicized spark plug militants who lead their followers toward bread-and-butter issues in shop-floor actions, and towards radical *revendications* in national political action." They caution that they do not see such workers as "disorganized, cursed with the disaffiliation and disaggregation that some scholars believe accompany rapid industrial advance." Instead they suspect only that the shop floor did not become the locus of organization for such workers, who preferred neighborhood or town-based affiliations.[14]

Shorter and Tilly's modification of the common view is well taken; too often historians have read the more rigorous social statistics of the Third Republic period as mere continuations of the story told by Villermé, Blanqui, Reybaud, and Audiganne earlier in the century; all seem to confirm that the textile worker was the classic proletarian, without communal ties or history. Shorter and Tilly restrict this argument to the workplace; on the shop floor itself if not outside, in their view, the textile worker felt uprooted and directionless.

As interpretations of statistical evidence on strikes, population movements, and mechanization, there is some justice to these conclusions. Perrot, Stearns, Shorter, and Tilly are speaking comparatively; and, in comparison with printers, glassworkers, molders, or turners, it is correct to say that textile workers had fewer formal shop-floor organizations, had in some cases less historical experience to draw on in the exercise of their craft, and certainly went on strike with less preparation and forethought in the period 1870 to 1914.

It is difficult, in fact, to see how preliminary surveys of such a large and well documented terrain as the Third Republic could have arrived at different conclusions about the textile industry. With such great masses of data to deal with, these studies could not afford the leisure of raising fundamental questions about individual trades. Previously there was not even a general view of the situation to reflect upon. Now, standing on others' shoulders, it is possible to entertain alternative explanations of a known range of phenomena. Closer examination will always, of course, raise problems of detail. But an attempt will be made here to go further still, and use such problems of detail to open a door on an entirely different way of seeing the passionate strikes of the *belle époque*. The reason historians have seen textile laborers as uprooted and disorganized, it will be argued here, is that – like most historians of industrial society – they have accepted as a background assumption that market society works more or less as it is supposed to, or at least that the terms of market culture are adequate for describing it.[15]

A problem of detail with these characterizations of French textile workers is that there is much evidence of social continuity rather than uprootedness in mill towns of the *belle époque*. The major centers of textile production in 1914 were virtually the same as in 1830. What differences there were in the map resulted from the decline of old centers like Cholet, Cambrai, or Rouen – and the German annexation of Alsace – not from the appearance of new ones. It is true that certain towns, Reims, Lille, Roubaix, Armentières, experienced substantial growth after 1870; but not on a scale that ever required them to draw raw recruits into the industry. Net fertility in the textile towns was well above the French average.[16] Furthermore, the final snuffing out of handloom weaving for almost all grades and varieties of cloth between 1860 and 1890 provided a steady stream of immigrants from the countryside to fill new power-loom mills. Rural weavers, when forced to abandon their cottages, moved a minimum distance; the mills that replaced them grew up in the nearby towns where they had marketed their cloth since the eighteenth century, and it was to these towns that they brought their families in search of work. This is what census data from the town of Armentières show. Eighty-one percent of immigrants to that town during the period of rapid mechanization of linen weaving from 1860 to 1885 came from the surrounding traditional linen-producing area. (Less than 3 percent came from Lille or Roubaix, only 10 miles away.) Yet the town's population tripled in these same years.[17]

Roubaix is often cited as the paradigmatic new industrial center in this context. Its rapid expansion attracted a constant flow of thousands of new arrivals from the countryside. By 1886, 53 percent of the town's population were Belgian citizens, an impressive sign of the community's newness, like an American city, as has so often been said. But a closer look at the figures shows that 24,000 of the town's 54,000 Belgian citizens had been born in Roubaix. A great number of the remainder, it appears, were French speakers from very nearby.[18] (Roubaix is almost on the border.) They spoke a version of the same dialect that native Roubaisiens used. Laurent Marty reports that newcomers quickly learned to take pride in Roubaix and to join in the singing and composing of dialect songs.[19] Flemish speakers established their own neighborhoods.[20] Even they were from not very distant parts of Belgium, all within a region that had been dominated by domestic textile production for centuries. Roubaix's own merchant manufacturers, before the onset of the power loom, had put out weaving in large parts of this area.

These people may have been new to the factory but they were already familiar with the products, the firms, and even many of the tasks they would be expected to perform. Piecing yarn, installing warps, sizing, and evaluating cloth were all carried out in much the same way in the mill as in the cottage. Once they found work in the towns, moreover, these new workers showed little inclination toward further movement. Rare evidence on one Armentières weaving mill from 1903 shows that 63 percent of laborers over 25 years of age had been at work in that mill for over 10 years; even among those 21 to 25 years of age, 58 percent had been in the mill over five years.[21]

Yet these settled populations with long experience of the trade appear in strike statistics as volatile, angry, and unpredictable. Against a continuous background of frequent localized conflict, these towns were swept every 10 years or so by strike waves that engulfed whole regions in 1880, 1889–90, and 1903–4. These were the "epidemics" referred to by Perrot. Those of 1889 and 1903 in particular affected small towns, rural mill villages and dwindling handloom centers where one was hardly likely to find disoriented workers new to the industry.[22] The great exception to the rule was the city of Lille. Expanding very rapidly, with a diversified industrial base, Lille harbored a working population that might more plausibly be called dislocated, at least by comparison with other textile towns. Yet, it was less often involved in strike epidemics than any other major center.[23] Close examination of the geography and demography of the industry, in other words, yields findings that seriously challenge the whole notion of disorganization as the underlying cause of textile strike patterns.

Utilizing the abundant evidence of the Third Republic era, applying sophisticated quantitative measures, historians have elaborated, in effect, carefully nuanced variations on the classic notion of proletarianization – but variations with a serious flaw. Textile laborers have been seen as massed together, deprived of skill or qualification, unknown to each other, ignorant of the forces that oppressed them, and capable of exhibiting no more than the most primitive forms of collective human response to adversity – impulsive waves of riotous resistance. The problem is that, on balance, there does not seem to have been enough movement or dislocation to make this view plausible; and, even more telling, the waves of protest seem to have affected areas where social disruption was less marked or even where its opposite, industrial stagnation of an old center, prevailed.

What actually underlay these patterns of strike behavior was the opposite of disorganization. Not industrialization in an exemplary form, but the exemplary unfinished nature of the French textile trade's transition to capitalism, even by 1900, accounts for the way textile laborers acted. It was the laborers' very rootedness and the particular nature of organization of their community life that gave rise to these forms of collective action. These laborers acted as they did because they were all but captives of their local communities, not free enough to feel even a tug from competing alternatives, unable to realize in practice even a shadow of the freedoms that they enjoyed in law as citizens of a democracy. Utterly dependent on the will of small owner oligarchies, they lived out their lives almost like medieval serfs, except that they were now learning to act out a shallow travesty of market relations that has somehow, unbelievably, never been questioned. This is the context in which they felt grievances and protested, not that of uprootedness or free competition.

Despite the new attitudes of laborers toward wages that are evident in records of conflict by the late 1860s, despite another full round of growth and technological advance, despite the liberalizing legislation of the Republican regime, both workplace and community continued to display the distinctly nonmarket features already identified in earlier chapters:

1. Tasks continued to be strictly segregated by age and sex, with earning levels reflecting age-old assumptions about the distribution of duties among family members. Wage differentials based on age and sex in turn continued to encourage mill owners to use women and children in equal proportion to adult males, employing in effect not individuals but whole communities of families.[24]

2. Methods of payment changed little after the abolition of discounts and fees following the 1848 Revolution. This meant that laborers' piece-rate earnings continued to be linked to the proper operation of the work process, the quality of raw material, the good repair of the machinery, and the perfection of the product. These factors continued to stand as impediments to any simple equation between time at work and earnings (even though such equations came to serve by common consent as a means of calculating piece rates). If the use of subcontracting had been buried once and for all, nonetheless owners continued to depend on an almost proprietary involvement of their laborers in the smooth running of the shop, rather than on discipline or direct control, as the principal element of their labor management strategy.[25]

3. Associated with these conditions was the continued exercise – Republic or no Republic – of extensive informal social and political authority by owners within the textile towns. If anything, such authority became more visible as it came under challenge from the rising socialist parties and union federations. Owners now had to fight to retain their hegemony within the towns, but their fights were usually successful.

The persistence of these three factors throughout the pre–World War I era created a context that determined both the content and style of labor conflict. Laborers' grievances as before concerned work processes, family employment patterns, social deference – all matters that fit only poorly the commodity concept of labor. Their methods of expressing these grievances, likewise, were a poor fit for the legal definition of the strike as the withholding of a service by one party to a free contract. Owners succesfully blocked practical realization of the Republic's liberal reforms of labor law. If the government recognized unions after 1884, mill owners did not. They fired militants, blacklisted all leaders and spokesmen, refused negotiations, abrogated agreements. Intransigence was the keynote of their strategy for dealing with any sign of independent initiative. If intransigence failed, bad faith was a ready recourse. All this was, of course, no secret at the time and is quite well known to specialists even now.[26] Yet some fail to see the obvious consequence that, against such opponents, it was impossible to fulfill a modern ideal of "rational" strike behavior.

It must also be underscored that such owner strategies for neutralizing Republican reforms placed militants in a most difficult position. That militants existed at all was a result of the minimal enforcement of a few Republican liberties, and their impact on industrial life sets this period apart from those that preceded it in a most dramatic way. Yet, this impact can only be understood if one holds in mind the severe handicaps under which they labored.

Public expression of socialist or anarchist views was a dangerous thing engaged in only by the hardy few. These few in turn banded together for comfort and protection, creating a certain distance between themselves and the rest of the laboring community. This distance did not preclude tacit support from that community, however; and as time went on militants were increasingly able to find a livelihood in the operation of neighborhood bars, consumers' cooperatives, "unions" of very restricted membership, and (especially after 1890) in elective office. They were marked by their politics because of the unfree atmosphere of these towns, therefore, very much like songwriters in the Nord, they eventually succeeded in making their politics a profession.[27]

But, whatever brand of socialism or anarchism they embraced, they failed to understand the insurrectionary tone of textile strikes. Their analysis of wage labor remained a classical one: It was because of competition that the laborers suffered, suffering was caused by low remuneration, therefore textile strikes were short-term (and usually irrational) outbursts of discontent.

This is not to say that socialists were uncritical in their acceptance of political economy. On the contrary, they waged continuous polemical warfare against it. But in doing so, they used the language of market culture; they spoke in terms of costs, prices, competition, standard of living, accepting the utility of such terms in the same general way that social investigators had before them. They did so from the days of their first emergence following the repressive period of the 1870s. Paul Lafargue, for example, in a four part series in *L'Egalité* in 1882 called "Capitalist Production," drew extensively and uncritically on the writings of Villermé, Adolphe Blanqui, Audiganne, and Reybaud to demonstrate the terrible ravages of wage competition. Gustave Rouanet in the premier issue of *La revue socialiste* in 1885 contributed a piece called "The Economic Crisis" in which he decried the current "chaotic state" of competition; workers were forced to rent their services at too low a price, he explained, resulting in widespread pauperism and crises of overproduction. Symptomatic of this limited outlook was the fact that all socialist factions, and after 1896 the syndicalist Confédération générale du travail as well, constantly emphasized wages and hours in their programs and electoral platforms.[28]

Few militants, as a result, found it necessary to inquire closely into the causes or motives behind unplanned, spontaneous textile strikes. These were self-evident; laborers' suffering and degradation were so extreme that they occasionally gave in to overwhelming impulses to act. Such impulses had to be channeled in more effective directions; to some, more effective directions meant the ballot box, to others it meant revolution. But in either case, militants' views closely paralleled the later interpretations of historians.

Jules Guesde in particular, the most popular ideologue among the militants of textile towns, taught that strikes were best seen as schools of revolution in which the worker would learn the futility of seeking partial or short-term relief. Party discipline must reign during the struggle for state power; therefore spontaneous strikes were to be restrained if possible, or if not possible then to be used as occasions for the dissemination of propaganda. These views ensured that Guesdists were the worst of all the socialist factions in their mishandling of strikes.[29] The more reformist factions, who tried to steer strikes toward successful conclusions, were not much better, however, since they consistently misread the underlying social meaning of strike activity.

A RITUAL JACQUERIE

This view of the meaning of textile strikes cannot be substantiated by means of statistical evidence, not because there is anything wrong with statistics as such, but because all the numbers available were produced by an officialdom under the sway of state-mandated categories. It is easy to find in the archives the forms that local police filled out for the Office du Travail's statistical reports on strikes.[30] The Office du Travail's form had blanks for number of days, number of strikers, demands, results, wages before, wages after, and so on. It had no blank to check when the event in question did not fit into the definition implied by the other blanks. It had no blank to check when a collective action involved a struggle over the organization of work or the status of family members or the intransigence of the owners. For outcomes one had to check "victory," "defeat," or "compromise," terms often meaningless when applied to complex, community-wide struggles.

The only alternative approach is careful examination of specific incidents. But this method necessarily limits one to an extremely small proportion of the hundreds of well documented cases of textile conflict from this period. Because the aim is to appreciate the tenor of relations in the community of the trade overall, however, it would certainly be safe to look at some of those strike epidemics that occasionally broke out across whole textile regions. These incidents will be instructive if for no other reason than that they involved so many people in the trade one does not have to worry over their representativeness. One of these incidents, the linen-industry strike of 1903, was chosen for more careful investigation because of the availability of uniquely informative materials from the 1906 census that allow one to say how often family members worked together in the same mills.

The first of the Third Republic strike waves occurred in 1880; major strikes virtually closed down the towns of Lillebonne and Bolbec in Normandy; Roubaix, Tourcoing, and Armentières in the Nord; and Reims in Champagne. Smaller, partial shutdowns affected Lille, certain Rouen suburbs, and outlying mill villages surrounding Roubaix. About fifty thousand laborers were involved at its peak.[31]

Some obvious factors made 1880 a likely time for such an occurrence.[32] Recent political changes had contributed to a mood of expectancy. Republican forces were now firmly in control of the government; certain laws restricting freedom of expression and of assembly, while not yet repealed, were no longer being actively enforced. For the first time since the Commune, open meetings of socialists and anarchists were being tolerated. Certain pieces of Lille dialect literature discussed in chapter 9 suggest that laborers at this time approved of the Republic and expected great things from it. Local Chambres syndicales were springing up. (This term, usually translated as union, means literally chamber of spokesmen.) In 1878 a national labor congress was organized. At its second meeting a year later in Marseille, an obscure young radical named Jules Guesde spearheaded a socialist takeover. To the displeasure of a strong minority, the Congress of Marseille voted for the abolition of capitalism and established a political party to work toward this end. Delegates to the Congress also discussed practical goals for immediate labor action, including the 10-hour day.

The first strike began at Lillebonne and Bolbec on April 20. Twenty-nine hundred weavers walked out of area mills. Local mill owners had announced abolition of a long-standing incentive pay scheme; 10 percent bonuses (paid to weavers who made their output targets) were to be discontinued. Like the rest of the Normandy cotton industry, the Bolbec–

area mills were in trouble; their number had shrunk by over 50 percent in the previous 20 years. Obsolete equipment, unimaginative direction, and English competition had plagued the region since 1860; only control of the protected Algerian market had allowed production to continue.[33] The end of production premiums, which may be traced back to the "tâche" system, was now seen as a further unwanted sign of decline. The weavers had come to count on their bonuses by now.

It was the first disturbance of any kind in the area in a number of years; a Paris newspaper correspondent remarked with surprise that there was no Chambre syndicale; no committee was formed, no demands formulated, no delegates named. The weavers marched through Lillebonne singing the "Marseillaise." The following day a group of weavers set out for Paris to ask for a reinstatement of protective tariffs, since mill owners had insisted on their helplessness before English competitors.[34] They returned empty-handed on 2 May; a day later, all were back at work. Obviously this was no disorganized mass new to industry, but a well established community clinging to a declining trade and attempting to exercise its new Republican rights without experience or guidance.

It is not known why the strike at Reims began; but the timing suggests that news of the Lillebonne walkout may have acted as a trigger. The strike started on the twenty-third, the day after newspapers published the first report on the Normandy conflict. No one knew what the strike was about; after 7,000 weavers had walked out of the town's woolen mills, owners insisted bitterly that they had not been presented with any demands and, therefore, had no obligation to recognize the strike.

But a weaver named Baudelot provided the strike with an issue the following day. He was head of the local Chambre syndicale formed three years before; he had attended the Congress of Marseille and embraced its new socialist stance with enthusiasm.[35] He called a meeting on 24 April and told 2,000 weavers gathered in a field outside town that they should demand the 10-hour day. He read out to them an adjusted piece-rate schedule that would allow them to maintain earnings despite the shorter hours. The weavers applauded. From this point on, the 10-hour day became their official strike aim.

In subsequent days the weavers, meeting in their field, heard forceful arguments that they should stay out until their "last resource" had been expended. Baudelot explained that, if they returned to work out of hunger, it would not be a defeat but only a truce. Another speaker said that "if the owners saw us come back tomorrow, they would hide behind the doors and laugh at us!"[36]

In a speech on 4 May, Baudelot elaborated on the 10-hour demand. It would give us time to care for our children, he said. When our daughters are forced to work:

It means for them the loss of their honor. When they are pretty, clerks and others seduce them and in the end they abandon their work and give themselves over to prostitution. That is the fate dealt out to our children, our daughters. And that is why we demand the amelioration of our condition as well as of theirs. Who dare blame us?[37]

The following day Baudelot and a number of weaver delegates had a fruitless meeting with the owners. During this second week of the strike, weavers had begun filtering back to work; by 13 May, over three thousand had returned to the mills. Meanwhile the remaining strikers were attempting to save the movement by means of street demonstrations. On the fourteenth, a crowd of 700 parading through the streets singing the "Marseillaise" were met by Baudelot who had rushed out to calm them down and avert violence. Troops were called into the town. The following day the subprefect announced to a gathering of 1,200 strikers that the owners would be willing to consider negotiating on their demands eight days after the resumption of work, with "absolute forgiveness" for all strikers. However, the weavers appeared less than mollified by this offer.

Three days later the strike took a strange shift in direction. At a meeting on the seventeenth the demand for a 10-hour day was dropped. The weavers decided they would accept 11 hours until such time as the working day was reduced by legislation. In addition, a whole list of further demands was drawn up of which not a word had previously been spoken. These demands all concerned machine operation and pay procedures in the mills. The weavers wanted lower lateness fines; they wanted factory doors to remain unlocked during the day. They wanted acceptance of cloth to be "definitive" – that is, no additional fines for flaws to be allowed after the initial inspection. They wanted the owners to specify exactly which kinds of machine breakdowns were the weaver's fault (and therefore subject to fine). They listed a series of flaws in cashmere and other varieties of cloth that resulted from poor raw materials; these should never be charged to the weaver. The weavers demanded that owners pay them 2 francs a day in cases where machine repair forced them to remain idle for more than six days, and 75 centimes for each third of a day they were idled for other causes. (In other words they were willing to accept up to six days without pay in cases of machine repair only.) Finally, they wanted to be able to smoke and wished to receive a receipt for all work they turned in.[38]

Here is an indication of how distant work conditions and weavers' concerns remained from the notion of wage labor held by Baudelot and the Congress of Marseille. At first the weavers had not resisted the idea that their strike was for the 10-hour day, a demand strictly appropriate to a wage–laborer's interests. They had listened patiently to Baudelot's preaching (à la Villermé) about the moral degeneracy that resulted from long hours and low pay. But as the effort began to fail and owner intransigence on hours became clear, the remaining strikers insisted on a complete change of emphasis; and suddenly the issues which, from their point of view, most urgently needed addressing came out. Just as in the July Monarchy, their concerns focused on the terms of exchange of the finished product, the quality of raw material, and machine repair. Their demand to be compensated for idle time suggests that they wished to be treated more like wage laborers, whose time is the only thing they have to sell. Yet they were still willing to remain idle up to six days without compensation if a machinery breakdown were involved. This is a very generous allowance from a wage laborer.

The owners quickly agreed to a few of these demands: "definitive" acceptance was conceded, as was the demand for written receipts; weavers were never to be fined for machine breakage that was not their doing. The rest of the demands were rejected. The strikers who were still out did not know what to do. No one had the expertise necessary to represent them vigorously on the issues that really mattered to them. Within two days their number had dwindled to 400; the following day, the newspapers announced that the strike was effectively over.

Everything indicates that, as in Lillebonne, an air of novelty and uncertainty surrounded this action for the weavers. They did not know exactly what a strike was nor how the government or the owners would react. When Baudelot got up and told them authoritatively what to demand and why to demand it they were at first content. Doubtless a 10-hour day without loss of pay would have been a wonderful improvement for them. There is no reason to suppose, either, that they were not concerned about their daughters' moral well-being. But the struggle dragged on, and a point was reached when it had to take a new direction or else fail; then the long list of practical concerns about work were finally put forward. Doubtless they were among the original triggers of the walkout, although there is no reason to suppose that any individual weaver could have said at the beginning why all his fellows had left work. Baudelot's initial effort to interpret their aims for them had not worked very well, but it took time to ascertain that this was so.

There is no indication that Baudelot ever sensed anything inappropriate about his direction of the strike, despite the remarkable shift near the end. Needless to say, he had been marked as a leader several years earlier and had not been able to work in the mills since that time. On 19 May, he explained to a police inspector who came to talk to him that he was glad violence had been avoided. He did not think that the workers were ready for it. Next time they would be armed, however. It would take another year or two before the revolution began, he thought. Word would come from Belgium and Switzerland. In the meantime he planned to start

301

collecting money to start a socialist newspaper in a few months (once the weavers had paid off some of their strike debts to local shopkeepers). For the present he had burned all his papers and was waiting to be arrested. (The government did not, however, act against him.)[39]

Leaders like Baudelot have rightly inspired historians to speak of this period in French history as the heroic age of the strike; the obvious commitment and intense visions of a revolutionary future displayed by thousands of now obscure local militants have attracted much attention and admiration. But this should not blind us to their enforced social isolation or their highly schematic view – borrowed from a middle-class tradition – of capitalism and of the laborer, that "beast of burden," in Baudelot's words, whose character was debauched by poverty.[40] Not that they were at fault for misreading their fellows' social position; every circumstance conspired to lead them down this path. The ruthless denial of jobs to these pioneers cut them off from direct experience of work, and the heady privilege of literacy introduced them to a whole received intellectual culture that spoke of laborers strictly in terms of markets and moral degeneracy.

Roubaix weavers had experienced one townwide strike effort before in 1867, and the local leader of their Chambre syndicale, named Bonne, was one of the moderates who had resisted the socialist takeover of the Congress of Marseille; his outlook on strikes was highly practical and gradualist. But events there in 1880 were no simpler or more satisfying in their outcome than in Reims.

In Roubaix weavers had walked out of a few mills on 1 May. They were moved exclusively by the Reims example, without any urging or intervention on the part of Bonne. The movement spread quickly. By 4 May, 66 mills had been closed; by the sixth, 80 establishments were affected and about 25,000 laborers out of work. Between the seventh and the eleventh of May a further 10,000 laborers struck Tourcoing spinning mills and all of Armentières' 25 weaving mills were closed. The towns were quiet; laborers strolled the streets in small bands. There were daily gatherings in designated fields just across the Belgian border (an easy walk from any of these towns) where police could not pry. Armentières laborers gathered near Ploogsteert; Roubaix weavers met in a field near Mont-à-Leux that they called "le Ballon."

At first the press carried wild stories about these meeting places: It was said that vast sums were being siphoned to the workers from London. Conspirators from the International were secretly directing the whole movement. But these rumors were groundless. Bonne and his associates took no part in the meetings. He had opposed the strike from the beginning, as he explained to a correspondent from *Le Temps* on 10 May. His idea had been to target the lowest paying firms separately, to negotiate wage increases or declare partial strikes against these firms, and to use dues from working weavers to support the strikers. Now, he lamented, they would all go back to work defeated after a week.

Perhaps because of Bonne's opposition to the strike, no formal list of demands was ever drawn up. Bonne knew what the weavers' grievance was, however: during the previous winter, owners had arranged unofficial wage cuts by imperceptibly increasing the number of yarns installed on looms so that weavers were actually producing a finer grade of cloth (and tending more yarns per meter) than they thought they were. (Apparently there was nothing new in the practice.) Now, however, business was good; wool prices had soared giving many owners large paper profits on their current stocks. Laborers wanted rectification of the yarn counts.[41]

Bonne did actually organize a group of delegates and engage in discussion with the mayor; but their sole public pronouncement was to urge an end to the strike on 12 May. Bonne felt the owners were not about to move, and he was right on this point. At first, the owners had wanted to slap fines for absence on every striking weaver and drag each one before the Conseil des prudhommes for quitting without notice; the owners wished to express their extreme displeasure at the manner in which their employees had walked out of the mills without deigning to speak to them. "The old principles of respect, of obedience, of hierarchy have disappeared," said one owner. "Now begins the '93 [i.e., the Reign of Terror] of industry."[42] But the mayor succeeded in dissuading them from this hard-line stance. By the middle of May they were letting it be known that after the return to work newly adjusted piece rates might be posted. But like their fellows in Reims, they refused even to consider the idea of discussion while the work stoppage continued.

What did the laborers do in their daily meetings if they were not naming delegates or formulating demands? The records are scanty; the laborers actively drove out the curious and the newspaper reporters. Apparently the daily excursions across the border had quickly become occasions for organized contraband. Coffee, tobacco, groceries, and fuel were all cheaper across the border. When the laborers brought large quantities back with them into France for resale, they always returned in groups of a thousand or more. The border guards prudently refrained from acting against them.

> I've got good tobacco
> In my tobacco pouch.
> I've got good tobacco
> And you won't be getting any!

So one crowd is said to have taunted the guards.[43] Laborers were reportedly able to net up to 4 francs per trip in this way.

But most of the laborers' energies were concentrated on how to keep the mills closed for as long as possible and how to impress the owners with their resolve. Hence at the daily meetings, news must have been passed about attempts to reopen, suggestions made for the proper response, speeches delivered about the overall situation. Later, back in town, crowds would gather to throw stones at the reopened mill or to march chanting and singing to the central square. On the fourteenth in Roubaix a number of groups tramped through the streets chanting the following verse in dialect:

Si ne veutent pon nous renquerir	If they won't give us more pay
In va bentôt tout démolir.	We'll demolish it all one of these days.
Si ne veutent pon nous augminter	If they won't give us a raise,
Nous allons les égorger.	We're going to slit their throats.
Si les patrons n'augmintent pas	If the owners don't raise the rates,
In leur mettra la tête en bas.	We'll see their heads roll.
Nos délégués sont aux Ballons	Our delegates are at le Ballon
Aveuque une caisse de six millions.	With a treasury of six million.[44]

This kind of action with all its dramatic flare has often made prime material for romantic reconstructions. Thus, in Zola's novel *Germinal*, striking miners meet in the moonlight in an obscure rural retreat where their forefathers once planned *jacqueries*. When they leave this place, they become a disorderly mob sweeping across the plain; the mob is likened to a storm or a flood leaving death and destruction in its wake. The miners are depicted as drunk on gin, beyond control.

A sympathetic account of the Roubaix strike of 1880 has recently appeared in book form. Its authors have taken full advantage of the dramatic possibilities; they took their title from the first stanza of the just-quoted verse.[45] The Roubaix weavers' utter contempt for the mills and everything they stand for is highlighted, as is the owners' unreflective intransigence. With inspired accuracy, the authors have characterized the Roubaix owners' notion of authority; they were *"un patronat du droit divin"* ("an owning class by divine right"). What the authors fail to ask is how far the dramatic element was self-consciously played up by the strikers themselves. The verse that was chanted through town on 14 May, for example, was obviously an exaggeration intended to play upon upper-class fears. The weavers did not have 6 million francs or even 600 for their strike and they knew it. They made no attempt to demolish the mills. Because an owner had already been quoted in the newspapers referring to the strike as "the '93 of industry," the weavers could not resist making a veiled reference of their own to the guillotine. The chant and march were consciously staged.

What else could the weavers have done? Joining Bonne's Chambre syndicale meant losing one's job. Yet without some organization, they could not attempt the strategies he recommended. Short of such coordinated effort, there was no way to force the owners into bargaining either singly or collectively. An individual approaching his employer with a wage or other demand was simply fired. But the owners could not fire the whole lot of them, so they had to go out all at once, without planning. They had to try to intimidate; it was the only option open to them. This Roubaix strike may well have been a form of collective bargaining by riot, but if so, it is important to remember that the weavers' actual demand (for restoration of accepted piece rates) was only a minor issue in the affray.[46] Most of everyone's energy was wrapped up in the struggle over how a demand ought to be expressed and what form of collective action was legitimate. The owners' position added up to a refusal to admit demands in any form; they did not even admit to having increased the warp yarns. The weavers attacked this position by a number of highly lurid gestures, all of which were within their reach with only a minimum of formal coordination (and individual risk). They in effect paid the owners in their own coin; if they were treated as being too uncivilized and low to be listened to, they would act the part.

Both Baudelot and Bonne – both the revolutionary and the reformist – misunderstood the extent to which the weavers' position was still not that of wage laborers disposing of a service in an open market, whatever the law or the intellectual tradition said. Both, therefore, misinterpreted the weavers' intent. In Reims, Baudelot went along with the insurrectionary mood, mistaking it as a sign of the beginning of the end, when in fact it was appropriate to a situation in which capitalism, as he imagined it, had not yet properly begun. In Roubaix, Bonne interpreted similar action as lack of self-control and poor planning, when in fact, the laborers were pressuring their employers in the only way the employers left open.

The Roubaix strike ended in much the same way as had the one at Reims. By mid-May mills had begun reopening and a significant drift back to work was under way. Within a week, the strike had ended. No record exists to show whether the owners followed through on their promised rate adjustments.

THE SUCCESS OF GUESDIST INDIFFERENCE

Ten years later, in 1890, the first May-Day celebration in France sparked another improvised strike wave in the Nord. By this time the political complexion of the socialist movement had changed. Jules Guesde's enduring popularity with militants in the Nord had led him to turn Lille into his base of operations, and it was quickly becoming his bastion. Many towns in the Lille region had recently gained their own sections of Guesde's Parti ouvrier français (POF); affiliated with each section was at least one Chambre syndicale. Usually both were headquartered in a bar which, as soon as possible, would be reorganized into a consumer's cooperative. But real support was still narrow; Guesdist showings at the polls remained negligible. By 1890, in other words, an infrastructure was in place but as yet it had not found a large following.[47] Up to this time the Guesdists had not cared about their repeated electoral failures. Electioneering, Guesde explained, was merely an occasion for getting a message across; success was not to be measured by counting office holders. But the Guesdist strategy was about to take a sharp turn in response to a sudden growth of voter interest. The fizzling of the Boulanger affair in 1889 left many industrial workers in France – who were by now thoroughly fed up with the republicans in power – hungry for a new direction. A wave of electoral support was turning toward socialists of all factions.[48] (There were at this stage three other major currents besides Guesdism.) One of the earliest signs of the new mood was in fact the startling success of the May-Day idea, which the Guesdists took the lead in promoting within France for the first time in 1890.[49]

The aim was to make of the first of May a great celebration of proletarian unity and resolve. Workers were to strike for one day, their official demand being institution of the eight-hour day without wage cuts. At the first congress of the Second International in 1889 socialists from every country had pledged to make a major organizing effort to prepare for the demonstration. For the Guesdists, it was to serve as a vehicle for consciousness raising. A one-day demonstration for a symbolic set of demands fit their idea of the strike perfectly; the aim was not to achieve practical results but to prepare morally and organizationally for a greater struggle to come. Those socialists in France who prided themselves on being gradualists and oriented toward practical results dissociated themselves from the May-Day plan entirely. For them the eight-hour day was an impossible aim and therefore the whole project was to be rejected as a waste of the workers' energies. But again, as in 1880, neither the reformists nor the revolutionaries properly understood the meaning of the event for textile laborers.

In the days before the first of May, there were reports that the laborers' response to the idea in the Nord was enthusiastic. Guesdist organizers were surprised and pleased at this enthusiasm, anticipating a level of participation far beyond their original hopes. In Roubaix, many laborers went to work as usual on the morning of 1 May, but by noon the town had shut down.[50]. Five thousand gathered in front of the town hall to cheer their delegates as they went in to present their demands formally to the mayor. In the rest of the Nord, the turnout was less impressive; Tourcoing followed Roubaix's lead to some extent, but in Lille perhaps only two thousand stayed away from the mills; in Armentières only one mill was actually closed down. The response in Roubaix was heartening enough, however, to make up for these disappointments. Guesde and his followers were euphoric.

What happened next, however, the organizers had not expected. Most laborers in Roubaix went back to work as usual the next morning; but a group of several thousand stayed out; they gathered in the streets and began marching from mill to mill crying "Strike! Strike! Death to the owners!" They cut telegraph lines into the mills, broke windows, caved in doors, and brought their fellows out. By midday, 90 mills had closed; by evening 70,000 laborers were on strike in Roubaix, Tourcoing, and surrounding communes.

Saturday 3 May was calm but no one returned to work. A large crowd gathered at le Ballon in Belgium; the meeting was boisterous. There was talk of a general strike. Laborers asked their delegates to demand a 40 percent pay increase as well as the eight-hour day. Simultaneously over one hundred mill owners were meeting at the Chamber of Commerce. There they passed a resolution redolent with pedagogical intent. They agreed to grant a 10-hour day and the elimination of night work but only on condition that an international law was passed in various countries imposing identical limits everywhere.

The Guesdists were unsure of what direction to take; nothing had prepared them for this. On Sunday, 4 May, they met with a delegation of 15 mill owners. They decided to scale down their demand to the 8-hour day with a smaller 15 percent wage increase. When the owners said no, they did not insist. The following day they issued a proclamation that revealed their complete confusion about what was happening: "Your delegates, having fulfilled their mandate, tender their resignation and leave you free to act however you see fit."[51] In the meantime, a small band of laborers had tried to sabotage the Roubaix water supply at its source in nearby Bousbecque, an act that would have shut down every steam engine in the town for an indefinite period; but they were headed off by troops.

The government was equally unsure of how to respond. On Monday, after their public resignation, two leading delegates, both Guesdist militants, were arrested in their homes and their papers seized and searched. Both were released later when it became clear that they had played no role in setting off the 2 May strike. Police also sought for an anarchist connection and on 7 May arrested Jules Leroux, "a Parisian anarchist" who was in town. There does seem to have been some evidence of anarchists encouraging the laborers in their course; but nothing was ever found to show that anyone had actually conspired to foment this strike. Its outbreak remained a mystery to contemporaries.

The general thrust of militant activity was decidedly against the strike. Before the strike ended, a string of political leaders addressed the laborers on the folly of their current course of action. The president of the Paris Bourse du Travail (the term means Labor Exchange, a combination union hall and municipal placement office) in a speech on 5 May told the laborers to go back to work, to join their Chambres syndicales, and allow them to formulate demands and coordinate actions. On Tuesday the popular deputy Emile Moreau, in a proclamation posted throughout town, delivered a similar message. He told the laborers that certain leaders had turned their brilliant demonstration into a general strike, but that the moment was poorly chosen. They should, instead, form Chambres syndicales to defend their interests. The law was on their side, he said; no one could stop them. Two more deputies addressed a meeting of strikers on Wednesday, and told them to go back to work.[52] By the end of the week, the laborers began to follow the advice of these multifarious voices. The strike collapsed and the town returned to normal.

Before this "quasi-revolutionary movement" as one correspondent called it, neither reformist nor revolutionary socialists knew exactly what to do. In their uncertainty they fell back on the idea that the laborers were hotheaded and misinformed as to their basic rights and interests. They washed their hands of the strike after a single meeting with the owners; they found speakers to address the laborers – as if they were children – about the simplest legal and economic facts of their situation. That they were wage laborers who should organize unions and defend their economic interests seemed to be ideas as yet unknown to them. But the reason such ideas were alien to them was that they were severely incomplete. The reality of their relationship to the owners remained quite a bit more complicated than these ideas suggested. The 1890 strike, like so many other demonstrations before it, turned into a dramatic denial of deference, a flagrant rejection of submission and obedience on the part of a working population from whom deference and obedience were extracted without reference to their formal rights – in return for paternalistic favors that could not be measured in terms of francs and centimes.

To promote their own view of proper social order, owners in Roubaix had by this time begun backing the activities of a Catholic group called Notre Dame de l'Usine (Our Lady of the Factory) who came into the mills and into laborers' homes to promote religious observance. Known socialists were of course systematically blacklisted. To further counter the socialist threat, they tried setting up what were called mixed unions (mixed because the owner and his foremen also joined), sponsored Christian unions and Catholic political organizations. In 1894, the Catholics set up a "House of Good Works" to rival the socialist cooperative, providing free books, medical and legal services, visits to the sick, and job placement.[53] Of course this could all be interpreted as merely a bargaining ploy aimed at keeping wages down. But it must be asked: What kind of bargaining is it when one rejects bargaining, when one supports the idea that parties to an exchange are merely part of one big family under God's suzerainty; when one backs people who preach moderation and submission and fires forthwith those who suggest that bargaining should be possible? Would such a sales pitch work on the floor of the New York Stock Exchange? Why, further, would someone continue to use such a pitch year after year even though the response was at best unenthusiastic, unless selling was not his real (or his only) motive? These efforts in Roubaix had success only among a small minority of laborers, yet they were continued without letup throughout the 1890s.[54]

A strike in this context could not be expected to lead to real negotiations; it could only be a form of symbolic protest against the stance of the owners. The strike of 1890 was not a bargaining maneuver, it was a gesture in an ongoing struggle over the legitimacy of certain ideas about authority and submission. Doubtless this is why the weavers were perfectly content with their socialist leaders even when those leaders refused to lead the strike and told them all to go back to work. Once the gesture had had its effect, they obeyed. The following year, when Paul Lafargue was arrested in connection with the May-Day demonstration in Fourmies, Roubaix elected him to the Chamber of Deputies.[55] In 1892, they put the Guesdists in control of City Hall, and sent Guesde himself to Paris as their representative in 1893. The socialists articulated a desire for another form of legitimacy, for the complete expropriation of the owners; and they confidently predicted a revolution in the near future. Their attractiveness stemmed directly from the owners' refusal to admit the rules of the market game inside the doors of the factory. If they had done so, doubtless a very different working-class movement would have grown up in Roubaix. As it was, the violence of Guesdism and the gentle ironies of popular dialect culture came closer to being integrated there than anywhere else. The details of Guesde's watered-down Marxist vision were not really relevant to the situation. Nor did it really matter that Guesde was indifferent to strikes. He was right about them in his own way; they could not possibly make any difference.

A TOTAL VICTORY IN DEFEAT

Thirteen years later, in 1903, a third strike wave surged across the Nord. For this episode there is precise information on the grievances that motivated it; and this information demonstrates clearly how deference, community structure, and the family life cycle (not hours or wages) lay at the foundation of laborer discontent. A fundamentally noncompetitive, informally respected pattern of job distribution was under challenge; the laborers made clear by their action that their deference and obedience were conditioned on its being maintained. The owners could not enjoy the benefits of having a subordinate caste of laborers without accepting the responsibilities this entailed.

The center of this strike was not Roubaix but Armentières. The 1906 French census enumerators' lists, which are quite exceptional in providing name of employer, allow one to explore the family-based system of labor deployment in that town at the time of the strike.[56] In 1906, 50 percent of all laborers in weaving mills in Armentières lived with a close relative who worked at the same mill as himself. (Of course, if measured over laborers' whole lives instead of at a single moment this percentage would have been much higher.) A certain class of weavers in these mills were assisted by apprentices whom they hired and paid themselves. The census suggests that weavers regularly hired their own sons, or if sons were lacking, they hired their wives and daughters for these jobs, keeping the income within the family. The owners, according to their own testimony confirmed by census figures, filled preparation and finishing shops by preference with weavers' wives and daughters as well.[57]

Piece rates paid within the mills reflected this pattern of family employment. To show this it is necessary to subject these piece rates to a careful dissection.[58] The Piece-Rate Schedule of 1889, conceded by linen mill owners in that year after a brief general strike, sets comparatively low rates to weavers working on the finest grades of cloth and comparatively high rates to those working on the coarsest grades. To discover this relation, one assumes loom speed to be a constant two-shuttle strokes per second; and assumes that the weaver wants to earn at least 21 francs per week (a figure culled from a contemporary source as a "good week"); and one then calculates how much down time is allowed to the weaver by the piece rate in question.[59] For example, a weaver working on fine linen of 23 threads per centimeter and one meter in width received 19 centimes per meter of cloth woven, according to the Piece-Rate Schedule of 1889. To earn 21 francs per week at this rate he had to keep his loom in operation a minimum of 58 percent of the time he was at work. Warp changes, yarn repair, shuttle recharging, machine lubrication, and other maintenance tasks had to be limited to 42 percent of the time at work. By the same Schedule, a weaver working on a coarse grade of cloth of the same width, having, say, only 7 threads per centimeter, earned 6 centimes per meter of cloth woven – about one-third the rate paid for the finer grade. But, because the loom produced a meter of this coarse cloth about three times faster (there being less than one-third as many shuttle strokes per meter), this meant that the weaver on the coarser grade could enjoy roughly the same amount of down time (45 percent to be exact). Yet he had far fewer threads to install, repair, or remove than his fellow on the finer grade, and these threads were larger and easier to handle. The principal cause of down time, handling thread, was far less onerous for him. Weavers of equal skill could therefore have earned much more working coarse grades. Why this peculiar, apparently unfair pattern?

The answer must lie in the linen weaver's career pattern. Loom tending was easy to learn but difficult to perfect. Older weavers with great experience and with growing sons at home were apparently assigned to the fine grades and brought in their sons to help them. Younger weavers who had just completed their apprenticeships were assigned to coarser grades. The Piece-Rate Schedule compensated partially for their slower pace of work. The advantage enjoyed by the experienced weavers with apprentices far outweighed the disadvantage created by the Schedule.[60] In many mills certain weavers under 18 were still termed "apprentices" even if they had their own looms; they were paid half price for their work, thus eliminating the advantage built into the Schedule.[61] But once over 18, the Schedule gave them a boost making it possible for them to earn wages commensurate with adult status, despite the skill differential that separated them from their elders.

When the weavers went out on strike in 1903, they called for enforcement of the Piece-Rate Schedule of 1889. "The Schedule of '89!" was the battle cry of the bands that marched along the roads from mill to mill. It was easy to suppose, therefore, that this was a wage dispute, but in fact it was a conflict over the apprenticeship system. Three partial strikes earlier in the year had opposed the laying off of apprentices.[62] The mill owners had a new generation of looms on hand that operated more smoothly; they anticipated needing fewer weavers in the future, and felt that current weavers needed fewer assistants. Apprenticeship had to go. The layoffs were accompanied by doubling up on looms and toying with piece rates in ways not anticipated by the old Schedule.[63] From the weavers' point of view, enforcement of the Schedule of 1889 would prevent this changeover from occurring. It would prevent the owners from profiting by higher loom productivity; they would therefore not invest in the new looms. The demand was very similar in effect to that put forward by Lille mule spinners in 1848, claiming for themselves the added productivity of improved machinery. If they won this demand, the weavers would be able to protect their family income level and ensure their sons access to a job in their native town.[64] The issue was the way of life of the working community. A structure of expectations based on informal hiring practices and reflected in the peculiarities of the 1889 Piece-Rate Schedule was under siege. The laborers felt betrayed by their paternal employers who, like those in Roubaix, sent nuns to visit their wives and had prayers said morning and evening in the shop, who had set up a mixed union and had dominated local politics for decades before 1900. Why should they put up with prayers when their sons and daughters were being thrown out on the streets?[65]

When a group of weavers at one mill initiated a walkout on 3 October 1903, they were able to bring the rest of the town out with them in a matter of hours. They broke windows, turned over tram cars, sang the "Internationale," and called for the "Schedule of '89!" Once this unplanned general walkout had begun, however, and spread through the surrounding valley, the weavers' original grievance was lost sight of as the strike itself and the procedures for dealing with it became the subject of an intense political struggle. The weavers quickly turned for leadership to the strong Guesdist faction that by then existed in Armentières, a group for which the owners felt the deepest antipathy. As a result, the paramount question soon became whether the owners could be brought to negotiate. The subsequent course of the strike deserves close attention; for it reveals that each of the various actors – owners, laborers, and Guesdists – had startlingly different conceptions of what was at issue.[66]

As in other northern factory towns, the local socialists had enjoyed steady electoral advances in the 1890s, culminating in their capture of the municipal government in 1900 in both Armentières and its working-class suburb, Houplines.

The strike thus broke out while the socialist municipal councils, led by their two mayors, Désirée Daudrumez (Armentières) and Emile Sohier (Houplines) were serving their first terms, hopeful of proving worthy of their constituents' trust. This was the high tide of Guesdist success in the Nord; socialist response to this crisis, at a time when they were at their strongest, is therefore particularly revealing. Daudrumez and Sohier immediately recognized that the strike would be a decisive test for them. They had not wanted it. The official word from the party leadership in Lille had been to put off all strikes until the eve of the upcoming elections in April 1904, so that the struggles would be in progress as voters went to the polls. (There was no better way of enforcing on the electorate a consciousness of its need for sympathetic officials.)[67] Once it had begun, however, the socialists in Armentières realized that their political future rested on their ability to bring the strike to a successful conclusion. Daudrumez and Sohier quickly formed a strike committee; by 6 October they had elaborated a list of demands including a 6 percent pay hike over the levels indicated in the Schedule of 1889, pay increases for workers in the spinning departments, and compensation for the new 10-hour day soon to be imposed by law. Presumably, these demands were meant as a bargaining position since they went well beyond the weavers' own stated wishes. Daudrumez, furthermore, urged his fellow socialists to quit the Guesdist organization and appeal for help to Guesde's principal rival in the socialist movement, Jean Jaurès. Jaurès' practical orientation and his strong position in the Chamber of Deputies made him appear as a highly desirable ally in this moment of crisis, since the government's attitude toward the strike might well prove decisive.

For a week, the laborers of the town watched quietly as the strike committee tried to initiate negotiations with the mill owners. At first, the owners denied that a strike existed, claiming that criminal threats from a small group had forced them to close their mills. Undaunted, Daudrumez approached the president of the local Chamber of Commerce, a man named Miellez, to ask him to convey the strike committee's demands to the mill owners. Miellez, after consultations, responded that he would, provided that delegates of employees at each mill would simultaneously submit the list of demands separately to their own employers. Daudrumez quickly organized the necessary delegates. The demands were submitted in correct fashion by Saturday afternoon, 10 October, one week after the strike had begun.

Sunday passed with no word from the employers. On Monday there was still no word. At an open-air meeting attended by several thousand strikers Monday evening, mayor Sohier issued a harsh warning to the mill owners, promising "the revolution with all its consequences!" if the owners did not respond in short order. The following morning, Miellez indicated that a response would be delivered within hours. But Miellez then went off to attend a funeral. By 11:30 A.M., a dense crowd had been packed in front of the Armentières town hall waiting for the promised response for over two hours. At that moment, a part of the crowd broke away and dashed down a side street. They attacked display salons, warehouses, and private homes belonging to the mill owners (the mills themselves were being guarded by troops). Rocks were thrown, fires set (unsuccessfully); rolls of linen were taken and stretched across the streets to be used as barricades against the gendarmes. Others were piled up in the gutters. A bank office was sacked. Sporadic rioting continued throughout the day. A slum landlord's house was burned down; firemen refused to save it.

Late in the afternoon, Miellez in haste finally delivered the mill owners' response: The Schedule of 1889 was accepted (without alteration), no word was spoken about the shortened workday or pay increases for the spinning departments. In effect, what this response implied was that the spontaneous battle cry of 3 October had been conceded, but at the same time the formulated demands of the socialist strike committee were passed

The town hall of Armentières, 13 October [1903] at 11:30 A.M." From *L'Illustration*, 24 October

Figure 8. "The rue Bayard in Armentières, evening of 13 October: on the pavement and sidewalks, rolls of linen strewn about by the strikers." From *L'Illustration*, 24 October 1903.

315

Figure 9. "The rue Sadi-Carnot: view of buildings invaded and pillaged by the strikers." From *L'Illustration*, 24 October 1903.

M. Daudrumez, maire d'Armentières.

M. Sohier, maire d'Houplines.

Les deux maires cabaretiers d'Armentières et d'Houplines.

LA GRÈVE D'ARMENTIÈRES ET D'HOUPLINES

Dans notre dernier numéro, nous avons déjà publié des documents suggestifs au sujet des actes de vandalisme et de pillage commis à Armentières pendant la déplorable journée du 13 octobre ; d'autres nous ont été communiqués depuis, qui les complètent et achèvent d'attester la gravité de l'émeute.

Parmi les vingt établissements industriels saccagés, les plus éprouvés ont été ceux de M. Henri Bocquart, que dirige M. Demanne-Dupanchel, désignés les derniers à la fureur des émeutiers. Ceux-ci, après avoir pillé la maison de vente, située à l'angle des rues de Lille et Bayard, ont tenté à plusieurs reprises de l'incendier. A la suite de leur passage, les magasins du rez-de-chaussée, développant une façade de 50 mètres  en bordure de la rue Bayard, présentaient un aspect lamentable : la porte par où s'était ruée la bande était défoncée ; aux fenêtres, en partie démolies, il ne restait plus une seule vitre. Les incendiaires avaient mis le feu en jetant des paquets entiers d'allumettes de provenance belge sur les pièces de tissus, préalablement recouvertes, pour faciliter la combustion, de papier et de toile d'emballage imbibés de pétrole. En somme, ils ont brûlé ou rendu impropres à la vente 192 pièces de toile.

Voilà un exemple trop caractéristique des conséquences' immédiates de la grève encouragée par M. Daudrumez, maire d'Armentières, et par M. Sohier, maire d'Houplines, tous deux socialistes militants et tous deux cabaretiers. Ces magistrats municipaux protestent énergiquement contre l'intervention de la force armée, qui a d'ailleurs été bien peu efficace en cette circonstance. L'autorité n'en a pas moins cru prudent de maintenir jusqu'à nouvel ordre les troupes cantonnées dans les usines, et les localités occupées demeurent comme en état de siège.

Le jeudi 22, M. Jaurès, vice-président de la Chambre, voulut apporter aux grévistes le réconfort de son éloquence. A Houplines, sur la place de la République, contre la Maison de la Coopérative ouvrière, une estrade avait été dressée, dont les dimensions, dépassant de beaucoup celles d'une tribune ordinaire, permirent à l'éminent orateur de se mouvoir librement et de souligner sa parole véhémente de gestes pleins d'ampleur. Et il se fit acclamer de près de dix mille ouvriers bravant la pluie pour écouter les exhortations par où il les engageait à persévérer dans la voie où, dès le début, ils ont montré — ce sont ses propres termes, — « tant de vigueur et de décision ».

over in silence. Daudrumez rightly perceived this response as an attempt to undercut the strike committee, to go around it with a generous offer, to buy the laborers' loyalty away from the socialists. The mill owners' principal aim was to avoid bargaining with the committee at all costs.

Daudrumez decided that the owners must be given a dramatic demonstration of the laborers' commitment to the socialist strike committee; otherwise they would never agree to negotiate. In arranging such a demonstration, he received help from an unexpected quarter. The violent riots had attracted national attention, prompting the government to take a direct hand in restoring order; and within two days of the outbreak of rioting the prefect of the Nord agreed with Daudrumez to hold a referendum in Armentières on the mill owners' offer. The prefect, to make the offer even more attractive, added to the referendum, on his own authority, a provision to compensate laborers for the shortened work day soon to go into effect. (Through all these preparations the owners said nothing.) On Sunday, over nine thousand strikers voted seven-to-one against the proposed settlement, just as Daudrumez and Sohier had asked them to.

It was a resounding affirmation of support for the strike committee, all the more clear in that the proposal rejected was precisely what the laborers had set out to obtain. The message was clear: Recognize our committee, or we shall not accept any settlement. Support was broad, even the women had joined in. A local journalist remarked the novel prospect of devout working women walking straight from mass on Sunday morning to the voting place. (Women had never been allowed to vote for anything before.)[68]

Daudrumez was confident that this irresistible proof of support would induce the mill owners to negotiate. Again he approached them. He was informed that the strike committee could meet with a delegation of owners on 21 October at 10 A.M. at the town hall. The socialists smelled victory. To their surprise, however, at the meeting the delegates explained that they were not empowered to negotiate any issue. Their mandate was merely to reiterate the mill owners' response of the previous week. They would recognize the Schedule of 1889; they were willing to discuss a new schedule of piece rates for preparations. But that was all. Daudrumez asked for another meeting; he wished to talk this over with his constituents. The owner delegates informed him that they were authorized to hold only one meeting. Daudrumez asked, then, that this one meeting be suspended and resumed after 24 hours. To this, the owner delegates agreed.

The following day, the socialist committee began offering sweeping concessions to the owners, which they multiplied in vain over the next week; they would set aside the issue of spinning-department pay raises, they would not insist on a 6 percent pay increase. They asked only that the proposed rate increase to compensate for the shortened day be instituted at once (instead of waiting six months until the new law went into effect). The owner delegates merely reiterated that they were not empowered to negotiate. The meeting broke up.

In the following week, some owners began to reopen their mills. There were stories of foremen walking through the poor neighborhoods, threatening widows and single women with discharge if they did not return to work. A number of female workrooms did go back into operation. Daudrumez and Sohier, fearing defeat, rushed to Paris to ask Jaurès for help. On 28 October he interpellated the government in the Chamber on the issue of the mill reopenings. He denounced the high-handed tactics employed. The prefect quickly responded by threatening to withdraw troop protection if such actions continued against the strikers. All the mills closed down again. Jaurès sponsored a bill to establish a parliamentary commission of inquiry into the textile industry; it passed with only two dissenting votes. The Jaurès connection had proved useful in the end.

With all the mills again safely closed, however, the owners still did nothing. Two prominent liberal owners were pushing strongly for real negotiations, although they refrained from any public statement and would not act without the support of all 30 of their colleagues.[69] As the strike began its second month, the socialist committee wrapped itself in gloomy inactivity. Sohier no longer appeared at the daily meetings. Daudrumez could think of nothing better to do than counsel patience. Having proved that he had the laborers' full support, having demonstrated complete flexibility, having won close government collaboration, he had run out of ideas. Yet, without some added concessions from the owners to prove that he was worthy of the laborers' overwhelming support, he knew that the strike would end in failure for himself, even if the owners did honor their promise to follow the Schedule of 1889.

In the first week of November, the prefect in an angry public letter to the mill owners remarked that the only remaining point of difference between them and the strike committee was exactly when to start paying compensation for the shortened work day. In money terms, he added, this difference amounted to no more than one week's pay for the average weaver. The following day, as if to spite the prefect's words, the mill owners countered with an offer to give each weaver an extra week's pay on their return to work. At this, Daudrumez and his committee were incensed; it was an insult, a slap in the face, another blatant attempt to undercut their position. Daudrumez' sense of vulnerability was increased by discord in the ranks of his followers. A faction within the strike committee had begun to murmur against him, criticizing his handling of the strike, demanding a renunciation of the Jaurès connection.[70] This was the first sign of a split in the socialist ranks that was soon to divide them into two irreconcilable camps, ensuring their failure at the polls the following spring.

On 10 November, a number of owners met with the prefect and assured him that their offer of one week's extra pay had not been intended in any way as an insult. This statement was seized on by Daudrumez, who went before the strikers declaring he was in favor of accepting the offer on these grounds. A return to work was voted; Daudrumez hailed the victorious end of the struggle. The end of the strike came on 14 November. But the laborers' mood was far from enthusiastic. The laborers and their leaders were bitterly aware that they had stayed out four extra weeks beyond the time of the owners' initial offer of 13 October and had nothing to show for it but one week's pay. Furthermore, the socialists recognized that the mill owners had successfully avoided any appearance of recognition for, or negotiation with, the strike committee. Even worse, spinning-mill workers (mostly women and young boys) remained on strike another two weeks until the strike committee finally advised them to return to work, as they were unlikely to win anything and were only endangering their jobs by prolonging the strike.

The following year, the two socialist factions ran separate lists in the municipal elections and went down to defeat together. Although their support had dropped slightly, unity could still have ensured them victory. But they refused cooperation even on the second ballot. Many workers stayed away from the polls. A new clerical right group, the "Patriotic League," which had made a strong bid for worker support, was also defeated. The coalition that bested them both was formed, on the secret, direct instigation of the prefect, from various centrist elements under the leadership of the two prominent liberal mill owners mentioned above; one of them, Henri Chas, became the new mayor.[71] That fall the mill owners came to a final, and quite generous, agreement with their weavers on the apprenticeship issue. Labor unrest did not occur again in Armentières before the war. The socialists of Armentières remained divided to the bitter end. Not even the unification of Guesdists and Jaurèsists in a new, single socialist party in 1905 (the Section française de l'Internationale ouvrière) was enough to reconcile the two factions.[72]

In order to understand the full significance of this episode, a number of points must be spelled out.

First, the fundamental grievance of the laborers, the desire to retain the apprenticeship system, was based on their attachment to a nonmarket mode of labor distribution. Weavers in Armentières did not choose their jobs on the basis of a calculation of supply and demand pressures within a larger market. In fact it would hardly be appropriate to say that they "chose" their jobs at all. Being a weaver was more of an ascribed status than an achieved one, the result of parental expectations, combined with informal assumptions in the workplace that the sons of weavers became weavers. And this is precisely what the weavers were fighting to protect.

The system was informal and therefore unenforceable because law defined the wage relation as a free contract obligating the employer to do no more than pay wages. Competition in the linen industry after 1900, moreover, was forcing the mill owners to adopt new methods of labor organization that struck at the heart of this informal system, requiring fewer apprentices and soon fewer weavers, than the community's demographic structure provided.[73] The owners were free to stand on the narrow legal definition of wage labor and deny that they had any obligation to employ weavers' sons. But the weavers refused to allow them to do this with impunity. The weavers resisted being treated as wage laborers in the strict and narrow sense whenever it suited the mill owners' convenience, while the rest of the time they were expected to be loyal, deferential members of a subject laboring community. In return for deference, however grudgingly delivered, they considered that the mill owners must care for the whole way of life of the community, which entailed obligations well beyond the mere paying of wages.

Second, although going on strike was a perfectly legal act well within the laborers' rights, it was, nonetheless, experienced as a full-fledged rebellion. The explanation of this follows directly from what has already been said. The weavers knew they were breaking with unwritten reciprocal obligations, but they believed the owners had already broken them. Hence they employed the ritual of popular insurrection when the strike began, singing the "Internationale" as they marched from mill to mill, calling for the final general strike that was to end capitalism, overturning tram cars, storming mill entrances as if they were Bastilles resisting the popular will. The laborers did not feel that they were engaging in bargaining or in a market maneuver; they expressed their intention of imposing their will on a tyrannous minority whose failure to live up even to their own conservative notions of owner–laborer reciprocity had forfeited their last claim to tolerance.

Third, the owners' response was to deny that a strike was underway and to refuse bargaining of any kind. This response was dictated in part by the rebellious tenor of the laborer's actions, in part by the owners' habitual refusal to recognize all of the implications of wage labor strictly defined. Because the laborers expressed through their actions a desire to break with the obligation of deference and to impose their will on the owners, the owners realized that any expression of a willingness to negotiate would amount to a tacit admission that the laborers were in the right, that they had been inconsistent, that if the letter of the wage relationship was imposed in one area (laying off of apprentices) it had to be imposed in another (good-faith bargaining).[74] The owners wished to be able to lay off at will and reorganize the workplace while continuing to exercise a special authority over a subject population whose whole lives from cradle to grave were in their hands.

Fourth, within this struggle the socialists' role first and foremost was to serve the laborers as symbols of disloyalty. If you force us to, the laborers were in effect saying, we shall turn our loyalties toward these enemies of property, for strictly speaking, it is our right. This implicit threat was extremely effective. In their blind determination to undermine the socialist strike committee, the owners conceded the main demands of the weavers – even if the concessions were made in a backhanded manner. Once the socialists were defeated at the polls, moreover, the mill owners offered further guarantees on the apprenticeship question. They overcame the socialist threat but not without paying the price of deference, which was to maintain social stability at the expense of profits.

To serve as the symbol of disloyalty, the socialists merely had to stand publicly for the overthrow of private property and to offer themselves as spokesmen for the community on strike. The specific strategy they adopted was not very important. But the strategy that Daudrumez did adopt turned out to be disastrous for his own personal prestige (especially among the socialists themselves).

This was because Daudrumez misread the situation. Unwittingly he took upon himself the task of attempting to get both parties (to this struggle over unwritten rules and informal loyalties) to act as if France actually were a market society governed by a liberal democracy, in which people exercised their rights untrammeled by informal sanctions and were free to bargain over the price of their services. He set out an initial set of demands that would allow for plenty of concessions once negotiations began. When the owners refused all sign of recognition, he willingly sought intermediaries. The angry and destructive riot of 13 October he denounced (rather lamely) as the work of "outsiders." To prove that he had the laborers' support, he organized a referendum, as if ballots in a box would have an overwhelming moral effect on the owners. When this gambit failed, he gave up all his demands except for one symbolic concession that he had to win from the owners in order to vindicate his direction of the strike. He eventually did win this concession, but in a form that amounted to a slap in the face (that is, as one week's extra pay, offered to the prefect in response to a call from the prefect). Daudrumez would have done better if he had followed a more strictly Guesdist strategy – enfolding himself in revolutionary intransigence and leaving to the owners the problem of taking the initiative. But revolutionary intransigence would have meant giving up the hope of government help, a real advantage since the Left Bloc government in power was in debt to Jaurès' socialists for their support in the Chamber. Government support would only come along legal lines, however, and legally wage earners and employers were defined as parties to a free contract. It was a difficult call; Daudrumez did not anticipate the depth of owner intransigence. His reading of the community before him, however, must be traced at least in part to his own schooling in socialist ideology which taught that the proletariat was miserable because of the laws of supply and demand (not in spite of them), because of free contracts concluded between employer and employee (not because of the forces that denied laborers the ability to bargain or to seek competing alternatives). Socialism taught that Republican rights were too limited (when in fact even those limited rights were never really granted). Inadvertently, he became the champion of voting, of bargaining, of liberalism itself, believing, as he did, that the society before him was a liberal one.

THE LIBERAL BOX

Consideration of these three strike waves provides a picture in microcosm of the French industrial community under the Third Republic, as well as of the peculiar position of socialism within it. This was an illiberal society stuffed into a liberal box. Here is what made up the box: Law, policy, and intellectual tradition were formulated in conformity to liberal principle; in times of crisis or struggle, when actors wished to ensure the backing of the state, they turned to market principles to justify their actions. But apart from this, there was very little about life in French industry that fit the market mold. Here are the illiberal elements: Laborers were by and large subject to extensive informal authority inside and outside the workplace. Owners used every possible means to deny them the opportunity to act or bargain collectively or to exercise their political rights (with the precious exception after 1870 of the ballot box). Laborers depended heavily on informal arrangements in the workplace to steer a secure course through life's various stages and continued to feel a proprietary interest in the work process itself. It is impossible to understand the illiberal aspects of this form of community without studying, with care, the very limited sphere within which liberal principles were applied. It is further impossible to understand why only this limited sphere felt the application of such principles unless one realizes that market language blinded people to the need to go any further. Those who were reflective about society persisted in interpreting the fundamental social relationships they saw around them in market terms – in terms of property rights, labor as a commodity, competition, supply and demand. To observers on the scene, there was no doubt that Armentières was in the grip of a strike over wage levels, or that the owners were resisting the demands of the committee because of their desire to maximize profits, or that the laborers' spontaneous outburst was ill-advised and immature. Contemporary observers – from all parts of the political spectrum – found every one of these strike waves to be astounding and inexplicable; and historians have by and large echoed this feeling.

It was just this kind of narrow certainty – just the confident use of these terms as if they comprehended all possible parameters of the situation: markets, strikes, wages, demands, profits, and so forth – that constituted the liberal box into which industrial life was being forcibly but unsuccessfully pressed. Laborers did not act in markets; all their legal freedoms were hedged about by informal limits. In practice, unquestioning obedience was expected of them. To indicate a desire to bargain, to utter a word deemed disrespectful meant almost certain dismissal, blacklisting, unemployment, loss of income, probable ostracism from one's town and trade.[75] Yet when changes in industrial organization threatened laborers' vital informal arrangements in the shops, they were told that they were free to go elsewhere. For all that they demanded from the laborers, the owners claimed to owe only wages in return.

The socialists suffered from illiberal discrimination, yet they were as much blinded by the liberal vision as anyone else. From both these factors, both discrimination and blindness, an uneasy distance resulted between laborers and militants, a lack of understanding that shows up in a multitude of tactical miscues and false steps. The socialists opposed capitalism as capitalism was described in theory not as it actually worked in practice. They misread the laborers' intentions in moments of collective action tending to go in one of two false directions. Either these collective actions were taken as proof of the inherent radicalism of the laborers, giving heart to those with revolutionary hopes; or else they were taken as proof of the laborers' immaturity of judgment and lack of appreciation of capitalist reality, in which case the reformist was encouraged in his efforts to organize and rationalize. All too often socialists inadvertently ended up, like Daudrumez, working hard to make society more liberal.

Finally the liberal state collected vast amounts of information on strikes and riots in this period, all of it filtered through market categories. Plenty of hard numbers now became available that fit perfectly with the assumptions informing debates at union and socialist congresses, in newspapers, and in Parliament. Historians, as a result, have too readily fallen victim to the categories embedded in their sources (and, for that matter, impregnated in our very language by the end of the nineteenth century), repeating the misguided judgments of contemporaries, perpetuating the liberal myth. Real progress in understanding (and therefore in changing) industrial society will not be possible until the power of this myth is once and for all dissipated.

Conclusion

During the Armentières strike of 1903, Jean Jaurès came for a brief visit to boost the morale of his new allies and address the strikers. Despite a steady rain, thousands of them came to the railroad station to meet his train from Paris and lined the streets to cheer him as he proceeded in a carriage toward the square where he was to speak. On the way, he made a prearranged stop in a neighborhood full of tenements along the border between Armentières and Houplines. There the two socialist mayors escorted him into three different buildings so that he could inspect some working-class dwellings. In a speech in another town on the following day he described what he had seen. He saw:

> poor households of weavers . . . poor apartments, narrow, minuscule, a few square meters, where miserable families with seven and eight children are piled up without air, without light, without furniture, without anything that gives human life some dignity, some price.
> . . . in this town of Armentières, the queen of linen, we saw beds that had not a scrap of linen to cover the nudity and modesty of infants. The queen of linen could not spare a bed sheet to cover these poor people.

The problem was laid directly on salary levels.

> That is the crime . . . these salaries of 14 and 15 francs a week, these salaries of famine and misery, these households so poor lodged in apartments so small that mother, father, son, grandmother, young daughter and infants, that old age and puberty all lie down *pêle-mêle* in a miserable promiscuity where vice cannot help but germinate.

He denounced the long hours in the mills.

> For these work days immeasurably long that uproot man from human life, that tear women indefinitely from the home, that shatter and disperse the family, that exhaust the muscular force and cerebral vitality of the laborer . . . These days prolong the servitude of the working class. And when in his home, which he only sees at intervals, the laborer encounters unrelieved misery, then comes the temptation of alcoholism.[1]

326

Conclusion

The pedigree of these ideas is clear; the description might have been taken directly out of the pages of Villermé or Reybaud or any of their disciples. It is all there: the lack of furnishing and light, the invocation of incest and alcoholism, the tight link between physical deprivation and moral depravity – all blamed on low salaries, themselves the result of the "anarchic capitalist regime." An insufficiency of money, the result of unrestrained competition, reduced the working class to an inhuman level. The most learned and most large-spirited representative of French socialism of his time had come to the Nord and immediately been conducted by two working-class leaders on a brief empirical investigation of the impact of economic law. By this time, it was almost a ritual; the forms and expectations were now deeply set in the minds of a great number of people. Market society was understood to have a certain preordained form, the same one which Dupin and Dunoyer, among others, had outlined 80 years before. No one had ever really questioned whether this was true or not; conviction was reinforced by the ease with which evidence, apparently compatible with the model, could be gathered, at a moment's notice, as it were, between the train station and the town square.

Endless sophistications and qualifications have been put forward about the market model by economists and others over the last 200 years. Its characteristics, its utility, its implications have been debated endlessly by experts. This tradition of intellectual reflection has had a great impact on political and social conditions, and it has been necessary to consider it in detail at certain points in the present study. But what is really under examination here is the much simpler, much more vague idea of the market that has taken hold of everyday life and everyday language in France and elsewhere in the course of those same two centuries and that shows very few signs of letting go even today. This idea remained as inappropriate to the social reality of Armentières in 1903 as it had been to that of Rouen in 1752, or Lille or Mulhouse in 1835. The major difference was that it had gradually gained currency among a new class of owners, in public opinion, and finally among the laborers themselves in the intervening years and that certain practices within the mills had been brought into line with the notion of labor as a commodity. But even these changes added more confusion than clarity to the conduct of social life.

Market forces had only an indirect relationship, at best, to the condition of textile laborers, because no market for labor had ever come into existence. Immorality and low pay were not inherently linked in their lives. Family solidarity was not under challenge; it was one of the keys to their survival and, therefore, also one of the central features of their predicament. It made the low wages of many of the laborers possible.

Conclusion

The market was segmented according to sex and family status. The need of individuals to pool resources in order to get along dampened mobility, restricting job choice and life chances. But these conditions remained just enough in line with age-old peasant and artisan work habits and just tolerable enough that the laborers were willing to submit to them. In doing so, they necessarily yielded great power over their lives to their employers, who sought to legitimate this power by a ready adaptation of available notions of authority and rank, and who sought to extend it into the political realm quite successfully, by and large, in spite of the socialist challenge of 1848 and its renewal under the Third Republic. This power was far more than merely economic in nature, nor was it wielded purely for purposes of profit. Textile mill owners had an inveterate sense that their continued existence, and also their ability to continue making profits, was wrapped up with the maintenance of their special status. They saw power as a single complex of ends, not a means to the end of profit, because profit could only be, after all, a means to the end of rank and authority. To maintain this power, and as a sign of its existence, by the end of the nineteenth century, they sent nuns to visit their employees' homes in the evening, had prayers recited in the female workrooms, adamantly refused all forms of negotiation (in a manner utterly incompatible with the idea of the market), waged unrelenting war against socialist electoral hopes, offered generous concessions when necessary (but at a time of their own choosing), and drew their laborers into involvement in work with carefully formulated piece-rate schemes and informal hiring and work arrangements. They had to make sure that the family survival strategy continued to work; the immobility and dependence of their labor force were founded on it. They had to make sure, therefore, that forms and levels of pay bore a minimum of compatibility with the notions of age and family status that informed the way of life of the laborer. Piece rates became a male preserve and were calculated in accord with male notions of age and rank. Owners and directors went into their shops and inspected work right alongside of the laborer, they argued about it, they preached about it. They fired socialists and troublemakers with brusque indifference. They built imposing private homes, gave to the church, had large families, and cursed the anticlerical Republic.[2]

After 1848, laborers accepted such treatment only sullenly and half-heartedly. But the alternative they longed for was not clearly formulated. This is why the strike developed among them in such a paradoxical form. It was a market maneuver allowed by the law but condemned by the owner. To use it was to rebel against the owner's authority and just insofar as strikes became little rebellions they failed to be successful bargaining ploys – except in the much larger and uncertain sense that owners were sensitive to any threat to their power and might be moved

328

to make backhanded concessions, as they often were. The strike became a ceremony of resistance, a promise of future liberation, and, confusedly, an attempt to win specific demands all at the same time. Since laborers were not really in a purely monetary exchange relationship with owners, it was impossible for the strike to be simply part of a negotiating strategy.

But the market idea, particularly as it was worked out by Republican law and socialist common sense, obscured the nature of the laborers' predicament and the complex motives for their actions. Inadvertently socialist leaders were forced either to discipline their followers and struggle with owners and the state to make the strike idea work or else to declare their indifference to all collective action short of the final seizure of power. This latter strategy, which was the dogma that Guesde preached to his followers, was actually closely attuned to certain features of the laborers' situation. In his harangues, Guesde regularly castigated the owners with great violence; he constantly predicted a revolutionary showdown just over the horizon. What he approved of about strikes was that they "frightened the owners" and hardened the workers' resolve.[3] Without thinking the matter through, he played on those feelings of injustice and resentment that arose out of the owners' very noneconomic power over the laboring community. The manner in which he disapproved of strikes encouraged their continuation in their current ambiguous form.

It would be easy enough to dismiss all these particular features of textile mill towns at the end of the nineteenth century as anomalous or peculiar. The textile industry was by this time an aging one, no longer on the cutting edge of technical or social change. The form of paternalism that mill owners adopted in this period was the product of a particular time and place, not to be confused with other, newer forms of labor management appearing in steel, machine building, or chemicals. The Guesdists, too, were an odd and ephemeral phenomenon; their intellectual sterility and dogmatism naturally prevented them from appreciating the subtle forms of dominance and accommodation around them.

All of this is true as far as it goes. But it can also be argued that these were peculiar manifestations of much more general features of industrial society. Where has there ever been a class of entrepreneurs that did not successfully wield great political power in their own localities and large influence beyond? Where has there ever been a population of laborers who were perfectly free to change jobs and did so regularly in response to shifting price signals, who could bargain singly or collectively as they chose without fear of repression? Where has there ever been a work situation that did not amount to an informally arranged way of life worked out through painful compromises between worker aspiration, technical requirements, and managerial constraints? If situations could be found that answered to all these requirements, they would be the anomalies needing explanation. One could not find them in the steel mills of Gary, Indiana, Saint-Chamond, or Essen, not in the mines of the Pas-de-Calais or the Ruhr, not in Carmaux, not in the machine-building trades of Chicago or Berlin, not even in the casual-labor pools of the great capital cities.[4] Everywhere one turns, even in situations of great geographic mobility or high job turnover, one finds countervailing factors – emotional, political, familial, technical – that prevented such mobility from allowing supply and demand to have free play, that gave employers de facto authority, gave them formal and informal power that made a travesty of any notion of equal bargaining. Of course, any of this can be assimilated to the market model. Anything in the world can be assimilated to the market model including slavery, or husband-wife relationships in a hunter-gatherer society. But what is the utility of doing so? It necessarily leads one to ignore or play down the importance of central features of human social experience.

The reason Armentières' piece rates had such a complex structure, the reason Lille mule spinners were willing to pay for steam power between 1830 and 1848, the reason eighteenth-century urban weavers held so determinedly to their guilds is that a life of work is a complex, multi-dimensional experience that slips like quicksilver out of the conceptual boxes of market language. Quantification of its features in terms of money values that can be compared and canceled out – the foundation on which capitalist rationality has been built – can never square with the immediate human experience of transforming nature, however nicely it may allow accountants' ledgers in certain times and places to discover one more margin of profit. Enterprises that succeed or go under solely on the basis of whether the numbers are positive or negative at the end of the year always stand to benefit from changes that reduce unit costs. Owners who do not do the work themselves do not face any trade-off in making such changes. If they fail to make them, the enterprise will soon stop existing. But those who have direct experience of work, the laborers, when faced with technical and managerial change in the name of profit, are always left with the difficult task of reconciling profitable methods with the diverse, nonquantifiable demands of human life. The failings of market language are always shifted onto the laborers' backs. The accountant demonstrates to him that, because he now has twice as many spindles he should be happy with a 50 percent cut in piece rates. Two plus two equals four. Calculations with money values are always at bottom rhetorical in nature, part of a struggle over the structure of human relationships. But one of the strengths of this rhetoric is that the existence of a rhetorical dimension is not admitted. Market language poses as exact and objective. Laborers, however, by virtue of their place, can never be convinced.

This helps to explain why throughout the century-and-a-half under consideration, as in so many other times and places, laborers struggled unremittingly to retain every scrap of independence that they could, first as independent artisans, then as subcontractors within the mills, finally as savvy evaluators of piece-rate systems. Some have attempted to explain such behavior among laborers in the nineteenth century as the result of a commitment to a moral economy, a set of values and moral standards that were violated by technical and commercial change. Laborers are depicted as hanging on to vestiges of a doomed way of life. Their protest against laissez-faire policies, against the minute subdivision of labor, against cheap technical tricks that diluted skill requirements was reasoned and cogent. But their face was always turned toward the past. The idea that laborers defended a culture of work that can be characterized as a moral economy is valid beyond doubt for many of the cases to which it has been applied. But it is also necessary to recognize that defense of such moral standards need not have been motivated by memory of the past. The inadequacy of market language was constantly being brought to the laborer's attention by the very conditions of work. There were so many things before his very eyes every day that money calculations could not be applied to. The struggle for independence within the workplace was a struggle to retain the freedom to respond to these things.

It would be easy to suppose that eighteenth-century urban masters resisted rural production out of a desire to protect their income. Rural weavers undercut them because they worked for less. But this cannot possibly explain all facets of guild members' behavior. As individuals, any one of them stood to gain by the end of guild restrictions that limited the kinds of products they could make, the number of looms they could operate and apprentices they could employ, the hours they could work, and the places they could buy and sell in. They appreciated, rather than resisting, these limits because such limits were necessary to prevent them from feeling the prick of profit-seeking. Thanks to these limits, they could take an extra moment to piece a broken yarn properly without asking themselves whether the extra quality would pay off. Thanks to these limits, they were free to go to the cafe on Monday afternoon without asking themselves whether the expense of lost production should be attributed to the profit or the wages account. Thanks to these limits, they were free to work alongside their journeymen without feeling the constant need to control their every move. It would be wrong to romanticize eighteenth-century guild working conditions; but what was most painful about them for weavers was that the old guild way of life was becoming impossible to sustain. They stuck with guild regulations to the end be-cause they knew that only these regulations made it possible for them to be weavers both when they were at work and when they marched in procession through the streets. Without them, they were merely individuals who happened to weave.

In the spinning mills of Rouen at the beginning of the July Monarchy, mule spinners resisted with equal determination the imposition of a piece-rate scheme linking pay levels to output quotas. Under the previous pay system, they had received flat rates for yarn solely on the basis of what grade of yarn it was. Of course there were inequities involved. Some machines broke down more than others; some batches of cotton were dirty or brittle; some spots in the shop did not get enough light. It was up to the spinner alone to coordinate his team in overcoming these difficulties (or in enjoying temporary or accidental advantages). Once a certain amount was done each day (less at the beginning of the week), he could choose to slack off, to take more time lubricating the spindles, to talk with a friend down the line while the foreman was in the office. To play, joke, sing, flirt, or daydream. If he got a bad batch of cotton one week, he could make do with a little extra effort. But under the *tâche* system, he was forced to be aware every moment he let up on the pace that all of his output for the week would be worth less to him. He did not just forgo, as before, the pay for the final amount, but gave up a supplement for the whole amount. This was painful, because it forced the spinner to calculate his gain in a more refined manner, it forced added resentment on him when the machine ran poorly or his new piecer made mistakes. It made life incrementally less tolerable; it made the benefits inherent in the routine of the shop (participation in the life of the group, for example) more difficult to enjoy. Had gain been his only motive, there would have been no resistance; the spinners resisted being forced to think in terms of a fine-tuned trade-off between their pace of work and their income. The violation was invisible to anyone who did not stand in front of the machine and know what it was like to live there. But for those who did, it was not necessary to hark back to old traditions or values, or to a golden moral standard of the past in order to feel the sense of loss at the new constraints on action.

Mule spinners of Lille and Rouen in 1848 demanded flat-rate yarn prices in spite of the inequities this would cause due to new, larger mule jennies that were coming into the mills. They preferred that those who had to tend an extra 200 spindles be paid at the same rate for every bit of extra yarn they produced. The extra 200 spindles all had to be supplied with roving, lubricated, watched for breaks, nursed through the winding on. The level of concentration necessary was much greater, the necessary down time much longer. How much of the added output was due to the spinner's own work? The same proportion as before, was the spinners' answer. This answer would allow them to continue with much the same habits of work, or even to slow up a bit to compensate for the higher level of concentration and attentiveness. It was the owners' idea, not theirs, to recalculate all piece rates on the basis of targeted daily averages, a procedure which injected the abstract idea of effort into pay calculations more clearly than before. Again, mule spinners did not have to yearn for a lost artisanal status of the past in order to value the small bit of independence they were losing. Its advantage was built into the routine of work and involved not money, but the freedom to think about what they wanted to do with life from one hour to the next. Even inside the Satanic Mill their lives had scope for those lovely "distributive passions" that Fourier so masterfully evoked – flitting from one job to another, making a cabal with others, enjoying for a moment the way the yarn wound onto the cop (instead of rushing on to the next stretch).

During the mid-century boom, textile laborers learned to calculate piece rates with much greater expertise and admitted, for the purposes of bargaining, that work should be evaluated as time and effort. But with the mechanization of weaving, a new category of mill workers emerged who, down to the end of the century, fought bitterly the same kind of fights as mule spinners had before. Roubaix weavers in 1867 refused two-loom work at any level of pay; Reims wool weavers in 1880 wanted fair cloth-measurement procedures (not unlike Lille spinners in 1839) and refused to go any longer than six days without pay if their machines had trouble. These demands suggest how closely weavers continued to associate the justice of pay with output instead of effort, and the extent to which they wished to be left to their own devices at the machine, to make their own decisions about when to start, when to stop, when to fix, when to set up, when to lubricate, when to stare out the window. Human consciousness has all its dimensions, from metaphysical to physiological, at every moment of its existence. This is why people continue to want independence from the finely calculated management of others. Managers want it, so do shopkeepers, so do machine-tenders. (How much venture capital is squandered every year by people who just want to be their own boss?)

In Armentières, linen weavers in 1903 fought for an apprenticeship system that ensured a coherent relationship between available jobs and family needs. This was another constant of textile laborers' existence throughout the century. The piece-rate structure with which the apprenticeship system was associated reflected the high levels of skill that were attainable in these jobs. Most textile jobs in the nineteenth century were skilled in this sense; they could be learned in two weeks, but expert work took years to master. This is evident in the endless complaints of mill owners about the inadequate facility of their employees and also in the highly selective patterns of recruitment into the trade; new mill hands almost always came from rural textile areas. This was difficult, specialized work that made complex demands and gave birth to complex identities.

The point here is not to argue that textile laborers did not want more money, or would not have liked fewer hours. The claim being made is not that they enjoyed their work, or loved to work alongside other members of their families, or were endlessly fascinated by the coarse yarns and cloths they produced. The claim being made is that they resisted trading off money for certain categories of things, especially limited control over their own bodies and routines and a coherent structure for the family life cycle. They resisted trading off money for these things because these things had an importance they did not wish to quantify. Competitive pressures in product markets forced mill owners repeatedly to violate these desires. Market language, insofar as it came into play, blinded people to the existence of such desires, thereby advantaging the mill owners in the ongoing struggle.

Something like a moral economy is bound to surface anywhere that industrial capitalism spreads. It arises directly out of the impact of entrepreneurial cost cutting on work routines and the inability of the commodity concept of labor to render employer–employee relations coherent. It should not be thought that the motive forces behind conflict in the French textile industry between 1750 and 1900 represent merely the peculiarities of an early stage of capitalism. The conflicts examined in this study, from the Rouen food riot of 1752 to the Armentières strike of 1903, are quite diverse in form. What they all reflect, however, is the need of people to make the varied requirements of a life of work fit together with their own varied needs. In this respect, they are no different from, for example, metalworkers' resistance in the early twentieth century to the introduction of scientific management, or the subtle forms of sabotage that assembly-line workers constantly engage in, or the resistance to collectivization of agriculture in Eastern Europe in the 1950s, or the popularity of plant takeovers in Western Europe in the 1970s.

The great failing of reformers and revolutionaries of every persuasion throughout the nineteenth century and into the twentieth has been that (with the exception of rare and isolated voices), they have never provided a cogent critique of market categories. Elements of such a critique may be found in the works of hundreds of thinkers, not just Fourier, but Carlyle, Ruskin, Marx, Jaurès, Durkheim, Gramsci, and many others. But seldom were these critiques formulated in such a way as to reveal that the ongoing struggles in the very heart of mechanized industry were motivated by the weaknesses of market categories. The trend has been firmly in the direction of believing that these categories had triumphed, that the new language was now sovereign. Resistance was to be organized on the grounds that a present state of defeat before the market system had to be alleviated or overturned. On the contrary, the reality has always been that damage to society results from the failure of market language to apply even to the realm it reigns over with such apparent completeness. In defiance of the market system's attempt to divide all of life up into separate spheres of production and consumption, people have continued to consume as they produce and produce as they consume; like the cook who is constantly tasting his own pastries, we become what we do. The problem is to discover a new language that takes this into account and that can guide society in shaping those market forces that it wants instead of letting itself be shaped by market forces into a grotesque facsimile of market society.

The assumptions of market language, even among the most outspoken critics of industrialism, have encouraged an extremely oversimplified view of the conditions of collective unity as well. The self-evident interest everyone has in earning more and spending less, all things else being equal (but all things else are never equal), has induced students of industrial society to suppose that common economic interest is easy to discover and an obvious basis for collective action. Nothing could be further from the truth. Because experience is multidimensional, because some people can find satisfaction in growing lilies while others need to act on the stage, because the human spirit is capable of creating many languages utterly different from each other, unity of any kind is always difficult to create. Knowing what another wants and why he wants it takes work. Even in a society like this one where money is absolutely indispensable to existence, people make the most complex compromises of their divergent desires, as Alexandre Desrousseaux did, in order to get the money they need. There is no reason why any one person's compromise should coincide perfectly with all those of a crowd of people who happen to work in the same industry.[5] As a result, no one – historian, politician, economist, worker – can afford to ignore the difficulty of interpreting other people's motives. The indifference to this problem which market culture encouraged helped give rise to the peculiar forms of collective action that were gradually worked out among French textile laborers between 1830 and 1900, as well as to a complaisant historiography that explained away all such forms as signs of immaturity. The laborers' own motives for protesting were much too complex to be contained within the narrowly defined strike of law and economic common sense. Yet, no one offered them a better explanation of what they wanted than the one implicit in the market model. By mid-century, market language provided the only public code within which they could work as individuals to understand what they as a group wished to do. As a result, their actions were deformed into a half-conscious compromise between market and nonmarket forms of behavior. But then, this has been true of most industrial conflict in most countries over the last century or so. In the long run, there is no solution available to the current dilemma from that direction. Only conscious reflection on the limitations of market language can provide the starting point for a new, genuinely free, social order.

Notes

Except where otherwise indicated, all translations of quoted matter from the French were done by the author.

Preface

1. E. P. Thompson's *The Making of the English Working Class* (New York, 1963) fired the first salvo in this struggle to rewrite the history of industrialization. For further references see Bibliographical Note, section entitled "Recent Studies of Industrialization."
2. See Neil Smelser, *Social Change and the Industrial Revolution* (Chicago, 1959); Michael Anderson, *Family Structure in Nineteenth-Century Lancashire* (Cambridge, 1971); John Foster, *Class Struggle and the Industrial Revolution: Early Industrial Capitalism in Three English Towns* (London, 1974); H. I. Dutton and J. E. King, *"Ten Percent and No Surrender": The Preston Strike, 1853–54* (Cambridge, 1981); Craig Calhoun, *The Question of Class Struggle: Social Foundations of Popular Radicalism in the Industrial Revolution* (Chicago, 1981); Patrick Joyce, *Work, Society and Politics: The Culture of the Factory in Later Victorian England* (New Brunswick, N.J., 1980); William H. Lazonick, "Industrial Relations and Technical Change: The Case of the Self-Acting Mule," *Cambridge Journal of Economics* 3 (1979):231–62; H. Catling, "The Development of the Spinning Mule," *Textile History* 9 (1978):35–57; H. I. Dutton and J. E. King, "The Limits of Paternalism: The Cotton Tyrants of North Lancashire," *Social History* 7 (1982):59–74.
3. On Lyon, see Fernand Rude, *L'insurrection lyonnaise de novembre 1831: Le mouvement ouvrier à Lyon de 1827 à 1832*, second edition (Paris, 1969); Robert J. Bezucha, *The Lyon Uprising of 1834: Social and Political Conflict in the Early July Monarchy* (Cambridge, Mass., 1974); Yves Lequin, *Les ouvriers de la région lyonnaise (1848-1914)*, 2 vols. (Lyon, 1978); Robert Liebman, "Labor Market Structure and the Production of Solidarity Among Nineteenth-Century Lyon Workers," paper presented to the Davis Center Seminar, Princeton University, April 1982; George J. Sheridan, "The Political Economy of Artisan Industry: Government and the People in the Silk Trade of Lyon," *French Historical Studies* 11 (1979):215–38; idem, "Household and Craft in an Industrializing Economy," in John M. Merriman, ed., *Consciousness and Class Experience in Nineteenth-Century Europe* (New York, 1979), 107-28; Laura Struminger, "Les canutes de Lyon (1835–1848)," *Le mouvement social* no. 105 (1978):59–85.

4. Christopher H. Johnson, "Patterns of Proletarianization: Parisian Tailors and Lodève Woolen Workers," in Merriman, ed., *Consciousness and Class Experience*, pp. 65–84.
5. See Suzannne Berger and Michael J. Piore, *Dualism and Discontinuity in Industrial Societies* (Cambridge, 1980); Jill Rubery, "Structured Labor Markets, Worker Organization, and Low Pay," *Cambridge Journal of Economics* 2 (1978):17–36; Glen G. Cain, "The Challenge of Segmented Labor Market Theories to Orthodox Theory: A Survey," *Journal of Economic Literature* 14 (1979): 1215–57; Jacques Magaud, "Vrais et faux salariés," *Sociologie du travail* 16 (1974):1–18. See also the special issue of *Revue économique* 29 (1978), no. 1, "Emploi et Chômage"; and the special issue of *Revue d'économie politique* 89 (1979), no. 1, "Les nouveaux problèmes de l'emploi," in particular the article of Jean Vincens "Les nouveau aspects du problème de l'emploi," pp. 7–41 in that issue, which places segmentation theory in the larger context of Keynesian and neo-classical debate over labor markets. According to Vincens (p. 12), "Le temps semble révolu où, en économie du travail, ceux qui n'étaient pas néoclassiques ne pouvaient être que de plats empiriques."
6. Lester Thurow, *Generating Inequality: Mechanisms of Distribution in the U.S. Economy* (New York, 1975); Michael J. Piore and Peter B. Doeringer, *Internal Labor Markets and Manpower Analysis* (Lexington, Mass., 1971).

Introduction

1. Karl Polanyi, *The Great Transformation* (New York, 1944); T. S. Ashton, *The Industrial Revolution, 1760–1830* (Oxford, 1948).
2. E. J. Hobsbawm, *The Age of Revolution, 1789–1848* (New York, 1962).
3. George Lefebvre, *Quatre-vingt-neuf* (Paris, 1939) (translation by R. R. Palmer: *The Coming of the French Revolution* [Princeton, N.J., 1947]); idem, *La révolution française*, 2nd edition (Paris, 1957) (translation by Elizabeth Moss Evanson, John Hall Stewart, and James Friguglietti: *The French Revolution*, 2 vols. [New York, 1964–1965]); Albert Soboul, *Précis d'histoire de la Révolution française* (Paris, 1962) (translation by Alan Forrest and Colin Jones: *The French Revolution, 1787–1799, From the Storming of the Bastille to Napoleon* [New York, 1975]).
4. Among the prominent critics: Alfred Cobban, *The Social Interpretation of the French Revolution* (Cambridge, 1964); George V. Taylor, "Noncapitalist Wealth and the Origins of the French Revolution," *American Historical Review* 72 (1967):469–96. More recent attempts at synthesis include: Colin Lucas, "Nobles, Bourgeois and the Origins of the French Revolution," *Past and Present*, no. 60 (August 1973):84–126; William Doyle, *Origins of the French Revolution* (Oxford, 1980).
5. E. P. Thompson, *The Making of the English Working Class* (New York, 1963) pp. 234–313, 472–602.
6. See Bibliographical Note, section entitled "Recent Studies of Industrialization." See also Louise Tilly and Joan W. Scott, *Women, Work and Family* (New York, 1978); Michel Frey, "Du mariage et du concubinage dans les classes populaires à Paris (1846–47)," *Annales. économies. sociétés. civilisations* 33 (1978):802–29; Michelle Perrot, "De la nourice à l'employée, travaux de femmes dans la France du XIXe siècle," *Le mouvement social* 105 (1978): 3–10; idem, "Quelques éléments de bibliographie sur l'histoire du travail des femmes en France (principalement au XIXe siècle)," *Le mouvement social* no.

105 (1978): 127–131; Louise A. Tilly, "Structures de l'emploi, travail des femmes et changement démographique dans deux villes industrielles, Anzin et Roubaix (1872–1906)," *Le mouvement social* 105 (1978):33–58; Sally Alexander, *Women's Work in Nineteenth-Century London 1820–1850* (Littlehampton, England, 1982); Robert Liebman, "Labor Market Structure and the Production of Solidarity Among Nineteenth-Century Lyon Workers," paper presented to the Davis Center Seminar, Princeton University, April, 1982; Marie-Hélène Zylberberg-Hocquard, "Les ouvrières de l'Etat (Tabac et Allumettes) dans les dernières années du XIXe siècle," *Le mouvement social* no. 105 (1978):87–107; Thierry Leleu, "Scènes de la vie quotidienne: les femmes de la vallée de la Lys (1870–1920)," *Revue du Nord* 63 (1981): 637–666; Theresa M. McBride, *The Domestic Revolution: The Modernization of Household Service in England and France, 1820–1920* (New York, 1976); Madeleine Guilbert, *Les femmes et l'organisation syndicale avant 1914* (Paris, 1966); idem, *Travail féminin et travail à domicile* (Paris, 1956).

7. E. P. Thompson, *The Making of the English Working Class* (New York, 1963), pp. 269–313.

8. Duncan Bythell, *The Handloom Weavers, A Study in the English Cotton Industry During the Industrial Revolution* (Cambridge, 1969), reviews contemporary discussion and criticizes elements of Thompson's analysis, but the overall picture remains little changed. See also Maxine Berg, *The Machinery Question and the Making of Political Economy* (Cambridge, 1980), pp. 226–52.

9. Quoted by Simon Rottenberg, "On Choice in Labor Markets" in John F. Burton, Jr., Lee K. Benham, William M. Vaughn, III, and Robert J. Flanagan, eds., *Readings in Labor Market Analysis* (New York, 1971), p. 41.

10. See, for example, Gary S. Becker, *The Economic Approach to Human Behavior* (Chicago, 1976).

11. Robert J. Lampman, "On Choice in Labor Markets: Comment," in Burton et al., eds., *Readings in Labor Market Analysis*, pp. 53–60; Lester Thurow, *Generating Inequality: Mechanisms of Distribution in the U.S. Economy* (New York, 1975), viii.

12. This contention of Thompson's is disputed by Bythell, in *The Handloom Weavers*, pp. 251–272, who offers only circumstantial evidence to counter Thompson's impressionistic evidence. That a substantial number of weavers suffered reduced life expectancy due to the decline of the trade, and that a substantial number never left it are indisputable facts. The only question is exactly how many; no sources exist to resolve this question without a vast demographic survey.

13. See Berg, *The Machinery Question*, pp. 226–52; R. M. Hartwell's comments in his introduction to Bythell, *The Handloom Weavers*, xi; also ibid., pp. 139–75. At best the case has been seen as one in which the new system worked with tragic slowness; see Ashton, *The Industrial Revolution*, pp. 80–82; Malcolm I. Thomis, *The Luddites: Machine-Breaking in Regency England* (Hamden, Conn., 1970), pp. 11–40, 56–60; J. L. Hammond and Barbara Hammond, *The Skilled Laborer* (London, 1919), pp. 1–11.

14. The flow of illegal Mexican labor into the U.S. has been cited as an example of the market mechanism distributing labor. But of what benefit is it to use the same model for a shift of labor in which a century goes by and still wages on each side of the border are not brought to equilibrium, and exchanges of stocks that result in a new equilibrium price literally within

seconds? Surely the difference is more than one of time or efficiency; surely it is a difference in kinds of systems of distribution?

15. Eric Hobsbawm, "Custom, Wages and Work-Load in Nineteenth-Century Industry," in *Laboring Men: Studies in the History of Labor* (London, 1964), pp. 344–70.

16. See Keith Burgess, *The Origins of British Industrial Relations* (London, 1975); H. A. Turner, *Trade Union Growth, Structure, and Policy* (London, 1962); C. K. Harley, "Skilled Labor and the Choice of Technique in Edwardian Industry," *Explorations in Economic History*, series 2, 11 (1974): 391–414; David Montgomery, "Whose Standards? Workers and the Reorganization of Production in the United States, 1900–20," in idem, *Workers' Control in America* (Cambridge, 1981), pp. 113–38; Joan W. Scott, *The Glassworkers of Carmaux* (Cambridge, Mass., 1974), 72–166; Michael P. Hanagan, *The Logic of Solidarity: Artisans and Industrial Workers in Three French Towns, 1971–1914* (Urbana, Ill., 1980), esp., pp. 3–32, 62–72, 93–120, 129–50, 178–84; Charles More, *Skill and the English Working Class* (New York, 1980); Richard Price, *Masters, Unions and Men: The Struggle for Work Control in Building and the Rise of Labor, 1830–1914* (Cambridge, 1980), pp. 129–235.

17. See William H. Sewell, *Work and Revolution in France: The Language of Labor From the Old Regime to 1848* (Cambridge, 1980), 146-61; Richard Roehl, "L'industrialisation française, une remise en cause," *Revue d'histoire économique et sociale* 54 (1976): pp. 406–27.

18. See Henry Mayhew, "The Tailors" and "The Boot and Shoe Makers," in Eileen Yeo and E. P. Thompson, eds., *The Unknown Mayhew* (New York, 1971), 181–280; E. J. Hobsbawm and Joan W. Scott, "Political Shoemakers," *Past and Present* no. 89 (November 1980):86–114; Johnson, "Patterns of Proletarianization"; Philippe Perrot, *Les dessus et les dessous de la bourgeoisie: Une histoire du vêtement au XIXe siècle* (Paris, 1981), 69–109; Jacques Rancière, *La nuit des prolétaires: Archives du rêve ouvrier* (Paris, 1981), 36–60.

19. Thompson, *The Making of the English Working Class*, pp. 234–68; Iorwerth Prothero, *Artisans and Politics in Early Nineteenth-Century London: John Gast and His Times* (Baton Rouge, La. 1979), especially pp. 22–70, 210–64; Price, *Masters, Unions and Men*, pp. 19–128; Martin Nadaud, *Mémoires de Léonard, ancien garçon mason*, ed. Maurice Agulhon (Paris, 1976), pp. 100–08, 265–71; Dudley C. Barksdale, "Parisian Carpenters and Changes in Forms of Work, Culture, and Protest, 1789–1848" (Masters thesis, University of North Carolina, 1978); William H. Sewell, "Social Change and the Rise of Working-Class Politics in Nineteenth-Century Marseille," *Past and Present*, no. 65 (November 1974): 75–109; Alain Corbin, *Archaïsme et modernité en Limousin au XIXe siècle*, 2 vols. (Paris, 1975).

20. Compare Nadaud, *Mémoires*, 83–100, for example, with *Report from the Committee on the Bill to Regulate the Labor of Children in the Mills and Factories of the United Kingdom* (London, 1832)(the so-called Sadler Report). Or Thomas Holcroft, *Life of Thomas Holcroft*, ed. E. Colby (London, 1925) – whose father was a peddler – with Agricole Perdiguier, *Mémoires d'un compagnon* (Geneva, 1854–55), a journeyman joiner; or with G. Désert "Les mémoires d'un travailleur bas-normand (Première moitié du XIXe siècle) – Souvenirs de jeunesse," *Annales de Normandie* 19 (1969):59–78, whose father was a coppersmith in the 1830s. Such evidence is extremely difficult to use, but the comparison nonetheless suggests what one would expect, that proper

apprenticeship in a skilled trade was far less onerous than, say, spinning-mill work.

21. Of course the argument was soon advanced that children were not free agents; but this only meant that their labor power was exploited for profit all the more efficiently – or so the argument went. See Samuel Kydd, *The History of the Factory Movement* (London, 1857); Charles Wing, *Evils of the Factory System* (London, 1837); J. T. Ward, *The Factory Movement, 1830–55* (London, 1962); Patrick Joyce, *Work, Society and Politics: The Culture of the Factory in Later Victorian England* (New Brunswick, N.J., 1980), pp. 50–64.

22. AN F^{12}4704, France, Chambre des Pairs, Séance du 29 juin 1847, *Rapport fait à la Chambre par M. le Baron Charles Dupin au nom d'une commission spéciale chargée de l'examen du Projet de loi relatif au travail des enfants dans toutes les manufactures, fabriques, usines, chantiers et ateliers*, p. 5.

23. AN, F^{12}4704, response of the Chambre de Commerce de Rouen, 1837.

24. See references in note 11. Albert O. Hirschman has tried to introduce other possible motives into the systematic study of economic behavior; see his *Exit, Voice and Loyalty: Responses to Decline in Firms, Organizations and States* (Cambridge, Mass., 1970). See also idem, *The Passions and the Interests* (Princeton, N.J., 1977); or the foreword by Joan Robinson to Alfred S. Eichner, ed., *A Guide to Post-Keynesian Economics* (New York, 1978), xi-xxi.

25. See Raymond William, *The Country and the City* (Oxford, 1973) for a telling discussion of the ambiguities of dominant values and the uses to which they can be put.

26. See Hirschman, *The Passions and the Interests*; Williams, *The Country and the City*, 60–67. Joyce Oldham Appleby suggests that the development of economic thought was arrested between 1690 and 1713 at just the moment when the issue of motives was explicitly broached; see her *Economic Thought and Ideology in Seventeenth-Century England* (Princeton, 1978), 183–93, 244–46. See also Donald Winch, "The Emergence of Economics as a Science 1750–1870," in Carlo Cipolla, ed., *The Fontana Economic History of Europe*, vol. 3, *The Industrial Revolution* (London, 1973), 507–73, especially 514–19. The impact of mechanistic models on economic thought in the eighteenth century is evident from passages like the following from Turgot, who described the aim of economic inquiry as follows: "to discover the hidden causes and effects of that multitude of revolutions [in commerce] and their continual variation; to return to the simple principles whose actions, always in combination and often disguised by local circumstances, direct all the operations of commerce; to recognize those unique and primitive laws, founded on nature, by which all values existing in commerce balance each other and are fixed at a determinate level just as bodies abandoned to their own weight arrange themselves according to their specific gravity." Anne-Robert Jacques Turgot, "Eloge de Vincent de Gournay," in *Ecrits économiques* (Paris, 1970), p. 82.

27. Furthermore one must understand the conflicts in which political economy was used in order to see how market culture came into existence. European society did not embrace the new theory unconditionally; but there was a general, tacit agreement to argue by using its terms, its theoretical language. This process is now attracting the attention of a growing number of social historians. See, for example, Gareth Stedman Jones, "The Language of Chartism," in James Epstein and Dorothy Thompson, eds., *The Chartist Experience: Studies in Working-Class Radicalism and Culture, 1830–1860* (London, 1982), pp. 3–58; Sewell, *Work and Revolution in France*, 194–

242; Joan W. Scott, "Men and Women in the Parisian Garment Trades, Discussions of Family and Work in the 1830s and 40s," forthcoming; James Epstein, *The Lion of Freedom: Feargus O'Conner and the Chartist Movement, 1832–1842* (London, 1982), pp. 7–59. See Introduction note 36 for further references.

28. By comparison, the Christian schema would divide individual acts up into sinful and virtuous; each of these would have subcategories: avarice, lust, envy; charity, faith, obedience. A crucial step in the emergence of market culture involved the mapping of Christian and market categories: production became virtue; consumption, sin. See R. H. Tawney, *Religion and the Rise of Capitalism* (New York, 1947), esp. 164–270; E. P. Thompson, "Time, Work Discipline and Industrial Capitalism," *Past and Present*, no. 38 (December 1967):56–97. For other schemas of individual action, see Clifford Geertz, "Person, Time and Conduct in Bali," in *The Interpretation of Culture* (New York, 1973), pp. 360–411; Michelle Z. Rosaldo, *Knowledge and Passion: Ilongot Notions of Self and Social Life* (Cambridge, 1980).

29. Clifford Geertz, "Religion as a Cultural System" in *The Interpretation of Culture*, pp. 87–125.

30. Thompson, "Time, Work Discipline and Industrial Capitalism"; Michelle Perrot, "The Three Ages of Industrial Discipline in Nineteenth-Century France," in John M. Merriman, ed., *Consciousness and Class Experience in Nineteenth-Century Europe* (New York, 1979), 149–68; Denie Woronoff, "Le monde ouvrier de la siderurgie ancienne: note sur l'exemple français," *Le mouvement social* no. 97 (October–December 1976):109–19.

31. See Ivy Pinchbeck, *Women Workers and the Industrial Revolution, 1750–1850* (New York, 1930); Tilly and Scott, *Women, Work and Family*, 9–60; Olwen Hufton, *The Poor in Eighteenth-Century France, 1750–1789* (Oxford, 1974), especially pp. 11–127; Sydney Pollard, *The Genesis of Modern Management* (Cambridge, Mass., 1965); S. Paul Garner, *Evolution of Cost Accounting to 1925* (University, Al., 1954), pp. 27–90.

32. A fascinating exploration of management theory on this issue in France may be found in Bernard Mottez, *Systèmes des salaires et politiques patronales: Essai sur l'évolution des pratiques et des idéologies patronales* (Paris, 1966).

33. William H. Lazonick, "Industrial Relations and Technical Change: The Case of the Self-Acting Mule," *Cambridge Journal of Economics* 3 (1979):231–62; Burgess, *Origins of British Industrial Relations*; H. Catling, "The Development of the Spinning Mule," *Textile History* 9 (1978):35–57; Harley, "Skilled Labor and the Choice of Technique."

34. Jones, "The Language of Chartism," pp. 18–22.

35. Jones, "The Language of Chartism"; Epstein, *The Lion of Freedom*.

36. Bernard Moss, *The Origins of the French Labor Movement: The Socialism of Skilled Workers, 1830–1914* (Berkeley, 1976), pp. 31–70; Christopher H. Johnson, *Utopian Communism in France: Cabet and the Icarians, 1839–51* (Ithaca, N.Y., 1974), pp. 62–108, 158–68; Sewell, *Work and Revolution in France*, pp. 242–76. But see also Rancière's warnings about these views in *La nuit des prolétaires*. Other discussions include Christopher H. Johnson, "Economic Change and Artisan Discontent: The Tailors' History, 1800–48," in Roger Price, ed., *Revolution and Reaction: 1848 and the Second French Republic* (New York, 1975), pp. 87–114; Alain Faure, "Mouvements populaires et mouvement ouvrier à Paris," *Le mouvement social*, no. 88 (July–September 1974): 51–92; Alain Faure and Jacques Rancière, *La parole ouvrière, 1830–1851* (Paris, 1976).

37. The language of the Revolution has been extensively dealt with in, e.g., Albert Soboul, *Les sans-culottes parisiens en l'an II: Mouvement populaire et gouvernement révolutionnaire, 2 juin 1973-9 Thermidor, an II* (Paris, 1958); Mona Ozouf, *La fête révolutionnaire 1789-1799* (Paris, 1976), or Dominique Julia, *Les trois couleurs du tableu noir. La Révolution* (Paris, 1981); Dominique Julia, Michel de Certeau, Jacques Revel, *Une politique de la langue. La Révolution française et les patois: L'enquête de Grégoire* (Paris, 1975), Marie-Noëlle Bourguet, "Race et Folklore. L'image officielle de la France en 1800," *Annales. économies. sociétés. civilisations* 31, no. 4 (July–August 1976):802–823. Steven L. Kaplan has dealt with the language issue insofar as productive activity is concerned in "Réflexions sur la police du monde du travail, 1700–1815." But much remains to be done.

38. See especially Paul Ricoeur, "The Model of the Text: Meaningful Action Considered As a Text," *Social Research* 38 (1971):529–63; and Charles Taylor, "Interpretation and the Sciences of Man," *Review of Metaphysics* 25 (1971):3–51.

Part One: A world without entrepreneurs, 1750–1815

1. Quoted in Steven Marcus, *Engels, Manchester and the Working Class* (New York, 1974), p. 160.

2. Pierre Goubert, for example, refers to outworkers as "practically reduced to the condition of salaried employees," in *Beauvais et le Beauvaisis de 1600 à 1730* (Paris, 1960), 163; Georges Lefebvre referred to outworkers as a "rural proletariat" in *Les paysans du Nord pendant la Révolution française*, 2 vols. (Lille, 1924), I, 288–90. Jeffry Kaplow refers to outworkers as "wage laborers" and putters–out as "manufacturers" throughout his *Elbeuf During the Revolutionary Period: History and Social Structure* (Baltimore, Md., 1964), esp. p. 33. The forward-looking bias of much economic history of the period is evident in Pierre Léon, "L'élan industriel et commercial," in F. Braudel and E. Labrousse, eds., *Histoire économique et sociale de la France*, 4 vols. (Paris, 1970–82), II, 499–528; or David S. Landes, *The Unbound Prometheus* (Cambridge, 1969).

1. Commerce as conflict

1. Philippe Guignet, *Mines, manufactures, et ouvriers du Valenciennois au XVIIIᵉ siècle* (New York, 1977), pp. 557–76. For another example, see Paul Dupieux, "Les Brondes, manufactures de cotonnades et de liqueures (1762–1800)," in Commission de recherche et de publication des documents relatifs à la vie économique de la Révolution française, *Mémoires et documents* 6 (1933–34):59–104.

2. Of putting–out in general, Sydney Pollard remarks, "at each stage the product was marketable and its price therefore known" making management no different from routine merchant operations; see his *The Genesis of Modern Management* (Cambridge, Mass., 1965), p. 214, also pp. 14–37, 48–51. See also, for German cases, Hans Medick, " 'Freihandel für die Zunft,' ein Kapitel aus der Geschichte der Preiskämpfe in Württembergischen Leinengewerbe des 18. Jahrhunderts," and Jürgen Schlumbohm, "Agrarische Besitzklassen und gewerbliche Produktionsverhältnisse: Grossbauern, Kleinbesitzer und Landlose als Leinenproduzenten im Umland von Osnabrück und Bielefeld während des frühen 19. Jahrhunderts," both ar-

ticles in *Mentalitäten und Lebensverhältnisse. Beispiele aus der Sozialges-chichte der Neuzeit,* edited by colleagues and students of Rudolf Vierhaus (Göttingen, 1982), pp. 277–94 and 315–34 respectively.

3. The best general documentary sources on the Normandy cotton trade before 1789 are memoirs by M. Latopie (1773) in AN $F^{12}560$, Goy de Fontenoy (1782) in AN $F^{12}651$, idem (1787) in AN $F^{12}1365$, and a history of royal regulations composed in 1779 in AN $F^{12}658A$. Secondary sources of particular importance: Eugène Tarlé, *L'industrie dans les campagnes en France à la fin de l'ancien régime* (Paris, 1910); André Rémond, *John Holker, manufacturier et grand fonctionnaire en France au XVIIIe siècle, 1719–1786* (Paris, 1946); F. Evrard, "Les ouvriers du textile dans la région rouennaise (1789–1802)," *Annales historiques de la Révolution française* 19 (1947):333–52; M. M. Bouloiseau, "Aspects sociaux de la crise cotonnière dans les campagnes rouen-naises en 1788–89," in *Actes du 81e Congrès national des sociétés savants, Rouen-Caen, 1956. Section d'histoire moderne* (Paris, 1956), 403–28; Guy Lemarchand, "Les troubles de subsistances dans la généralité de Rouen (sec-onde moitié du XVIIIe siècle)," *Annales historiques de la Révolution française* 35 (1963):401–27; Gay Gullicksen Carens, "Cottage Industry and Women's Work: A Study of Auffay, France, 1750–1850 (Ph.D. thesis, University of North Carolina at Chapel Hill, 1978); Serge Chassagne, "La diffusion rurale de l'industrie cotonnière en France (1750–1850)," *Revue du Nord* 61 (1979):97–114.

4. See Goy de Fontenoy's memoir of 1782 in AN $F^{12}650$. Charles Engrand reports Rouen warps reaching the Aisne department in about 1800 and finds that 2,400 spinners in the Abbeville region were reported working for Rouen dealers before the Revolution. See his "Concurrences et com-plémentarités des villes et des campagnes: les manufactures picardes de 1780 à 1815," *Revue du Nord* 61 (1979):61–81. In the same article (p. 69) Engrand tries to reduce the variety of putting–out arrangements in Picardy's woolen industry to three basic patterns: (1) At Amiens urban independent weavers with shops of five to six looms shared local business with large-scale merchant manufacturers who put out warps in both town and country. Country weavers of these latter struggled to maintain access to alternative buyers. (2) At Crèvecoeur, weavers were independent, buying their own warps and selling their cloth to agents who handled fulling and other finishing on orders from urban merchants. (3) In the Grandvilliers area, merchant manufacturers operated much like certain of Goy's infor-mants, putting out fiber to be spun, warping the yarn, and putting it out to weavers; but they were much smaller, occupying an average of only eighteen weavers each. Charles Ballot pointed to cases of multiple-tiered putting–out noting that "the variety of organizations was infinite"; see his *L'introduction du machinisme dans l'industrie française* (Lille, 1923), 166. A memoir in AN $F^{12}654$, probably of the 1770s, describes the Saint-Quentin-area linen industry as controlled by a core of 30 merchants, with twenty or so more in town who often work as their agents, and "numerous *fabricants*" in the the countryside who receive raw material on consignment from them and put it out in turn to spinners and weavers. Because weaving operations had changed very little in Normandy by the 1830s, it is possible to cite the testimony of A. Caignard before a ministerial commission in 1834: "The worker living in town has his loom at home; we agree on a price either by the *aune* [unit of length] or by the piece. It is the same with weavers living in the country, with the difference that we use intermediaries called *porteurs*:

most are farmers [*agriculteurs*] who come once a week to fetch the warp and the weft yarn and bring us back the finished pieces; we pay them 3 or 4 francs per piece for this. And for those of our workers in diverse villages of the Somme, the Aisne, the Pas-de-Calais, the Eure, and the Marne departments we use agents ... We treat directly with these [agents]; we set the price when we send the raw material and accord them a commission for the production. Transport costs are covered by us." See ERDP, III, 254.

5. Especially good on these independents are Latopie's memoir (1773), AN F¹²560 and Goy's of 1782, AN F¹²650.

6. André Rémond, *John Holker*, 50, Paul Sement, *Les anciennes halles aux toiles et aux cotons de Rouen* (Rouen, 1931); Latopie in AN F¹²560.

7. Memoir of 1779 on regulatory history of Rouen bureau in AN F¹²658A.

8. The author is grateful for personal communication from James Epstein on this issue.

9. Pierre Goubert, *Beauvais et le Beauvaisis de 1600 à 1730* (Paris, 1960), 162–64; Chassagne, "La diffusion rurale"; see also Serge Chassagne, "Aspects des phénomènes d'industrialisation et de désindustrialisation dans les campagnes francaises aux XIXᵉ siècle," *Revue du Nord* 63 (1981):35–57. Guignet, *Mines, manufactures, et ouvriers du Valenciennois*, 211, notes the difficulty of distinguishing dependent from independent weavers. A related issue was the importance of textile earnings to the household; see Carens, "Cottage Industry and Women's Work"; Franklin Mendels, "Les temps de l'industrie et les temps de l'agriculture. Logique d'une analyse régionale de la proto-industrialisation," *Revue du Nord* 63 (1981):21–33.

10. See Goy's report on a putting–out operation near Yvetot in his 1782 memoir, AN F¹²650.

11. Specialized studies exist for most of these towns: François Dornic, *L'industrie textile dans le Maine et ses débouchés internationaux (1650–1815)* (Le Mans, 1955); Goubert, *Beauvais et le Beauvaisis*; Engrand, "Concurrences et complimentarités"; Guignet, *Mines, manufactures, et ouvriers du Valenciennois*; Jeffry Kaplow, *Elbeuf During the Revolutionary Period: History and Social Structure* (Baltimore, Md., 1964); Lynn Avery Hunt, *Revolution and Urban Politics in Provincial France: Troyes and Reims, 1786–1790* (Stanford, Calif., 1978); André Colomès, *Les ouvriers du textile dans la Champagne troyenne, 1730–1852* (Paris, 1943); Alain Lottin, *Chavatte, ouvrier lillois, un contemporain de Louis XIV* (Paris, 1979); Gérard Gayot, "Dispersion et concentration de la draperie sedanaise au XVIIIᵉ siècle: l'entreprise des Poupart de Neuflize," *Revue du Nord* 61 (1979):127–48. See also T. J. Markovitch, *Histoire des industries françaises*, I, *Les industries lainières de Colbert à la Révolution* (Geneva, 1976).

12. On Lille, see Lottin, *Chavatte, ouvrier lillois*, 40–105, 382–3; Christophe Dieudonné, *Statistique du département du Nord*, 3 vols. (Douai, 1804), II, p. 437.

13. See Guignet, *Mines, manufactures, et ouvriers du Valenciennois*, 32, 175–78, 202–09, 557–76.

14. Ibid., 32, 71–76, 494; Engrand, "Concurrences et complémentarités"; Caignard testimony in ERDP, III, p. 255.

15. On thefts of raw materials in woolen centers, see AN F¹²2337–2338: a dossier containing reports from the Revolutionary period through 1839. At Sedan in 1803, for example, merchants demanded enforcement of a 1739 ordinance that forbade all carters and shippers (*routiers et voituriers*) to buy wool from local workers. The local prosecutor had refused to pursue a case involving a

poor woman found with 200 pounds of wool of various grades in her cellar. This was just a more flagrant instance of a general and growing problem, in the merchants' view. See also reports of Scipion Mourgues at Sedan in 1803–04 in AN F¹²654; For further references, see note 17 and Chapter 3, note 37.

16. On fraud in wool weighing, see E. Maumené, *Mémoire sur les propriétés hygrométriques de la laine et sur les moyens d'obtenir la connaissance exacte de l'humidité qu'elle renferme* (Reims, 1849).

17. See note 15; Gerard Gayot reports that the Poupart de Neuflize firm found in 1760 numerous *fabricants* in the Limbourg area supporting their operations out of raw material pilfered by rural spinners from the consignments of large Sedan firms; see "Dispersion et concentration de la draperie sedanaise," 143. See also Calonne's special *arrêt* against such thefts of 1784, as in ADN C16008.

18. Guignet, *Mines, manufactures, et ouvriers du Valenciennois*, 130–37, 141.

19. Christopher H. Johnson, "Patterns of Proletarianization: Parisian Tailors and Lodève Woolen Workers," in John M. Merriman, ed., *Consciousness and Class Experience in Nineteenth-Century Europe* (New York, 1979), 76.

20. Gérard Gayot, "La longue insolence des tondeurs de draps dans la man-ufacture de Sedan au XVIIIᵉ siècle," *Revue du Nord* 63 (1981): 105–34; idem, "Dispersion et concentration."

21. That forms of control in the trade remained commercial in nature, reflecting merchant preoccupations, is reinforced by numerous comments in Chassagne, "Aspects des phénomènes d'industrialisation."

22. Rémond, *John Holker*, p. 64 note 146.

23. Marquis d'Argenson, *Journal et mémoires*, 9 vols. (Paris, 1859–67), VII, 206–7.

24. Rémond, *John Holker*, pp. 139–41.

25. This account is based on d'Argenson, *Journal et mémoires*, VII, 206–10; Amable Floquet, *Histoire du Parlement de Normandie*, 7 vols. (Rouen, 1840–42), VI, 414–15; ADSM, B, Parlement, Registre secret, 1751–52.

26. Several historians have referred to the 1752 incident as a food riot: R. B. Rose, "The French Revolution and the Grain Supply," *Bulletin of the John Rylands Library* 39 (1956–57):171–87; George Rudé, *The Crowd in History: A Study of Popular Disturbances in France and England, 1730–1848* (New York, 1964), pp. 22–3; Lemarchand, "Les troubles de subsistance."

27. See Carens, "Cottage Industry and Women's Work." On spinners' earnings, see Tarlé, *L'industrie dans les campagnes*, pp. 19, 35; Evrard, "Les ouvriers du textile," p. 341; files of the Bureau d'encouragement of Rouen in AN F¹²658A. On female heads of households, see Olwen Hufton, *The Poor in Eighteenth-Century France, 1750–1789* (Oxford, 1974), pp. 69–107; on unmarried women, Guignet, *Mines, manufactures, et ouvriers du Valenciennois*, pp. 271–9.

28. Records of this interrogation are in ADSM, B, Parlement, Registre secret, 1751–2.

29. See Steven L. Kaplan, *Bread, Police, and Political Economy in the Reign of Louis XV*, 2 vols. (The Hague, 1976), I, 1–8.

30. The phrase is from Eric Hobsbawm, "The Machine Breakers," in *Laboring Men: Studies in the History of Labor* (London, 1964), pp. 5–22.

31. On shop size and similar controversies, see Lottin, *Chavatte, ouvrier lillois*, 85–97; Guignet, *Mines, manufactures, et ouvriers du Valenciennois*, 475–80.

32. Ibid., 483–85.

33. On the moral spirit underlying guild structure, see William H. Sewell, *Work and Revolution in France: The Language of Labor From the Old Regime to 1848* (Cambridge, 1980), 16-39; Lottin, *Chavatte, ouvrier lillois*, esp. 97–105.
34. Jules Flammermont, ed., *Remontrances du Parlement de Paris au XVIIIe siècle*, 3 vols. (Paris, 1888-89), III, 368-88; Sewell, *Work and Revolution in France*, 72–7; Edgard Faure, *12 mai 1776, La disgrâce de Turgot* (Paris, 1961), 452–4.
35. Ibid., p. 451.
36. See the summary report, "Extrait des avis …" in F^{12}654; also Harold T. Parker, *The Bureau of Commerce in 1781 and Its Policies With Respect to French Industry* (Durham, N.C., 1979), 31–7; Guignet, *Mines, manufactures, et ouvriers du Valenciennois*, 90-93, 102–23.
37. From "Extrait des avis … ," AN F^{12}654.
38. Latopie discusses this problem in his 1773 memoir in AN F^{12}560; see also Goy's report of 1787 in AN F^{12}1365; the Laverdie edict of 1765, as in ADN C8655; the review of regulation history of 1779 in AN F^{12}658A.
39. Some of the extensive files on this court battle are in ADN C194, C197, C200, C201.
40. The best introduction to this literature is Fernand Carton's edition of François Cottignies, dit Brûle-Maison, *Chansons et pasquilles* (Arras, 1965). See also Lottin, *Chavatte, ouvrier lillois*, pp. 81–2.
41. The *pasquille* on the lad who ate the spider is a genuine work of Cottignies'; the others mentioned here are anonymous, attributed to him, written probably in the 1780s. All are in F. de Cottignies, *Les chansons et histoires facétieuses et plaisantes de feu F. de Cottignies, dit Brûle-Maison* (Lille, 1856).
42. Guignet, *Mines, manufactures, et ouvriers du Valenciennois*, pp. 480–532.
43. Ibid.; Johnson, "Patterns of Proletarianization"; Dornic, *L'industrie textile dans le Maine*, 54; Colomès, *Les ouvriers du textile*, pp. 34–5, 41–5.
44. That such renunciation was a real possibility and perhaps on the increase among guild members in the eighteenth century is suggested by Jacques-Louis Ménétra, *Journal de ma vie*, ed. Daniel Roche (Paris, 1982). Nonetheless, the evidence of urban weavers' attachment to guild regulation is also abundant.
45. The *arrêts* of 1725 and 1749 are in AN F^{12}784–5; a summary of the 1731 regulations is in AN F^{12}658A, memoir of 1779.
46. On Colbert's policies, see T. J. Markovitch, "Le triple tricentennaire de Colbert," *Revue d'histoire économique et sociale* 49 (1971):305–24; Parker, *The Bureau of Commerce*, pp. 16–19.
47. See dossiers cited in note 39. See also AN F^{12}761, containing a complaint against merchants of a Lille guild in 1766. The lawyer who wrote this complaint stopped to explain that he usually represents the defendants, giving us a rare glimpse of the all-pervasive role of legal counsel in these battles. In 1763–65, the local *intendant* refused to promulgate the new edict creating freedom for rural producers; finally an exemption was won for the Lille Chatelenie, only lifted in 1776. See, on this phase of the struggle, AN F^{12}657 and the memoir "Picardie, Artois, Hanault, Flandre" in AN F^{12}650. Further relevant information is in ADN C1658, C1660.
48. See the Roubaix memoir of 1780 in AN F^{12}657.
49. The Roubaix petition of 1789 is in ADN, C194; on the Armentières battle, see ADN C159, dossier of 1752.
50. See Chassagne, "Aspects des phénomènes d'industrialisation"; Guignet, *Mines, manufactures, et ouvriers du Valenciennois*, pp. 32–45, 90–123,

491–501; Dornic, *L'industrie textile dans le Maine*; Engrand "Concurrences et complémentarités"; Gayot, "Dispersion et concentration."

51. See especially Goy's two memoirs, of 1782 in AN F¹²560 and 1787, AN F¹²1365; also Chassagne, "Aspects des phenomènes d'industrialisation."
52. Guignet, *Mines, manufactures, et ouvriers du Valenciennois*, p. 207.
53. Rouen regulatory history in AN F¹²658A.
54. Latopie estimated the trade volume that escaped royal inspection at one-third of total production in 1773, in AN F¹²560.
55. See Tarlé, *L'industrie dans les campagnes*, 4; Parker, *The Bureau of Commerce*, 27; Engrand, "Concurrences et complémentarités," p. 63.
56. A copy is in ADN C8655.
57. Anne-Robert Jacques Turgot, "Eloge de Vincent de Gournay," in *Ecrits économiques* (Paris, 1970), p. 85.
58. From François Quesnay, "Sur les travaux des artisans. Second dialogue," in *François Quesnay et la Physiocratie*, 2 vols., Institut national des études demographique, ed. (Paris, 1958), II, p. 890.
59. Ibid., p. 896.
60. Turgot, for example, distinguished land from other capital on the grounds that its return on the investment of money and labor depended more on the way they were invested than on how much was invested. Obviously this is to neglect entirely the potential impact of mechanization on productivity. See his "Réflexions sur la formation et la distribution des richesses," in *Ecrits économiques*, pp. 121–188. Jean-Claude Perrot has analyzed the Physiocrats' exclusive and careful attention to estate accounting practices in "La comptabilité des entreprises agricoles dans l'économie physiocratique," *Annales. économies. sociétés. civilisations* 33 (1978):559–79. For further considerations, see Elizabeth Fox-Genovese, *The Origins of Physiocracy* (Ithaca, N.Y., 1976); Kaplan, *Bread, Police, and Political Economy* I, 97–163.
61. The disinterest of the French elite in such matters, by comparison with their English equivalents, is notorious; see Taylor, "Non-capitalist Wealth"; Lucas, "Nobles, Bourgeois and the Origins of the French Revolution"; Robert Forster, *Merchants, Landlords, Magistrates: The Depont Family in Eighteenth-Century France* (Baltimore, Md., 1980).
62. See William M. Reddy, "Modes de paiement et contrôle du travail dans les filatures de coton en France, 1750–1848," *Revue du Nord* 63 (1981):135–146; Rémond, *John Holker*, 139–41; BN, fond Joly de Fleury, Ms. 362, fol. 40–3; report of inspector de la Genière, 1779, in AN F¹²658A; Goy, in his 1787 memoir, remarks the uniformity of reels in Holker's Rouen shop as a noteworthy oddity, AN F¹²1365.
63. According to Rémond, Holker was thoroughly discouraged by 1763, but began meeting with somewhat better reception after the Seven Years War ended; Rémond, *John Holker*, pp. 80–5; see also the disparaging report on his 1764 tour of Languedoc by a local *subdélégué* in AN F¹²557.
64. Kaplow, for example, remarks that Elbeuf merchant manufacturers were "immensely proud of the quality of their cloth and therefore reluctant to adopt any procedures that might harm it." Kaplow, *Elbeuf During the Revolutionary Period*, p. 141.
65. This was done at Caen, for example; see Jean-Claude Perrot, *Génèse d'une ville moderne: Caen au XVIIIᵉ siècle*, 2 vols. (Lille, 1974), I, p. 453.
66. See, for example, Roubaix complaints against the Treaty of 1786 in ADN C201, petition of 1787.
67. Albert Soboul, *The French Revolution, 1787–1799* (New York, 1975), p.

127. See also, for example, the cahiers of two Rouen merchant guilds, the Marchands Merciers Quincailliers and the Marchands Fabricants de Bas in M. Bouloiseau, ed., *Cahiers de doléances du Tier Etat du bailliage de Rouen pour les Etats généraux de 1789*, 2 vols. (Paris, 1957), I, pp. 84–9, 173–80. Both guilds called avidly for sweeping reform but envisioned continuation of a guild structure.

68. See Guignet, *Mines, manufactures, et ouvriers du Valenciennois*, pp. 95–7; on calls for a return of regulation under Napoleon, see AN $F^{12}654$, $F^{12}2337$–2338, and $F^{12}679$, among others; this issue is discussed in greater detail in Chapter 3.

69. Goy remarked the problem in 1782, AN $F^{12}650$; see also Guignet, *Mines, manufactures, et ouvriers du Valenciennois*, p. 200.

70. See Guignet, *Mines, manufactures, et ouvriers du Valenciennois*, 105; Parker, *The Bureau of Commerce*, 29–46; AN $F^{12}654$.

71. On implementation of the "système intermédiaire," see AN $F^{12}654$, and ADN C16006, C1660, C6733.

72. See Dornic, *L'industrie textile dans le Maine*; Lottin, *Chavatte, ouvrier lillois*, 382–83; memoir entitled "Picardie, Artois, Hainault, Flandre," in AN $F^{12}650$.

73. See memoir "Picardie, Artois, Hainault, Flandre," in AN $F^{12}650$; Lottin provides a brief glossary taken from Savary des Bruslons, *Dictionnaire universel du commerce*, 3 vols. (Paris, 1741) in *Chavatte, ouvrier lillois*, pp. 381–4. The lengthy entries on these terms in Bruslons' dictionary are revealing of the difficulty of reconstructing the precise meaning of cloth terms of the period. See also Lottin's discussion (p. 41) of the distinction between *sayeteurs* and *bourgeteurs* in Lille, and his summary (pp. 86–94) of a conflict of the 1660s over whether a *bouracan* was a *changeans*, i.e., a cloth governed by a regulation of 1557.

74. *Drap de Levant* was a term used for Midi *drap* intended for export to the eastern Mediterranean, including a wide range of qualities; Elbeuf and Sedan *draps* were exclusively higher quality, made from imported Spanish wool; see Kaplow, *Elbeuf in the Revolutionary Period*, pp. 25–51; Gayot, "Dispersion et concentration." How much experience did it take to recognize a Spanish wool on sight, however?

75. AN $F^{12}654$, for example, contains long tabular lists of varieties of cloth subject to royal regulation in various towns as of 1779, with number and grade of yarns in warp and weft, drawn up in connection with the application of Necker's reforms.

76. Mentioned in Goy's memoir of 1787 in AN $F^{12}1365$.

77. Forster, *The Depont Family*.

78. Kaplan, *Bread, Police, and Political Economy*, especially I, pp. 164–214; II, pp. 563–8.

79. See Rudé, *The Crowd in History*; Louise Tilly, "The Food Riot as a Form of Political Conflict in France," *Journal of Interdisciplinary History* 2 (1971):23–58.

2. The design of the spinning jenny

1. The following account of Hargreaves' invention is based on C. Aspin and S. D. Chapman, *James Hargreaves and the Spinning Jenny* (Preston, 1964).

2. Ibid. contains a report on the experiment.

3. On the earliest improvements, see ibid., p. 16 and plate opposite p. 45. Andrew

Ure commented as follows about early textile inventors: "Among this motley gang, ... if anything went amiss with their machine, each of them endeavored to supply the deficiency with some expedient borrowed from his former trade; the smith introduced a piece of iron, the shoemaker had recourse to leather, and the hatter to felt; whereby valuable suggestions were obtained." See his *The Cotton Manufacture of Great Britain Systematically Investigated*, 2 vols. (London, 1836), I, p. 272. On Crompton, Ure (I, p. 277) quoted a certain John Kennedy as saying, "It would be vain to enumerate all the little additions to Crompton's original machine; also, as they arose so much out of one another, it is impossible to give every claimant what is exactly his due for improvements." See also H. Catling, "The Development of the Spinning Mule," *Textile History* 9 (1978):35–57.

4. David S. Landes, *The Unbound Prometheus* (Cambridge, 1969), pp. 41–123, provides an excellent survey of England's distinctive characteristics, although it is sometimes overstated. The laissez-faire reforms of 1800–1815 had a powerful impact; at the same time they were only the end point of a long development. See also Raymond Williams, *The Country and the City* (Oxford, 1973); E. P. Thompson, *The Making of the English Working Class* (New York, 1963); William H. Sewell, *Work and Revolution in France: The Language of Labor from the Old Regime to 1789* (Cambridge, 1980); Pierre Goubert, *The Ancien Regime: French Society, 1600–1730* (New York, 1974).

5. The prophetic nature of this insight is brought out in E. A. Wrigley, "The Process of Modernization and the Industrial Revolution in England," *Journal of Interdisciplinary History* 3 (1972):225–59.

6. See Charles Ballot, *L'introduction du machinisme dans l'industrie française* (Lille, 1923), p. 45.

7. The Amiens firm of Morgan, for example, bought its first jennies from Holker; there were apparently no local suppliers; see Charles Engrand, "Concurrences et complémentarités des villes et des campagnes: les manufactures picardes de 1780 à 1815," *Revue du Nord* 61 (1979), p. 74. On the feud with the Holkers, see various references in the writings of Roland's wife, Marie-Jeanne Roland de la Platière, *Mémoires de Madame Roland* (Paris, 1821).

8. Report of 23 February 1777 in AN F^{12}654.

9. Aspin and Chapman, *James Hargreaves*, give a clear idea of how subsequent improvements and centralization were related.

10. Serge Chassagne ("La diffusion rurale de l'industrie cotonnière," p. 104) reports that Holker built 106 jennies between 1771 and 1786; by 1780 there were others manufacturing the machine, such as the Hall brothers, former Holker associates, who had set up on their own. See the Hall memoir of 6 May 1783 in AN F^{12}1340; also Ballot, *L'introduction du machinisme*, pp. 47–9. There are virtually no indications of spontaneous taking up of jenny production by common carpenters and clockmakers as in Lancashire.

11. J. R. Harris reports that the word *perfection* "becomes ironically familiar to all readers of the primary material of French industrial history in this period." See his "Attempts to Transfer English Steel Techniques to France in the Eighteenth Century," in Sheila Marriner, ed., *Business and Businessmen: Studies in Business, Economic, and Accounting History* (Liverpool, 1978), pp. 199–233; quote from p. 211. (The author is indebted to Professor Harris for his correspondence on this and other issues.)

12. For examples of such applications, see AN F^{12}658A, 1365, 1340, 1341 among many others.

13. See Holker's memoir of 1773 on the jenny in AF F^{12}2295; on other techniques introduced by Holker, see Chapter 1.
14. See André Rémond, *John Holker manufacturier et grand fonctionnaire en France au XVIIIe siècle, 1719–1786* (Paris, 1946), pp. 97–8. The Milnes who introduced the carding technology, are the subject of a large file in AN F^{12}1340.
15. See Holker's memoir of 1773 in AN F^{12}2295; Ballot, *L'introduction du machinisme*, p. 48; Aspin and Chapman, *James Hargreaves*.
16. Holker's memoir of 1773, AN F^{12}2295; Dubet's memoir of 1780, AN F^{12}1340.
17. Ballot estimates total jennies in operation by 1789 at nine hundred (*L'introduction du machinisme*, pp. 47–8).
18. See Pickford's memoir of 1790 for these estimates (AN F^{12}1341). Pickford was not aware that the first mule had been imported from England by Morgan at Amiens in 1788 (see Engrand, "Concurrences et complémentarités," p. 74). Chassagne ("La diffusion rurale de l'industrie cotonnière en France (1750–1850)," *Revue du Nord* 61 [1979]:97–114) reports (p. 104) that the Milnes had built 17 machine sets by 1790.
19. On this mill, see ibid.
20. Goy memoir of 1787, AN F^{12}1365, p. 39.
21. For other comments in the same vein, see files of the Rouen Bureau d'encouragement from 1788 in AN F^{12}658A.
22. Holker memoir, 1773, AN F^{12}2295.
23. See ibid.; also plan for a spinning school, no date, in same dossier, several proposed *tarifs* of 1788 in AN F^{12}658A. For further evidence, see Chapter 3.
24. See the files of this agency in AN F^{12}658A; also Ballot, *L'introduction du machinisme*, p. 46.
25. Excerpt of proceedings of 17 April 1788, AN F^{12}658A.
26. Ibid., 14 August 1788 *arrêt* for expenses on jennies completed.
27. This report is in the Bureau's files, AN F^{12}658A; it has no date but prices on Manchester were quoted as of 14 September 1788.
28. See F. Evrard, "Les ouvriers du textile de la région rouennaise (1789–1802)," *Annales historiques de la Révolution française* 19 (1947):333–52; Evrard reports that earnings had been occasionally high enough to attract adult males into the trade in some of Rouen's poor neighborhoods (p. 341).
29. See Marc Bouloiseau, ed., *Cahiers de doléances du Tier Etat du bailliage de Rouen pour les Etats généraux de 1789*, 2 vols. (Paris, 1957).
30. Ibid., II, p. 383.
31. Ibid., p. 295.
32. See ADSM 202 BP 13 (*cote provisoire*) for records of such incidents.
33. On this incident, see ADSM 202 BP 12 (*cote provisoire*). Ballot (*L'introduction du machinisme*, p. 20) has identified this shop as that of Debourges et Calonnes. In AN F^{12}1340 there is a claim filed by George Garnett for compensation of damages incurred in a raid on the morning of 14 July. From the details it is clear that Garnett was the manager of the shop referred to in the depositions in the Rouen archives.
34. See ADSM 202 BP 12; Ballot, *L'introduction du machinisme*, pp. 20–1.
35. Ballot, *L'introduction du machinisme*, pp. 20–1; Christophe Dieudonné, *Statistique du département du Nord*, 3 vols. (Douai, 1804), II, p. 250; AN F^{12}1340.

3. New terms and old practices

1. See François Dornic, *L'industrie textile dans le Maine et ses débouchés internationaux (1650–1815)* (Le Mans, 1955), 245–71; France, Commis-

sion de recherche et de publication des documents relatifs à la vie économique de la Révolution française, *L'industrie*, Charles Schmidt, ed. (Paris, 1910); two dossiers in the AN, $F^{12}1405B$, $F^{12}679$, contain particularly revealing information on the overall commercial situation of the 1790s. For an overview, see Albert Soboul, "Le choc révolutionnaire, 1789–1797" in Fernand Braudel and Ernest Labrousse, eds., *Histoire économique et sociale de la France*, 4 vols. (Paris, 1970–82), III, part 1, 5–64.

2. See Alfred Cobban, *The Social Interpretation of the French Revolution* (Cambridge, 1964), p. 39; William Doyle, *Origins of the French Revolution* (Oxford, 1980), pp. 205–6.

3. Although guilds were not explicitly mentioned in the decree of 11 August, nonetheless, the clear intention of the Assembly as shown, for example, in article 4 of the Declaration of Rights of Man and Citizen was to exclude them from the new order. From 4 August on, guild law was widely considered a dead letter. See William H. Sewell, *Work and Revolution in France: The Language of Labor from the Old Regime to 1848* (Cambridge, 1980), p. 86.

4. See Steven L. Kaplan, *Bread, Politics, and Political Economy in the Reign of Louis XV*, 2 vols. (The Hague, 1976); Edgar Faure, *12 mai 1776, La disgrâce de Turgot* (Paris, 1961); Jean Egret, *Necker, ministre de Louis XVI* (Paris, 1975), pp. 91–2, 229–30.

5. Necker's reform of guild regulations in 1779–81 constituted the last round before 1789; see Chapter one above. See also Steven L. Kaplan, "Réflexions sur la police du monde du travail, 1700–1815," *Revue historique* 261 (1979):17–77.

6. These reform efforts and institutional novelties have been endlessly narrated; a good, detailed account is Jean Egret, *La pré-révolution française, 1787–1788* (Paris, 1962).

7. Georges Lefebvre describes the strategy of making all interests suffer equally in *The Coming of the French Revolution* (Princeton, N.J., 1947), 135–6. Of course, *privilege* had gradually become a dirty word in the previous two years of political discussion; on the other hand, many privileges were widely seen as forms of property and therefore "sacred"; see ibid., p. 140. There is wide agreement among historians that the resolutions of 4 August were highly summary in nature and ran into many difficulties of interpretation in succeeding days. See Sewell, *Work and Revolution in France*, pp. 84–6; Patrick Kessel, *La nuit de 4 août 1789* (Paris, 1969); H. Methivier, *La fin de l'ancien régime* (Paris, 1970).

8. Albert Soboul, *The Sans-Culottes* (New York, 1972) has abundantly documented the perceived split between large and small property interests in Paris in the 1790s. He fails, however, to see the real antagonism between profit-seeking and subsistence-oriented management that underlay this split.

9. William H. Sewell, "Ideologies, States, and Social Revolutions: Reflections on the French Case," paper presented to the meeting of the American Historical Association, December, 1981.

10. Sewell, *Work and Revolution in France*, 86–91; Kaplan, "Réflexions sur la police du monde du travail."

11. Quoted in E. Levasseur, *Histoire des classes ouvrières et de l'industrie en France*, 2nd edition, 2 vols. (Paris, 1903–4), I, 21–2.

12. Report of the Academy's proceedings of 21 December 1785 in AN $F^{12}1340$; André Rémond, *John Holker manufacturier et grand fonctionnaire en France au XVIIIe siècle, 1719–1786* (Paris, 1946), p. 113, note 364, reports the demonstration at Versailles.

13. Roland de la Platière, *L'art du fabricant de velours de coton* (Paris, 1780); idem, *Encyclopédie méthodique. Manufactures, arts et métiers*, 4 vols. (Paris, 1784–90), Tome premier, partie II, p. 14.

14. On revolutionary governments' efforts to promote jenny spinning, see Charles Ballot, *L'introduction du machinisme dans l'industrie française* (Lille, 1923), pp. 91–8; AN F^{12}654, 2195, 2204.

15. Quoted in Commission de recherche et de publication des documents relatifs à la vie économique de la Révolution française, *L'industrie*, p. 103.

16. Ibid., p. 129.

17. Quoted by Henri Hauser, "Grégoire, Chaptal et le procès de la machine," in France, Commission de recherche et de publication des documents relatifs à la vie économique de la Révolution française, *Mémoires et documents*, 6 (1933-34), 279–85.

18. France, Commission de recherche et de publication des documents relatifs à la vie économique de la Révolution française, *L'industrie*, p. 114, 183–200.

19. See the discussion of Sieyès' pamphlet "What is the Third Estate?" in Sewell, *Work and Revolution in France*, pp. 77–84. Sieyès describes society as made up of classes, each with a distinct productive or service function; the term *class* does not yet have a hierarchical connotation. On Say's thought, see William Coleman, *Death is a Social Disease: Public Health and Political Economy in Early Industrial France* (Madison, Wis., 1982), pp. 65–74.

20. Jean-Baptiste Say, *Traité d'économie politique*, 6th edition (Paris, 1841), pp. 78–9. It is important to note that the conservative de Bonald was also speaking of the "bourgeois" and "proletarian" classes at just this time. See Vincenza Petyx, "Borghesia e proletario in Bonald," *Il pensiero politico* 12 (1979):410–31. (Daniele Derosa brought this article to the author's attention.)

21. On the dismantling of the old inspector system, see Julien Hayem, "Les inspecteurs des manufactures," in France, Commission de recherche et de publication des documents relatifs à la vie économique de la Révolution française, *Mémoires et documents*, 2 (1912):227–86; several administrative questionnaires are reproduced and discussed in idem, *L'industrie*.

22. Luc-Jacques-Edouard Dauchy, *Statistique du département de l'Aisne* (Paris, 1803), pp. 50–2.

23. Claude-Louis Bruslé de Valsuzenay, *Tableau statistique du départment de l'Aube* (Paris, 1803), pp. 64–8.

24. Jean-Baptiste-Charles Legendre, compte de Luçay, *Description du département du Cher* (Paris, 1803), pp. 41–3.

25. Christophe Dieudonné, *Statistique du département du Nord* 3 vols. (Douai, 1804), II, 247–8, for example, reports the total number of kilograms of cotton yarn produced yearly in the department as follows: 3500 jennies producing 150 kilograms per year yield 500,000 kilograms (note the arithmetical error); 288 wheels still operating produce 25 kilograms per year, total 7,200 kilograms; grand total 507,200 kilograms. Yarn consumption for weaving various grades of cloth is estimated (e.g. 11,000 kilograms for stockings or 244,975 kilograms for *nankins*) adding up exactly to 507,200 kilograms.

26. Gabriel-Joseph Jerphanion, *Statistique du département de la Lozère* (Paris, 1803), p. 54.

27. Bruslé, *Statistique du département de l'Aube*, p. 61.

28. Dieudonné, *Statistique du département du Nord*, II, p. 254. But similar conditions must have prevailed in other trades, too, as his description of

Lille camelot weaving (II, p. 437); Roubaix cotton weaving (II, p. 326); or Avesnes tricot and serge weaving (II, p. 431) show.

29. This discussion based on Serge Chassagne, "L'enquête, dite de Champagny, sur la situation de l'industrie cotonnière française au début de l'Empire (1805–1806)," *Revue d'histoire économique et social* 54 (1976):336–370.
30. See the dossier of 1791–92 marked "Pétitions pour le rétablissement de la règlementation" in AN F^{12}1429.
31. Request in AN F^{12}1560.
32. Petition in AN F^{12}679.
33. Memoir in AN F^{12}1560.
34. Several reports by Scipion Mourgues from Sedan in AN F^{12}654.
35. See France, Commission de recherche et de publication des documents relatifs à la vie économique de la Révolution française, *L'industrie*, 183–200; J. Chaptal de Chanteloup, *De l'industrie française*, 2 vols. (Paris, 1817), II, 341–53. On Necker's 1781 labor regulations, see AN F^{12}654.
36. On the founding and jurisdiction of Conseils des prudhommes, see Levasseur, *Histoire des classes ouvrières*, I, 390, which includes a list of towns where they were founded up to 1814. Eleven out of the first 22 were textile centers.
37. On the activities of Conseils des prudhommes in woolen centers, see AN F^{12}2337-2338; AMR F II (ga) 1: complaint (undated) of 1816 signed by numerous merchant manufacturers against weavers who use *ancrachage* to enhance raw material weight to aid pilferage; AMR F II (ga) 2: règlement sent from the firm of Payenneville-Queval, a Rouen putting-out operation.
38. See the first two references in note 35.
39. Levasseur, *Histoire des classes ouvrières*, I, 506–07; Sewell, *Work and Revolution in France*, pp. 163–6.
40. On restraint of movement, see, for example, AN F^{12}4648, report from Reims, 10 April 1846, on a weaver whose *livret* was retained by his foreman; numerous similar cases are documented in ADN M604/3. On Roubaix's tight enforcement of *livret* law and novel uses of its Conseil des prudhommes (including creation of piece-rate lists, unemployment relief, lay-off regulation, etc.), see ADN M604/2, AMR F II (ga) 1–3. Compare ADN M606/3 on Armentières' use of *livrets* for outworkers. See also the complaints of the weaver Charles Noiret, *Mémoires d'un ouvrier rouennais* (Rouen, 1836), pp. 56–7.
41. Two recent studies provide indispensable background information on the economy of the Napoleonic period: Louis Bergeron, *Banquiers, négociants, et manufacturiers parisiens du Directoire à l'Empire* (Paris, 1978) and Geoffrey Ellis, *Napoleon's Continental Blockade: The Case of Alsace* (Oxford, 1981). See also the useful study by Serge Chassagne, *Oberkampf, un entrepreneur capitaliste au siècle des lumières* (Paris, 1980).
42. These estimates are based on Serge Chassagne's partial figures from 1806 in "L'enquête, dite de Champagny," 348, note 32; as well as on Dieudonné's tally of 3500 jennies for the Lille area and his price quotes in *Statistique du département du Nord*, II, 247–50; and Maurice Lévy-Leboyer, *Les banques européennes et l'industrialisation internationale* (Paris, 1964), p. 59.
43. On this turn to cotton, see Lévy-Leboyer, *Les banques européennes*, 57; Charles Picard, *Saint Quentin, de son commerce et de ses industries*, 2 vols. (Saint Quentin, 1865), I, 227–31; Charles Engrand, "Concurrences et complémentarités des villes et des campagnes: les manufactures picardes de 1780 à 1815," *Revue du Nord* 61 (1979), p. 57.
44. Oberkampf's printing establishment at Jouy near Versailles pioneered chlor-

ine bleaching and roller printing; see Lévy-Leboyer, *Les banques euro-péennes*, p. 55 and p. 78n; Chassagne, *Oberkampf*, pp. 157–60. On the smuggling of mules, or use of English prisoners of war to build them, see AN F¹²2195, 2204. See also Achille Penot, *Statistique générale du département du Haut Rhin* (Mulhouse, 1831), p. 352; and Jean Vidalenc, "L'industrie dans les départements normands à la fin du Premier Empire," *Annales de Normandie*, 7, Nos. 3–4 (October–December, 1957):281–307. On roller printing in Alsace, see Ellis, *Napoleon's Continental Blockade*, p. 187.

45. Chassagne, "L'enquête, dite de Champagny," pp. 354–5, reports 350,000 spindles were added, 1806–10, in Rouen alone (but his estimates on Seine-Inférieure capacity by 1800 seem low); see Lévy-Leboyer, *Les banques eu-ropéennes*, pp. 58–9; Jean-Pierre Hirsch, "Un fil rompu? A propos du crédit à Lille sous la Révolution et l'Empire," *Revue du Nord* 61 (1979):181–92, esp. p. 182.

46. On Tarare and the Vosges, see Lévy-Leboyer, *Les banques européennes*, 74–5; on Cholet, Chassagne, "La diffusion rural de l'industrie cotonnière," p. 108; on Saint-Quentin and Cambrai, Philippe Guignet, "Adaptations, mutations et survivances proto-industrielles dans le textile du Cambrésis et du Valenciennois du XVIIIᵉ au debut du XXᵉ siècle," *Revue du Nord* 61 (1979):27–59, esp. p. 38. See also AN F¹²1581, Etat of September 1811 from Saint-Quentin. On Normandy, see M. Roussel, "Mémoire sur l'in-dustrie des tissus en lin, chanvre, et coton de pays de Caux depuis plusieurs siècles jusqu'à nos jours," *Annuaire normand*, 1878, 391–3.

47. See Lévy-Leboyer, *Les banques européennes*, pp. 56–7, 79; Ellis, *Napo-lean's Continental Blockade*, pp. 180–1, 187–8.

48. On Ternaux, Douglas (whose machines Ternaux used), and Cockerill, see Ballot, *L'introduction du machinisme*, pp. 183–200. See also Bergeron, *Banquiers, négociants, et manufacturiers parisiens*, pp. 201–2.

49. An older standard work on the collapse of 1810–11 is Odette Viennet, *Napoléon et l'industrie française, la crise de 1810–11* (Paris, 1947); see also Ellis, *Napoléon's Continental Blockade*, pp. 219–63; Bergeron, *Ban-quiers, négociants, et manufacturiers parisiens*, pp. 292–7; numerous re-ports in AN F¹²1670–85; ADN M 433/6–7; Roussel, "Mémoire sur l'industrie des tissus,"393–5.

50. See Chassagne, "L'enquête, dite de Champagny," 361–62, for these figures.

51. AN F¹²1585, "Etat des métiers à filer le coton," January, 1814.

52. The following technical discussion of the mule jenny and its operating re-quirements is based on H. Catling, "The Development of the Spinning Mule," *Textile History* 9 (1978):35–57; Walter English, *The Textile Industry: An Account of the Early Inventions of Spinning, Weaving, and Knitting Machines* (London, 1969); Andrew Ure, *The Cotton Manufacture of Great Britain Systematically Investigated*, 2 vols. (London, 1836), II, 149–99; Oger, *Traité élémentaire de la filature du coton* (Mulhouse, 1839); C. E. Jullien and E. Lorentz, *Nouveau manuel complet du filateur* (Paris, 1843), pp. 89–108; A. Prestwich, *Young Man's Assistant to Cotton Spinning* (Manchester, 1887); Paul Dupont, *Aide-mémoire pratique de la filature du coton* (Paris, 1882); C. Aspin and S. D. Chapman, *James Hargreaves and the Spinning Jenny* (Preston, 1964). See also the illuminating discussion in Anthony F. C. Wallace, *Rock-dale: The Growth of an American Village in the Early Industrial Revolution* (New York, 1978).

53. See AN F¹²2195, report of 1788 on English machines and prices, assortment order of the year 9, report of an English shop operator at Saint-Marie-aux-

Mines in 1806 – which had two pairs of cards and 1,700 spindles, or about eight mules for each pair of cards. See also the discussion of assortments in Jullien and Lorentz, *Nouvel manuel*, p. 115; Oger, *Traité élémentaire*, pp. 311–349. Fohlen reports that the Méquillet-Noblot firm in Héricourt purchased the equipment of a bankrupt Paris spinning mill in 1819. In contrast to the English shop mentioned above, this assortment included eight coarse carders and 12 fine carders for 21 jennies (4,564 spindles), in other words, one set of cards for every two jennies. This was an extraordinary amount of carding capacity, but not unusual for Empire firms. See Claude Fohlen, *Une affaire de famille au XIXe siècle: Méquillet-Noblot* (Paris, 1955), 30, 121–2.

54. AN F^{12}2195, report of 1788 on English machines, the French inspector states: "It is absolutely necessary to have skilled operators [for carding machines], otherwise they will spoil the cotton and the cards."

55. On the quality of different grades of cotton, see Dieudonné, *Statistique du département du Nord*, II, 245–50; Chassagne, "L'enquête, dite de Champagny," p. 342; Jullien and Lorentz, *Nouvel manuel*, pp. 12–13.

56. AN F^{12}1585, Etat (coton), 4e trimestre 1815.

57. On Alsace, see AN F^{12}1583, letter of *maire adjoint*, Mulhouse, 2 June 1811, and attached report. From some secondary sources one learns that the Nord had 180,000 to 200,000 mule spindles by 1810 (Chassagne, "L'enquête, dite de Champagny," p. 357; Lévy-Leboyer, *Les banques européennes*, 59); elsewhere that there were only 69 shops in the area (Ballot, *L'introduction du machinisme*, 122). Can these two reports be combined? T. Leuridan, *Histoire de la fabrique de Roubaix* (Roubaix, 1863), p. 134, reports that Roubaix had 53 mills in 1824 with only 360 mules spinning fine numbers – only seven per establishment.

58. On these giant firms, see Chassagne, "L'enquête, dite de Champagny," idem., "la diffusion de l'industrie cotonnière," p. 106; Ballot, *L'introduction du machinisme*, pp. 103–112, 183–200; Bergeron, *Banquiers, négociants, et manufacturiers parisiens*, 205–22.

59. See Bergeron, *Banquiers, négociants, et manufacturiers parisiens*, esp. pp. 167–204, 299–316, or the concluding remarks of Ellis, *Napoleon's Continental Blockade*, pp. 264–73.

60. On power requirements, see especially Catling, "Development of the Spinning Mule."

61. See Penot, *Statistique générale*, pp. 322–23; Lévy-Leboyer, *Les banques européennes*, p. 60; ERDP, III, 273, 415; Ballot, *L'introduction du machinisme*, pp. 125–6, 192. See further discussion in Chapter 4.

62. Catling, "Development of the Spinning Mule," is particularly penetrating on the Roberts and Sharp design; see also Oger, *Traité élémentaire*, p. 241.

63. Several of these points are based on extrapolating backwards from July Monarchy sources discussed fully in the next two chapters. See also references in note 64.

64. Pay procedures, as described by Jullien and Lorentz, *Nouveau manuel*, pp. 89–90, or Oger, *Traité élémentaire*, pp. 273–5, may be inferred from details included in Dieudonné, *Statistique du département du Nord*, II, 244–50.

65. On the Manchester reel, Holker's promotion of it, and other yarn rating systems in the eighteenth century, see Rémond, *John Holker*, pp. 139–40; report of Etienne Lafont in AN F^{12}557 (dated 1764), memoir by Holker in AN F^{12}1341; BN, fond Joly de Fleury, Ms. 362, fol. 40–3; "Mémoire de E. L. Ponchet sur le besoin d'introduire l'uniformité dans les dévidoirs,"

1788 in AN F^{12}658A; report of de la Genière at Castres, 16 June 1799 in AN F^{12}1341. In the Nord, an older rating system was still in use in 1802; see Dieudonné, *Statistique du département du Nord*, II, 244–5; Leuridan, *Histoire de la fabrique de Roubaix*, 126.

66. See Oger, *Traité élémentaire*, pp. 241–4, 255, 258; Dupont, *Aide-mémoire pratique*, pp. 110–16.
67. Dieudonné's description of a jenny shop is a good case study in questions not asked; see *Statistique du département du Nord*, II, 244–6.
68. See output-per-spindle estimates discussed extensively in Chapter 4.
69. See Lévy-Leboyer, *Les banques européennes*, p. 57; Ballot, *L'introduction du machinisme*, p. 107; Chassagne, *Oberkampf*, pp. 186–225. See also Fohlen, *Une affaire de famille*, pp. 18–19, on efforts to spread cotton production in the Vosges; and Dornic, *L'industrie textile dans le Maine*, pp. 282–6, on the spread of cotton production there after 1797.
70. See Roussel, "Mémoire sur l'industrie des tissus," pp. 391–4.
71. Ballot, *L'introduction du machinisme*, pp. 248–52.
72. Roussel, "Mémoire sur l'industrie des tissus," pp. 395–6.

Part Two: Uses of the market idea, 1816–1851

1. See J. C. L. Simonde de Sismondi, *Nouveaux principes d'économie politique, ou de la richesse dans ses rapports avec la population*, 2 vols. (Paris, 1819); on Sismondi, see William Coleman's discussion in *Death is a Social Disease: Public Health and Political Economy in Early Industrial France* (Madison, Wis., 1982), pp. 74–80.
2. See, for example, ERDP, III, 276, 360, 380, 522–4; or AN F^{12}4476A, reports on the commercial situation of 1838–42.

4. The first crisis of management

1. See J. Lucas-Dubreton, *Le culte de Napoléon, 1815–1848* (Paris, 1960); also the revealing anecdote in Martin Nadaud, *Mémoires de Léonard, ancien garçon mason*, edited by Maurice Agulhon (Paris, 1976), p. 108.
2. See ERDP, III, p. 367 (quote by Roman), p. 258 (quote by Rouen merchant Adolphe Caignard).
3. See Lucas-Dubreton, *Le culte de Napoléon*, p. 132; Philippe Perrot, *Les dessus et les dessous de la bourgeoisie: Une histoire du vêtement au XIXe siècle* (Paris, 1981); pp. 56–63; Henriette Vanier *La mode et ses métiers: Frivolités et luttes de classes, 1830–1870* (Paris, 1960), pp. 13–52.
4. ERDP, III, 408–20.
5. Maurice Lévy-Leboyer, *Les banques européennes et l'industrialisation internationale* (Paris, 1964), pp. 97–8.
6. Roussel, "Mémoire sur l'industrie des tissus en lin, chanvre, et coton du pays de Caux depuis plusieurs siècles jusqu'à nos jours," *Annuaire normand*, 1878, p. 355, indicates that the calico trade did not pick up after the 100 days; see also Caignard's testimony in ERDP, III, 251–4; Lévy-Leboyer, *Les banques européennes*, p. 120, on cachemires; and Paul Sement, *Les anciennes halles aux toiles et aux cotons de Rouen* (Rouen, 1931), pp. 30–3.
7. Lévy-Leboyer, *Les banques européennes*, pp. 117-18; Claude Fohlen, *Une affaire de famille au XIXe siècle: Méquillet-Noblot* (Paris, 1955), pp. 121–2.
8. ERDP, III, 271, 567.

9. Ibid., p. 349; Serge Chassagne, "La diffusion rurale de l'industrie cotonnière en France (1750–1850)," *Revue du Nord* 61 (1979), p. 104.

10. On calico price cuts in Normandy, see ERDP, III, 252–4; Roussel, "Memoire sur l'industrie des tissus," 396–9; at Saint-Quentin, Charles Picard, *Résumé d'une étude sur la ville de Saint-Quentin* (Saint-Quentin, 1880), 125–6, and ERDP, III, 522–4; at Tarare, ERDP, III, p. 318; in Alsace, ERDP, III, p. 354 and Lévy-Leboyer, *Les banques europeennes*, p. 80. On immigrant Swiss weavers in Alsace, see Marie-Madeleine Kahan-Rabecq, *La classe ouvrière en Alsace pendant la Monarchie de Juillet* (Paris, 1937), pp. 18–19.

11. On 1825 price fluctuation, see ERDP, III, 522–4, 632; Achille Penot, *Statistique générale du département du Haut-Rhin* (Mulhouse, 1831), p. 320.

12. For wool prices, see testimony of Henriot in ERDP, III, 398–402, who reports that Reims consumes 3.5 million kilograms of raw wool per year, at a cost of 34.5 million francs, and sells its products for a gross of 50 million francs.

13. Lévy-Leboyer, *Les banques européennes*, p. 97, gives 30 francs per *aune*, an *aune* being about 1.2 meters.

14. France, Ministère de l'agriculture, du commerce, et des travaux publics, Conseil supérieure du commerce, de l'agriculture et de l'industrie, *Enquête. Traité de Commerce avec l'Angleterre*, III, Laine (Paris, 1861), pp. 213–31.

15. Lévy-Leboyer, *Les banques européennes*, 124; ERDP, III, p. 403.

16. On *circassiennes*, see ERDP, III, p. 453.

17. On *napolitaines*, see Lévy-Leboyer, *Les banques européennes*, p. 124; ERDP, III, 398, 470.

18. Ibid., pp. 406, 453, 455, 470; the merchant was Adolphe David of Reims.

19. On *guinghams*, see Penot, *Statistique générale*, 320; D. Risler, *Histoire de la vallée de Saint-Marie-aux-Mines, anciennement vallée de Liepvre* (Saint-Marie-aux-Mines, 1873), pp. 160–73; Lévy-Leboyer, *Les banques européennes*, p. 75.

20. Lévy-Leboyer, *Les banques européennes*, pp. 161; ERDP, III, 403; Leuridan, *Histoire de la fabrique de Roubaix*, pp. 141–2.

21. Leuridan, *Histoire de la fabrique de Roubaix*, pp. 143–7; Lévy-Leboyer, *Les banques européennes*, pp. 128–9. A. Mimerel was the first to combine cotton and wool at Roubaix; see ADN, M581/170^A.

22. Picard, *Résumé d'une étude*, pp. 113–14; ERDP, III, 450; Lévy-Leboyer, *Les banques européennes*, p. 125.

23. On *marchands de nouveautés*, early department stores, and the development of *confection*, see Vanier, *La mode et ses métiers*, pp. 101–03; Perrot, *Les dessus et les dessous de la bourgeoisie*, pp. 69–109; Michael B. Miller, *The Bon Marché: Bourgeois Culture and the Department Store* (Princeton, N.J., 1981), pp. 19–28.

24. Lévy-Leboyer, *Les banques européennes*, p. 104, quotes Michelet (in *Le Peuple*): "Today the poor worker covers his wife in a flowery dress for the price of one day's work." A skilled cotton printer of Rouen in an 1852 pamphlet remarked, "One sees, it is true, many young people of both sexes who are quite smartly dressed; but their outfits consist for the most part of light cotton or other cloth of low price; and most ... have to deprive themselves of food in order to save up the necessary sum." (From *La verité sur la position actuelle des classes laborieuses et sur la principale cause de leurs malaises*, by Gobelin, ouvrier imprimeur en indienne; a copy is in AN F^{12}2370.)

25. Perrot, *Les dessus et les dessous de la bourgeoisie*, pp. 31–8.

26. Ibid., p. 38; for some vivid descriptions of Revolutionary dress, see Christopher Hibbert, *The Days of the French Revolution* (New York, 1981).
27. Lévy-Leboyer, *Les banques européennes*, pp. 77–80.
28. ERDP, III, 254–6; Lévy-Leboyer, *Les banques européennes*, 67.
29. ERDP, III, 349. According to N. Koechlin, "On calcule assez généralement la façon par pièce, tout compris; c'est ainsi qu'on traite avec les entrepreneurs des campagnes," in ERDP, III, p. 621. See also Risler, *Histoire de la vallée de Saint-Marie-aux-Mines*, p. 173; Penot, *Statistique générale*, p. 326; Fohlen, *Une affaire de famille*, pp. 31–2.
30. On Elbeuf loom shops, see revealing records of conflicts there in AN BB^{18}1442 (2135) and ADSM 10MP2001; these are considered in detail in Chapter 7.
31. On Roubaix's Conseil des prudhommes and its control of weavers, see ADN M604/2; in 1838, 25 percent of Roubaix weavers still did not have *livrets*; see Lévy-Leboyer, *Les banques européennes*, p. 130. On use of housing tracts, see T. Leuridan, *Histoire de la fabrique de Roubaix* (Roubaix, 1863), p. 151; and ADN M620/12, report of 1 July 1846. See also Martine Le Blan, "Notes sur une étape dans la génèse d'une espace industriel: la construction des 'forts' roubaisiens dans la première moitié du XIXe siecle," *Revue du Nord*, 63 (1981):67–72.
32. On Elbeuf, see references cited in note 30; on fashion and price cuts in general, see references cited in note 10 and also ERDP, III, 195, 296–7, 402, 419, 453. On weavers' costs, see Charles Noiret, *Mémoires d'un ouvrier rouennais* (Rouen, 1836), p. 10. Noiret, himself a Normandy cottage weaver, also mentions bargaining over prices at time of reception of warp (p. 33) and constant changing of suppliers by weavers. Most, he said, do no more than one or two warps for any one merchant; those who stay out a year are very rare (p. 34).
33. Lévy-Leboyer, *Les banques européennes*, 96–104. Johnson believes that, in the case of Lodève, labor militancy deterred investors from committing new funds to the region; see his "Patterns of Proletarianization: Parisian Tailors and Lodève Woolen Workers," in John M. Merriman, ed., *Consciousness and Class Experience in Nineteenth-Century Europe* (New York, 1979), 65–84. See Chapter 6 for further discussion.
34. Claude Fohlen, *L'industrie textile au temps du Second Empire* (Paris, 1956), pp. 161–253, gives a good overview of the spread of power looms.
35. ERDP, III, 252–3.
36. See Leuridan, *Histoire de la fabrique de Roubaix*, pp. 137–49; AMR, F II (ga) 2; Peter N. Stearns, *Paths to Authority: The Middle Class and the Industrial Labor Force in France, 1820–48* (Urbana, Ill., 1978), pp. 157–8. This was, of course, entirely illegal.
37. Penot, *Statistique générale*, pp. 322–3.
38. Kahan-Rabecq, *La classe ouvrière en Alsace*, p. 33, gives figures showing 4 kilograms per spindle per year of No. 28 cotton yarn as the Alsace average in 1815, and 20 kilograms by 1835, an improvement of 400 percent. But this latter figure is impossibly high; see the section of Chapter 4 entitled "Theory and Practice at the Mule." Hand-cranked mules were eliminated in Alsace by 1825, according to her evidence (p. 32).
39. The first steam engine was installed in a Normandy spinning mill in 1817; the figure of 10 by 1825 is extrapolated from data in J. A. Delerue, "Documents pour la statistique de la production industrielle du département de la Seine-Inférieure," *Annuaire normand*, 1844, 327–51. See also Lévy-Leboyer, *Les*

banques européennes, 88–90. Roubaix's first steam engine was installed in 1820; water shortages remained a problem until 1828; see ADN M581/170ᴬ.

40. ERDP, III, 354–5.
41. Ibid., pp. 210–1.
42. On credit problems and prices in 1827–32, see ibid., pp. 360, 632–3; on the structure of these crises in general, see Lévy-Leboyer, *Les banques européennes*, pp. 594–9.
43. ERDP, III, 211, 520.
44. This interpretation of the response of survivors has been recently (and quite independently) proposed for Lille in Charles Engrand, "Les industries lilloises et la crise économique de 1826 à 1832," *Revue du Nord* 63 (1981):233–51.
45. They may all be found in AMR F II (ga) 1–4.
46. See ADN M581/170ᴬ; Leuridan, *Histoire de la fabrique de Roubaix*, 134–5.
47. Article 6 of the rules of the Vernier-Delaoutre mill, filed 13 May 1830; on *levées* see C. E. Jullien and E. Lorentz, *Nouveau manuel complet du filateur* (Paris, 1843), 88–90.
48. See Article 4 of the rules of the Dazin mill, filed 17 March 1836; Article 2 of the rules of the Ernould-Bayart mill filed 1 July 1839; and Article 12 of the rules from the Duflos et Annebicque mill, filed 1 October 1847. All are in AMR F II (ga) 3.
49. Oger, *Traité élémentaire de la filature du coton* (Mulhouse, 1839), 344–5. On keeping of good Monday in Alsace, see AN F¹²4704, copy of Société industrielle de Mulhouse pamphlet of 1835, p. 13: "Beaucoup d'ouvriers, et surtout ceux qui travaillent à la piece, font le bon lundi, ainsi que cela se voit dans toutes les villes de fabriques; c'est-à-dire, qu'ils prennent sur eux de rester hors des ateliers, durant tout ou partie de la journée, ceux qui s'y rend ne font que peu de besogne." On singing in the mills, see L.-B. Horemans, *Etudes de moeurs lilloises, comprenant: le fileur de coton, l'histoire d'un filtier, la brodeuse de tulles, etc., etc.* (Lille, 1886). For further discussion, see Chapter 6.
50. ERDP, III, 569. The firm in question, M. Pihet, had perfected a line of bobbin-and-fly frames by 1825. On these preparation machines, see Andrew Ure, *The Cotton Manufacture of Great Britain Systematically Investigated*, 2 vols. (London, 1836).
51. On installation of steam engines in Normandy, see J. A. Delerue, "Documents pour la statistique de la production industrielle de la Seine-Inférieure," pp. 336–47; in Lille–Roubaix, see *ERDP*, III, p. 192; for Saint-Quentin, Picard, *Résumé d'une étude*, 111, and *ERDP*, III, p. 517. The Méquillet-Noblot firm of Héricourt installed steam power and new bobbin-and-fly frames in the same period, 1832–1834; see Fohlen, *Une affaire de famille*, pp. 45–6.
52. Lévy-Leboyer, *Les banques européennes*, 89–90.
53. ERDP, III, 519, 583.
54. Roussel, "Mémoire sur l'industrie des tissus," 400–3.
55. Oger, *Traité élémentaire*, 207–11.
56. Jullien and Lorentz, *Nouvel manuel*, p. 108. Estimates from this manual are also about 40 percent lower than those made by Ure, *Cotton Manufacture*, II, p. 172, who is, however, like Oger, giving technical capacity.
57. ERDP, III, 269–81.
58. Ibid., pp. 603–33.
59. Ibid., pp. 346–81.
60. Ibid., pp. 484–95.

61. On piecers spelling crank operators, see ADN M611/3, 1840 letter of the Lille Chamber of Commerce. For further discussion, see Chapter 6.
62. ERDP, III, p. 356.
63. Ibid., p. 486.

5. Spinners on guard

1. The following account is based on records in ADSM, 10MP2001; on reports in the *Journal de Rouen* of 28 August–12 September 1830; those in *Gaz. Trib.*, of 14 September and 12, 16 October 1830, and 13 February 1831, and on a report in AN BB[18]1189(4344). Jean-Pierre Aguet has provided an account of this incident in his *Les grèves sous la Monarchie de Juillet: Contribution à l'étude du mouvement ouvrier français* (Geneva, 1954), pp. 38–42.
2. Charles Noiret, *Mémoires d'un ouvrier rouennais* (Rouen, 1836), pp. 2–4; for further discussion, see Maurice Lévy-Leboyer, *Les banques européennes et l'industrialisation internationale* (Paris, 1964), pp. 89–93; Peter N. Stearns, *Paths to Authority: The Middle Class and the Industrial Labor Force in France, 1820–48* (Urbana, Ill., 1978); Davis S. Landes, *The Unbound Prometheus* (Cambridge, 1969), pp. 158–66.
3. See David H. Pinkney, *The French Revolution of 1830* (Princeton, 1972); Gilette Ziegler, *Paris et ses révolutions* (Paris, 1970); Maurice Dommanget, *Histoire du drapeau rouge des origins à la guerre de 1939* (Paris, 1967).
4. Quoted in William H. Sewell, *Work and Revolution in France: The Language of Labor from the Old Regime to 1848* (Cambridge, 1980), p. 195; see also Edgar Leon Newman, "What the Crowd Wanted in the French Revolution of 1830," in John M. Merriman, ed., *1830 in France* (New York, 1975), pp. 17–40; Alain Faure, "Mouvements populaires et mouvement pouvrier à Paris," *Le mouvement social*, no. 88 (July–September, 1974): pp. 51–92; Octave Festy, *Le mouvement ouvrier au début de la Monarchie de Juillet* (Paris, 1908).
5. See the circular from the Ministry of War in ADSM 10MP2001.
6. Prefect to minister of the interior, 28 August 1830, in ADSM 10MP2001.
7. In ADSM 10MP2001.
8. Christopher H. Johnson, "The Revolution of 1830 in French Economic History," in John M. Merriman, ed., *1830 in France* (New York, 1975), 152.
9. *Journal de Rouen*, 30 August 1830.
10. See AN F[12]4704, report of the Société libre de l'émulation de Rouen; same dossier report of the Chambre de commerce de Rouen. For further discussion, see Chapter 6.
11. Prefect to minister of the interior, 29 August 1830, ADSM 10MP2001.
12. ADSM 10MP2001; the paper holding the piece-rate schedule lies under a letter from the mill owner Vaneyenne, saying he has enclosed a copy of his "work rules."
13. See the account of Drely's trial in the *Journal de Rouen*, 12 September 1830; it is discussed further on in this section of Chapter 5.
14. The letter is in ADSM 10MP2001.
15. According to Drely's testimony, *Journal de Rouen*, 12 September 1830.
16. *Gaz. Trib.*, 14 September 1830.
17. Report of Maréchal de Camp to prefect; report of prefect to minister of the interior, 5 September 1830, ADSM 10 MP 2001.
18. *Gaz. Trib.*, 13 February 1831.
19. Ibid.
20. *Gaz. Trib.* 14 September 1830.

21. AN BB[18]1189(4344).
22. ADN M137/54 and M620/4 for police reports on the events; *procureur's* reassurances in AMR F II (ga) 2.
23. Marie-Madeleine Kahan-Rabecq, *La classe ouvrière en Alsace pendant la Monarchie de Juillet* (Paris, 1937), pp. 333–5; AN BB[18]1192(4666); ADHR 10M8, mayor of Mulhouse to prefect, 24 September 1830 is also relevant.
24. The scanty evidence is also removed in time. Pay records surviving from 1847–1848 suggest widespread and long-standing use of premiums there; see ADHR 10M8, pages from pay book of Koechlin-Dollfus et Frère, dated 22 July 1848. See Chapter 7.
25. See the letter of the mayor of Roubaix of 9 October 1857 in ADN M606/6: "Those who adopted the new motor [i.e., the steam engine] did not change their piece-rate schedule [*tarif des façons*], but withheld 9 francs per week from spinners to turn the mules." This charge "grew as it got older" to as high as 18 francs in some mills by 1848. Demands that the practice be abolished in Lille appear in the grievances of the Société républicaine des fileurs de Lille of June 1848 in ADN M605/3. See also letter of Tourcoing mill owners of January 1849 in ADN M620/14. For further discussion, see Chapter 7. References to charges for steam power appear in work rules of the following mills in Roubaix: De Grendel, Article 2 (filed 1 November 1835), Dazin, Article 3 (filed 17 March 1836), Ernould-Bayart, Article 3 (filed 1 July 1839), A. Mimerel, Article 3 (filed 1 January 1844), and Duflos et Annebicque, Articles 16 and 22 (filed 1 October 1847). In the last of these work rules, the steam charge was set at 14 francs. In most cases, the article gives notice that the steam charge will continue to be due even when the spinner is absent. All of these rules are found in AMR, F II (ga) 3.
26. See Chapter 3, note 40; Noiret, *Mémoires*, 10, 33–4.
27. ADN M620/4.
28. Aguet, *Les grèves sous la Monarchie de Juillet*, p. 49.
29. Aguet (in ibid., pp. 50–2) treats this incident as having occurred in a spinning mill; but close reading of surviving records shows a loom shop was involved. See AN BB[18]1217, reports of the local *procureur*, 16 July through 30 September 1833; AN F[7]6782(15), report of the Gendarmerie to minister of the interior, 16 July 1833.
30. On the Place de Grève, see Jacques Hillairet, *Dictionnaire historique des rues de Paris*, 2 vols. (Paris, 1963), II, 648–50. For examples of use of the word by Parisian journeymen, see Aguet, *Les grèves sous la Monarchie de Juillet*, 32–4; Remi Gossez, *Les ouvriers de Paris*, I, *L'organisation, 1848-1851*, Bibliothèque de la révolution de 1848, vol. 23 (La Roche-sur-Yon, 1967), p. 273 (for which example, the author thanks William H. Sewell); Y. Efrahem, *De l'insurrection des ouvriers de tous les corps d'état* (Paris, 1833), and Gisquet, *Mémoires du Préfet de police* (Paris, 1840), III, p. 170 (these two examples, thanks to Michelle Perrot). For uses of the word to mean unemployment or casual labor, see Gossez, *Les ouvriers de Paris*, p. 377; Adolphe Blanqui, *Des classes ouvrières en France pendant l'année 1848* (Paris, 1849), 15, 28, 47, 108–09.
31. Personal communication from Cynthia Truant; see also Jacques-Louis Ménétra, *Journal de ma vie* edited by Daniel Roche (Paris, 1982), 63, 69–72, for two examples.
32. But see Octave Festy, *Le Mouvement ouvrier*; Maurice Agulhon, *Une ville ouvrière au temps du socialisme utopique: Toulon de 1815 à 1851* (Paris, 1970); Faure "Mouvements populaires et mouvement ouvrier à Paris."

33. *Gaz. Trib.*, 6 September 1833; see also the issue of 20 June and Aguet, *Les grèves sous la Monarchie de Juillet*, 70.
34. All subprefect's reports on this incident are in ADM 194M9; see also AN BB¹⁸1226; *Gaz. Trib.* 1–2, 4, 8 September 1834; Aguet, *Les grèves sous la Monarchie de Juillet*, p. 150.
35. Report in ADM 194M9.
36. ERDP, III, 403, testimony of Henriot; Lévy-Leboyer, *Les banques européennes*, pp. 123–4.
37. Subprefect to prefect, 24 August 1834, ADM 194M9.
38. Text of song is in ADM 194M9; *Gaz. Trib.*, 1–2 September 1834 indicates tune of "La Parisienne" was used for this or some other text.
39. Subprefect to prefect, 31 August 1834, ADM 194M9.
40. *Commandant de la gendarmerie* to prefect, 31 August 1834, ADM 194M9.
41. Subprefect to prefect, 3 September 1834, ADM 194M9.
42. See Festy, *Le mouvement ouvrier*; Aguet, *Les grèves sous la Monarchie de Juillet*; Agulhon, *Une ville ouvrière*; Robert J. Bezucha, *The Lyon Uprising of 1834: Social and Political Conflict in the Early July Monarchy* (Cambridge, Mass., 1974); Faure, "Mouvements populaires et mouvement ouvrier à Paris"; Christopher H. Johnson, *Utopian Communism in France: Cabet and the Icarians, 1839–51* (Ithaca, N.Y., 1974); Jacques Rancière, *La nuit des prolétaires: Archives du rêve ouvrier* (Paris, 1981); Sewell, *Work and Revolution in France*.
43. Sewell, *Work and Revolution in France*, pp. 143–93; Christopher H. Johnson, "Patterns of Proletarianization: Parisian Tailors and Lodève Woolen Workers," in John M. Merriman, ed., *Consciousness and Class Experience in Nineteenth–Century Europe* (New York, 1979), 65–84; Joan W. Scott, "Men and Women in the Parisian Garment Trades: Discussions of Family and Work in the 1830s and 40s," forthcoming; Rancière, *La nuit des prolétaires*.
44. See references cited in preface, note 3.
45. These comments based largely on Nadaud, *Mémoires*, especially 265–72, an account of Nadaud's brief experiment with subcontracting. See also the accounts of the carpenters' strike of 1845 in Aguet, *Les grèves sous la Monarchie de Juillet*, pp. 300–10.
46. Jacques Rancière, "Le mythe de l'artisan," paper presented to the Conference on Representations of Work in France, April 1983, sponsored by the Western Societies Program, Cornell University.
47. On this incident, see Auget, *Les grèves sous la Monarchie de Juillet*, pp. 108–9; Johnson "Patterns of Proletarianization," pp. 72–3.
48. Johnson, "Patterns of Proletarianization," p. 73; Aguet, *Les grèves sous la Monarchie de Juillet*, pp. 326–36.

6. Visions of subsistence

1. Martin Nadaud, *Mémoires de Léonard, ancien garçon mason*, Maurice Agulhon ed. (Paris, 1976), pp. 265–71.
2. Jacques Rancière, "Le myth de l'artisan," paper presented to the Conference on Representations of Work in France, April 1983, sponsored by the Western Societies Program, Cornell University.
3. Quoted in Henriette Vanier, *La mode et ses métiers: Frivolités et luttes des classes, 1830–1870* (Paris, 1960), pp. 13–14.
4. David Ricardo, *Principles of Political Economy and Taxation* (London,

1817). On his influence in contemporary England, see Barry Gordon, *Political Economy in Parliament, 1819–1823* (London, 1976); Mark Blaug, *Ricardian Economics* (New Haven, 1958). On Ricardo's views on machinery as fixed capital, see Maxine Berg, *The Machinery Question and the Making of Political Economy* (Cambridge, 1980), pp. 43–74. Berg disputes the pessimism of Ricardo's own thought – but not that of his followers. On the rhetorical power of economic thinking, see Simon Dentith, "Political Economy, Fiction, and the Language of Practical Ideology in Nineteenth-Century England," *Social History* 8 (1983), pp. 183–199.

5. This conclusion follows inescapably from William Coleman, *Death is a Social Disease: Public Health and Political Economy in Early Industrial France* (Madison, Wis., 1982). It will be developed further in the sections of this chapter entitled "Imaginary Budgets" and "Fourier on Guard."

6. Especially credulous in the use of such sources is Benigno Cacérès, *Le mouvement ouvrier* (Paris, 1967); but see also, for example, Vanier, *La mode et ses métiers*, pp. 36–9; or Georges Duveau, *La vie ouvrière en France sous le Second Empire* (Paris, 1946), pp. 351, 510, 535; or the textbook by A. Jardin and A. J. Tudesq, *La Frances des notables*, 2 vols. (Paris, 1973), II, *La vie de la nation*, pp. 158–62; or Jean Sandrin, *Enfants trouvés, enfants ouvriers, 17ᵉ-19ᵉ siècles* (Paris, 1982). The views of Louis Chevalier, *Classes laborieuses, classes dangereuses à Paris pendant la première moitié du XIXᵉsiècle* (Paris, 1958) are widely acknowledged to be extreme. But the sources are still not generally approached with the skepticism they deserve.

7. See remarks in, for example, Francois Furet, *Penser la Révolution française* (Paris, 1978); William H. Sewell, *Work and Revolution in France: The Language of Labor From the Old Regime to 1848* (Cambridge, 1980), pp. 5–14, 219–36; Jacques Rancière, *La nuit des prolétaires: Archives du rêve ouvrier* (Paris, 1981), pp. 8–12; Coleman, *Death is a Social Disease*, pp. 15–21.

8. These two figures are chosen for careful attention here because of their direct roles in the controversy over child labor in the 1830s. Fuller discussion of developments of the 1820s may be found in Coleman, *Death is a Social Disease*; Chevalier, *Classes laborieuses et classes dangereuses*. See also Peter N. Stearns, *Paths to Authority: The Middle Class and the Industrial Labor Force in France, 1820–48* (Urbana, Ill., 1978), especially pp. 111–172.

9. *Forces productives et commerciales de la France*, 2 vols. (Paris, 1827).

10. His preoccupation with the moral plane dates, not surprisingly, from 1830; see his pamphlet *Discours sur le sort des ouvriers considéré dans ses rapports avec l'industrie, la liberté, et l'ordre public* (Paris, 1831), or his later work *Du travail des enfants qu'emploient les ateliers, les usines, et les manufactures* (Paris, 1847).

11. *L'industrie et la morale considérées dans leurs rapports avec la liberté* (Paris, 1825). (Ricardo was translated by 1819.)

12. Dunoyer, *L'industrie et la morale*, p. 373.

13. Ibid., p. 381.

14. Ibid., p. 389.

15. Alexandre-Jean-Baptiste Parent-Duchâtelet, *Essai sur les cloaques de la ville de Paris* (Paris, 1824); Tanneguy Duchâtel, *La charité dans ses rapports avec l'état moral et le bien-être des classes inférieures de la société* (Paris, 1829).

16. J. C. L. Simonde de Sismondi, *Nouveaux principes d'économie politique, ou de la richesse dans ses rapports avec la population*, 2 vols. (Paris, 1819); on Saint-Simon and Comte, see Frank E. Manuel and Fritzie P. Manuel, *Utopian Thought in the Western World* (Cambridge, Mass., 1979), pp.

590–614, 717–34. Manuel and Manuel report that Dunoyer attended Comte's first lecture series in 1826 (pp. 719–20).

17. Coleman repeatedly emphasizes that a general, if undeveloped commitment to political economy underlay the work of social investigators, in *Death is a Social Disease*, especially pp. 207, 277–306.
18. *Discours sur quelques recherches de statistique comparée faites sur la ville de Mulhouse* (Mulhouse, 1828). (Read to the Industrial Society on 26 September 1828.)
19. See "Rapport de la commission spéciale concernant la proposition de M. Jean-Jacques Bourcart," BSIM (1828), pp. 328–38.
20. Compare the actions of the Conseil des prudhommes of Roubaix during the slump of 1827–32 (collective control of weaver pay rates organized for the benefit of merchant manufacturers) with the Mulhouse mill owners' Society, launched in those same years. On Roubaix, see AMR F II (ga) and ADN M604/1.
21. In Rouen the Société libre d'émulation came to fulfill some of the same functions as the Mulhouse Society; see its *Bulletin* of 1837. In Lille, the Chamber of Commerce played this role. In Roubaix, Auguste Mimerel turned himself virtually into a one-man public-relations project; see his pamphlet *Du paupérisme dans ses rapports avec l'industrie en France et en Angleterre* (Lille, no date) exonerating French mill owners from any responsibility in working-class conditions. Mimerel organized the Association pour la défense du travail national as a national import-prohibition lobbying group in 1846; see Marie-Madeleine Kahan-Rabecq, *Réponses du département du Haut-Rhin à l'enquête faite en 1848 par l'Assemblée nationale sur les conditions du travail industriel et agricole* (Paris, 1939), pp. 21–3, on this group. The differences between industrialists' policy concerns and those of other notables come out clearly in the important survey by Andre-Jean Tudesq, *Les grands notables en France (1840–1849)*, 2 vols. (Paris, 1964) II, 566–668.
22. According to the BN catalogue *Périodiques*, bulletins of *sociétés industrielles* began publication in each of these towns on the following dates: Reims (1858), Elbeuf (1859), Saint-Quentin (1869), Rouen (1873), Lille (1873). (This does not capture all the societies, however, or dates of foundation: a *société industrielle* was founded in Saint-Quentin before 1837; see its report and pamphlet in AN F¹²4704.)
23. *De la misère des ouvriers et de la marche à suivre pour y rémédier* (Paris, 1832). A good introduction to the whole investigative tradition is Michelle Perrot, *Enquêtes sur la condition ouvrière en France au 19ᵉsiècle* (Paris, 1972).
24. Morogues, *De la misère*, p. 43.
25. Ibid., pp. 52–3.
26. *Economie politique chrétienne*, 3 vols. (Paris, 1834).
27. Ibid., I, 309–28.
28. Ibid., p. 293.
29. In fact, publication of wage data became routine for local statistical studies by the late 1830s; see, for example, Amédée Lecointe, "Statistique de la fabrication et du commerce des rouenneries en 1842," *Annuaire normand* (1844), pp. 317–23. Achille Penot, stung by critiques of his 1831 statistical study of the Haut-Rhin department because it included no wage information, provided abundant figures in his later *Recherches statistiques sur Mulhouse* (Mulhouse, 1843).
30. A copy of the pamphlet is in AN F¹²4704.
31. That Villermé spoke with Barrois is almost certain; see Louis Villermé,

Tableau de l'état physique et moral des ouvriers employés dans les man-ufactures de coton, de laine, et de soie, 2 vols. (Paris, 1840), I, 83.

32. Ibid., pp. 139–56.
33. Examples of historians who have used Villermé's evidence freely are in-cluded in note 6. But further examples can be cited to give an idea of the pervasiveness of his influence: E. Levasseur, *Histoire des classes ouvrières et de l'industrie en France,* 2nd edition, 2 vols. (Paris, 1903–04), I, 223–34; Paul Louis, *La condition ouvrière en France depuis cent ans* (Paris, 1950), pp. 9–18; Edouard Dolléans, *Histoire du travail* (Paris, 1943), pp. 84–9; Marie-Madeleine Kahan-Rabecq, *La classe ouvrière en Alsace pendant la monarchie de Juillet* (Paris, 1937). It can fairly be said that this single source has dominated the historiography of working-class conditions as far as the July Monarchy is concerned.
34. Villermé, *Tableau,* I, 93.
35. Ibid., p. 97.
36. Ibid., p. 99.
37. Ibid., pp. 99–100.
38. Ibid., p. 93.
39. See Maurice Lévy-Leboyer, *Les banques européennes et l'industrialisation internationale* (Paris, 1964), p. 163; Pierre Pierrard, *Les chansons en patois de Lille sous le Second Empire,* Publications de la Société de dialectologie picarde, vol. 8 (Arras, 1966), p. 170.
40. Villermé, *Tableau,* I, 107–15.
41. Alain Lottin, *Chavatte, ouvrier lillois, un contemporain de Louis XIV* (Paris, 1979) brings out the intense sense of self and guild-focused social life among weaver inhabitants of this quarter in the late seventeenth century.
42. Louis Vermesse, *Dictionnaire du patois de la Flandre française ou wallonne* (Lille, 1867), pp. 228–9.
43. Villermé, *Tableau,* I, 87–8.
44. One may follow the paths of conspirators in a plot to raise wages, for example, as they move in and around Lille in the 1850s, described in William M. Reddy, "The *Batteurs* and the Informer's Eye: A Labor Dispute Under the French Second Empire," *History Workshop Journal* No. 7 (Spring, 1979):30–44. See also Chapter 9.
45. On this affair, see ADN M137/54.
46. For some examples of mule-spinner wage reports, see ERDP, III; Lévy-Leboyer, *Les banques européennes,* p. 91; Kahan-Rabecq, *La classe ouvrière en Alsace,* pp. 222–45; and others cited in note 49. For additional budgets, see Villermé, *Tableau,* I, p. 44 (for Mulhouse), p. 126 (Saint-Quentin), p. 144 (Rouen).
47. Ibid., II, p. 319.
48. Ibid., pp. 342–3.
49. These figures are from, respectively, ERDP, III, 350 (Roman); Kahan-Rabecq, *La classe ouvrière en Alsace,* p. 230 (Koechlin); AN $F^{12}4704$ (pamphlet of the Société industrielle de Mulhouse, 1837); Penot, *Recherches statistiques sur Mulhouse,* p. 152; Kahan-Rabecq, *Réponses du département du Haut Rhin,* 80–1 (Dolfuss-Meig).
50. C. E. Jullien and E. Lorentz, *Nouveau manuel complet du filateur* (Paris, 1843), pp. 88, 108, explain how to calculate piece rates on the basis of ideal output levels.
51. Stearns argues that manufacturing wages went up in this period in *Paths*

to *Authority*, 71–80; Kahan-Rabecq maintains the opposite for Alsace in *La classe ouvrière en Alsace*, 222-45. (Both may be right, of course.)

52. This was especially true of bobbin winders (called *bobineuses*, or *épeuleuses* in weaving shops) and bobbin-and-fly-frame operators; see Roman's comments in ERDP, III, 352; 1830 pay book excerpt in ADSM 10 MP 2001; demand of Armentières spinning preparations workers for abolition of piece rates in 1903 discussed in William M. Reddy, "Family and Factory: French Linen Weavers in the Belle Epoque," *Journal of Social History* 8 (1975):102–112.

53. Pay book excerpt in ADSM 10MP2001.

54. Villermé, *Tableau*, I, 141–2.

55. This is why No. 30 cotton yarn was so widely produced. It was fine enough for calico; it resulted in the least waste fiber; it was strong and cheap. For a long time, it was the only grade used on power looms. See Oger, *Traité élémentaire de la filature du coton* (Mulhouse, 1839), p. 292.

56. A copy may be found in documents stemming from the 1849 conflict in Tourcoing in ADN M620/12.

57. See Roubaix work rules in AMR F II (ga) 1–4; *vrilles, mols retors, boutons* (flaws resulting from over- or undertwisting) are always fined. On the spinner's discretion in twisting, see Oger, *Traité élémentaire*, p. 240.

58. Jullien and Lorentz in all capacity calculations in *Nouveau manuel* assume water-powered mills work an average of only 250 days per year. See also, on water shortages, Claude Fohlen, *Une affaire de famille au XIXᵉ siècle: Méquillet-Noblot* (Paris, 1955), pp. 30–1. On variability of wages, see Francis Demier, "Les ouvriers de Rouen parlent à un économiste en juillet 1848," *Le mouvement social*, No. 119 (April–June 1982): 3–31.

59. By following the quarterly reports on industry from the Aisne department (location of Saint-Quentin) from 1838 through 1841 – a particularly rich series – in AN F¹²4476A, one discovers how extraordinarily sensitive wages were to the general pace of affairs.

60. On the issue of needs varying with life cycle, see Louise Tilly and Joan W. Scott, *Women, Work and Family* (New York, 1978), 104–145.

61. Marriage records for Darnétal, a Rouen suburb, from 1830 to 1837 show that 58 percent of spinners' fathers were domestic weavers and that 70 percent of mill operatives had been born in the commune itself, Rouen, or another Rouen suburb. (See Archives communales de Darnétal, E11 to E15.) Francis Demier also reports local origin, high stability of Rouen-area workers in "Les ouvriers de Rouen parlent à un économiste." On Reims see Georges Clauses, "Les cardeurs et fileurs de laine à Reims en 1812: origine et moralité," in *L'industrie, facteur de transformations politiques, économiques, sociales et culturelles* (Association interuniversitaire de l'Est, xvii; Colloque de Metz, 17–18 November 1972. Lunéville, 1974), 59–70. On origins of Roubaix immigrants, see Jean-Claude Bonnier, "Esquisse d'une évolution sociale: Roubaix sous le Second Empire (1856–1873)," *Revue du Nord*, 62 (1980): 619–636. Discussions in ERDP, III, 485–6, 613–16, imply that spinners were overwhelmingly of local origin. Mulhouse was exceptional in having drawn unemployed domestic weavers from neighboring Swiss regions following the import prohibition of 1816; see Kahan-Rabecq, *La classe ouvrière en Alsace*, pp. 154–7.

62. Eric Hobsbawm, "Custom, Wages and Work-Load in Nineteenth-Century Industry," in *Laboring Men: Studies in the History of Labor* (London, 1964), pp. 344–70.

63. Tilly and Scott, *Women, Work and Family*, 81–145.
64. On spinners hiring own piecers, see letter of Motte-Bossut firm (Roubaix) to prefect of the Nord, 9 January 1853, in ADN M613/1, or Dupont report and accompanying police report on Martini firm (Lille) of 29 October 1858 in ADN M613/16, both discussed further in the section of Chapter 8 entitled "Gradgrind in the Factory."
65. Established kin ties revealed by an employee roll from a Rouen mill in 1830 (the same as discussed in Chapter 5 in the section entitled "The Prefect's Coalition") and another from the Tourcoing mill of Darras-Lemaire in 1853 (in ADN M581/143) show that at least 34 percent and 38 percent respectively of employees were related to each other. These are bare minimums, however, since in the first case piecers were not listed; in the latter case, the percentage only includes those both related and living together. (The Tourcoing figure might have been as high as 51 percent, based on last-name recurrences.) Hence the estimated range of 40 to 60 percent. See also evidence from the 1837 Bureau of Manufactures inquiry, discussed in the section of this chapter entitled "The Rhetoric of Subsistence."
66. On the number of overlookers per department, see Oger, *Traité élémentaire*, pp. 351–2; references to "mon contre-maître" in the singular in work rules in AMR F II (ga) 1–4.
67. Roman in ERDP, III, 350. See also Stearns, *Paths to Authority*, pp. 64–7.
68. ADSM 6MP5150.
69. Ibid.
70. See Tilly and Scott, *Women, Work and Family*, pp. 81–6, 123–36.
71. Ibid., pp. 106–116.
72. See the report of Theodore Barrois in AN F^{12}4705 and the 1837 pamphlet of the Société industrielle de Mulhouse in AN F^{12}4704.
73. List of the Darras-Lemaire mill in ADN M581/143.
74. Oger, *Traité élémentaire*, p. 53.
75. For a point of comparison, see Reddy, "Family and Factory," which provides census figures on employment by family for a whole town in 1906.
76. Norbert Truquin, *Mémoires et aventures d'un prolétaire à travers la Révolution, l'Algerie, la République Argentine et le Paraguay* (Paris, 1888), 70, quoted in Michelle Perrot, "Une expérience de travail au XIXe siècle, à travers une autobiographie ouvrière (Norbert Truquin)," paper presented to a conference on Representations of Work in France sponsored by the Western Societies Program, Cornell University, April 1983.
77. T. Barrois in 1837 complained that his laborers "collaborate to arrange for the time needed to take their three meals and for various breaks." See his report in AN F^{12}4705; see also the previous discussion of Oger's comments on discipline in Chapter 4.
78. The term is Olwen Hufton's from *The Poor of Eighteenth-Century France, 1750–1789* (Oxford, 1974), pp. 69–127.
79. See the pamphlet by Gobelin, *La vérité sur la position actuelle des classes laborieuses et sur la principale cause de leurs malheurs* (1853) in AN F^{12}2370. In the Lille dialect there was a verb for makeshift work: *manoquer* (one who engaged in it was a *manoqueux*); see Vermesse, *Dictionnaire du patois de la Flandre française*, p. 325; and Pierrard, *Les chansons en patois de Lille*, p. 170.
80. On the textile crises see Kahan-Rabecq, *La classe ouvrière en Alsace*, pp. 246–69, or the superb account in Lévy-Leboyer, *Les banques européennes*, pp. 537–89.

81. Leutner in ERDP, III, 295.
82. Mimerel in ibid., p. 577.
83. Sanson-Daviller in ibid., p. 486.
84. See references in note 61.
85. See, for example, Marie Pascal Buriez, "Le mouvement de la population dans le département du Nord au XIXe siècle," Diplôme d'études supérieures, Université de Lille, Faculté des lettres, 1970; Charles Engrand, "Les ouvriers lillois de 1829 à 1832" Diplôme d'études supérieures, Université de Lille, Faculté des lettres, 1957; Bonnier, "Esquisse d'une évolution sociale."
86. Lévy-Leboyer, *Les banques européennes*, p. 119.
87. For a case study of such job shifting, see Reddy "The *Batteurs* and the Informer's Eye."
88. J.-J. Bourcart, "Proposition sur la necessité de fixer l'âge et de reduire les heures du travail des ouvriers des filatures," BSIM (1828), p. 327.
89. "Rapport de la commission spéciale concernant la proposition de M. Jean-Jacques Bourcart," BSIM (1828), 332–4; "Rapport de la commission chargée d'examiner la question relative à l'emploi des enfants dans les filatures de coton," BSIM (1837), 481–501.
90. See "Rapport de la commission chargée d'examiner la question relative à l'emploi des enfants"; and Kestner-Rigau, "Raport fait au nom de la commission spéciale chargée d'examiner les question relatives au travail des jeunes ouvriers des fabriques," BSIM (1833), 339–51. For an excellent review of public debate leading to passage of the law, see Tudesq, *Les grands notables*, II, 581–98.
91. A printed copy of the speech may be found in AN F^{12}4704.
92. On this law's legislative history, see Emile Durand, *L'inspection du travail en France de 1841 à 1902* (Paris, 1902). Results of inquiries by the Bureau of Manufactures are in AN F^{12}4704–05; ADN M611/3. See also France, Ministère du commerce, Conseil général de l'agriculture, du commerce et des manufactures, *Procès-verbaux résumés, 1837–38*, pp. 120–143.
93. Villermé, *Tableau*, compare, e.g., I, p. 24; II, p. 43, 110–25, 316–26.
94. Ibid., II, 36–9.
95. Ibid., II, 112.
96. See questionnaire responses of the named groups in AN F^{12}4704–05.
97. Coleman, *Death is a Social Disease*, p. 174, indicates that Villermé had access to government files – a common experience for social investigators in the period.
98. Villermé, *Tableau*, I, 82–3.
99. Steven Marcus, *Engels, Manchester, and the Working Class* (New York, 1974); Chevalier, *Classes laborieuses, classes dangereuses*.
100. Jean-Louis Flandrin, *Familles, parenté, maison, sexualité dans l'ancienne société* (Paris, 1976), pp. 92–5; Natalie Z. Davis, "Proverbial Wisdom and Popular Errors" in idem, *Society and Culture in Early Modern France* (Stanford, 1975), pp. 227–67.
101. Hufton, *The Poor in Eighteenth-Century France*, pp. 50, 62–3, 171.
102. See responses of the organizations named in AN F^{12}4704–05.
103. AN F^{12}4705.
104. Ange Guepin and E. Bonamy, *Nantes au XIXe siècle. Statistique topographique, industrielle, et morale, faisant suite à l'histoire de Nantes* (Nantes, 1835), pp. 483–4.
105. Pamphlet of the Société industrielle de Mulhouse in AN F^{12}4704.
106. Villermé, *Tableau*, I, 27–8.

107. "Rapport ... concernant la proposition de M. Jean-Jacques Bourcart," BSIM (1828), 329–330.
108. Pamphlet of the Société industrielle de Mulhouse in AN F^{12}4704.
109. Penot, "Rapport ... relative à l'emploi des enfants dans les filatures de coton," BSIM (1837), pp. 488–9.
110. Pamphlet of Société industrielle de Mulhouse in AN F^{12}4704.
111. Villermé, *Tableau*, I, 25–6.
112. Ibid., I, 26, 27.
113. Penot, *Recherches statistiques sur Mulhouse*, p. 135.
114. The shift was not unrelated to the appearance of Louis Blanc's *Organisation du travail* (Paris, 1840), which drew heavily on the investigative literature. See, e.g., the counter-arguments of Auguste Mimerel in his pamphlet, *Du paupérisme dans ses rapports avec l'industrie*. On Blanc, see Sewell, *Work and Revolution in France*, pp. 232–6.
115. See, e.g., Jean-Paul Brunet, *Saint-Denis, la ville rouge, 1890–1939* (Paris, 1980), pp. 99–100, where he draws on one of Villermé's later disciples: Jacques Valdour, *Ateliers et taudis de la banlieue de Paris* (Paris, 1923). The simple mason Martin Nadaud had no idea how bad working-class life was before he had read Villermé and Adolphe Blanqui; see his autobiography, *Mémoires de Léonard, ancien garçon mason*, edited by Maurice Agulhon (Paris, 1976), p. 314.
116. Adolphe Blanqui, *Des classes ouvrières en France pendant l'annee 1848* (Paris, 1849), pp. 97, 99.
117. This comment is in a letter to Hugo reproduced in Victor Hugo, *Oeuvres complètes*, 42 vols. (Paris, 1909–50), vol. 38, *Actes et Paroles I*, 434–8.
118. Ibid.
119. Quoted in Hufton, *The Poor in Eighteenth-Century France*, 113.
120. Villermé, *Tableau*, I, 84–5.
121. On Fourier's distributive passions, see Albert Fried and Ronald Sanders, eds., *Socialist Thought, A Documentary History* (New York, 1964), pp. 129–35, where texts from various places are gathered together. A brief definition of each of the distributive passions may be found in Charles Fourier, *Oeuvres complètes*, 12 vols. (Paris, 1966–68), II, 145–6. This passage is translated in Jonathan Beecher and Richard Bienvenu, eds., *The Utopian Vision of Charles Fourier* (Boston, 1971), pp. 219–20. Fourier, of course, discerned several other major sorts of passions, all of which would be put to constructive use in a properly ordered society. See Manuel and Manuel, *Utopian Thought*, pp. 641–75.

7. A search for identity

1. Martin Henkel and Rolf Taubert, *Maschinenstürmer: Ein Kapitel aus der Sozialgeschichte des technischen Fortschritts* (Frankfurt, 1979), 9-30.
2. See discussions in Chapters 1 and 2.
3. Craig Calhoun, *The Question of Class Struggle. Social Foundations of Popular Radicalism During the Industrial Revolution* (Chicago, 1982), has attempted to make a bold revision of current understanding of modern social movements on the basis of this distinction. Something like this is surely called for.
4. Jean-Pierre Aguet, *Les grèves sous la Monarchie de Juillet: Contribution à l'étude du mouvement ouvrier français* (Geneva, 1954), frankly applied the term to a vast variety of different forms of action. Edward Shorter and

Charles Tilly, *Strikes in France, 1830–1968* (Cambridge, 1974), begin their history significantly with the year 1830 and draw directly on Aguet's compilation. Alain Faure, "Mouvements populaires et mouvement ouvrier à Paris," *Le mouvement social*, no. 88 (July–September 1974):51–92, is also content with the label, strike. The point is not that the term is always inappropriate, only that it has been used too loosely, obscuring an array of fascinating issues.

5. Indicative of their pervasive influence is Hobsbawm's notion of "collective bargaining by riot," later taken up by Shorter and Tilly and others. Hobsbawm put forward the idea as a counter to the notion that machine breaking is necessarily backward. But the way he exonerated this form of action was to see a bargaining rationality (and market forces) as hidden beneath the outwardly violent form of protest. See Eric Hobsbawm, "The Machine Breakers," in *Laboring Men: Studies in the History of Labor* (London, 1964), pp. 5–22. Again, collective bargaining by riot is certainly possible, but can it be taken for granted that this is what laborers are doing in any particular case?

6. Charles Noiret, *Aux travailleurs* (Rouen, 1840), p. 4.

7. On the crises of 1837 and 1839, see Maurice Lévy-Leboyer, *Les banques européennes et l'industrialisation internationale* (Paris, 1964), 551–84, 595–6; AN F^{12}4476A, quarterly reports on the economic situation from prefects, see especially those from the Eure, Marne, and Nord departments. Figures on the cotton trade in Guillaumin, *Dictionnaire du commerce et des marchandises*, 2 vols. (Paris, 1841), I, p. 711, are also useful.

8. A number of detailed reports by the *procureur* of nearby Les Andelys in AN BB^{18}1379(8426) are the basis of this account.

9. *Echo du Nord*, 22 September 1839. André Lasserre has also remarked the ambiguity of extant accounts, in *La situation des ouvriers de l'industrie textile dan la région lilloise sous la Monarchie de Juillet* (Lausanne, 1952), pp. 218–26.

10. Tribunal correctionel de Lille, session of 9 October, as reported in *Echo du Nord*, 12 October 1839.

11. See *procureur*'s views expressed in AN BB^{18}1378–9 reports of 24 September and 28 August 1839.

12. *Commissaire de police*, Lille, report of 19 August 1839 in ADN M617/9; the other police agent's report, same date, is in ADN M620/70.

13. The charter is in ADN M617/9.

14. Prefect's report of 23 September 1839 in ADN M617/9.

15. Codron's lawyer is quoted in *Echo du Nord*, 13 October 1839; see also *procureur général*'s report of 25 September in AN BB^{18}1378–9.

16. Théry's and Codron's comments both in *Echo du Nord*, 12 October 1839 (excerpts reprinted in *Gaz. Trib.*, 16 October 1839).

17. See Codron's claims about his contacts with the mayor of Lille in *Echo du Nord*, 13 October 1839; and mayor's letter to prefect, 24 September 1839, in ADN M617/9.

18. Mayor's letter to prefect, 24 September 1839, in ADN M617/9.

19. Trial testimony quoted in *Echo du Nord*, 12 October 1839.

20. On the Toussaint incident, see police reports of 19 September and a report from the Gendarmerie of 21 September in ADN M617/9.

21. See reports in ADN M617/9, and account in *Echo du Nord*, 21 September 1839.

22. Report of *commissaire central de Lille*, 21 September 1839 in ADN M617/9.
23. *Procureur*'s report in AN BB[18]1378–79.
24. Prefect's report in ADN M617/9; see also report from the Gendarmerie, 21 September, same dossier.
25. Maurice Agulhon, *La république au village* (Paris, 1970); see especially his discussion of the "archaism of municipal unanimity" in the uprising of 1851, pp. 450–5.
26. Quoted in Christopher H. Johnson, *Utopian Communism in France: Cabet and the Icarians, 1839–51* (Ithaca, N.Y., 1974), p. 170; see also on Codron, pp. 205, 241.
27. Conflicts occurred in January in Furville and Neufchâtel (reports in ADSM, 10MP2001); in March in Armentières (ADN M606/3, mayor's report of 2 and 8 March 1837); in Reims in April (ADM 194M9, reports of Gendarmerie and subprefect; AN F[12]6781(12), report of Gendarmerie; Aguet, *Les grèves sous la Monarchie de Juillet*, p. 157); in Roanne (ibid., 158); in Mulhouse in late April – apparently after the price break (Marie-Madeleine Kahan-Rabecq, *La classes ouvrière en Alsace pendant la Monarchie de Juillet* [Paris, 1937], pp. 335–6).
28. Marches on public buildings: Furville, Neufchâtel, Armentières; notice violations: Neufchâtel, Armentières, Mulhouse. (See sources listed in note 27.)
29. See prefect's report of 29 April 1839, ADSM 10MP2001; AN BB[18]1259(7754); Aguet, *Les grèves sous la Monarchie de Juillet*, 177.
30. AN BB[18]1259(7754), *procureur*'s report, 29 May 1839; Aguet, *Les grèves sous la Monarchie de Juillet*, 177.
31. Claude Fohlen, *L'industrie textile au temps du Second Empire* (Paris, 1956), pp. 161–253.
32. On the Cholet incidents of both 1840 and 1841, see AN BB[18]1396(2571); Aguet, *Les grèves sous la Monarchie de Juillet*, p. 254.
33. *Journal de Maine-et-Loire*, as quoted in the *Gaz. Trib.*, 10 October 1841.
34. Report of *procureur général*, Anger, 7 October 1841 in AN BB[18]1396(2571).
35. Same official, report of 9 October, ibid.
36. *Journal de Maine-et-Loire* as quoted in the *Gaz. Trib.*, 10 October 1841; see also *Gaz. Trib.* reports of 11, 15 October.
37. Prefect, Maine-et-Loire, report of 16 October 1841, AN BB[18]1396(2571).
38. See Agulhon's discussion of *chambrées* in *La république au village*, pp. 207–45.
39. On Roanne incidents of 1837, 1842, and 1847, see Aguet, *Les grèves sous la Monarchie de Juillet*, pp. 158, 267, 342; also AN BB[18]1250(5984), BB[18]1408(5769), BB[18]1455(4304). On Cholet, 1846, see Aguet, *Les grèves sous la Monarchie de Juillet*, p. 337, and AN BB[18]1439(1650). On Roubaix, 1843, see Aguet, *Les grèves sous la Monarchie de Juillet*, p. 257; AN BB[18]1410(6141); and ADN M606/4. Claims made here about the intentions of weavers are based on original documents, not Aguet's accounts. On Roubaix, 1846, see AN BB[18]1440(1738); ADN M620/11, report of mayor, 21 February 1846, report of Gendarmerie, 25 February 1846; Aguet, *Les grèves sous la Monarchie de Juillet*, p. 338. On Bitschwiller, AN BB[18]1456(4621); Kahan-Rabecq, *La classe ouvrière en Alsace*, p. 339; Aguet, *Les grèves sous la Monarchie de Juillet*, p. 343.
40. On Lillebonne, see AN BB[18]1456(4625) and Aguet, *Les grèves sous la*

Monarchie de Juillet, p. 343. On Romorantin, see Aguet, *Les grèves sous la Monarchie de Juillet*, p. 188.

41. ADM 194M9, reports of subprefect, 16, 17, 21, 23 August 1841.
42. AN BB¹⁸1446(2671); Aguet, *Les grèves sous la Monarchie de Juillet*, p. 341.
43. Johnson, *Utopian Communism*, p. 103.
44. On both Elbeuf incidents, see AN BB¹⁸1442(2135); ADSM 10MP2001, reports of mayor of Elbeuf, 8–11, 16 October, of *commissaire de police*, 24 October 1846; *Gaz. Trib.*, 29 October 1846; Aguet, *Les grèves sous la Monarchie de Juillet*, 340–1.
45. See numerous reports in ADN M610/4, 5 and M433/48.
46. Kahan-Rabecq, *La classe ouvrière en Alsace*, pp. 394–7.
47. See John M. Merriman, *The Agony of the Republic: The Repression of the Left in Revolutionary France, 1848–51* (New Haven, 1978) on the gradual process of repression. Through the greater part of 1849, laborers continued to enjoy freedom to engage in strictly economic or professional activities; see the circular in ADN M617/1. But by 1850, pretexts for breaking up their organizations had been found and the old law on coalitions was back in force. See also the classics on the regional history of the revolution, two by Maurice Agulhon, *La république au village* and *Une ville ouvrière au temps du socialisme utopique: Toulon de 1815 à 1851* (Paris, 1970); another by Philippe Vigier, *La Seconde République dans la région alpine* (Paris, 1963). Also useful, Ronald Aminzade, *Class, Politics, and Early Industrial Capitalism: A Study of Mid-Nineteenth Century Toulouse, France* (Albany, N.Y., 1981), pp. 149–91.
48. Not just the maneuverings of opponents but also mutual misunderstandings plagued those who circled in Blanc's orbit; see William H. Sewell, *Work and Revolution in France: The Language of Labor from the Old Regime to 1848* (Cambridge, 1980), pp. 243–72; Remi Gossez, *Les ouvriers de Paris*, I, *L'organisation, 1848–1851*, Bibliothèque de la révolution de 1848, vol. 23 (La Roche-sur-Yon, 1967).
49. See André Dubuc, "Frédéric Deschamps, commissaire de la République en Seine-Inférieure (février-mai 1848)," *Actes du Congrès historique du centenaire de la révolution de 1848* (Paris, 1948), pp. 381–95.
50. Ibid., p. 387.
51. Ibid., p. 388.
52. Maromme petition, 29 February 1848, ADSM 10MP2001.
53. Dated 6 March, in ADSM 10MP2001.
54. Petition in ADSM 10MP2001.
55. Notice in ADSM 10MP2001.
56. ADSM 10MP2001; see also the account in Dubuc, "Frédéric Deschamps," p. 388.
57. Ibid., p. 392.
58. ADSM 10MP2001.
59. Petition from Oissel, in ADSM 10MP2001.
60. All these petitions in ADSM 10MP2001.
61. Letter in ADSM 10MP2001.
62. Dubuc, "Frédéric Deschamps," p. 394; Merriman, *Agony of the Republic*, pp. 17–21; Jacques Toutain, *La révolution de 1848 à Rouen* (Paris, n.d.); AN BB³⁰365, "Trouble du 27 avril 1848 à Rouen."
63. Merriman, *Agony of the Republic*, pp. 156–7; Toutain, *La révolution de 1848 à Rouen*; Aminzade, *Class, Politics, and Early Industrial Capitalism*,

pp. 161–87; on Reims, see the section entitled "Limiting Cases" in this chapter.

64. ADN M606/3.

65. For a copy of the decree, see ADN M605/2; for evidence of misunderstandings about the meaning of the word *marchandage*, see responses to question no. 7 of the 1848 inquiry into working conditions in agriculture and industry, AN C944–969; Marie-Madeleine Kahan-Rabecq, *Réponses du département du Haut-Rhin à l'enquête faite en 1848 par l'Assemblée nationale sur les conditions du travail industriel et agricole* (Paris, 1939), pp. 262–3; project for a "reorganization of work" by a Tourcoing physician proposing (1) fewer hours, (2) minimum salary, (3) old-age pensions, March 1848, in ADN M605/1.

66. ADN M606/3, letter of 23 March 1848. The mayor called it "the principle of equality pushed to the absurd."

67. ADN M605/3 has a copy of the charter.

68. Ibid.

69. Ibid.

70. Numerous reports on this strike are in ADN M605/3 and AN BB^{30}360(4).

71. Comments of Roubaix mill owners in ADN M620/14.

72. Reports in ADN M620/14; AN BB^{30}360(4).

73. Report of the mayor of Roubaix, 28 October 1848, ADN M620/14.

74. These proposals in ADN M620/14.

75. Ibid.

76. ADN M595/3.

77. Reports in ADN M620/12.

78. Reports of the mayor of Roubaix, 5, 7 May 1849 in ADN M620/12.

79. Numerous reports in ADN M595/3.

80. See reports of mayor of Roubaix, 3, 8 October 1849, in ADN M595/3.

81. *Procès-verbal* of *commissaire de police*, Tourcoing, 20 October 1849, in ADN M595/3.

82. Report of mayor of Roubaix, 17 December 1849, in ADN M595/3.

83. On conditions in Mulhouse mills, see numerous reports in ADHR 10M8.

84. Parts of pay registers (but not enough to deduce the whole pay system) may be found in ADHR 10M8.

85. Report of the *sous-commissaire*, Altkirch, 5 August 1848, in ADHR 1Z513.

86. See Gustave Laurent, "Les événements de l'année 1848 à Reims et dans la Marne," Comité départemental marnais de célébration du centenaire de la révolution de 1848, *Le département de la Marne et la révolution de 1848* (Châlons-sur-Marne, 1948), 23–78.

87. Ibid., pp. 49, 56–7.

88. Ibid., pp. 73–6.

89. Reports of *lieutenant de gendarmerie*, 13, 15 October, 8, 11 November 1849; subprefect's reports of 2 February, 19 March 1849 in ADM 194M9.

90. As elsewhere, rural weavers in Seine-Inférieure voted with the peasants: conservative in April 1848 (when Deschamps' total votes, 47,000, were fewer than the total number of weavers in the department), Bonapartist in December 1848 (when Ledru-Rollin got fewer than 6,000 votes to Napoleon's 135,000), and shifting slightly toward *démoc-soc* in 1849. See Toutain, *La révolution à Rouen*, pp. 72, 94–6, 106; Merriman, *Agony of the Republic*, xvii; Edward Gary Berenson, "Populist Religion and the Republican Left in France, 1848–1851: The Diffusion of the *Démocrate-*

socialiste Ideology in the French Countryside," Ph.D. dissertation, University of Rochester, 1980.
91. On the inquiry's findings, AN C944–969; Kahan-Rabecq, *Réponses du département du Haut-Rhin.*
92. Agulhon, *La république au village*, p. 467, also stresses that the creative, close relation between the laboring poor and middle-class leaders was nonetheless one involving extensive mutual misunderstanding.

Part Three: Unquestioned assumptions, 1852–1904

1. Michelle Perrot, *Les ouvriers en grève, France 1871–1890*, 2 vols. (Paris, 1974).

8. The clock time of the Second Empire

1. On the coup d'état, see Maurice Agulhon, *La république au village* (Paris, 1970), pp. 436–67; Ted W. Margadant, *French Peasants in Revolt: The Insurrection of 1851* (Princeton, N.J., 1979); Pierre Pierrard, *La vie ouvrière à Lille sous le Second Empire* (Paris, 1965), pp. 428–98; Ronald Aminzade, *Class, Politics, and Early Industrial Capitalism: A Study of Mid-Nineteenth-Century Toulouse, France* (Albany, N.Y., 1981), pp. 193–220; Yves Lequin, *Les ouvriers de la région lyonnaise*, 2 vols. (Lyon, 1978), II, 169–72; Georges Duveau, *La vie ouvrière en France sous le Second Empire* (Paris, 1946), pp. 63–102; Thomas R. Forstenzer, *French Provincial Police and the Fall of the Second Republic* (Princeton, N.J., 1981).
2. All these remarks based on Theodore Zeldin, *The Political System of Napoleon III* (New York, 1971).
3. On machine builders and back orders, see report of the Chambre de commerce de Rouen, 11 August 1852 in AN $F^{12}4476$–C; on the boom in general, see David H. Pinkney, *Napoleon III and the Rebuilding of Paris* (Princeton, N.J., 1958); Claude Fohlen, *L'industrie textile au temps du Second Empire* (Paris, 1956); François Crouzet, "An Index of French Industrial Production in the Nineteenth Century," in Rondo Cameron, ed., *Essays in French Economic History* (Homewood, Ill., 1970), pp. 245–78.
4. Wage figures may be found in France, Ministère de l'agriculture, de commerce, et des travaux publics, Conseil supérieure du commerce, de l'agriculture, et de l'industrie, *Enquête: Traité de commerce avec Angleterre*, 8 vols. (Paris, 1860–2); Pierrard, *La vie ouvrière à Lille*, 200; Duveau, *La vie ouvrière*, 310–17.
5. On department stores, crinoline, and suits, see Philippe Perrot, *Les dessus et les dessous de la bourgeoisie: Une histoire du vêtement au XIXe siècle* (Paris, 1981), pp. 111–154; Michael B. Miller, *The Bon Marché: Bourgeois Culture and the Department Store* (Princeton, N.J., 1981); Henriette Vanier, *La mode et ses métiers: Frivolités et luttes de classes, 1830–1870* (Paris, 1960), pp. 186–220. On masons, see Pinkney, *Napoleon III and the Rebuilding of Paris*, pp. 157–62; on using oil to fry potatoes, see Pierre Pierrard, *Les chansons en patois de Lille sous le Second Empire*, Publications de la Société de dialectologie picarde, vol. 8 (Arras, 1966), pp. 171–3.
6. Pierrard, *La vie ouvrière*, pp. 428–98; Zeldin, *Political System*, pp. 75–7, 91.
7. France, Ministère de l'agriculture, de commerce, et des travaux publics,

Conseil supérieure du commerce, de l'agriculture, et de l'industrie, *Enquête*; AN F¹²4722, Enquête sur le travail des enfants, 1867.

8. On the surprise, see T. Leuridan, *Histoire de la fabrique de Roubaix* (Roubaix, 1863).

9. Armand Audiganne, *Les populations ouvrières et les industries de la France*, 2nd edition, 2 vols. (Paris, 1860); Louis Reybaud, *Rapport sur la condition morale, intellectuelle, et matérielle des ouvriers qui vivent de l'industrie de coton* (Paris, 1863).

10. Marie-Madeleine Kahan-Rabecq, *Réponses du département du Haut-Rhin à l'enquête faite en 1848 par l'Assemblée nationale sur les conditions du travail industriel et agricole* (Paris, 1939), pp. 80–5.

11. Audiganne, *Les populations ouvrières*, I, p. 192.

12. Ibid., p. 194.

13. Ibid.

14. Ibid.

15. Ibid., pp. 193–4.

16. Reybaud, *Rapport sur la condition morale*, p. 695.

17. Ibid., p. 698.

18. Louis Villermé, *Tableau de l'état physique et moral des ouvriers employés dans les manufactures de coton, de laine, et de soie*, 2 vols. (Paris, 1840), I, 103–07.

19. Audiganne, *Les populations ouvrières*, I, 21–6.

20. Ibid., pp. 29–30.

21. Ibid., p. 28.

22. Reybaud, *Rapport sur la condition morale*, p. 840.

23. Ibid., p. 841.

24. Steven Marcus brilliantly analyzes similar forms of equivocation about Manchester in *Engels, Manchester, and the Working Class* (New York, 1974), 28–66.

25. See Chapter 6, note 117, on Hugo; Martin Nadaud, *Mémoires de Léonard, ancien garçon mason*, edited by Maurice Agulhon (Paris, 1976), 314–15; John M. Merriman, *The Agony of the Republic: The Repression of the Left in Revolutionary France, 1848–51* (New Haven, 1978), p. 56, gives another, provincial example.

26. Reybaud, *Rapport sur la condition morale*, p. 660.

27. Audiganne, *Les populations ouvrières*, I, 32.

28. Ibid., pp. 66–7.

29. Ibid., p. 33.

30. Ibid., p. 20.

31. Ibid., p. 21.

32. Records of Dupont's activities are in ADN M613/1–16.

33. Report of 3 June 1854 on Halluin, ADN M613/16.

34. On all these matters, see also his reports of 26 April 1857 on Wambrechies (M613/16); 15 March 1853, 6 February 1859, 25 October 1866, 7 December 1866 – all on Tourcoing – (M613/14); 9 February 1866 and 10 April 1857 on Tourcoing and 21 April 1856 on Roubaix (M613/16). See also Pierrard, *La vie ouvrière à Lille*, pp. 173–8, 340.

35. Letter of Motte-Bossut et Cie., 9 January 1853, ADN M613/1; reports of 7 December 1866 and of October 1857 in ADN M613/16.

36. France, Ministère de l'agriculture, du commerce, et des travaux publics, Conseil supérieure du commerce, de l'agriculture et de l'industrie, *Enquête*, IV, 33, 68, 82, 572.

37. Ibid., pp. 55–63.
38. For examples, see note 35. Morris B. Morris has documented very similar informal habits in Bombay spinning mills before 1920; see his *The Emergence of an Industrial Labor Force in India* (Berkeley, 1965).
39. Report of 29 October 1858, ADN M613/16.
40. AN F^{12}4722, response of the Chambre de Commerce de Lille; Pierrard, *La vie ouvrière à Lille*, p. 176.
41. Report of 12 February 1859, ADN M613/16; report of 20 January 1860, ADN M613/14.
42. Report of 9 October 1857, ADN M613/16.
43. Report of 24 March 1861 in ADN M613/14.
44. Report of the Conseil général du Nord, AN F^{12}4722.
45. Pierrard, *La vie ouvrière à Lille*, p. 181; Emile Durand, *L'inspection du travail en France de 1841 à 1902* (Paris, 1902).
46. Reybaud, *Rapport sur la condition morale*, pp. 633–4.
47. Fohlen, *L'industrie textile*, gives an in-depth account of the cotton famine.
48. Much discussion of self-actors and their limitations is found in France, Ministère de l'agriculture, du commerce et des travaux publics, Conseil supérieure du commerce, de l'agriculture et de l'industrie, *Enquête*, IV.
49. See ibid., vols. III, IV, and V; for specific page references on the task of weaving, see note 69.
50. Reports in ADN M581/141.
51. The informer was named Vermesse; his reports are in ADN M581/164.
52. Reports in ADHR 10M9.
53. Ibid.
54. Ibid., report of 24 April 1860.
55. For mention of early traces of Roubaix weavers' resistance to two-loom work, see report of the *commissaire de police*, Roubaix, 5 February 1867, ADN M619/1; Fohlen, *L'industrie textile*, 420; and reports in AN BB^{18}1609 (2780).
56. See petition of 3 March 1862 in AN F^{12}2370.
57. Petition in AN F^{12}2370.
58. Reports in AN BB^{18} 1606(2542).
59. Reports in AN BB^{18} 1675(9105).
60. Petition of October 1855 in ADN M606/15.
61. Two petitions of 31 October and 29 November 1855, ADN M606/6.
62. Numerous reports on the *liard au franc* discount in ADN M606/6 and AN F^{12}2370.
63. Response of Chambre de commerce of Rouen to 1867 child-labor inquiry, AN F^{12}4722.
64. Report in AN B^{18} 1609(2780).
65. Pierre-Léon Fournier, *Le Second Empire et la législation ouvrière* (Paris, 1911), 207–18, 226.
66. Michelle Perrot, *Les ouvriers en grève: France, 1871–1890*, 2 vols. (Paris, 1974) I, 36, 74–80.
67. Pierrard, *La vie ouvrière à Lille*, pp. 477–9.
68. Perrot, *Les ouvriers en grève*, I, p. 78.
69. On weaving, see report of *commissaire de police* of Roubaix, 13 April 1867 in AN F^{12}4652; France, Ministère de l'agriculture, du commerce, et des travaux publics, Conseil supérieure du commerce, de l'agriculture, et de l'industrie, *Enquête*, III, 229–38, 407–15, 617–30; IV, 21, 85–8, 163–7, 185, 395–6, 407, 577; V, 247–54.

70. Report of 13 April 1867 in AN F¹²4652.
71. The account that follows is based on numerous reports in AN F¹²4652; ADN M619/1; *Journal de Roubaix*, 18–20 March 1867. See also Fohlen, *L'industrie textile*, 412–16.
72. *Commissaire de police*, Roubaix, report of 20 February 1867, ADN M619/ 1.
73. Copy may be found in ADN M619/1.
74. Fohlen, *L'industrie textile*, p. 413.
75. But according to one report, the weaver might be asked to give notice if he refused; see Fohlen, *L'industrie textile*, p. 415.
76. Grievance list repeated in Fohlen, *L'industrie textile*, p. 437.

9. The moral sense of farce

1. C. Brochet, "Le Branle-Bas" (Lille, no date, probably early Third Republic), BN Ye 971(61).
2. The original reads: "Les infants qu'minch'nt à faire tapage / In dijant quoich' qu'ell' veut qu'mander; / Cheull'femme tout' saisie n'ose pu bouger d'plache, / L'fille et l'garchon, furieux comme des loups, / Li dijot'nt in li crachant au visache, / T'aros mieux fait d'mette eun' corde à tin cou … Te couch'ra dins l'lit d'tin garchon, / Faut point t'faire de l'bill, va pour cheull' viell' sotte, / Tous les jours au soir on m'ttra dins tins lit / Eun bouteille in gré tout remplie d'iau cautte, / Pour cauffer tes pieds si t'as frod par nuit."
3. H. Andraud, untitled (Lille, 1868), BN Ye 971(3).
4. Original reads: "Si vou pernez unn fimme, / Qu'elle a un panari, / Ch' n'est point au bout de neuf jours / Qu'ell' porat ête gueri.
5. Rancière, "Le mythe de l'artisan," paper presented to a Conference on Representations of Work in France, April 1983, sponsored by the Western Societies Program, Cornell University; see also his *La nuit des prolétaires. Archives du rêve ouvrier* (Paris, 1981).
6. Pierre Pierrard, *Les chansons en patois de Lille sous le Second Empire*, Publications de la Société de dialectologie picarde, vol. 8 (Arras, 1966), provides a catalog of the songs, a detailed survey with numerous lengthy quotations, and discussion of the identities and biographies of about thirty known authors. Pierrard also draws on the songs extensively in his *La vie ouvrière à Lille sous le Second Empire* (Paris, 1965).
7. Laurent Marty, *Chanter pour survivre: Culture ouvrière, travail et techniques dans le textile Roubaix, 1850–1914* (Lille, 1982).
8. The richest collections are in municipal libraries. The BN also has a great number but scattered almost at random through the disorderly Ye series. The author has searched the Ye series by calling broadsheets of known composers (listed in the general catalog) and examining the others that are bound in the same folder. Usually place and period are preserved to some extent in individual folders. The best recent editions of known authors are those edited by Fernand Carton, whose introductions are full of precious information. See his editions of François Cottignies dit Brûle-Maison, *Chansons et pasquilles* (Arras, 1965) and Jules Watteeuw, *Pasquilles et chansons du Broutteux* (Tourcoing, 1967). See also Carton's "Recherches sur l'accentuation des parlers populaires dans la région de Lille" (Thèse, Faculté des lettres, Université de Strasbourg, 1970).
9. Pierrard, *Les chansons*, 21. Carton in his introduction to Cottignies, *Chansons*, 72, doubts the extent to which the Second Empire saw a revival. The

tradition of signing all compositions with the name of Brûle-Maison continued up until 1820; these are usually difficult to date, as a result. But if quantity did not increase after 1852, certainly the character of the literature went through a marked change.

10. Pierrard provides a brief but vivid biography in *Les chansons*, pp. 9–15.
11. Numerous Desrousseaux pieces deal with the pain of absence from Lille, especially in the military; see the section on "Themes of the Dialect Literature" for further discussion.
12. ADN M620/15, various reports of 1–22 August 1848; John M. Merriman, *The Agony of the Republic: The Repression of the Left in Revolutionary France, 1848–1851* (New Haven, 1978), 159–60.
13. Pierrard, *La vie ouvrière*, pp. 48–9.
14. Pierrard, *Les chansons*, p. 15.
15. This collection, like the first two, is attributed to "T. Desrousseaux," *Chansons et pasquilles lilloise. Troisième recueil* (Lille, 1849), BN Ye 20196. All the songs in it may also be found in the 1865 edition: Alexandre Desrousseaux, *Chansons et pasquilles lilloises*, 2 vols. (Lille, 1865).
16. See the 1855 edition: Alexandre Desrousseaux, *Chansons et pasquilles lilloises suivies d'un vocabulaire*, 2 vols. (1855).
17. Desrousseaux, *Chansons* (1855 edition), II, 49–53.
18. Desrousseaux, *Chansons* (1865 edition), I, 189–98.
19. One of his earliest poems, "L'R'vidiache" (1849) concerned a christening ceremony. See Desrousseaux, *Chansons* (1865 edition), I, 47–55 for a copy of it. And, of course, he had written many on young love and marriage.
20. Pierrard, *Les chansons*, pp. 16–21; Marty, *Chanter pour survivre*, 125–33. Hundreds of singing clubs have left behind membership lists, indicating cafes where they met, in ADN M222.
21. "Histoire de Brûle-Maison," in T. Desrousseaux, *Chansons et pasquilles lilloise pour faire suite au recueil publié en November 1848* (Lille 1849), pp. 5–9. On Charles Descottignies, Pierrard, *Les chansons*, pp. 18–20; on Catrice, Marty, *Chanter pour survivre*, p. 150.
22. Originally published in 1849, may also be found in Desrousseaux, *Chansons* (1865 edition), I, 139–44.
23. Anonymous, no date, no title, may be found in BN Ye 7182(127).
24. Gustave Bizard, "Les Femmes et les Cartes," no date, BN Ye 971(30).
25. Desrousseaux, *Chansons* (1865 edition), I, 20–3.
26. Jean-Baptiste Lefebvre, "Le Plaisir des Femmes" (Lille, 1861) BN Ye 7182(519); cited by Pierrard in *Chansons*, p. 229.
27. Desrousseaux, *Chansons* (1865 edition), I, 60–65, 159–61.
28. Jules Fouques, "L'Gardin d'Saint-Sauveur," BN Ye 7182(44), as cited in Pierrard, *Chansons*, p. 132.
29. Charles Descottignies, as cited in Pierrard, *Chansons*, 132.
30. Florimond Caby, untitled (Roubaix, 1862), BN Ye 971(73).
31. Anonymous "La Bière d'Armentières," BN Ye 971(16).
32. Desrousseaux, *Chansons* (1855), II, "Curiosités Lilloises."
33. As cited in Pierrard, *Chansons*, pp. 120–1.
34. BN Ye 971(22).
35. Louis Longret, "Rue de la Gare" (Lille, 1870), BN Ye 971(400).
36. Anonymous, "Les Nouveaux Quartiers d'Armentières" (Armentières, no date), BN Ye 7182(641).
37. Anonymous, untitled (Lille, 1859), BN Ye 971(112).
38. Edouard Prévost, untitled (Lille, 1858), BN Ye 7182(672).

39. Anonymous, untitled (Lille, 1841), BN Ye 7182(150).

40. On this, see Pierrard, *Chansons*, 172–5; or Anonymous "Le Malheur des Marchands" (Lille, no date), BN Ye 7182(183bis); or Louis Longret, "Les Marchands de Pomme de Terre" (Lille, no date), BN Ye 971(406).

41. Desrousseaux, *Chansons* (1865), I, 28–30.

42. As cited in Pierrard, *Chansons*, pp. 174–5.

43. Louis Longret, "L'Marchand des Quatre Saisons" (Lille, no date), BN Ye 971(407).

44. Pierrard, *Chansons*, pp. 170–2.

45. Ibid., pp. 85–8.

46. Anonymous, "Les Consolations d'un Conscrit" (Roubaix, no date), BN Ye 971(44).

47. (Lille, no date), BN Ye 7182(563).

48. (No place, no date), BN Ye 971(36).

49. Oscar Descottignies (Roubaix, no date), BN Ye 971(263).

50. Other songwriters did occasionally try their hands at this style; see, for example, Louis Longret's "Le Jour de Bonheur" (Lille, no date), BN Ye 7182(563); or Charles Descottignies' "Bottes de Lin" cited in Pierrard, *Les chansons*, 85. Jules Wateeuw made it his own later in the century.

51. Alexandre Desrousseaux, *Moeurs populaires de la Flandre française*, 2 vols. (Lille, 1889).

52. "Le Broquelet d'Autrefois" first appeared in the *Troisième recueil* (1849).

53. All the traditional local festivals are listed in the song "Le Carnaval" in *Chansons* (1855 edition). See also "Le Bistocache de Saint Catherine" in the second collection of *Chansons et pasquilles* (1849); "Le Lundi de Pacques" and "Un Episode à la Foire de Lille" in the *Troisieme recueil* (1849).

54. Marty, *Chanter pour survivre*, pp. 133–45.

55. "Ro Bot!" first appeared in the second collection of *Chansons et pasquilles* (1849); "Le Broquelet d'Autrefois" also appears in *Chansons* (1865 edition), I, 72–6.

56. Desrousseaux, *Chansons* (1855 edition), II, 203–05.

57. See Pierrard, *Les chansons*, pp. 230–3; Marty, *Chanter pour survivre*, p. 142.

58. Cited in Pierrard, *Les chansons*, p. 232.

59. Louis Vermesse, *L'amusement d'un lillois* (Lille, 1855), pp. 16–24.

60. Pierrard, *Les chansons*, 233; Alexandre Desrousseaux "Les Marionnettes," in *Chansons* (1865 edition), I, 127–31; Gustave Bizard, "Le Théâtre Impérial" (Lille, 1870), BN Ye 971(27).

61. William M. Reddy, "The *Batteurs* and the Informer's Eye, A Labor Dispute Under the French Second Empire," *History Workshop Journal*, No. 7 (Spring 1979):30–44.

62. Anonymous, untitled (Lille, no date), BN Ye 7182(171).

63. (Lille, no date), BN Ye 971(404).

64. Joseph Bonte (Tourcoing, 1879), BN Ye 971(433).

65. Watteeux, *Chansons*.

66. Note that the author of this song was a woman, Irenée Roumieux, "Pour la Patrie" (Tourcoing, 1895), BN 4° Ye Pièce 483.

67. Henri Thérin, "L'Actualité Roubaisienne" (Roubaix, 1895), BN 4° Ye Pièce 545.

68. Marty, *Chanter pour survivre*, 106-07, 134–6, 149–55.

69. Ibid., p. 126.

70. Ibid., p. 155.

71. Pierrard, *La vie ouvrière à Lille*, pp. 338–418. For a discussion of very similar developments in the Pas-de-Calais, see Yves-Marie Hilaire, *Une chretienté au XIXe siècle?: La vie religieuse des populations du diocèse d'Arras, 1840-1914* (Villeneuve-d'Ascq, 1977).
72. Yves-Marie Hilaire, "Les ouvriers du Nord devant l'église catholique (XIXe et XXe siècles)," *Le mouvement social*, no. 57 (October–December 1966), pp. 181–201.
73. Pierrard, *Les chansons*, p. 16.
74. Marty, *Chanter pour survivre*, pp. 226–9.

10. Little insurrections

1. There were major government inquiries into the industrial and commercial situation (1870–2), into working conditions in industry (1885), into the tariff system (1890), and into the textile industry (1904). The Office du Travail after 1890 carried out investigations into salaries and hours in industry (1893–7), into the history and development of unions (1899–03), into domestic manufacturing (1907-11), the artificial flower industry (1913), and the boot and shoe industry (1914). For a comprehensive list of these inquiries and others, see M. de Crecy, *Bibliographie analytique des enquêtes 1800–1918*, a BN catalog, call number: "Economiques 70. Bureau." See also the reviews of sources in Edward Shorter and Charles Tilly, *Strikes in France, 1830–1968* (Cambridge, 1974), 351–9; Michelle Perrot, *Les ouvriers en grèves: France, 1871–1890*, 2 vols. (Paris, 1974), I, 15–47.
2. See ibid.; Shorter and Tilly, *Strikes in France*, Edgard Andréani, "Les grèves et les fluctuations de l'activité économique de 1890 à 1914 en France," Thèse, Faculté de droit, Paris, 1965; Peter N. Stearns, *Revolutionary Syndicalism and French Labor: A Cause Without Rebels* (New Brunswick, N.J., 1971). For the period after World War I, see Annie Kriegel, *La Croissance de la C.G.T., 1918–1921* (Paris, 1966); Robert Goetz-Girey, *Le mouvement des grèves en France, 1919–1962* (Paris, 1965).
3. Perrot, *Les ouvriers en grève*, I, p. 352.
4. Ibid., II, p. 723.
5. Ibid., I, pp. 352, 397, 401, 405.
6. Shorter and Tilly, *Strikes in France*, 151, 198; William M. Reddy, "Laborers and Their Families: Community, Kinship and Social Protest in a French Factory Town in 1903" (Ph.D. thesis, University of Chicago, 1974), p. 23.
7. Reddy, "Laborers and Their Families," 19-20.
8. Shorter and Tilly, *Strikes in France*, pp. 198, 208, 221.
9. Perrot, *Les ouvriers en grève*, I, 352.
10. Ibid., pp. 355, 361.
11. Ibid., p. 356.
12. Daniel Vasseur, *Les débuts du mouvement ouvrier dans la region Belfort-Montbéliard, 1870–1914* (Paris, 1967), p. 75.
13. Peter N. Stearns and Harvey Mitchell, *Workers and Protest: The European Labor Movement, the Working Classes and the Origins of Social Democracy* (Itasca, Ill., 1971), 144.
14. Shorter and Tilly, *Strikes in France*, p. 216.
15. Certainly the guiding thesis of Shorter and Tilly's work, for example, is that all these episodes of conflict represent, fundamentally, forms of economic or political bargaining which are more or less efficacious according to the level of organization achieved by the bargaining groups. Perrot, by contrast, felt

that strikes represented something more than this; she discussed extensively the "impediments to the economic rationality" of strike behavior (*Les ouvriers en grève*, I, 150-99) and described the noneconomic features of strikes with great care. From here it is only a short step to hypothesize that economic rationality may have itself been one of the things which laborers resisted by striking.

16. See Louise Tilly, "Structure de l'emploi, travail des femmes, et changement démographique dans deux villes industrielles, Anzin et Roubaix (1872–1906)," *Le mouvement social*, 105 (1978):33–58; E. A. Wrigley, *Industrial Growth and Population Change: A Regional Study of The Coalfield Areas of Northwest Europe in the Later Nineteenth Century* (Cambridge, 1961); Georges Franchomme, "L'évolution démographique et économique de Roubaix dans le dernier tiers du XIXe siècle," *Revue du Nord* 51 (1969):201–47; Marie Pascale Buriez, "Le mouvement de la population dans le département du Nord au XIXe siècle," Diplôme d'études supérieures, Université de Lille, 1970.

17. Reddy, "Laborers and Their Families," pp. 46, 50.

18. Franchomme, "L'évolution démographique," 207-10.

19. Laurent Marty, *Chanter pour survivre: Culture ouvrière, travail et techniques dans le textile Roubaix, 1850–1914* (Lille, 1982), 77–8. But the political drawbacks of having so many resident aliens in the town must also be held in mind; see Judy Reardon, "Belgian Workers in Roubaix, France, in the Nineteenth Century" (Ph.D. dissertation, University of Maryland, 1977).

20. Franchomme, "L'évolution démographique," 212; Marty, *Chanter pour survivre*, 77.

21. See ADN M625/12, letter of Villard to prefect, 3 December 1903.

22. Reddy, "Laborers and Their Families," 11–14; Perrot, *Les ouvriers en grève*, I, 358–9.

23. Lille remained relatively undisturbed in 1889–90 and in 1903; the 1904 strike, called in Lille by the Guesdists, was disappointing; see ADN M607/30. Inspection of the 1906 *listes nominatives* suggests much less frequent employment of family members by the same mill for Lille and its suburbs than for Armentières; the *listes nominatives* are in ADN M474 (communes listed alphabetically).

24. See Jules Houdoy, *La filature de coton dans le Nord de la France* (Lille, 1903); Marty, *Chanter pour survivre*, pp. 17–66, provides a highly sensitive description of work routines in the Roubaix woolen industry that is suggestive about how different tasks were associated with male or female personality characteristics. See also Reddy, "Laborers and Their Families," 75–94, 250–3; Tilly, "Structures de l'emploi"; Madeleine Guilbert, *Les fonctions des femmes dans l'industrie* (Paris, 1966).

25. See the discussion of a weaver's pay record in William M. Reddy, "Entschlüsseln von Lohnforderungen: Der *Tarif* und der Lebenszyklus in den Leinenfabriken von Armentières (1889–1904)," in Robert M. Berdahl et al., *Klassen und Kultur* (Frankfurt, 1982), pp. 77–107.

26. See Claude Willard, *Le mouvement socialiste en France (1893–1905). Les guesdistes* (Paris, 1965); Jacques Marseille and Martine Sassier, "*Si ne veulent point nous renquerir, in va bientôt tout démolir*" (Paris, 1982); Peter N. Stearns, "Against the Strike Threat: Employer Policy Toward Labor Agitation in France," *Journal of Modern History* 40 (1968): 474–500.

27. See Willard, *Les guesdistes*, 229–42; Marty, *Chanter pour survivre*; Robert P. Baker, "Socialism in the Nord, 1880–1914," *International Review of Social History* 12 (1967):357–89; Robert Pierreuse, "L'ouvrier roubaisien

et la propagande politique, 1890–1900," *Revue du Nord* 51 (1969):249–73; Michelle Perrot and Annie Kriegel, *Le socialisme française et le pouvoir* (Paris, 1966); Jean-Paul Brunet, *Saint-Denis, la ville rouge, 1890–1939* (Paris, 1980), 34–57; Joan W. Scott, "Social History and the History of Socialism: French Socialist Municipalities in the 1890s," *Le mouvement social*, No. 111 (April–June, 1980):145–53.

28. Paul Lafargue, "La production capitaliste," in *L'Egalité*, 30 July–27 August 1882; Gustave Rouanet, "La crise économique," *La revue socialiste* 1 (January–June, 1885):6–24. The eight-hour day was made the official demand of the first May Day in 1890; the CGT took this demand over after its formation in 1896, and used it as the centerpiece for its insurrectionary 1906 May-Day demonstration. Wage and hour legislation figured in virtually all socialist electoral platforms and were major targets of Millerand's first ministry; see Paul Dramas, "Les conditions du travail et les décrets Millerand du 10 Août 1899," *La revue socialiste* 38 (July–December 1903):287–315. See Conclusion for further discussion. On May Day 1906, see Georges Lefranc, *Grèves d'hier et d'aujourd'hui* (Paris, 1970).

29. On Jules Guesde and his followers' view of strikes, see Willard, *Les guesdistes*, 33, 49–50, 195–6; Pierreuse, "L'ouvrier roubaisien," 264, 266; Georges Lefranc, *Le mouvement socialiste sous la Troisième République*, 2 vols. (Paris, 1977), I, 53; Leslie Derfler, "Reformism and Jules Guesde." *International Review of Social History* 12 (1967):66–80. On Guesdist handling of strikes, see Willard, *Les guesdistes*, 482–3, 567–71.

30. See, for example, those in ADN M619.

31. The following account is based on reports in AN F^{12}4664; ADM 194M10; *Le Temps*, 24 April–27 May 1880; *L'Indépendent Rémois*, 24 April–May 1880; and *Courier de la Champagne*, 24 April 1880. Perrot, *Les ouvriers en grève* gives numerous useful comments on the strike wave. (These are indexed at II, 879.)

32. On the political situation, see Lefranc, *Le mouvement socialiste*, I, 32–48; Aaron Noland, *The Founding of the French Socialist Party (1893-1905)* (Cambridge, Mass., 1956), pp. 1–9; Bernard H. Moss, *The Origins of the French Labor Movement: The Socialism of Skilled Workers* (Berkeley, 1976), pp. 71–102.

33. See G. Halu, "Rapport sur la fabrication des tissus dans l'arrondissement d'Yvetot, et sur la position des tisserands," *Annuaire normand* 44 (1878):379–87; and a special report in *Le Temps*, 29 April 1880.

34. *Le Temps*, 29 April 1880.

35. On Baudelot, see especially material in ADM 194M10; comments in *Le Temps*, 8 May 1880.

36. *L'Indépendent Rèmois*, 3 May 1880.

37. Ibid., 5 May 1880.

38. Ibid., 19 May 1880.

39. See report of *inspecteur en mission* Paire of 19 May 1880 in ADM 194M10.

40. The prevalence of highly schematic views of capitalism and the consequences of social isolation have been brought out especially forcefully by Willard, *Les guesdistes*, pp. 159–221, 237–42; see also Lefranc, *Le mouvement socialiste*, I, 57.

41. *Le Temps*, 12 May and 25 May 1880.

42. Ibid., 26 May 1880.

43. Ibid., 13 May 1880.

44. Ibid., 16 May 1880.

45. Marseille and Sassier, *"Si ne veulent point nous renquerir, in va bientôt tout démolir"* is the whole title.
46. See numerous interesting reflections on this issue in Edward Shorter and Charles Tilly, "Le déclin de la grève violente en France de 1890 à 1935," *Le mouvement social,* 76 (1971):95–118. Doubtless violence as a bargaining point was an idea not at all alien to many laborers in France by this point; but it is important, as well, to remember that any gesture can carry more than one meaning.
47. On the Guesdist infrastructure in the Nord, see Baker's insightful remarks in "Socialism in the Nord"; Willard, *Les guesdistes,* 222-60; Pierreuse, "L'ouvrier roubaisien"; Nicolle Quillien, "La S.F.I.O. à Roubaix de 1905 à 1914," *Revue du Nord* 51 (1969):275-89; Reddy, "Laborers and Their Families," pp. 136-45.
48. On the sudden upsurge in support for socialists, see especially, Brunet, *Saint-Denis, la ville rouge,* pp. 34–57; Joan W. Scott, *The Glassworkers of Carmaux* (Cambridge, Mass., 1974). On the Guesdist shift in electoral strategy, see Willard, *Les guesdistes,* pp. 59–75; Noland, *Founding of the French Socialist Party,* pp. 26–33.
49. Willard, *Les guesdistes,* pp. 45–8.
50. For this and subsequent details, see especially *Le Temps,* 29 April–9 May 1890.
51. Ibid., 7 May 1890.
52. Accounts of these addresses in ibid., 7–9 May 1890.
53. Pierreuse, "L'ouvrier roubaisien," pp. 251–2, 268.
54. Ibid.
55. Lefranc, *Le mouvement socialiste,* I, p. 55.
56. Full presentation of the results of a census sample is in Reddy, "Laborers and Their Families."
57. See owner testimony and comments of an *inspecteur du travail* in France, Chambre des Députés, Huitième Législature, Session de 1904, *Procès-verbaux de la commission chargée de procéder à une enquête sur l'état de l'industrie textile et la condition des ouvriers tisseurs,* 5 vols. (Paris, 1906), I, 17, 33–59, 86, 111.
58. The following analysis summarizes a full discussion in Reddy, "Entschlüsseln von Lohnforderungen."
59. Actually, the assumed loom speed used was 1.86 shuttle strokes per second, derived from extrapolation on the basis of piece-rate variation with cloth width; further discussions in ibid. Assumed speed agrees with contemporary technical data in, e.g., C. P. Brooks, *Weaving Calculations* (London, 1893). See also sources in Chapter 8, note 69.
60. On the role of skill in weaving, see Reddy, "Entschlüsseln von Lohnforderungen"; France, Chambre des Députés, Huitième Législature, Session de 1904, *Procès-verbaux,* I, 33–59, 111.
61. See records on strikes leading up to the October strike of 1903, especially at Mahieu in May and at Dulac in August, in ADN M619/30.
62. Ibid.
63. *L'Avenir d'Armentières,* 4 October 1903; Reddy, "Laborers and Their Families," pp. 147–52.
64. Evidence of attachment to Armentières may be seen in demands of 1906 that returning servicemen be allowed to get their old jobs back (see ADN M154/87 and M625/78, report of 8 October 1906), as well as in the massive

return of inhabitants to the town after World War I and their loving re-construction of it, even though the mills were never rebuilt.

65. On these practices, see France, Chambre des Députés, Huitième Législature, Session de 1904, *Procès-verbaux*, I, 79–81; Reddy, "Laborers and Their Families," especially pp. 199–210.

66. The best sources on the course of the strike include *La Gazette d'Armentières*, 23 September–17 November 1903; *L'Avenir d'Armentières*, 4 October–15 November 1903; and ADN M619/30, M625/8, 11, 12.

67. See ADN M625/11, report of Delbove, 1 October 1903.

68. *Gazette d'Armentières*, 20 October 1903.

69. See letter of Villard to prefect, 9 November 1903, in ADN M625/11; telephone report of Delbove, 26 October 1903, ADN M625/8.

70. See account of strike meeting of 31 October in *Gazette d'Armentières*, 2 November 1903.

71. On the election, see *Gazette d'Armentières*, 15 March–4 April 1904.

72. Splits of this kind, and electoral disenchantment, were a common fate of socialist municipal governments in the early days. Roubaix was lost to a mill owner in 1900 (Marty, *Chanter pour survivre*, pp. 204–6); Carmaux to Radicals in 1896 (Scott, *Glassworkers*, pp. 162–4); Saint-Denis to a similar moderate coalition in 1896 (Brunet, *Saint-Denis, la ville rouge*, pp. 80–96).

73. Between 1894 and 1903, the excess of births over deaths recorded in Armentières and Houplines, ranged from 5 to 11 per thousand inhabitants, producing a potential population increase of 1 percent per year; ADN M475/158.

74. The owners went to great lengths to avoid any appearance of bargaining, dealing always with the prefect unless he specifically requested that they meet with the strike committee. Even when dealing on an individual basis with their own employees they went no further than listening to requests; it was they who then made the decisions and issued them as authoritative resolutions. Not even the appearance of equality between parties was respected. See Reddy, "Laborers and Their Families," pp. 147–151, 229–320. On their way of life, style of management, and outlook, see Jean Lambert-Dansette, *Quelques familles du patronat textile de Lille-Armentières, 1789–1914* (Paris, 1954).

75. See the inquiry into dismissals, and the discussion of the weaver Brullois' wages in France, Chambre des Députés, Huitième Législature, Session de 1904, *Procès-verbaux*, I, 33–59; see, for further discussion, Reddy, "Entschlüsseln von Lohnforderungen," pp. 96-102.

Conclusion

1. Jean Jaurès' speech was published in *La revue socialiste* 38 (July–December 1903):578–602.

2. See the fascinating study of the place and experience of women in the mill-owning families by Bonnie Smith, *Ladies of the Leisure Class: The Bourgeoises of Northern France in the Nineteenth Century* (Princeton, N.J., 1981).

3. Robert Pierreuse, "L'ouvrier roubaisien et la propagande politique, 1890–1900," *Revue du Nord* 51 (1969): 266.

4. See Michael P. Hanagan, *The Logic of Solidarity: Artisans and Industrial Workers in Three French Towns, 1871–1914* (Urbana, Ill., 1980); David Montgomery, *Workers' Control in America* (Cambridge, 1981); Michelle Per-

rot and Annie Kriegel, *Le socialisme française et le pouvoir* (Paris, 1966); Joan W. Scott, *The Glassworkers of Carmaux* (Cambridge, Mass., 1974); Klaus Tenfelde, *Sozialgeschichte der Bergarbeiterschaft an der Ruhr im 19. Jahrhundert* (Bonn, 1977); Wolfgang Rensch, *Handwerker und Lohnarbeiter in der frühen Arbeiterbewegung, Zur sozialen Basis von Gewerkschaften und Sozialdemokratie im Reichsgrundungsjahrzehnt* (Göttingen, 1980); Gareth Stedman Jones, *Outcast London: A Study in the Relationship Between Classes in Victorian Society* (Oxford, 1971); David Stark, "Class Struggle and the Transformation of the Labor Process," *Theory and Society* 9 (1980): 89–130.
5. See the important new study on this issue by Charles F. Sabel, *Work and Politics: The Division of Labor in Industry* (Cambridge, 1982).

Bibliographical note

I. MANUSCRIPT SOURCES

In the Archives nationales, series F^{12} contains reports and internal memoranda on commercial and industrial matters from the seventeenth through the nineteenth centuries. The records of the Bureau of Commerce contain reports from inspectors of manufactures and intendants, files on guild regulations and law suits, petitions from inventors and manufacturers. F^{12} is less useful for the nineteenth century; quarterly prefectural reports are spotty but often informative. Files of workers' petitions from the Second Empire give evidence of conflicts not noticed by the police. Records of the 1837 and 1867 inquiries into child labor are also in this series.

Series BB^{18} contains reports from prosecutors and the Gendarmerie on local disturbances and political activity. These reports sometimes make incidents appear simpler than they actually were; subordinates are reporting to ministries in Paris that have no local on-the-ground experience. The need of local officials to appear knowledgeable and in control is often evident. The series is, nonetheless, indispensable for the period 1820 to 1860.

In departmental archives, series M usually includes a number of dossiers on industrial conflict, papers from the files of the local prefect that are often the most important sources of information. Series M also covers population, public health, politics, voluntary societies, commerce and industry, technology, working conditions. In all these areas, the Archives départementales du Nord are inexhaustibly rich and therefore contributed by far the most information to this study. Particularly important were the dossiers on textile technology (M571 to 594), on singing clubs (M222), wages and working conditions (M604 to 616), and strikes (M616 to 630). In the departments of Haut-Rhin, Marne, and Seine-Maritime, dossiers on industrial conflict are far less extensive, but precious reports on the period 1830 to 1849 were available.

387

Bibliographical note

As for local archives, war and fire have destroyed the bulk of records from the nineteenth century in many towns, including Rouen, Reims, Lille, and Armentières. Roubaix's Archives municipales, however, are quite good and in good order. The papers of the Conseil des prudhommes (rarely preserved elsewhere) are particularly rich.

II. PUBLISHED PRIMARY SOURCES

Much has already been said in the text about the value and limitations of government inquiries and investigative literature (especially in Chapters 3, 4, 6 and 8). Footnote 1 to Chapter 10 mentions the principal government inquiries after 1870 not explicitly discussed in the text. By far the most useful inquiries are those that consist of oral testimony and cross-examination before government commissions, like that of 1834 (France, Minstère du commerce, *Enquête relatif à divers prohibitions établies sur l'entrée des produits étrangers, commencée le 8 octobre 1834 sous la présidence de M. T. Duchâtel, ministre de commerce*, 3 vols. [Paris, 1835]) or that of 1904 (France, Chambre des députés, Huitième Législature, Session de 1904, *Procès-verbaux de la commission chargée de procéder à une enquête sur l'état de l'industrie textile et la condition des ouvriers tisseurs*, 5 vols. [Paris, 1906]).

A good number of private studies of textile centers were published in the course of the nineteenth century. For the most part they hardly touch on politics and social issues, aiming to pay homage to a local audience of businessmen. But they are indispensable sources of detailed information about the scale of industry and the tenor of mill-owner communities. Especially useful are T. Leuridan, *Histoire de la fabrique de Roubaix* (Roubaix, 1863), Achille Penot, *Statistique générale du département du Haut-Rhin* (Mulhouse, 1831); Charles Picard, *Saint-Quentin, de son commerce, de ses industries*, 2 vols. (Saint-Quentin, 1865).

On machinery, the most useful sources were two technical manuals of the July Monarchy, Oger, *Traité élémentaire de la filature de coton* (Mulhouse, 1839) and C. E. Jullien and E. Lorentz, *Nouveau manuel complet du filateur* (Paris, 1843). Other sources are listed in Chapter 3, note 53. Perhaps the best introduction in English to nineteenth-century textile technology is Andrew Ure, *The Cotton Manufacture of Great Britain Systematically Investigated*, 2 vols. (London, 1836). Ure goes through the history of machine development and describes each step in the manufacturing process in abundant detail with numerous illustrations.

Before 1860, newspaper reports on local conflicts are often disappointingly summary and vague. Other aspects of working-class life are very seldom mentioned. The *Gazette des Tribunaux* is a useful starting point for this period, because it picked out and reprinted reports from the provincial press both on petty crimes and obscure fights and on major upheavals. Detailed accounts of trial testimony usually followed in later issues. After the 1860s, the national dailies became much more attentive to major local incidents. *Le Temps* can be counted on to give in-depth coverage. And eventually a working-class press appeared; the *Reveil du Nord* (Lille) and its affiliates, *L'Avenir d'Armentières* and *Le Travailleur* (Roubaix) are good on local political and industrial developments for the period 1895 to 1905. Useful on Guesdist policy and platforms is their central organ, *Le Socialiste*.

Pierre Pierrard's guide to dialect songs, *Les chansons en patois de Lille sous le Second Empire*, Publications de la Société de dialectologie picarde, vol. 8 (Arras, 1966), provides a complete catalog of 800 pieces, including call numbers in the BN. The BN's collection is in great disarray, organized only loosely by time and place. One can easily search for songs from a particular area, however, by calling broadsheets of a known author and finding out what else is bound in the same folder. Author's names for those songs of interest may then be checked in the general catalog to see what else by that author the library has. By this means, it is possible to find numerous pieces with relative speed. Both Lille and Roubaix have extensive collections of local songs in their own municipal libraries, however.

III. SECONDARY SOURCES ON THE FRENCH TEXTILE TRADE

Despite the great abundance of studies on this subject, a relatively small number of works constitute the indispensable research tools. For the ancien regime, André Rémond, *John Holker, manufacturier et grand fonctionnaire en France au XVIIIe siècle, 1719–1786* (Paris, 1946) is a mine of information. Still useful for a quick overview is Eugene Tarlé, *L'industrie dans les campagnes en France à la fin de l'ancien régime* (Paris, 1910). The most important recent work is undoubtedly Philippe Guignet, *Mines, manufactures et ouvriers du Valenciennois au XVIIIe siècle* (New York, 1977); the work is not only informative but full of highly intelligent observations. Harold Parker, *The Bureau of Commerce in 1781 and its Policies with Respect to French Industry* (Durham, N.C., 1979) gives an inside look at the agency that generated most of the documents.

For the first half of the nineteenth century, the vast survey provided by Lévy-Leboyer is the best starting place: Maurice Lévy-Leboyer, *Les banques européennes et l'industrialisation internationale* (Paris, 1964). A useful entree into sources on the industry in this period is Peter N. Stearns, *Paths to Authority: The Middle Class and the Industrial Labor Force in France, 1820–1848* (Urbana, Ill., 1978). Claude Fohlen, *L'industrie textile au temps du Second Empire* (Paris, 1956) picks up the story with equal detail for the period 1848–1871. No comparable work has been done on the textile trade of the Third Republic, however.

On local conditions there is nothing for any other city that matches Pierre Pierrard, *La vie ouvrière à Lille sous le Second Empire* (Paris, 1965) that draws extensively on the rich series M in the ADN.

On labor conflict, three works cover the century and give excellent discussion of sources. Jean-Pierre Aguet, *Les grèves sous la Monarchie de Juillet: Contribution à l'étude du mouvement ouvrier français* (Geneva, 1954) is an exhaustive survey of sources located in Paris for the period 1830–1847. Aguet misses departmental sources and thus overlooks up to 20 percent of conflicts that can be documented at the departmental level. His accounts often go into great detail. In some cases, however, they were found to be too summary. For the Third Republic, Michelle Perrot, *Les ouvriers en grève: France, 1871-1890*, 2 vols. (Paris, 1974) is sometimes difficult to use because individual strikes are never discussed separately. The overall picture is rich and trustworthy; the vast array of sources drawn on makes it a sure guide. Edward Shorter and Charles Tilly, *Strikes in France, 1830–1968* (Cambridge, 1974) is based on a computerized survey of quantitative material and provides a map of the terrain that is the indispensable starting point for any study of industrial conflict in France.

A new work on the investigative tradition gives a thorough history of Villermé's career: William Coleman, *Death is a Social Disease: Public Health and Political Economy in Early Industrial France* (Madison, Wis., 1982).

On the Guesdists there is a remarkable in-depth analysis, Claude Willard, *Le mouvement socialiste en France. Les guesdistes* (Paris, 1965).

IV. RECENT STUDIES OF INDUSTRIALIZATION

The last twenty years have seen a burgeoning of interest in artisans and industrial workers of the nineteenth century. A few titles representing works that directly or indirectly provide information and reflection on nineteenth-century industry in England and France are given below. This list can hardly pretend to be exhaustive, especially for England, but suggests the richness of recent literature in this area. (A few further titles on women and work are given in note 6 of the Introduction.)

On French economic developments, see T. J. Markovitch, "L'industrie française de 1789 à 1964," *Cahiers de l'Institut de Science Economique Appliquée*, series AF, 4, 6, and 7 (1965–66); François Crouzet, "An Annual Index of French Industrial Production in the Nineteenth Century," in Rondo Cameron, ed., *Essays in French Economic History* (Homewood, Ill., 1970), 245-78. For general discussions of their findings, see Christopher H. Johnson, "The Revolution of 1830 in French Economic History," in John M. Merriman, ed., *1830 in France* (New York, 1975), 139–89; William H. Sewell, *Work and Revolution in France: The Language of Labor From the Old Regime to 1848* (Cambridge, 1980), 146–61. See also for more recent discussion: François Crouzet, "Quelques problèmes de l'histoire de l'industrialisation au XIXe siècle," *Revue d'histoire économique et sociale* 53 (1975):526–40; and Richard Roehl, "L'industrialisation française, une remise en cause," *Revue d'histoire économique et sociale* 54 (1976):406–27; P. O'Brien and C. Keyder, "Les vois de passage vers la société industrielle en Grande Bretagne et en France (1780–1914)," *Annales. économies. sociétés. civilisations* 34 (1979):1284–1303.

For England: Duncan Bythell, *The Handloom Weavers: A Study in the English Cotton Industry During the Industrial Revolution* (Cambridge, 1969); idem, *The Sweated Trades: Outwork in Nineteenth-Century Britain* (New York, 1978); James Epstein, "Some Organizational and Cultural Aspects of the Chartist Movement in Nottingham," in James Epstein and Dorothy Thompson, eds., *The Chartist Experience: Studies in Working-Class Radicalism and Culture, 1830–1860* (London, 1982), 221–68; C.K. Harley, "Skilled Labor and the Choice of Technique in Edwardian Industry," *Explorations in Economic History*, series 2, 11 (1974):391–414; Royden Harrison, ed., *Independent Collier: The Coal Miner as Archetypal Proletarian Reconsidered* (New York, 1978); Gareth Stedman Jones, *Outcast London: A Study in the Relationship Between Classes in Victorian Society* (Oxford, 1971); Charles More, *Skill and the English Working Class* (New York, 1980); Richard Price, *Masters, Unions and Men: The Struggle for Work Control in Building and the Rise of Labour, 1830–1914* (Cambridge, 1980); Iorwerth Prothero, *Artisans and Politics in Early Nineteenth-Century London: John Gast and His Times* (Baton Rouge, La., 1979); Raphael Samuel, "The Workshop of the World: Steam Power and Hand Technology in Mid-Victorian Britain," *History Workshop Journal* 3 (Spring 1977):6–72; David Smith, "Tonypandy 1910: Definitions of Community," *Past and Present*, no. 87 (May 1970):158–84; Malcolm I. Thomis, *The Town Laborer and the Industrial Revolution* (New York, 1974); idem, *The Luddites: Machine-Breaking in Regency England* (Hamden, Conn., 1970); A.J. Taylor, "The Subcontract System in the British Coal Industry," in L.S. Pressnell, ed., *Studies in the Industrial Revolution* (London, 1960), 215–35; H.A. Turner, *Trade Union Growth, Structure and Policy* (London, 1962).

For France: Maurice Agulhon, *La république au village* (Paris, 1970) (translation by Janet Lloyd: *The Republic in the Village* [Cambridge, 1982]); idem, *Une ville ouvrière au temps du socialism utopique: Toulon de 1815 à 1851* (Paris, 1970); Ronald Aminzade, "The Transformation of Social Solidarity in Nineteenth-Century Toulouse," in John M. Merriman, ed., *Consciousness and Class Experience in Nineteenth-Century Europe* (New York, 1979), 85–105; idem, *Class, Politics and Early Industrial Capitalism: A Study of Mid-Nineteenth-Century Toulouse, France* (Albany, N.Y., 1981); Robert J. Bezucha, *The Lyon Uprising of 1834: Social and Political Conflict in the Early July Monarchy* (Cambridge, Mass., 1974); Maurice Bouvier-Ajam, *Histoire du travail en France*, 2 vols. (Paris, 1969); Jean-Paul Brunet, *Saint Denis, la ville rouge, 1890–1939* (Paris, 1980); Pierre Cayez, *Métiers jacquard et hauts fourneaux: Aux origines de l'industrie lyonnaise* (Lyon, 1978); Serge Chassagne, *Oberkampf, un entrepreneur au siècle des lumières* (Paris, 1980); J.P. Courthéoux, "Privileges et misères d'un métier sidérurgique au XIXe siècle: le puddleur," *Revue d'histoire économique et sociale* 37 (1959), 161–84; Alain Faure, "Mouvements populaires et mouvement ouvrier à Paris," *Le Mouvement social*, no. 88 (July–September 1974):51–92; Alain Faure and Jacques Rancière, *La parole ouvrière, 1830–1851* (Paris, 1976); Alain Faure, "L'épicerie parisienne au XIXe siècle, ou la corporation éclatée," *Le mouvement social*, no. 108 (July–September 1979):113–30; Patrick Fridenson, "Une industrie nouvelle: l'automobile en France jusqu'en 1914," *Revue d'histoire moderne et contemporaine* 19 (1972):557–78; Remi Gossez, *Les ouvriers de Paris*, I, *L'organisation, 1848–1851*, Bibliothèque de la révolution de 1848, vol. 23 (La Roche-sur-Yon, 1967); Michael P. Hanagan, *The Logic of Solidarity: Artisans and Industrial Workers in Three French Towns, 1871–1914* (Urbana, Ill., 1980); Christopher H. Johnson, *Utopian Communism in France: Cabet and the Icarians, 1839–51* (Ithaca, N.Y., 1974); idem, "Patterns of Proletarianization: Parisian Tailors and Lodève Woolens Workers," in Merriman, ed., *Consciousness and Class Experience*, 65–84; Tony Judt, *Socialism in Provence, 1871–1914: A Study in the Origins of the Modern French Left* (Cambridge, 1979); Steven L. Kaplan, "Réflexions sur la police du monde du travail, 1700–1815," *Revue historique* 261 (1979):17–77; Bernard Legendre, "La vie d'un prolétariat: les ouvriers de Fougères au début du XXe siècle," *Le mouvement social*, no. 98 (January–March 1977):3–41; Yves Lequin, *Les ouvriers de la région lyonnaise 1848–1914*, 2 vols. (Lyon, 1978); John M. Merriman, "Incident at the Statue of the Virgin Mary: The Conflict of Old and New in Nineteenth-Century Limoges," in Merriman, ed., *Consciousness and Class Experience*, 129–48; Bernard Mottez, *Systèmes des salaires et politiques patronales: Essai sur l'évolution des pratiques et des idéologies patronales* (Paris, 1966); Aimée Moutet, "Les origines du système de Taylor en France. Le point de vue patronal (1907–1914)," *Le mouvement social*, no. 93 (October–December 1975):15–49; Lion Murard and Patrick Zylberman, *Le petit travailleur infatigable ou le prolétaire régénéré*, No. 25

of *Recherches* (November 1976); Rémy Pech, *Enterprise viticole et capitalisme en Languedoc-Roussillon* (Toulouse, 1975); Michelle Perrot, *Les ouvriers en grève: France, 1871–1890*, 2 vols. (Paris, 1974); Philippe Perrot, *Les dessus et les dessous de la bourgeoisie: Une histoire du vêtement au XIXe siècle* (Paris, 1981); Pierre Pierrard, *La vie ouvrière à Lille sous le Seconde Empire* (Paris, 1965); Jacques Rancière, *La nuit des prolétaires: Archives du rêve ouvrier* (Paris, 1981); Jacques Rougerie, "Composition d'une population insurgée: l'exemple de la Commune," *Le mouvement social*, no. 48 (July–September 1964):31–47; Jean Sagnes, "Le mouvement de 1907 en Languedoc-Roussillon: de la révolte viticole à la révolte régionale," *Le mouvement social*, no. 104 (July–September 1978):3–30; Joan W. Scott, *The Glassworkers of Carmaux* (Cambridge, Mass., 1974); idem, "Men and Women in the Parisian Garment Trades: Discussions of Family and Work in the 1830s and 40s" forthcoming; William H. Sewell, "Social Change and the Rise of Working-Class Politics in Nineteenth-Century Marseille," *Past and Present*, no. 65 (November 1974):75–109; idem, *Work and Revolution in France*; George J. Sheridan, "The Political Economy of Artisan Industry: Government and the People in the Silk Trade of Lyon," *French Historical Studies* 11 (1979):215–38; idem, "Household and Craft in an Industrializing Economy," in Merriman, ed., *Consciousness and Class Experience*, 107–28; Edward Shorter and Charles Tilly, *Strikes in France, 1830–1968* (Cambridge, 1974); J. Harvey Smith, "Work Routine and Social Structure in a French Village: Cruzy in the Nineteenth Century," *Journal of Interdisciplinary History* 5 (1975):357–82; idem, "Agricultural Workers and the French Wine-Growers' Revolt of 1907," *Past and Present*, no. 79 (May 1979):101–25; Peter N. Stearns, *Lives of Labor: Work in a Maturing Industrial Society* (New York, 1975); Rolande Trempé, *Les mineurs de Carmaux, 1848–1914*, 2 vols. (Paris, 1971); Henriette Vanier, *La mode et ses métiers: Frivolités et luttes des classes, 1830–1870* (Paris, 1960); Daniel Vasseur, *Les débuts du mouvement ouvrier dans la région Belfort-Montbéliard, 1870–1914* (Paris, 1967); Jean Vial, *L'industrialisation de la sidérurgie française 1814–1864*, 2 vols. (Paris, 1967). See also two special issues of *Le mouvement social*, no. 97 (October–December 1976), "Naissance de la class ouvrière," presented by Roland Trempé; 99 (April–June 1977), "Au pays de Schneider."

Index

395

Index

Index

Index

Paris (*cont.*)
insurrection of 1830 in, 114–15, 129, 132; of 1848 in, 210
Parti ouvrier français, 283, 306
Pavilly, 120, 122, 206–7
pay procedures: in spinning, 81, 118, 196–7, 207, 211, 213, 215; in weaving, 202–3, 300, 310–11; *see also* piece rates, wage levels
Pays de Caux, 98
peddlers and vendors: in dialect literature, 272–4; in putting-out system, 27, 31, 33
Penot, Achille, 100–1, 107–8, 145–6, 157, 177–80
Perriers-sur-Andelle, 58–9
Perrot, Michelle, 225, 246, 290–1
Physiocrats, 40–4, 46, 63, 65–6, 85
Picardy, 98
piece rates: in First Empire, 81; in July Monarchy, 118, 126–7, 128, 136, 157–62, 190, 192; in 1848, 200, 202, 206, 211–15, 219; in Second Empire, 244, 247; in Third Republic, 310–11, 328
Pierrard, Pierre, 256, 274, 287
Piore, Michael, xiii
Piscart, 214, 217
Polanyi, Karl, 2
political economy, 3, 5, 12, 17; common knowledge of, 144–5; in investigative literature, 149, 235; prescriptive use of, 70; Say's dissemination of, 66; socialists' use of, 296–7
power loom, 4, 99, 240–1, 273; *see also* weavers, power loom
price mechanism, 6, 49, 87–8
production standards, regulation of, 35, 36–8, 44–5, 71, 72
productivity of labor, 7–8, 42–3, 51–3, 83, 142
profit, 22, 34, 48, 88, 328; textile laborers' earning of, 20, 35, 58, 211; views of, 42, 66, 68, 323
puppet shows of Lille, 278–80

Quesnay, François, 41–2

Radepont, 188–91
Rancière, Jacques, 135, 139
ready-to-wear garments, 96

Reims: dwellings in, 171; industry of, 27, 71, 75, 91, 94–6, 241, 293; labor conflict in, 130–3, 187, 202, 299–302; labor organization in, 219–21
Rémond, André, 31, 53
Renard et F. Masson fils, 206–7
Restoration, 75, 89, 94, 113; fashion in, 90–1; trade policies of, 90
Revolution of 1789, 2; economic impact of, 57, 61, 68; legal principles of, 66; and market language, 15–16; reforms of, 62–3, 84–5
revolution of July 1830, 113–15
revolution of 1848, 204–223
Reybaud, Louis, 229, 231–3, 235, 253, 288, 296, 327
Ribeauvillé, 243
Ricardo, David, 139–40, 143
Richard-Lenoir et Dufresne, 77, 83
Roanne, 60, 200
Roberts and Sharp, 79
"Ro Bot!" (Lille dialect song), 258, 276
Roland de la Platière, 51, 65
Roman, 90, 157
Rouanet, Gustave, 297
Roubaix: child labor in, 172, 236–7, 239; dialect literature of, 268, 283; industry of, 39, 75, 77, 93, 96–7, 101–3, 105, 241, 293; in investigative literature, 153–5, 235; labor conflict in, 125, 200, 203, 213–18, 243, 247–50, 302–9; work discipline in, 103–4
Rouen: *cahiers de doléance* of, 58–9; industry of, 24, 26, 36, 38–40, 54, 56, 76–7, 293; in investigative literature, 150, 158–9, 173, 234; labor conflict in, 31–3, 38, 40, 59–60, 114–24, 187, 199–200, 205–10, 243, 250; merchant manufacturers of, 71, 90, 98; mill owners of, 109, 113, 237
rouenneries (striped fustian of Rouen area), 45, 84, 92
Rousseau, Jean-Jacques, 62

Saint-Denis, 77
Sainte-Marie-aux-Mines, 95–6, 98, 128
Saint-Pierre-de-Franqueville, 60

Index

Index

Tilly, Louise, 162
Tourcoing: Catholicism in, 285; dialect literature of, 282–3; industry of, 37, 39, 161; labor conflict in, 216–18, 307
Tribout family, 22
Troyes, 60
Truquin, Norbert, 165–6
Turgot, Anne-Robert-Jacques, 40–1, 65

unions: forms of, 197, 298, 302, 305, 308; idea of, 185–6; legalization of, 246, 290

Valenciennes, 22, 26–7, 37, 39
valenciennes (lace of Valenciennes), 45
Vasseur, Daniel, 291
Vierzon, 68
Villeneuve-Bargemont, Jean-Paul-Alban de, 149–50
Villermé, Louis: influence of, 156, 180–2, 229–33, 296, 327; investigations of, 150–1; *Tableau* of, 171–5, 177–84; views of child labor of, 170; views of wages and markets of, 156–8
Villers-Ecalles, 206
Vosges mountains, 75, 98

wage labor, 20, 61, 69–70, 75, 84
wage levels, 5–6, 7; in investigative literature, 148–53, 156–9; legal minimum for 1848, 205–6; perceptions of, 323, 326–7; for women and children, 8, 10, 162–3; *see also* pay procedures; piece rates
wages, 4–5, 34, 228; employers' liens on, 71; of mule spinners, 157–62, 206–8; in programs of Confédéra-

tion générale du travail, 297; *see also* hours at work
Watteeuw, Jules, 282–3
weavers, handloom: in ancien regime, 24, 26–7, 34–8; conflicts and organizations of, 128–9, 135, 199–203, 219–21; decline of, 293; earnings of, 68–9, 127–8, 157; in England, 4–7, 10; in First Empire, 69, 72, 83–4, 93; quiescence of, 1848, 221; work schedules of, 237
weavers, power loom: conflicts of, 243–5, 247–50, 299–305, 309–23, 333, 335; geographical origins of, 293; task of, 241, 244, 247–8, 293, 303, 310–11
women: and customary wages, 8, 162; in dialect literature, 253–4, 262–3, 265–7, 270, 272, 285–7; in labor conflict, 243–5, 318; and Luddism, 1789, 59–60; as spinner entrepreneurs, 31–4, 57–9; and textile mill work, 162–5, 238, 241, 310–11
wool industry: in ancien regime, 26–7; decline of southern centers of, 99; and fashion, 94–5; mechanization of, 96, 241
work, discipline, 103–4, 110–11, 165–6, 209, 237–40; in dialect literature, 273, 275
work, diverse purposes of, 134–7, 223, 330–5

yarn: measurement of, 32, 103; output rates of, 107–11; prices of, 5, 56–60, 77, 87, 91, 160, 222, 240; rating systems for, 54, 81–2

Zickel, 170
Zola, Emile, 304

402

F